POWER, COMPETITION AND THE STATE
Volume 1: BRITAIN IN SEARCH OF BALANCE, 1940–61

POWER, COMPETITION AND THE STATE

Volume 1: Britain in Search of Balance, 1940–61

Keith Middlemas

Hoover Institution Press
Stanford University, Stanford, California

Hoover Press Publication 349

First printing, 1986

Printed in Hong Kong
90 89 88 87 86   9 8 7 6 5 4 3 2 1

Library of Congress Cataloging in Publication Data
Middlemas, Keith, 1935-
Power, competition, and the state.
Bibliography: v. l, p.
Includes index.
Contents: v. 1. Britain in search of balance,
1940-61.
1. Great Britain—Politics and government—
1945- . 2. Great Britain—Politics and government—
1936-1945. I. Title.
DA589.7.M53 1986   941.082   86-19987
ISBN 0-8179-8491-7 (v. l)

To my youngest daughter Annabel

To me those who condemn the quarrels between the nobles and the plebs seem to be cavilling at the very things that were the primary cause of Rome's retaining her freedom, and that they pay more attention to the noise and clamour resulting from such commotions than to the good effects which they produced . . . Every city should provide ways and means whereby the ambition of the populace may find an outlet, especially a city which proposes to avail itself of the populace in important undertakings.

N. Machiavelli
I Discorsi, Book 1, 4

Contents

Introduction   1

1 The Wartime State   17

2 Attitudes in War   46

3 Bargaining for Reconstruction   77

4 Managing Austerity 1945–47   112

5 Crisis and Austerity 1947–49   152

6 Which Way is Jerusalem?   180

7 Parties and Institutions 1951–56   212

8 Men and Issues   247

9 Threats to Equilibrium 1957–61   283

10 The New Opposition and the Old   316

11 Conclusion: 1961   335

Notes and References   356

Note on Sources   392

Index   394

Introduction

This book, the first of a trilogy about modern British government, starts with the making of a settlement in and after the Second World War. Conceived initially as a balanced, harmonious set of remedies for outstanding grievances from the inter-war years, and planned with increasing vigour as the great emergency receded, the settlement was modified to take account of a hostile economic post-war climate and then, through the affluent 1950s, maintained with much less difficulty than the authors had imagined would be possible. Questioned by some of the participants even before the good years ended, it was briefly revived at the start of the 1960s. At that point in the pattern this volume ends, leaving for the next the story of how the settlement was undermined and finally destroyed.

Six years ago, in *Politics in Industrial Society*, I described how the British political system adjusted to a complex pattern of crisis before and during the First World War; how by informal, even 'unconstitutional' means, labour and industrial organisations began to take (unequal) shares in the running of the modern state. This is not a sequel, although it covers in greater depth the period since 1940. *Politics in Industrial Society* should be seen, rather, as a preliminary essay, describing changing relations between increasingly significant and well-organised British institutions and the state which, in times of serious weakness, had to rely on them to help fulfil its aims, in ways not dreamt of when Dicey in the late nineteenth century canonised the doctrine of parliamentary sovereignty.

I wanted, afterwards, to trace the evolution of what I called 'corporate bias' – the tendency of industrial, trade union and financial institutions to make reciprocal arrangements with each other and with government while avoiding overt conflict – through its high peak and sporadic decline; and the fact that I had not (as helpful critics pointed out) given sustained treatment to the financial sector or the role of civil service departments as distinct areas of government, made it imperative to look again at the post-war period. Since then, however, contemporary political debates have

1

raised such deep questions about the nature and very existence of the post-war settlement that the work took on another, and to a historian somewhat disturbing dimension.

In today's climate of warring ideologies, so different from that of the 1940s and 1950s, post-war history seems to have been plundered or appropriated for anhistorical ends, to provide evidence for or against propositions about what is wrong with Britain – a conflict which the settlement's makers would have regarded as part of the problems they were trying to solve. At the same time it has become harder to defend the concept of a totality of politics, of a system, against those who, obsessed with decline, disintegration, and the symptoms of a 'blocked polity', echo Donne's complaint:

> The Sun is lost, and th'earth and no man's work
> Can well direct him where to look for it . . .
> 'Tis all in pieces, all coherence gone.

No historian can be free of or outside his subject matter. Mere proximity to the present does not, however, of itself increase his degree of personal involvement; nor conversely is there any reason to suppose that a historian observing a process conditions it, as does an observer of some experiments in the natural sciences. But his work may become part of contemporary debate: as Boris Pasternak suggested in 1937, he had become 'a particle of my time and state'. There is a temptation – and not intrinsically a bad one – to construct what Taine described as 'the lucid and persistent presentation of a quantity of individual facts, through an independent accumulation of isolated and juxtaposed documents . . . [to arrive at] a restricted circle, capable of being enlarged . . . inside which a man must know, not in order to know, but to act'.

It could be argued that the worst period for which to try to construct a systematic explanation of the nature of a modern nation's government is one as recent as this, when for the last thirty years since 1954 the state archives are closed. As far as documentation is concerned, the gap can partly be made good from other archives which are, in any case, necessary to complement government papers and offset the various sorts of administrative bias they contain. Beyond that lies the whole area of oral history, the immensely valuable but still under-used memories of participants and those recently retired from politics, business, civil service, or the labour and financial sectors, on which I have based a substantial part of this study. It is not intrinsically impossible to treat the recent past as if it had receded, nor for an historian to ask the same sorts of questions which other disciplines such as economics, political science, or legal studies do, to enter in fact the debate about political economy.

Because what follows grew out of it, I must briefly restate the theme of *Politics in Industrial Society*. I argued there that the emergence and institutional growth of central bodies representing management and labour, in the first half of the twentieth century in Britain, together with the reliance placed on them during two world wars by governments only too well aware of the weaknesses of the modern state to achieve victory without internal consensus and political harmony, were responsible for an enlargement and fundamental alteration of the political system. Erratically but conclusively, the party system and the informal relations of government and public altered in turn.

A threat to the nineteenth-century state had already developed before the First World War, which can be seen most clearly in the unprecedented strikes and industrial unrest that scarred employer-union relations, first in the late 1890s, then in the period 1911–14, the latter at a time when the British state found itself vulnerable to external threats, both in Ireland and Europe. Experience in the problems of conciliation showed Liberal Ministers the risks of allowing class conflict to erupt at such a time, and hinted, to Conservatives as well, how organised labour (as opposed to the small and somewhat quiescent Labour Party) might be bound into a parliamentary democracy which could not, according to prevailing theory, admit the legitimate existence of aggregates of power in unincorporated associations. In this inter-party competition, the potential prize was the votes of an as yet only partly enfranchised working class. 'Responsible labour,' properly organised in trade unions, held within the law by the system of immunities set out in the 1906 Trades Disputes Act, could be differentiated from agitation and revolutionary claims of syndicalists or guild socialists to a share in the disposal of government.

In the ferment of the last years of peace, civil servants, in particular in the Labour Department of the Board of Trade, as well as Ministers such as Lloyd George and Churchill, began to think about reform in terms of remedying the imbalance between capital and labour. But their advanced thinking was not reflected in the actual, disorganised state of industry and unions. No central organ of management existed.

Trade Associations tended to be characterised by a cartel mentality and restrictive practices, Employers' Organisations by an obsession with wage-costs; while, on the other side, the TUC remained a post-box, with a staff and resources tiny in comparison to those of major unions such as the miners or engineers. For a time it seemed to government that the Triple Alliance, the loose association of miners, railwaymen and transport workers whose power was not actually tested before 1921, presaged an alternative, revolutionary future.

World War in 1914 brought a double crisis of manpower shortages and inadequate munitions supply. Though government imported the skills of management and managers themselves, wholesale, and though trade unions conceded their privileges and the right to strike, in the 1915 'Treasury Agreement', the state was soon overstretched. Coercive powers proved useless in cases where large numbers of dissidents were involved, as in the South Wales miners' strike in May 1915, though rather more effective against individual leaders of the militant Clyde Workers' Committee. In all the stages of bargaining that followed, from demands for voluntary co-operation in recruiting men for the front, through the near-blackmail applied to unmarried men, to the Military Service Bill, progress towards full conscription ran parallel to the introduction of something akin to industrial conscription at home. Yet both were done, on the whole, by agreement with organised labour just as state direction of key industries like in engineering was with management, and the result can be compared very favourably with the efficiency and political harmony – or lack of them – in Germany, France, Russia or Italy during the terrible years 1916–18. The exceptions, such as failure to extend conscription to Ireland, war-weariness and declining production after the crisis of Spring 1918, and the messy compromises made to buy consent in different industries, exposed the state's weakness but did not damage its legitimacy.

Unlike their European counterparts, Coalition Ministers showed sensitivity to mass discontent. They used the reports of Industrial Unrest Commissioners in 1917 to increase wages, and offered planning for reconstruction, and pledges of a better world after, to substantiate an unprecedented effort to manage public opinion by propaganda at home. At the same time, through bargaining with government, central institutions representative of management took their twentieth-century form – in the case of the Federation of British Industries, partly as a result of government's instigation; in the case of the National Confederation of Employers Organisations, as a result of the need to overreach the bargaining advantages acquired in wartime by the TUC. These developments, and the changes which led the TUC in turn to institute its General Council in 1921, paralleled the Lloyd George Coalition's strategy of dividing 'respectable labour' from the Shop Stewards' Movement, the Communist Party and the Triple Alliance, all of which were indiscriminately lumped together by government as a threat to national stability in the strife-ridden, almost revolutionary years 1919–21.

Slump and the mass unemployment that destroyed the Shop Stewards' Movement at the end of 1921 completed the evolution of a political and economic organisation which left Britain radically different from her European counterparts. The Labour Party did not fragment into Communists and Social-Democrats in the aftermath of the Russian Revolution, and when faced with Lenin's Twenty-One Points. Instead, after Lloyd George's failure to establish a centre, governing majority, the Conservative Party, led by Stanley Baldwin, took Labour rather than the Liberals to be the real Opposition. Thus the party political system adapted itself in a novel way. Although Labour grew only slowly to become a genuinely national, cross-class party (the process being barely completed by the mid-1930s), the Conservative Party came to terms both with social reform and working-class aspirations, and as a direct result Britain was spared the rise of its extremist Fascist and Communist groups to mass-party status. The TUC likewise held together to become the largest and strongest movement in the industrial world. That power, however sluggishly articulated, or partially implanted in the workplace as a whole in conditions of slump and persistent mass unemployment, sufficed to hold off a sustained employers' campaign to cut wages in the middle 1920s. Later, after 1927, in conjunction with FBI and NCEO, it contributed both to the improved climate of opinion that favoured rationalisation of industry, and to the cartels, oligopoly and market-sharing practices which helped to keep employment, wages and demand alive in the depressed 1930s.

Corporate bias presumes a common interest not only in avoidance of major sources of conflict, but in the furtherance of a mixed economy. Argument would go on to the end of the 1930s over the desirable extent of state aid to the depressed regions, or about the advantages of balanced budgets as opposed to deficits in bad years. But after the 1926 General Strike (which should itself be seen as a conflict between archaic modes of thinking in the coal industry, rather than a struggle *à l'outrance* between 'capital' and 'labour') and more particularly after the economic and political crisis of 1931, ideas which implied acceptance of some degree of state ownership or regulation (for example, of the energy, transport and communications infrastructure, and recognition by all sides of the interdependence of profits, wages, investment and demand in the home and export markets) ceased to be mere abstractions and became increasingly part of the rational discourse of employers and trade unionists, government officials, Ministers and their economic advisers.

Organised labour remained on the margin of actual power until government needed it again in 1940, as it had in 1915–18. There was no neat symmetry between TUC and FBI or NCEO. Equally, in spite of growth in the central bureaucracies of management and unions, and some consolidation in peacetime of their First World War links with government departments, the relationships between each institution, the civil service and government developed haphazardly. Only in agriculture and aircraft production can origins of the 'sponsorship' system be found before 1939; and here, in the cosy partnership of the Air Ministry and aircraft manufacturers, or National Farmers' Union and Board of Agriculture, mutual interchange had deeply restrictive as well as supportive aspects. Elsewhere, civil servants developed their own forms of industrial diplomacy designed as much to protect their own sphere of activity as to prevent encroachment on government by producer groups. Government and industry treated each other warily, often on a basis of mutual ignorance, except where individuals like Lord Weir proved indispensable to both. Even the powerful Engineering Employers' Federation went cautiously, fearing to be held 'in restraint of trade'. Actual exponents of corporate bias behaved as if afraid that their deals might be exposed to the public or their own constituents and misinterpreted or misunderstood. Since parliament remained the one constitutionally legitimate forum, the corporatist models of the 1919 National Industrial Conference or the 'Tory corporatists', Oswald Mosley, and others in the mid-1930s, made little discernible impact.

Although in no sense the dominant trend – for the vastly enlarged, post-1914 state was obviously not captured by either capital or labour – corporate bias had nevertheless become an essential element in the extended political system before 1940. Grounded as it was in the fundamental change in size and nature of the state in the First World War, it ought to be seen as part of the explanation of change, and not as a mere symptom. On this, the political and economic organisation of Britain in the Second World War was to be erected. A general metamorphosis took place which also facilitated a greater openness to scientific management, amalgamation, standardisation and better accounting systems. Some aspects of this process may have retarded Britain's competitiveness, but overall it certainly ensured that the country was less strife-ridden, less prone to extremist ideologies than in the early 1920s and consequently better able to meet the external danger in 1939–40.

Subsequently, Britain developed in wartime a level of economic organisation, technological innovation and efficient production without parallel in modern history, and did so almost without political or social conflict. This involved an unprecedented extension in the power of organised labour, almost to the point of equivalence with management, and an integration of both into the wartime state, through their central and regional organisations. The experience shaped what became the idea of reconstruction and then the post-war settlement, and influenced subsequent events both directly, and as historic memory, indirectly, down to the present day.

I concluded (in 1979) that corporate bias was a characteristic of the modern British political system and, indeed, in different forms, of other Western industrial nations. It was a unifying phenomenon, since it allowed interests not directly represented in the formal democratic system to share in the operations of the state and hence to fulfil – or appear to fulfil – the various aims which bound each to its constituents. This sharing in the state led me to label them 'governing institutions', to differentiate them from mere lobbies or pressure groups which did not seek such permeation. But there could be no question of formal incorporation because each institution had to remain representative of its members' wishes, sensitive to their discontents, in order to survive. Except in wartime (when protest or alternative action was suspended) they proved unable to deliver the general consent of their members on issues that at various times were believed to be vital to government: such as wages, restrictive practices, cartels, or productivity and innovation. Corporate bias was therefore a tendency common to a particular stage of evolution in industrial society, prevalent but not necessarily dominant in industrial and political organisation, whose relatively efficient articulation had much to do with the absence of primary conflict in twentieth-century Britain. It was closely related to other phenomena, such as government's manipulation or management of public opinion, and the more or less successful ostracism of political movements designed to overthrow the system; but it was not an all-embracing explanation of that harmony. Because it was only one factor among several, I did not try to resolve the question whether political harmony was bought at the price of economic inefficiency and distortion of what classical economists took to be the proper operation of labour, industrial or financial markets.

I originally intended to do no more than study in detail Britain's extended political system at the peak of corporate bias in and after the Second World War, and to bring in as full as possible an analysis of the parts played by the Civil Service and the financial sector. But this intention soon changed, partly because of the great volume of material available, partly because the narrative grew too complex for such a straightforward scheme. The package of ideas which constituted the post-war settlement had become sufficiently discredited in the late 1950s for a serious attempt to be made to revise it in order to meet Britain's internal and external problems in the years after 1960, and this provided a logical point to divide the narrative into two volumes.

But beyond that, I realised that the questions raised by the material, particularly the oral evidence, were leading to a wide-ranging inquiry into the changing nature of the British state. Although it was reasonable to point up the lines of this argument initially, wherever they arose, to have developed it completely in the chronological framework would have overloaded the narrative with lengthy assessments of how the various bodies and organisations evolved their long-term attitudes, and clogged it with the development of what, inevitably, would be an abstract, even theoretical assessment of the state at various points in time.

Hence the third volume. Having described the several relations between government, different institutions and their memberships, it matters to try and relate them to the rest of the political system, not only physically, in terms of the political parties and the public as a whole, but conceptually, as part of a unified system of which politics, economics and indeed the legal system and the state are only aspects. Each relates to the other but there is an underlying logic to the whole. There need, for example, be no simplistic antithesis between the projection of a liberal democratic state and one in which corporate bias is prevalent: both are forms of pluralism, as I shall argue later. Nor in this analysis need there be the apparently clear divisions between free market, social market, and mixed economy which it suits ideologists and practitioners to use in their public language.

The development of the state constitutes an integral part of the narrative of interactions. It is not an abstraction, something neutral and impartial, but a major determinant of the way political, economic and social arrangements are organised. They, and the institutions which operate them, in turn affect the way the state actually works and condition the various forms in which it is conceived to exist. The state is not simply the fount of 'power' (although that is why the political parties compete to capture and control it). Industrial, trade union or financial institutions also compete, not so much to capture as to influence it; and the state itself changes as the various balances of power and the ways of thinking about the national interest which result from this competition also change. But changes in the state are not due simply to either level of competition because there are other areas within it (taking a necessarily wide definition) which have other sorts of power and influence, and whose ideas and ethos rest on much longer-term definitions of the national interest.

The state is therefore to be seen as constituted by the interactions of economic, social and political institutions of great diversity, parties, producer groups, bureaucrats and those like the Bank of England or the judiciary, who are guardians of a very specific concept of the national interest. Whereas the narrative of the period since 1940 will deal with a continuous series of relationships in a variety of planes (of which the party political one will often be less important than power-sharing between non-elected groups), the third volume will be concerned with the distinctive factors which shape institutions' behaviour over relatively long periods. Each develops a body of ideas about its functions, representativity, and proper place in the polity, as well as a doctrine about its rights and obligations. These are at once perceptions of itself and of the national interest which it seeks, consequently, to define in its own way, and then to impose, as part of the unending competition to define the orientation, if not the very nature of the state.

I shall ask whether that body of ideas, values, traditions and attitudes amounts to an ethos or, more coherently, to an ideology; how it was generated, how defended, modified, and transmitted to the next generation of members or officials; also, whether such analysis can be applied to the bureaucracy, or, more accurately, the mandarin elite of the civil service. The latter appears to lack corporate bias. Its formal accountability is to Crown in Parliament, its informal account to Cabinet as much as to individual Ministers. But despite the fact that the face it presents to institutions and general public as well as Ministers is agreed, ordered and intellectually coherent within the doctrine of accountability, it has in general a very highly developed awareness of the national interest and of what is proper to the efficient functioning of the state. In particular, it displays a set of often conflicting awarenesses, appropriate to the functions of different departments of state, whose polyarchic practice supplements and probably conditions the rest of the competitive process. Like the 'guardians', the Civil Service is manifestly an active part of the system and analysis must be wide enough to allow for all variants of its behaviour.

In assessing developments in the corpus of ideas, values and traditions in any institution, I assume that some definition of the national interest will take place. Because that is formulated by individuals, at various levels of membership and leadership, and filtered through an intellectual membrane composed of the self-interest of all members, past as well as present, no one institution's version can be exactly congruent with any other, although it may contain elements common to some or many. Definitions of the national interest are bound to be competitive in varying degrees. They resemble, at a 'higher' plane, what occurs as the institutions compete openly on the mundane, obvious self-interested level for scarce resources, status or political advantage.

Whether or not defined as class-based, competition thus defines which institutions are to be seen as 'governing'. Those who aspire to, and are able to compete at the 'altruistic' level of the national interest, enter the environs of the state. Those that do not, remain outside an invisible boundary, as self-interested, single-issue bodies, lobbies or pressure groups. But the governing institutions are not equal in their relative power or capacity to influence the final orientation of the state. Nor is their participation automatic, or granted on demand by some higher authority. Admission depends on the factors which define their power: size, coherence and activity of membership, possession of rare skills, expertise or specialised functions, popularity or other weighting with the general public. In addition, it requires a degree of recognition by government and the other competitors which depends not only on the preceding factors, but on the situation at any given time. Does the state, do the others, need them to achieve generally agreed aims?

The practical product of this competition is shown by the day to day orientation of the state, and the longer-term idea of the national interest represents its intellectual sum. Both are temporary, in the sense that nothing lasts for ever, but the latter tends to change only slowly. (One such cycle can be seen in the transition from defining full employment as a more important goal than inflation control in the 1940s, '50s and '60s, to inflation control as more important than employment in the 1970s and '80s.) In turn, both condition the ways in which institutional and party competition develops and, indeed, who will be the participants in future. Although it is axiomatic that a system in which corporate bias is prevalent will tend deliberately to avoid primary conflict in favour of a continual series of compromises, conditions can occur in which one or other of the participants reverts to the fundamental level of conflict in order to try and neutralise or even eliminate what it sees as its principal competitor by excluding it. An attempt to exclude the trade unions altogether from the governing level of competition occurred in the early 1920s and after 1979; attempts to alter permanently the rules in their favour were made in the mid-1970s. Whether de-recognition could occur, however, would depend on the excluded institutions' basic powers and motivation – the primary factors that gave it the power to compete at all.

To call Volume 3 a theory of the state may be to exaggerate its novelty and scope. But it is intended at least to provide a systematic framework in which to view the narrative, a framework which derives from the material itself and not from models, whether classical democratic, Marxist, or Weberian, based on earlier state formations.

To write a narrative fully to substantiate such a conclusion would require a series of complementary histories of the workings of each institution. This is clearly impracticable. I have tried to keep a reasonable balance between the role of leading individuals and the activity of the central organisations they served; no ethos is so strong that it conditions everything. But the activities of the branch or membership appear only infrequently. That is not to say that they are unimportant. They are clearly one of the main conditioning factors in institutional behaviour. But they belong to another sort of history and can only be hinted at here.

Individuals matter not only at particular times but as cohorts. The civil servants, officials or managers who devised and ran the wartime system retired, to be replaced by others who had only known it in their early years; who were followed by younger ones who had not known it at all and had therefore to reconstruct it from departmental memory. New men's formative experience did more than simply alter the ways government was run. When Britain's economic decline crept up on them, unawares, those who had not known the austerity-ridden 1940s found it at first an outrageous experience, but one for which solutions could be found. Later, the mid-1970s crisis invalidated for some their predecessors' creation and the Keynesian economic theories that funded it; for others, it confirmed a melancholy cynicism or a withdrawal into problem-solving, positions far from the general doctrine of thought as a preliminary to action laid down by Lord Haldane in 1918 as a fundamental principle – but one only fully utilised in the years immediately after 1940.

A connection between accelerating relative decline and the view of many contemporary political scientists that Britain has developed a blocked polity seems attractive but is actually hard to demonstrate. There is plenty of evidence below to suggest that the political system found it hard in the last half century to cope with long-term fundamental problems where the interests of industry, labour or finance conflicted. Deep questions were discussed at the end of the Second World War, about endemic weaknesses in management, investment, productivity or innovation, but they were too soon buried by governments intent on maintaining a high level of public and private consent. Macro-economic management derived some of its attractiveness from the evasion of precisely such hard and divisive matters. But that does not answer the question why economic policy failed (or worked) nor whether governments actually had the capacity they believed they possessed to achieve their aims.

Yet answers must exist in this general area of study. It may be that the degree of competition in the pluralist system was so high, the range of argument and luxury of choice so great, and the chances of reopening issues once decided so frequent that decisions were rarely made, but emerged, product of a process that ensured that all competitors were partially, and none totally, satisfied. Meanwhile the economic fruits of the post-war settlement were eaten greedily, as of right, while the plant grounded in the unwatered soil of political obligation withered.

This may serve better than the pendulum theory that no policy was ever pursued long enough, or the argument that in Britain the culture of government has been deeply inhospitable to enterprise. It fits also with the proposition that the post-war equilibrium was upset as much by party government's attempts from the mid-1960s first to control and then subordinate the interests outside the purely parliamentary arena as it was by broader economic or social causes. These debilitated the workings of the post-war system without regenerating party politics and thereby prepared conditions for much more abrupt changes a decade later.

But it is first necessary to demonstrate that there was a distinctive post-war settlement, deliberately conceived in wartime, modified as well as implemented after 1945. The history of the post-war Labour governments has recently been well covered using government archives and there is no need to retell it. Instead I ask a variety of questions about the settlement's origins in public demand and government activity; how far it was a product of parties, or individuals such as William Beveridge or Maynard Keynes; to what extent the attitudes dating from the 1930s persisted, and whether these gave support, from interstices of the political system, to that irregular but long reaction against the state's extended sphere of activity which first questioned the settlement and finally tried to replace it with another.

To take this narrative through to the present is to risk reducing the infinite number of past possibilities to something reflecting merely contemporary preoccupations, a danger aggravated by lack of perspective, inadequate documentation and the encroachment of bias or enthusiasm. An obvious deterrent need not, however, prohibit the attempt to connect where we are now with the recent, assessable past. Later historians will expose misdirections and show whether the trends discussed here are less significant than others. As Joseph Schumpeter put it: 'analysis . . . never yields more than a statement about the tendencies present in an observable pattern'.[1]

But the risk is only justifiable if there are sufficient sources which can be relied on. The 'thirty year rule' cuts us off from government archives closer in time than 1955, an almost irreparable loss not only to contemporary historians and political scientists but to politicians who have to learn the ministerial aspect of their profession by trial and error – a disability no other British profession imposes on its practitioners. The supplementary archives listed in the Note on Sources, however, do permit perspectives to be checked with government archives at least down to the early 1950s and then prolong accurate observation of the behaviour of institutions and political parties through the 1960s and in some cases here down to 1974. In addition, there exists a substantial number of excellent monographs to which a book like this must be heavily indebted.

Further justification, indeed almost a separate dimension, comes from the fact that 137 participants, distributed across the five main sectors (politics, the Civil Service, industry, unions, finance) and the whole forty-five years, agreed to be interviewed. It became possible not only to check details, fill gaps and uncover hidden episodes, but to test what the government and other documents purported to say – either to catch a glimpse of the multiplicity of things which do not appear in minutes or official correspondence (such as matters judged 'party political' by Cabinet Office officials); or to evaluate the bland prose designed to facilitate future discussion, not historians' later pursuit of minority views, blind alleys, decisions not taken; or to interpret key phrases, once the loose change of political conversation, whose significance has been overlaid by successive, depreciated currencies.

In the aftermath of the First World War, Maurice Hankey set out to write a 'peace book', to complement the War Book, that record of 1918 departmental and Cabinet practice which helped to reshape an emergency organisation in 1939. It was never done. A few departments subsequently commissioned internal, departmental histories; fewer still kept them up to date. A Civil Servant's working life of forty years apparently obviates the need of government to keep a written procedural memory alive. So, with his retirement and death, something irreplaceable vanishes. In bodies like the TUC or the CBI continuity is anyway less in demand, historic memory too often dependent on accident. Without access to this evanescent store of memory it would have been very hard to construct the accounts in Volume 3 of departments' and institutions' mentality. Even if all the documents which an inquiry into the workings of the extended state required had existed in easily available form, it would still have been more one-sided than the recollection of different individuals over a period of forty-five years.

The many problems of method and interpretation in oral history have been described adequately already.[2] A danger specific to the present book is that the selection, even of such a relatively large number to interview, might reproduce through the evidence a belief common to those who had participated in the political system under discussion that the system did indeed exist as described. (In the same way, government documents reflect certain preoccupations and assumptions which then became self-perpetuating.) As the list in Volume 3 suggests, they were carefully selected therefore to cover as wide a span of viewpoints as possible. In over 300 interviews, this diversity was maintained because those who agreed to discuss the questions were, almost without exception, prepared to probe into assumptions of this sort. Indeed, their insights did more to make me understand the ways in which political and other institutions behaved than I had originally hoped was possible. The common problem of failing memory for detail mattered less, since detailed chronology was rarely at issue.

But this accumulation and diversity of insights raises a serious difficulty when it comes to attributing sources. Some of the interview material used here would not have been given if the sources had been made plain so soon after the event. In other cases, where many respondents concurred on an interpretation, footnotes would have become unmanageably long; conversely, where I exercised a sort of Occam's razor on conflicting evidence, attribution might be simply presumptuous or unfair. Given that I chose twenty or more respondents as broadly representative of a particular sector over the period, it would, in any case, require inordinate explanation to justify every statement as equally 'representative'. With a handful of exceptions, on points either explicit or controversial, I decided against giving any references. Future historians may, however, find the records valuable, and they have been preserved.

To ask questions and receive answers is at one level a sort of academic theft. At minimal cost, the interviewer acquires a store of experience, a standard by which to evaluate the past, which has taken a lifetime to craft. There is no terminology of thanks appropriate to the willingness of so many to put one historian on the right tracks.

I owe therefore a debt which I cannot repay, only acknowledge to all who allowed me to ask questions, for their tolerance, courtesy, hospitality, and often friendship. They took the project seriously and will not, I hope, accept it as other than gratitude if I say that they helped to shape the book. I am also deeply indebted to those who granted me access to the archives listed here, often on privileged terms. My research fellow, Dr Neil Killingback, deserves my special gratitude, not only for unremitting work in the archives, but for his good humour and constant shrewd insights.

Four of those whose experience stretches back over many years kindly agreed to read the typescript for errors and misinterpretations and I should like to acknowledge their help: Sir Jasper Hollom, Sir Arthur Knight, Lord Murray of Epping Forest and Sir Douglas Wass. Their advice was most valuable, but the responsibility for the opinions expressed here is my own. I am most grateful for permission to quote from the archives listed in the Note on Sources and to the Comptroller of HM Stationery Office for permission to quote from the state papers deposited in the Public Record Office.

Any long research programme involving many archives and much travel requires financial assistance. I should acknowledge my thanks therefore, with a sense of humility towards other historians whose applications have been turned down in the present harsh climate, to the Social Science Research Council (now the ESRC) who made the major grant; to the Nuffield Foundation for grants for the pilot scheme of interviews and subsequent assistance; and to the Hitachi Foundation whose generosity to the University of Sussex facilitated further work and study leave. In addition, I owe much to the Hoover Institution and Stanford University where this first volume was written for the priceless gifts of time and a congenial, stimulating environment.

University of Sussex   KEITH MIDDLEMAS

1 The Wartime State

The needs of a nation fighting for survival, more than ideas about rational progress, have so far determined the main lines of state growth in modern Britain. Higher organisation of the war effort, reordered with amazing speed after the crisis of May 1940, lasted with few alterations until 1945 largely because it was both efficient and humane. It contrasted sharply with what had been achieved, haphazardly, during the First World War; but it owed its overriding symmetry to similar fears of invasion from Germany and chaos at home. In neither war did Britain indulge in total war planning from the outset. Long after 1940, indeed far into the post-war era, patterns of behaviour usually associated with the 1930s continued.

In a description of how the system worked there is no need to detail government's initial reluctance to adopt crisis measures or override 'normal trade' which survived even the invasion of Czechoslovakia in March 1939. So long as Neville Chamberlain and Lord Halifax, the Prime Minister and Foreign Secretary, believed it possible to avert war, there seemed no need, for example, to institute co-operation with organised labour, to match the arrangements already made with key sectors of industry (although Ernest Brown, Minister of Labour, was urging the Cabinet to consider how to deal with the lack of skilled manpower by talking to the TUC, and Conservative dissidents grouped around Churchill and Eden were discussing how to establish better links with the trade union movement). The general tone of government remained as hostile to these ideas as to the introduction of emergency provisions such as National Service or a Ministry of Supply. Chamberlain and his colleagues instead equated political equilibrium with financial stability and avoidance of wage inflation.

The argument that emergency legislation might frighten the City and destroy public confidence matched another, that concessions to unions in key industries would give them a lever to bargain with government. This theory drew weight from the way in which government conceded, almost precipitously, the miners' wage claim

17

in October 1939 in spite of its obvious consequences for wages and the cost of energy. Vast concessions had, on the other hand, already been made to the aircraft industry, and the Treasury failed to establish any real restraint on its excess profits until July 1939.

When war did come, Chamberlain and his government asked the TUC to co-operate. But they did not offer parity even of political esteem. Individual employers and industry collectively had been incorporated in the new departmental structure, chiefly in the Ministry of Labour and National Service (MLNS) and the Ministry of Supply. Representatives of the unions did indeed sit with management on the National Joint Advisory Council (NJAC), but in practice executive authority was confined to the latter. Thus the relative disadvantage trades unions had experienced through the inter-war years found expression in the new machinery of government. It is hardly surprising that they should blame it for the absence of firm direction of the war or for the unfair incidence of burdens on the public which swelled in the winter of 1939–40, as it had in 1915–16.

Lack of consultation about dilution of labour in engineering, manpower shortages in the coalmines (where over-enthusiastic recruiting among unemployed miners had seriously depleted the supply of skilled men), disruption of production, and the wages spiral, brought complaints also from industrialists. Neither side was permitted to take part in drawing up the key schedule of reserved occupations. Government proceeded as if waiting for events in Europe to convince labour, management, and public of the need for self-sacrifice, and ignored the arts of political management and propaganda. Its hostile view of trade unions complemented an antipathy to any form of association with the TUC or the Labour Party. Yet despite criticisms of unequal treatment made by Ernest Bevin and Walter Citrine, General Secretaries of the TGWU and the TUC respectively, Chamberlain somewhat patronisingly lectured the unions on their duties and made repeal of the Trades Disputes Act (which they asked for as a sign of the government's good faith) contingent on their wartime performance.[1] In this he showed less insight than Lloyd George in 1915.

Compared with the obvious advantage of co-opting prominent industrialists, trades unions seemed to the Chamberlain government to offer little, at that stage of the war. The TUC General Council indeed deliberately refrained from public protest, for fear of being taken to be 'in opposition'.[2] But unions' negative power can be gauged from the government's cautious progress towards conscription, which was finally only introduced on terms acceptable to the TUC, and from the way that the Control of Employment Act followed Ernest Bevin's suggested industry-by-industry approach. Industrial conscription, the great bogy of World War One, was not introduced at all, and the government ignored the Wolfe Report, published in January 1940, despite its forecast of extensive manpower shortages, for fear of having to bring in control of wages or compulsory direction of labour.

Progress towards economic, manpower and financial mobilisation followed a pattern dictated as much by sectional interests as the supposed national interest, in this period of 'phoney war', and inadequacies were not instantly remedied in May 1940 with the fall of Chamberlain's government. The new Coalition direction did, however to a great extent abolish earlier unwillingness to introduce control of civilian trade and consumption, labour mobility or capital movements, and to bring in full rationing, allocation of resources and dilution in munitions production.[3] It also brought into line government departments (Treasury, Board of Trade or Ministry of Labour) who until then seem to have resisted the more realistic adjustments to the crisis already made by institutions such as the Bank of England, Federation of British Industries (FBI) or TUC.

The efficiency and political harmony that are commonly recognised as leading characteristics of the wartime system did not stem simply from the Labour Party's entry into a coalition led by Churchill on terms of what Paul Addison calls 'moral equality', accompanied by near-parity in the War Cabinet. By Autumn 1940 when Ernest Bevin became Minister of Labour and manpower was designated as *the* essential resource and the basis of future planning, the trade union movement had been incorporated fully enough to mirror the roles of management and the financial sector in the war effort. Thus the energies of each sector were harnessed in a pyramidal structure from headquarters to firm or shop floor. Quite explicitly a political contract took shape, embracing agriculture and services as well as manufacturing industry, financial institutions as well as unions. It was backed by stringent powers of coercion, which were rarely if ever used – fortunately, since those over labour were more comprehensive and bore more heavily on the individual worker in industry than on others. Such an organisation, created voluntarily, had sufficient public prestige to tackle the essentially political issues of industrial or financial conscription, the new relationship of state to industry and labour, and the extent of liberty to be allowed to the individual. During two crucial years in which Britain's survival seemed doubtful, it complemented the fighting machine. In order of priority – and priorities were essential – manpower came first, followed by production, then finance; an exact inversion of the 1930s pecking order which was soon reflected in the machine of government itself.

After demarcation skirmishes with the Home Office, and more serious battles over distribution of skilled labour with Lord Beaverbrook at the Ministry of Aircraft Production, Bevin established for his Ministry of Labour (MLNS) near-total control of manpower. The principle of manpower budgeting, formalised in December 1942, ensured that his Ministry would, for the rest of the war, be the principal department of state. Bevin personally demanded voluntary acceptance of his terms of reference, at a delegate conference of all trade unions at Central Hall in May 1940; and this principle was repeatedly confirmed as government launched its Emergency Powers (Defence) Act 1940, with the wide range of Essential Work Orders. Trade unions (with a handful of exceptions, in contentious areas such as the docks, coalmines and shipbuilding) co-operated freely to implement direction of labour, dilution and cessation of official strikes. (Unofficial strikes continued sporadically throughout the war, but were of short duration and for the most part government dealt with them without using the full panoply of coercion.)

The Ministry of Labour had power not only to mobilise manpower across the whole country and control the pattern and conditions of engagements but, in effect, also to determine wages. Bevin could induce the Treasury, somewhat reluctantly, to remedy one injustice of World War One by raising the Excess Profits Tax to 100 per cent, and he negotiated effectively with other Ministries such as Food about food subsidies and rationing, or price control. In addition, he demanded and got, from Churchill, powers for MLNS to assist in organising production as well as manpower: tantamount to a licence to intervene in the areas of Production and Supply.[4] All this formed part of his grand design, conceived of as a political charter, to carry the assent of 'labour'. The TUC's General Council in return approved all MLNS orders, even the controversial Regulation 1AA, in 1944, with its stringent sanctions against unofficial strikers whom Bevin suspected to be under the influence of Trotskyites and other 'subversives'.

Bevin did not see himself as a trade union representative. He consulted employers and managers, sometimes to the annoyance of union bureaucrats who resented his easy-going pragmatism. But these consultations were substantive: Citrine and the Directors General of the FBI and British Employers Confederation (BEC) were able to comment on his May 1940 programme *before* it went to the War Cabinet. Later, it was discussed in the NJAC and referred to the Conference of Union Executives. Out of the largely advisory activity of the NJAC, Bevin then constructed his active, governing instrument, the Joint Consultative Committee (JCC) with seven-a-side representation of management and unions.[5] Here, the abrogation of collective bargaining (later to become Regulation 1304, which prohibited strikes and lockouts) was agreed and arrangements for voluntary joint regulation of wages in each trade or industry supplemented, when disputes occurred, by compulsory arbitration. The JCC met twice-monthly, usually with Bevin in the chair. While the NJAC receded into formalities, the two sides argued out intricate formulae like the dilution agreement for engineering.

Since 'labour matters' predominated on the JCC, it became the focus for the BEC while the FBI concentrated more on the similarly-balanced National Production Advisory Committee for Industry (NPACI), whose terms of reference included production, allocation of resources and what little remained of 'trade'. MLNS also had other means of regulating labour supply, wages and conditions, and separate links direct to individual trades unions. Bevin had left the union delegates in no doubt at his meeting in May 1940 that he would use every means he could to manage labour in wartime. Contemporary film shows him saying, 'I must have the co-operation of all employers' organisations and trades unions.' But he also declared that the nation would be best served if all workers, all employers joined such organisations.[6] Calling for service, like Lord Kitchener in 1914, he defined service in the collective sense.

Not all his methods were suited to union leaders' tastes. He would meet members of the General Council privately, circumventing TUC officials, and he once turned up to browbeat the General Council about a Yorkshire miners' strike in 1944. But the JCC was the nexus of the concordat with labour and management where the TUC was continually reassured (in the words of one MLNS official) 'that there would be equality of sacrifice among all sections of the community, and that more attention would need to be given to the questions of 1. profits, 2. the resources of taxation, 3. the relative levels of remuneration in different industries, 4. the practicability, even in wartime, of transferring purchasing power from the better to the less well paid'.[7]

Then and later, 'industry' lacked this clear access of unions to a single Minister. The FBI had opposed the idea of a Ministry of Supply in 1937–38, claiming that World War One had shown the efficacy of setting up committees of businessmen to oversee key industries, such as munitions production. FBI members, and the powerful Engineering Employers' Federation (EEF) wanted at all costs self-regulation under government aegis, not direct control by an alien Civil Service, which is what at first they took the Ministry of Supply to mean. But in talks with Sir John Anderson, they began to realise that it was better to deal with as few Ministries as possible. Hence they argued the importance of an employers' Advisory Panel, covering not just munitions but all manufacturing industry, whose powerful voice would speak to a single Minister of Supply.[8] In preparation for wartime, the FBI Council attempted from 1937–38 onwards to integrate the relevant trade associations in aircraft manufacture, machine tools and munitions. They aspired, explicitly, to become 'part of the transmission belt between the controller and the controlled'.[9]

Unlike the National Union of Manufacturers (NUM) (which seemed content to represent small businesses, mainly in the Midlands) and BEC which myopically stuck to its preoccupation with wages on the JCC and emphasised its old lines of demarcation, the FBI renovated its staff and services, and capitalised on its links with the Chamberlain government to the point at which it reached parity of esteem with the BEC, its old rival. Senior FBI men found themselves in government services in 1939–40 (to the dismay of the TUC who were told, blandly, that these posts were 'executive' not representative). They were concentrated, naturally, in the Ministry of Supply, whose organisation, by early 1940, confirmed FBI predictions that authority over the organisation of war production would be as far as possible decentralised down to industrialists, who 'know best what the capacity of an industry is, how an additional load of orders can be met, how a possible grouping of firms can be organised jointly to fulfil demands'.[10]

The supervised self-government of World War One thus found a broader base in World War Two and – like others recruited to the Ministry of Supply from academic life – Oliver Franks sat down and read the six-volume History of the Ministry of Munitions to find out how to write the rulebook of their association. Government retained complete power over the direction of raw materials, production, targets, and prices; but actual management lay in the hands of managers, no matter what the industry – iron and steel, non-ferrous metals, radio, engineering – with the exception of the government's own sectors such as Admiralty dockyards. In due course 'sponsorship' also developed with those industries and firms from whom Supply purchased its materials. In the end, the Ministry of Supply, together with Aircraft Production, covered almost all manufacturing. Regional Controllers acted as its tentacles, and dealt with local officials of the FBI and trade associations. Direct control was confined to a few basic industries and services, and even here, 'many of the official "controls" . . . were staffed by people from the industry itself. Such were scarcely distinguishable in composition from the pre-war head offices of trade associations'.[11]

Industrialists and businessmen found their vital role and received in return official recognition, as did the TUC in the labour field. Both were, quite simply, indispensable to the war effort, and both sides learned incalculable lessons from co-operation with each other and government. To match the NJAC the government set up the National Production Advisory Council (NPACI) in 1941. Despite reconstruction in 1942, the NPACI, however, always had a larger and more diffuse membership and never gave birth to an executive mechanism as straightforward as Bevin's Joint Consultative Committee. It included too many diverse interests and personalities, chairmen of the Regional Boards for Industry, and chairmen of a mass of sub-committees ranging from fuel allocation to emergencies. A parallel to the JCC can be found more easily in the network of Joint Production Committees, a form of line management stretching from the Production Authorities vertically downwards through each industry to the individual firm.[12]

Very many of the members of all these committees doubled up, the same individuals wearing different hats. Whatever the formal position (and 1940–42 was not a time for great formality), the new system incorporated the known best managers, businessmen and union leaders into the war effort, harnessing their skills and experience with the minimum of disruption. There was, of course, a price for the resultant harmony. What the institutions lost in independence, they gained in access to the innermost functions of the state. The FBI, for example, developed a technical expertise through handling war contracts, taxation, insurance and other agency work which was to serve its members well over many years of peace. Its liaison function developed to the point at which government relied on it almost completely for industrial co-operation. To member firms, complaining of the burden of paperwork, diversion of effort and loss of profit or civilian markets, this access to government provided clear compensation.

Well before the crisis of May 1940, the FBI had acheived a head start, in the eyes of both BEC and TUC. Later, something like equilibrium was restored, which the government seems to have deliberately preserved.[13] Far-sighted employers, too, took care not to repeat the errors of 1914–18 by offending public sentiment with high war profits and anti-union activity. The FBI modified its earlier opposition to government accountants' inspection of its members' books[14] and showed some pleasure when the Treasury at last controlled the aircraft manufacturers' monopolistic position and profits. Concentration of production required some firms to take the lead, others to shut down business altogether (see page 38) yet even in this somewhat disagreeable activity, with a cunning blend of altruism and self-interest the FBI kept alive the concept that industry served the national interest in wartime.[15] As a result, self-regulation and interdependence of all industrial sectors emerged from the closet of 1930s market-rigging to become the basis for rethinking about 'industry' in the reconstruction period. FBI and BEC may have failed to resolve their anomalous relationship, but both grew substantially in membership and funds.[16] Industry as a whole learned to live with government, and vice versa, each wrestling without final advantage, like Jacob and the angel.

Memories of mistakes made in World War One rankled in the financial sector, not least because British bankers had watched closely the Treasury's protracted struggle to stabilise the massive wartime debt, the debt to the United States, and the ultimate process of debt conversion in 1931–32. The banking system had been exposed also to much criticism not only for the way that that war had been financed, but for its alleged lack of service to industry (an accusation which came to a head in the Macmillan Committee's inquiries, 1929–31). This is not to say that any part of the City of London felt itself culpable – for each mounted, in its own way, a vigorous defence. But, just as the Bank of England and the main banks found it wise to rethink their attitudes to industry from about 1927, and in the process to set up new, intermediate institutions like the Securities Management Trust, Charterhouse, and the Bankers' Industrial Development Corporation, so they reacted, more swiftly than government departments and more pragmatically, to the threat of war.

On the industrial side, this impetus had been sustained in the 1930s by their reorganisation, as effective majority creditors, of industries such as steel and cotton; and work designed to bridge the so-called 'Macmillan gap' which culminated in the formation of ICFC and FFI in 1945. Banking organisation had already come into clearer focus, as far as government was concerned, since the Bank had evolved close liaison with the Committee of London Clearing Bankers (CLCB).[17] The Governor, Montagu Norman could, by the 1930s, supplement his 'disciplinary' powers over the City markets with advice based on a common understanding of the rapidly changing international scene. The Bankers' Information Service – a public relations organisation – meanwhile sought to ensure that the political left would not cry 'bankers' ramp' again.

Thus fortified, Norman and his deputy, Catterns, put considerable pressure on the Treasury, from 1937 on, to prepare for unpleasant measures such as exchange control and funding of a new, even vaster war debt. So long as hope lived in Chamberlain's appeasement policy, Treasury officials demurred.[18] The Bank instead conducted strategic planning on its own and used its facilities to help government through the abnormal conditions of May and October 1938 and January 1939 (for speculators accurately charted the failure of appeasement), thus preserving the reserves against a danger, the Chancellor, Sir John Simon, would not as yet admit.[19] Norman wanted fuller rearmament and emergency legislation in order to stabilise Britain's external position; denied both, the Bank conducted brilliant hidden manoeuvres to hold the value of sterling and succeeded, down to August 1939. At the same time (under cover of the Tripartite Monetary Agreement), Norman warned the US Federal Reserve of what would happen after, a wise provision safeguarding of American interests, which contained a long-term promissory note. Henry Morgenthau and the New York banks repaid this by policing the exchange-rate fixing agreements after 1939 and stopping black-market transactions, which amounted to mutual aid quite unacceptable to isolationist American opinion, possibly illegal under American law.

Since 1932 there had been a 'free but managed market' in sterling, mediated through the Exchange Equalisation Account. Simon and his Treasury officials remained wedded to freedom: 'The war would be over one day: London was banker to the world. Britain depended for her living on her freedom to trade with all parts of the world, and it would be suicidal to strangle current business by controlling every transaction.'[20] Instead of exchange control, the Treasury would control credit at home and, if necessary, deflate – a course which Norman regarded as a disastrous misreading of the lessons of the First World War. More realistic and flexible, the Bank and the CLCB prepared a far-reaching system of exchange control which was ready for immediate use when Simon gave way in August 1938.[21] The Stock Exchange conducted its own planning from mid-1937, which contributed to the institution of a Capital Issues Committee: again, regulated by the Stock Exchange, under Treasury consent. Here, as with control of savings, investments and new capital issues, the principle of voluntary co-operation was preserved, so long as government had 'first claim on all the resources of the capital market'.

The Bank's secret negotiations extended beyond the Stock Exchange, to Lloyd's, other City exchanges, and leading companies like Shell, BP and ICI, which had substantial overseas interests and assets. Arrangements were made by Catterns and Cobbold, by word of mouth only, for the insurance companies to invest their funds massively in government securities. Some directors objected, as did some bank chairmen. Bank of England officials used the consent of others, such as Barclays and Westminster, and the collapse of a discount house in December 1939, to weaken the opponents' position. By the time government came to legislate, this work – of immense importance in financing operations in the first two years of war – was almost complete. All the institutions by 1939 concurred that this should be a 'cheap money' war (with high levels of taxation, rather than War Loans which gave high returns to the *rentier* class), an agreement which other central bank governors extended to Australia, New Zealand and even, with some difficulty, Canada.

This hidden chapter (which included a sort of self-censorship) showed the City as surprisingly radical, and explains the ease with which the sterling area, the second prop of wartime finance, was created. Major holders of sterling (those who held reserves in sterling and could maintain exchange control) were invited into a novel imperial nexus where all internal transactions were free, all external ones tightly controlled, and capital outflow virtually forbidden in the interests of the whole. Canada raised more objections than any other prospective member, but in due course the central Commonwealth banks produced, under the Bank's consultation and tutelage, a flexible and remarkably unbureaucratic system. Given the fragmented state of Commonwealth political and public opinion on foreign policy and war in 1938–39, this financial and diplomatic achievement was remarkable. Its value to Britain's survival can scarcely be measured: the monetary union minimised Britain's dependence on dollar reserves, and helped to hold the pound until 1949, after its initial fall to $4.03 at the outbreak of war.

Everyone, at least in London, knew the price. Vast debts built up in 1939–41 to the Dominions, India, Egypt and the Argentine. But, thanks to the sale of $1000 million of government, corporate and private citizens' assets, and the loan raised by Niemeyer in New York, Britain survived. Whereas before 1940 the TUC or FBI had been able only to urge emergency preparations on the Ministry of Labour or the Board of Trade, the Bank and the financial institutions actually undertook the work, while the Chancellor hung back. Not till Kingsley Wood replaced Simon, in July 1940, did exchange control become wholly effective. Blocked channels were at once cleared to allow Treasury–City co-operation. Thereafter, during what R. S. Sayers calls 'the long haul', the Bank was content to work the new arrangements for capital issues, control of investment and government borrowing and to help, in a subordinate capacity, plan the war economy.

Although the Bank kept to its own sphere thereafter, unrepresented on any of the production or manpower organisations, it took a continuing interest in labour supply, industrial investment and the export–import balance, so that when reconstruction came, its collective opinion carried weight far beyond that of former individual Governors. In a real sense, by the date of his retirement in 1944, Norman had made the Bank into a Central Bank, and rendered nationalisation in 1946 otiose.

Much more than faces changed in May 1940. While the institutions had been pressing reluctant Ministers for action, in some cases for three years, civil servants had, themselves, worked out a new machinery of government in case the existing one should fail. The new range of departments: Supply, Food, Transport, Aircraft Production, lent themselves to novel thinking. Under the spur of emergency, a system of economic planning and direction grew up to maturity in less than a year, based on allocation of materials; controls of prices, shipping investment, building licences; direction of manpower; production targets, and, of course, the normal peacetime fiscal and monetary levers.

At the apex of government an intricate web of Ministerial committees came into being, complemented by committees of officials to conduct the preliminary work.[22] The Lord President's Committee gradually assumed a dominant and co-ordinating role, under the War Cabinet, though its voice was often disputed, with countervailing authority, by the War Cabinet's own Economic Secretariat also responsible to Sir John Anderson. Given that the new planning priorities began with manpower, continued with production, and ended with finance, it was natural that the Treasury should lose its peace-time primacy. The Chancellor ceased even to be a member of the War Cabinet for a time in 1940, and again in 1942–43; while his opinion on economic matters was often subordinated to that of the Economic Secretariat. (The original economic advisory committee, presided over by Lord Stamp, was divided in 1940 into the Central Statistical Office and the Economic Secretariat. Members of the latter, by far the youngest group seen in government since the days of Lloyd George's 'garden suburb', developed their original role of assembling information and processing it for ministers into a wide-ranging problem-spotting and brokerage of ideas which Lionel Robbins, its director, used to call 'the open conspiracy of economists in Whitehall'.)

The Treasury, however, retained control of the Permanent Secretaries' Steering Committee, and Treasury officials in their personal capacities preponderated on the official committees and working parties. By experience, if not sheer numbers, they still constituted an elite which Evan Durbin described as a majority among 'the 40 or 50 men and women in Whitehall . . . the "supreme economic authority" who keep under review the economic life of the nation and possess collectively great power to influence it'.[23] Though the Lord President's Committee co-ordinated war planning, the Treasury co-ordinated interdepartmental organisation, and thus retained a power in the interstices of bureaucracy which materially shaped the design of reconstruction.[24] One should not, therefore, exaggerate the *depth* of changes in 1940, but ask who ran the new ministries and committees. The influential Post-War Economic Issues Committee, for example, was largely staffed by officials with Treasury backgrounds. The 'forty or fifty' all became 'Poo Bahs', though few to the extent of Edward Bridges, Secretary to the Cabinet since 1938, who had become Head of the Civil Service and Treasury Permanent Secretary by 1945. As the Machinery of Government Committee noted, the war was organised chiefly by extending Ministers' and officials' authority – sometimes by subjecting them to excessive burdens – and this authority was not permanently prejudiced by the recruitment of outsiders from industry, banking or trade unions.

Meanwhile the idea of sponsorship, which had been a loose association or understanding confined to two or three areas of government before 1939, was formalised. Line management soon extended from War Cabinet to factory floor, through the whole geography of supply and production committees, in civil as well as military life. Controls, regulating even the tiny area outside government requirements, led to a form of organisation which, had it not been based in *practice* (though not in law) on voluntary commitment, should have been called totalitarian. The goal was collective: maximum war effort. Competition for private ends, black-marketeering, poaching, seepage, so prevalent in World War One, certainly existed but diminished during 1940: a virtuous cycle to be explained, indifferently, by altruism on the part of millions, fear at the danger across the Channel, and the comprehensive nature of state organisation.

Sponsorship implied departmental responsibility for a sector, knowledge of its affairs and, by derivation, sympathy for its problems; and frequently willingness to champion its grievances within a margin of prudence dictated by senior civil servants' awareness of the Whitehall debate on national needs. The system in fact constituted a microcosm of the state itself, corporate, almost Leninist in its prohibition of faction competition and lateral communication. Unions or trade and employers' organisations found it hard to co-ordinate any resistance to its scope, and were, in any case, tempted heavily to negotiate only upwards along the single line.[25]

The trade union movement naturally directed itself to MLNS as did the City institutions to the Treasury. Industry was fragmented, on sound enough functional lines, between Supply, Aircraft Production, Trade, as well as Transport, Food, and the defence departments. By 1942 the system had been perfected. Overlaps such as had bedevilled

Bevin's relations with Beaverbrook in 1940–41 had almost ceased to exist. Sponsors now acted as channels for government instructions (mediated, normally, as 'requests') and filters for demands on government. If the original models had been the cosy arrangements prevalent in late 1930s agriculture, or aircraft production, practice, in wartime, had to be attuned to the priorities of scarcity. Far more whittling down of sponsors' demands went on *inside* a department, before any negotiation took place with other departments or Ministers, than most industries realised.

When a department like MLNS, which had been rather moribund for almost twenty years found itself supreme in terms of the resource which it controlled, led by a Minister who effectively ranked as Deputy Prime Minister, the effect on its civil servants' outlook as well as on their status could be dramatic. Under such a system, newcomers were rapidly assimilated and imbued with an almost instant ethos and 'traditions' in departments even of only a few months' standing. Few of them, however, lost their peacetime affiliations. Lord Woolton, Minister of Food, was served by a mixture of businessmen and civil servants, most of whom went on to prolific careers in industry and government: they ranged from Ted Lloyd, who had written the 1914–18 history of the Ministry of Agriculture to Sir William Rooke who in 1941 bought up the entire West Indian sugar crop in the first purchase made possible under Lend–Lease. Sponsorship introduced a vigour and sometimes astonishing diversity in staid departmental life, yet at the same time bound its personnel, and its whole sector into a community within a larger interest. From their temporary submerging of lesser interests, reconstruction grew, in the hands of people who had learned how to work the machinery (and who also, once the worst of the emergency was over, felt increasingly free to take part). The shape of the 1940 state thus helped to determine what was done. Churchill put it, rather orotundly: 'the machinery of government should not change out of mere speculation or desire to achieve "unnatural symmetry". Nature is harmonious and not symmetrical. Departments grow like plants and acquire characteristics in the passage of time. Men direct themselves to this or that [one] . . . because of a general view that they have formed of its aspect. Brand-new groupings would not give the same vocational cue'.[26]

Self-evidently, the inner group of Coalition Ministers and officials in May 1940 intended that incorporation of so much outside experience, and the principle of voluntary commitment, should maximise political harmony as well as industrial efficiency.[27] If the price was a degree of monopolistic practice and lobby activity or special pleading, no one seems to have been inclined to complain, at least until after 1943. Coercion rarely occurred: the Betteshanger Colliery case in 1941, when striking miners were prosecuted, is notable for its uniqueness. Only a quarter of a million men and 90 000 women were directed, out of 4½ million serving under government powers; mostly in 'difficult' areas such as coalmining and agriculture. Some of the effects of long hours and stress which might otherwise have erupted into strikes were disguised by MLNS welfare work. Though the Defence Regulations laid down provision for wage determination, MLNS stood by the principle of self-regulation so far as possible, Bevin being most reluctant to use Regulation 1305. This strategy was greatly facilitated by price control, which kept the cost of living somewhat below the course of real earnings.[28] Only one third of the days of strikes lost in World War One were lost in 1939–45, and a mere 109 prosecutions took place. Elsewhere, for example in the financial sector, powers of direction were never used, and probably never threatened.

In the early days of war, the Ministry of Supply requisitioned frequently; later on, the system of allocation provided its own discipline. Consultation with sponsors, followed by hard bargaining, could be seen to achieve more than threats: especially if co-operation could later be rewarded by 'departmental assistance over scarce materials, foreign exchange, new capital, or by government contracts . . . where those concerned realise the likely value of being in good standing with departments from the point of view of obtaining specialist advice, assistance in the international sphere etc.'[29] Here was a sort of mutual association for the satisfaction of several aims. Yet during the years of extreme crisis, there is little evidence of abuse. State powers existed, in reserve, behind the bargaining and persuasive practice. On the other hand, consultation provided not only a mediating factor but a high degree of recognition amounting, for trade unionists at least, to a quiet revolution. Looking back, the FBI and BEC alike saw self-regulation as a tradition that the war had carved in stone.[30]

The physiology of the wartime state altered rapidly after May 1940. Firstly, even more than in World War One, the powers and scope of activity of the Prime Minister increased, for unlike Asquith or Lloyd George, Churchill found himself (at least till 1944) relatively unencumbered by rebellious Chiefs of Staff, unruly coalition colleagues or constraints in the House of Commons. His polymath nature could range across the whole direction of the war and the allocation of resources, questioning the efficiency of shipping control or steel production, or alerting the War Cabinet to the likely effect of Cripps' 1942 economy measures on civilian morale. Whether he championed public opinion against the war machine, or demanded of it even greater sacrifices, the machine itself served him, loyally and efficiently.

Within Whitehall (that is, leaving out the military aspect) Churchill and his colleagues relied primarily on the War Cabinet Secretariat headed by Sir Edward Bridges and Norman Brook, his deputy. For advice on economic problems, they turned to the Economic Section under Lionel Robbins, and Anderson's Lord President's Committee which together comprised that 'neutral territory . . . where economists of the higher standing should be'.[31] Although these two frequently disagreed, their arguments effectively replaced what in peacetime had been a rough overview provided for Ministers by the Treasury. As Maynard Keynes noted, the product amounted to much more than the lowest common denominator of departmental opinion, because the new economic centre had much less interest than the Treasury in living long-term with other departments or the financial institutions. Instead, looking simply at what was most expedient, in relation to winning the war, they acted as brokers of a clearly-defined national interest, in which the public – or rather civilian morale – also had a part.

Yet as Churchill's dictum about natural change indicates, he took considerable care in the running of government to avoid abrupt disruption and visionary schemes. The principle, 'All for the war, and nothing not for the war', which he laid down in 1943, curtailed what were becoming increasingly ideological arguments among Coalition partners about the shape of post-war Britain. Even in 1942, the terms of reference and composition given to the Machinery of Government Committee showed care to avoid undue radicalism, and to incorporate the main interest groups in Whitehall.[32] In spite of its apparent downgrading *vis-à-vis* Labour and the departments concerned with production, some observers like Max Nicholson reckoned that the Treasury retained much of its hold in central economic planning, just as it did over the official committees.[33]

From April 1941, with Keynes firmly ensconced and in increasingly close accord with Norman and Catto at the Bank of England, the Treasury began to perfect the first stage of demand management techniques, using that year's budget as a regulator to control prices and wages and thus assist industrial production and maintain employment.[34] Under the Chancellor, Kingsley Wood, this combination of officials cut loose from the old Treasury outlook sufficiently to constitute a revolution. Either because the system of manpower budgeting left them no alternative, or because the seniors and the Chancellor himself showed an unprecedented capacity to adapt, the Treasury came to occupy a technical and structural ground from which it was able to condition reconstruction planning and economic management for twenty years after the war. Although some Ministers still mistrusted the new practice of deficit budgeting within a long-term equilibrium, in November 1944 at its sixty-fifth meeting the committee agreed that, whatever other changes took place, the Treasury should remain at the centre of government.

In contrast to this subterranean survival, the Ministry of Labour's rise in the pecking order had an evanescent look about it, as if its lowly pre-war status prevented it achieving substantive rank. For a start, it had run against the trend by opposing wages control and industrial conscription in 1939. Although it established a schedule of reserved occupations at the same time as manpower priority, it had difficulty at first in consolidating these principles, especially in the munitions industry where poaching of skilled labour occurred most frequently. Unemployment had, of course, vanished, early in 1941. The system of allocation and control, based on comprehensive surveys of manpower needs and resources, was completed for skilled workers late in 1940, and was extended in the following year to the unskilled. The emergency gave it bargaining power even over the armed services; its concern about stress and loss of morale among civilian workers in mid-1942 led to cuts in services' manpower budget of a million men and women, to safeguard production – without any of the political warfare between generals and politicians which had bedevilled 1917–18. By 1943 it had become highly efficient, having achieved a point at which the entire population was so fully mobilised that wastages could not be made good. Such a triumph for MLNS officials left a profound legacy: the department became obsessed with the shortages of skilled labour that arose during cyclical upturns, and this conditioned policy at least down to the late 1960s.

Newer departments like Supply, Food or War Transport were assumed in Whitehall to be temporary, their functions ripe for incorporation afterwards in a reconstituted Board of Trade. Supply itself, with 60 000 civil servants, and 200 000 employees, sponsoring the bulk of manufacturing industry apart from the car factories (MAP) and shipyards, looked like a Ministry of Industry, but none of the civil servants who joined it from Trade (among whom the Import Duties Advisory Council (IDAC) officials became prominent) nor the industrialists on its Industry Committees imagined that they would remain in post long after the war ended. Nor did those in the Production Department, who fulfilled all the armed services' contracts and if necessary argued their suppliers' cases with MLNS or Supply. Production remained an executive rather than an administration. Yet for four crucial years, the Ministry of Supply controlled whole industries' exports and sales to private customers and in 1945 after long and acrimonious rivalry, it absorbed Aircraft Production as well. So wide was its orbit that many industries discovered a natural affinity, even if their formal sponsorship lay elsewhere.

By 1944 a case could be argued for retaining the essentials of this work under a reconstituted Board of Trade. But the members of Industry Committees (in effect a Who's Who of each industry) under Controllers such as Sir Andrew Duncan, Sir Cecil Weir, Oliver Lyttleton, Ashley Cooper, Lord Layton, were not men who could be held long in Whitehall. Ministry of Supply officials, however dedicated to their new job, probably never abandoned their original allegiance to Trade, Treasury or Inland Revenue. The Board of Trade, instead, came to be seen as the residuary legatee of 'industry', a conclusion approved by Treasury officials on the Machinery of Government committee. Thus the intellectual groundwork was laid down for a post-war triad of Treasury, Trade and Labour, in that order, an arrangement only quantitatively different from pre-war.[35]

If the Treasury were to manage demand and national income, and Labour to police the labour market, the Board of Trade (at least in the outspoken view its officials presented in 1943) would be responsible for industrial efficiency: 'except for the industries that have received the direct stimulus of war production . . . British industry will, unless efficiency is improved, be increasingly unable to sell its goods in competition with those of other countries, and they [BOT] are particularly afraid that industrialists (unwilling to see existing assets rendered obsolete) and trade unionists (unwilling to see the employment dislocation in particular industries which must follow the introduction of far-reaching labour-saving innovation) may join together to resist necessary improvements, and support themselves with the cry of full employment, unless the Government firmly take the long view and insist that industrial efficiency is essential to a long-term full employment policy'.[36] This *démarche* was later – regrettably – turned down by the War Cabinet. But, even if Trade was not to lay down terms of reference for the future, it is clear that these three Civil Service departments aspired each in its own way to run the post-war economy without benefit of the temporary personnel drawn in from outside.

The outsiders, from unions, banking, business or academic life were nominally temporary officials, and habituated themselves to working within a department ethos; but their former experience and attitudes inevitably conditioned how they worked, if not necessarily what they did. In daytime hours, as Oliver Franks noticed, they served the state; but at dinner, steel barons or petro-chemical experts reverted, among their colleagues, to discussing what the post-war world would be like for *their* industry. It is not enough to pick on key individuals like Keynes or Beveridge, therefore, fully to understand the matrix, beyond Durbin's 'forty or fifty' holders of collective power, which in all probability numbered four or five hundred. Some, like Bevin, Woolton, Anderson and Beaverbrook became temporary politicians as well as Ministers. Leaders of the institutions almost automatically took on a political dimension, and made friendships (like those between Norman and Keynes or Citrine and Churchill) which in peacetime might have seemed unlikely. To an extent which had simply not existed in World War One, Citrine, Tewson or Woodcock, Ramsay (BEC) and Kipping (FBI), and the officials of the Bank inhabited the same milieu as Ministers and Permanent Secretaries.

Not all senior civil servants did. Some, like Sir Frederick Leggatt and Harold Emmerson, in MLNS, rose with their department; others declined, out of incompetence, or too close association with the Chamberlain regime – Sir Horace Wilson being the most obvious case. The IDAC group occupied positions of prominence because of their familiarity with international trading patterns and the Empire Marketing Boards. Roughly speaking, anyone who had experience of exports, production, or finance had a head start – and certain skills such as accounting soon commanded a premium. Others, like Sir Norman Warren Fisher and Lord Hankey enjoyed an Indian summer, coming out of retirement to update the War Book of 1918 or the arrangements for censorship and control of information.

To say that the great majority were men of the 1930s conveys almost nothing about their wartime performance, although their intellectual framework became important once reconstruction entered the discussion. Old suspicions probably accounted for the reluctance of some officials to talk freely to union leaders; Treasury officials in particular saw no reason to grant trade union representatives automatic parity on committees.[37] Yet Norman Kipping, FBI Director General, ruminated on the profound changes war was bringing about: 'I do not believe that trade unions will in any future emergency accept the position that all Regional Board Chairmen are employers or ex-officials. It was easy to work this in 1942, before such jobs had been held by trade unionists. It is a very different thing now'.[38] If any market-rigging mentality survived wartime pressures to get things done expeditiously, it was among industrialists who would one day have to compete with each other again, rather than among Civil Service mandarins, diluted by a horde of academic economists and other luminaries, such as James Meade, Lionel Robbins, Henry Clay, Oliver Franks, Geoffrey Crowther, Hubert Henderson, Austin Robinson, John Jewkes, Alec Cairncross, Norman Chester, Max Nicholson, W. A. Robson, *et al*. Mostly men in their thirties and forties, the recruits introduced to longer-term thinking not only a bewildering heterodoxy but a solid, well-differentiated basis of research, ranging from PEP, NIESR, the Oxford Foreign Research and Press Service and the Institute of Statistics, to the Cambridge and LSE schools of economists to which Whitehall had previously been less than open.

There is little value in trying to categorise this heterogeneous elite on the lines of new or old men, insiders or outsiders. The chief criticism of Treasury authority, for example, came not from politicians or radical economists but from Sir Donald Fergusson, head of the Ministry of Agriculture. Too many able exceptions existed even to differentiate them by youth and age, and probably the only valid distinction is that adopted by Jose Harris, between adventurers and bureaucrats[39] – though perhaps this would be better put as adventurers and traditionalists. Few of them saw the war effort as a whole, being immured each in his own section, unable even on the highest committees to do much more than argue a departmental case. Only a handful in the War Cabinet Secretariat actually disposed of synoptic power, as Bridges did, for example, over selection for crucial Ministerial Committees, warning Churchill against choosing Herbert Morrison for the Machinery of Government Committee, despite his having greater experience than Anderson: 'there is a risk in matters of this kind, he might be influenced by the rather theoretical views of Mr. Harold Laski and Mr. Kingsley Martin'.[40] Keynes fitted happily at last into the Treasury framework; it was Beveridge, pushed out by Bevin who resented his claims to omniscience, who had to search out a novel competence. In a departmental sense, and in spite of the enormous changes wrought by the need to run a war economy, the men of the thirties did succeed in guarding certain tablets in the recesses of the temple. Later they saw in the reconstruction process a way to incorporate new methods, like tripartite consultation or demand management, as techniques to ensure stability without altering a more fundamental and ancient disposition of power.

The 'governing institutions' attempted, by enlarging their headquarters staff and extending services to members, to capitalise on their new influence with government, at the same time as they began to regiment members in order to display competence as agencies working on the government's behalf. The more the state needed them, the better services they could provide; and the more membership grew in numbers and satisfaction, the more they pleased Ministers. But a strict limit existed. To deliver bargains beyond what members were prepared under the various constraints to concede, risked schism or secession, as Lloyd George had discovered after 1916. BEC or FBI could not become corporations inside the state as some of the pre-war theorists had imagined.[41] On the other hand, they (and the TUC) were understood by member firms or unions to be the only substantive defence against complete state regulation.

The banks, Stock Exchange or insurance companies therefore found it expedient to listen more closely than usual to the Bank of England at a time when normal banking – other than private accounts – had ceased to exist. Not all aspects of the City looked for sponsorship to the Treasury: Trade retained responsibility for licensing of banks and insurance companies and company law. But as the Bank became a full Central Bank, so the Treasury established a position it guarded jealously thereafter, restricting communications other than through the Governor, who normally addressed himself to the Chancellor, but occasionally to Churchill himself.[42,43] At a lower level, Treasury officials began to talk to Bank officials, without admitting the legitimacy of other, possibly relevant viewpoints such as the Foreign Office.

BEC and FBI found it much harder to develop permanent links, because Supply and the other departments concerned with production were such patently temporary phenomena. Unsure what departments would be left, and divided among themselves by the old demarcation line between trade and labour questions (which now more or less confined the BEC to dealing with MLNS) industrialists had frequently to blur the line on the JCC and NPACI, if only to address themselves coherently to TUC representatives whose unions' membership ran across logical industrial boundaries. Their problems were complicated because the FBI had always been composed more of large single firms than trade associations whereas the BEC was wholly constituted of employers' organisations, each one habituated to wage bargaining. Unlike the latter, trade associations remained rather low-grade bodies, financially weak, and lacking authority – a legacy of their pre-war market-sharing arrangements and generally defensive mentality. The FBI itself, formerly regarded as 'soft' by BEC members, still lacked strong central direction and seemed preoccupied by a fear of becoming 'politicised' – another residue of the inter-war years. But the BEC, despite its strong and uninhibited focus in MLNS, under Sir Allan Smith's autocratic regime, failed to develop either a regional presence or a competent headquarters staff.

Under the centripetal force of wartime organisation, however, the FBI's varied access to Supply, Trade, MAP, and even Foreign Office and Treasury, turned out to be vital to firms living under the stable wage and manpower regime, much more preoccupied than before the war with materials, production and markets. For four years the BEC retired to the sidelines, where it muttered gloomily about the future and the rising influence of organised labour. Overstretched by a flood of new members clamouring for assistance, and trade associations who now saw that only association could ensure sponsorship advantages, the FBI had to multiply its committees to cope with allocation, excess profits tax and production targets. Simply to be able to advise industrial companies on technicalities of new laws and regulations, headquarters staff had to rely on civil servants for information and trade associations for co-operation.

Outside the Ministry of Supply, the government's principal link to trade associations and firms lay through the Production Executive, which was linked to the JCC and chaired by Bevin. The FBI tried to match this structure all the way down; but since departments also addressed themselves directly to trade associations, these grew in size and authority, coming at last closer to their pre-war American and German counterparts. Serious problems occurred when the War Cabinet decided to concentrate production on the main 'nuclei' firms in key industries, which were to take over their former competitors' plant to prevent waste and duplication.[44] Wisely retaining the voluntary principal, government threw this onus on to trade associations, not only to close down the weaker firms, but to devise a scheme to safeguard their interests for the future (usually by allowing them, under their own brand names, to distribute and market as before). Difficult and unpleasant as this job was, it greatly enhanced firms' sense of interdependence within an industry, and led the FBI to see trade associations as the logical guarantors of industrial self-regulation.

These changes, however, failed to compose all rivalries. Ministry of Supply Controllers found the steel barons still resentful at having had Sir Andrew Duncan and the Iron and Steel Board foisted on them by the banks in the 1930s; wool textiles on the other hand, an area of traditional rivalry and suspicion, came to trust another Controller, Sir Harry Shackleton. In mining and non-ferrous metals, motor cars and aircraft production, individualistic entrepreneurs waited; peacetime, they hoped would show how small had been the imprint of collective activity.

Employers' organisations and the BEC had more time to reflect and, at Lord Weir's instigation, a merger with the FBI was proposed in 1943, partly to reflect industry more comprehensively to government, partly to strengthen it against the rising tide of the trade union movement. W. H. Pilkington, more outspoken than most, declared: 'The FBI is regarded as obsolete and bureaucratic and afraid to act. The BEC has the reputation of being hopelessly obstructive and purely negative in its attitude to labour problems and has a very limited membership, quite unrepresentative of British industry.'[45] It was an accurate diagnosis: the FBI, though numerically larger, feared to be taken over by a body which had ever since 1919 shown itself more aggressive. Sir George Nelson told Hugh Dalton, in March 1944, that he would resist a combined Council 'with powers to issue orders to all British employers on any matter of general policy. He regards this constitution as fascist'.[46]

Government certainly did not envisage such a body, having learned by then to live with the inadequacies of both and the equal incapacity of the TUC to 'issue orders' to member unions. The TUC of course, after nearly twenty years under Citrine as General Secretary, possessed a competent staff, and a General Council dominated by the 'big six' which was, in many ways, practically and ideologically more coherent than either FBI or BEC. Densest in the world, the British union movement represented in 1940, 40.3 per cent of male workers, 17.1 per cent of female; this had risen to 45 per cent and 25 per cent by 1945 (though still less than it had been before the great slump began in

1921). Although no more than 84.7 per cent of the 1945 total was affiliated to the TUC, from 1939 the TUC monopolised all lines of communication with government.

Organised labour had an inestimable advantage in Bevin's membership of the War Cabinet. But, as one Treasury official wrote, this did not always give the TUC what it wanted: 'anything beyond what would be achieved by the informal influence of Mr. Bevin was not worth attempting'.[47] Bevin achieved his aims, unabashedly, by using whichever card suited him best, either with Citrine and the staff, or with pliant members of the General Council (and confronted by the Minister of Labour, few did not comply). Bevin seems to have disliked Citrine, for all his skills: he was, he told Dalton, 'always trying to be a super Foreign Secretary . . . but he doesn't run his office as well as old Charlie Bowerman [before 1921] and doesn't really get as much out of government'. This was unfair, as was Dalton's own comment, 'the GC, Bevin thinks, are a hopeless lot. They don't hold their end up against the employers in joint consultation, so that he himself often has to play the part of a union leader rather than a minister.'[48] Bevin disliked fixed procedures and could be highly autocratic; yet the TUC lived by procedures, which explains why Citrine sought endlessly to consolidate unions' fragile power (other than the power to call strikes) by formalising the tripartite arrangements of 1940–42. Naturally they quarrelled, sometimes seriously enough for Attlee to have to intervene.

Though Citrine's authority was rarely questioned on the General Council, and though the headquarters staff benefited (like those of the FBI) from unions' demands for information and assistance, their power was strictly limited by individual unions' – or general secretaries' – willingness to fulfil the TUC's requests. Citrine set himself to establish parity with the employers in all relations with government while the emergency still gave unions a measure of equivalence. Preoccupied with improving conditions and extending membership among the lowest paid and the ill-organised, on the other hand Bevin was often irritated by evidence of a bureaucratic mentality he instinctively disliked. But Citrine saw the political value of established channels in a pluralistic system, once labour had lost its temporary advantage, if the TUC could broaden its range of access beyond MLNS, and deepen it downwards through officials to regional authorities. For him, corporate bias represented the desirable state of affairs: 'in reconstruction matters . . . it will obviously be essential that the General Council should retain freedom of contact with the BOT, Ministry of Transport and Treasury'.[49]

The results were, at best, patchy, though Citrine did establish sympathetic links with some Conservative Ministers including Churchill and Beaverbrook. Treasury and Supply rebuffed the TUC's claims to parity with employers, and sometimes denied it even consultation, though this may have been due as much to administrative difficulty as political discrimination. Few union leaders reached senior *executive* positions, as distinct from membership of advisory committees. Their accumulation of experience, status, and effective power lagged behind that of industrialists; but, more importantly, Citrine had his reward when it came to membership of the committees planning reconstruction.

As with industry, a secondary line ran from MLNS to individual unions; and to supplement this at local level the TUC attempted to enlist Trades Councils – or rather those that had survived, battered and disciplined, the battles of 1934 with the Communist Party. To match the department's regional structure, it appointed Regional Advisory Committees. Less impressive than their titles suggest, these bodies provided useful services to unions, so that the TUC came to resemble a vast clearing house for information and advice, with an authority as the agent of government that had never existed in World War One. Bevin took care to ask the General Council and individual unions to approve Regulation IAA in 1944. The Government would, no doubt, have gone ahead in any case, but approval mattered to both sides, as it did in the dilution agreements in 1940–42, and the early collective wages agreements in the car industry.

Since Coalition Ministers had to devote their entire energies to the war effort, and were actively dissuaded by Churchill from introducing 'party politics' into the Cabinet or its committees, political party organisations were very largely excluded from the wartime system so long as the extreme crisis lasted, that is, from May 1940 to the early part of 1943.

On the Conservative side, the Research Department went into abeyance in 1940, apart from R. A. Butler's research programme, and activity remained desultory until nearly the end of the war.[50] With fewer agents, many constituency associations became moribund. Churchill, least party-political of all Conservative leaders, was not inclined to talk of future manifestos and took his advice rather from the War Cabinet staff or his friend Lord Cherwell. Thus very little discussion took place of the implications either of extensions to the state (which most party men imagined to be temporary, like that of 1914–18) or of those delayed ideological time-bombs left over from the 1930s such as regional industrial policy and planning (results of the Barlow report on the location of industry) or land usage (the Uthwatt report). Churchill's colleagues were inclined to let state intervention run, as long as the war was successful, and the right to manage industry was safeguarded. As far as trade unions were concerned, they recognised the need to seek TUC co-operation but hoped that MLNS and Board of Trade would take advantage to remove restrictive practices, and strengthen union officials against shop stewards and their power to call unofficial strikes.[51]

Labour Party officials woke up much earlier to the implications of the wartime state, but their chances to advise new and overworked Labour Ministers only came when reconstruction planning began. Also, unlike its Conservative counterpart, the Labour Research Department found considerable difficulty in coming to terms with corporate bias, at least insofar as it tended to downgrade the party *vis-à-vis* the TUC. In 1914–18, Arthur Henderson's simplistic distinction between the 'political' and the 'industrial' spheres had more or less been maintained. Now, Bevin was deputy Prime Minister in all but name with greater authority than Attlee, the party leader, or Herbert Morrison, before he even became an MP. The formalities were observed on the National Council of Labour and discussions occasionally took place between trade union MPs and the General Council; while the Council itself took care not to infringe on the Parliamentary Labour Party's sovereignty – if only to avoid giving Conservatives a hostage.[52] But nothing could disguise the fact that the TUC had a direct link to the War Cabinet and the main department of state. This may explain why Labour Ministers showed themselves remote, even standoffish, towards it.

This is not the place to discuss the parties' work in dealing with the public, nor the House of Commons' role in wartime as a clearing house for information and grievances. Government concerned itself closely with morale and sought to plumb it by every means available, open or covert ranging from Home Intelligence reports to the surveillance of suspicious groups by MI5 and Special Branch. Education and management of opinion became a branch of the war effort itself, and the radical wave of public opinion, which swelled in 1943–44, bent Ministers' and their officials' minds more to reconstruction than might otherwise have been the case. But no discontent existed on the scale of World War One to inspire another 1917 Industrial Unrest

Commission, nor was it necessary to restrain dissident opinion, after the inital internments of pre-war Fascists under Regulation 18B, and after the German invasion of Russia in June 1941 began what the Communist Party at once adopted as the 'great patriotic war'. The small Common Wealth Party, which achieved remarkable by-election results after 1943,[53] was quite other: a part of the radical wave, with 400 branches and 15 000 members, capable of publishing a striking and influential challenge to the party truce, *A New Social Order*, in 1944. Its support, however, seeped away into the Labour Party as the 1945 election approached, indicating that its social base, mainly among white-collar workers and technicians, had been insufficient to alter the traditional framework of voters' allegiance.

The existence and shape of the wartime system indicates how strong were the tendencies to work with government, inside an extended state, that corporate bias implies. It is easier, however, to describe its functioning than to assess its success. By comparison with Britain's 1914–18 experience, or the German or French cases, it has always been judged very highly as an 'experimental success'. Nevertheless, it was in the interests of each participating group subsequently to play up its part, emphasising the harmony of the whole, and a certain scepticism should be maintained. During the gas industry enquiry in 1944, one Board of Trade official wrote: 'Citrine has claimed more than once that the TUC is the most representative body of consumers in the country. My Minister, with Mr. Bevin's support, has consistently refused to accept this contention'.[54]

Official historians certainly recognised (and architects of the system on the Machinery of Government Committee utilised) the existence of corporate bias. They saw that the TUC, the BEC or FBI, as representative organisations or 'governing institutions', had a vested interest in dealing with government, while regulating their own members' affairs with the minimum of outside interference. Self-interest and a certain altruism, expressed as particular views of the general interest, went hand in hand. The Machinery of Government Committee actually dismissed the state's 'superior right' to introduce a distinct public interest. 'In so far as their members are representative of the industry . . . or are men of status accepted by the industry as capable of appreciating the industry's problems, their use clearly facilitates the application of measures of control and rationalisation which, however necessary, would be far more distasteful to the industry, and would be operated far less smoothly, if they were directly imposed by hands reeking of "Whitehall bureaucracy" or "party politics".[55]

This could serve as a Whitehall epitaph on the wartime system. Departments themselves assiduously justified corporate tendencies, not only as the best pragmatic solution to problems of supply and production, but as a necessary institutional buffer state between government (the political direction) and industry, labour or finance; and also between Whitehall and the general public.[56] Unless it is argued that such views were common at all times in modern industrial states (which is absurd) wartime practice in Britain seems to have reached a peak only marginally short of the corporate state. But that margin remained distinct and vital. Controls and sponsorship practice had, by 1943, reached a limit, in the opinion of survivors who ran the system. To have gone further would have alienated most interests and individuals. Whitehall had been stretched almost beyond endurance and probably could not have extended the system. As exhausted as their Ministers, civil servants reached 1945 in a sort of trance.

Dingle Foot, Minister for Economic Warfare, observed in 1943 that after twelve years in which industry and unions had pressed government to intervene to help them, there was now a need to preserve parliament, government and the civil service from further demands. Like his fellow-Liberal, Lord Haldane in 1918, he sought not only to simplify the process but to restore parliamentary control and supervision by the Civil Service Commission. It was the first cry against corporatism, echoing Bonar Law's 1923 complaints about Lloyd George's legacy, and pre-dating Aneurin Bevan's attack on Bevin; the first attempt to curb the new state, drawn from a radical who imagined war had spawned a machine that would permanently impair the political parties and debilitate democracy.[57]

Most participants suffered no such doubts – or kept quiet, accepting that unusual times needed men and remedies that would get things done quickly. The TUC took care always to emphasise that it had 'never challenged the rights of parliament as the final authority on legislation'. Others, like Beveridge, would have gone further and instituted fuller planning to achieve, in the people's interest, a 'people's peace'. The state, he thought, had directed employment but had not yet ensured fair distribution of rewards; instead, its intervention had vitiated the logic of private industry and collective wage bargaining. Nonetheless, he had to admit he preferred the system to any practical alternative: 'I at least want unions after the

British model, autonomous associations pursuing sectional ends, rather than unions after the Russian model, associations organised from above to secure the purposes of the state.'[58]

As for compliance by institutions, firms and the public, the limited number of cases where state coercion proved necessary,[59] suggests that, at most times, most played by the rules. After mid-1944, with the war nearly won, as the intensity of effort diminished and war-weariness set in (to be measured by falling production targets and productivity), the sense of common purpose and dedication began to evaporate; but that can hardly be blamed on wartime organisation.

Apparently untroubled by philosophical doubts, Attlee judged simply that wartime organisation 'had produced remarkable results . . . it is a natural step that the Government [in 1945] has recently taken, to reconstitute the NJAC . . . with a view to establishing a regular channel of communication between the government, the employers and workers.'[60] Stafford Cripps and Herbert Morrison concurred. Bevin later told Oliver Franks that the key was 'persuasion with power, but not power without persuasion'. A distinct, even categorical historic memory, uniquely favourable to the system was thus added to its more practical legacies, influencing, for example, Churchill's 1951 scheme for Cabinet 'overlords', as well as the official histories of the war written in the 1950s and '60s. It can be found in TUC minutes of the Tewson era, FBI memoranda, in Volumes 22 and 23 of Keynes' *Collected Works*, and in the transmitted memory which was the post-war Ministry of Labour's inheritance from MLNS. Here was a golden age of industrial relations, when the TUC's goodwill could be taken for granted, when a Minister ruled who did not need educating, when officials could oversee and control the national labour market as never before or since – an age to which subsequent officials looked back with nostalgia, even longing. Without being fanciful, one can say that wartime experience enjoyed a late flowering among those who backed the idea of the National Economic Development Council in 1961–64: politicians who had themselves observed the system from the First War front like Major Harold Macmillan, or the Second like Colonel Selwyn Lloyd and Colonel Edward Heath.

2 Attitudes in War

Absence of 'homes fit for heroes' and a general failure to meet the lavish promises of social reform in 1918 inhibit any historian from trying to argue that Christopher Addison and his Ministry of Reconstruction made a profound impression on living conditions in Britain. Assessing reconstruction planning during the Second World War raises a quite different problem: so much was accomplished by the 1945–51 Labour Governments, and so much of the preparatory work has been attributed to two notable protagonists, William Beveridge and Maynard Keynes, that the sense of more general activity in the Coalition government has almost disappeared. But what was done was not simply Keynes's and Beveridge's work; nor did it (as Kenneth Morgan has emphasised[1]) lead directly to the Labour Party's 1945 programme, even though Labour Ministers had substantial and perhaps predominant influence in the Ministerial Reconstruction Committee. Policy-making was a more general and complicated process that took place inside a many-layered matrix of ministers, civil servants and outside advisors; it grew out of the interweaving of different methods, clashes between older and newer ideas and conflicting ideologies. It is hardly surprising that the published outcome (in particular the 1944 White Paper on employment policy) seems timid in comparison with Beveridge's Reports; they *were* timid when set beside the vigorous Cabinet papers written by participants in the three-year-old process of argument.

Reconstruction was a coherent process, an intrinsic consequence of the changes of 1940–41; it was not an afterthought or a sop to raise public morale as in World War One. Precisely because the wartime system allowed all the substantive interests and institutions a degree of access to and influence within government, ideas about the future germinated early and vigorously, albeit at a level below that of the War Cabinet. The planning of reconstruction therefore provides a vital test of how the system worked, and of the attitudes and aspirations of each participant. Its legacy comprised not just the regimes of a welfare state or full employment but the concept of a post-war settlement, guaranteed under a reformed state.

In the earliest stages, 1940–41, reconstruction planning lay in the hands of a very few senior civil servants sitting in key committees on Reconstruction, Machinery of Government, and Post-War Economic Problems, or representing their departments on the NJAC, NPACI, Production Authority, or Capital Issues Committee. Their attitudes naturally reflected individual ideas about the economy and society which had been formulated in the inter-war years. Although they realised that the post-war world would be very different, they tended to assume that post-war problems would be ones of accommodation, which could in due course be solved, and that the major evils, to which they should address themselves, would still be those they had experienced before. The senior men in industry or among bankers and trades unionists with whom they came in contact had similar assumptions. Knowing that planning was starting (even if they had not been invited by government in the interests of the war effort), the latter would have had every self-interest in seeing that their views on such momentous subjects were not ignored. Between 1940 and 1945 a window slowly opened on to what, for most of them, was an unimaginable world. At an exceptionally fluid time, normal barriers to political discourse had been lifted; the future was to be discussed and competed for, in a contest where the stakes were limited only by external factors, and where the rules (that this activity was strictly conditional on the greater business of winning the war) were plain but simple.

Competition for the future thus ranged across the whole field of rewards which institutions could expect for public wartime service: from tangible, material gains in wages or wealth and positional goods to political advantage, from legal security to market opportunity. Naturally, in a finite economy, no one interest could expect to scoop the pool nor did any of them intend a revolution. They were bound, therefore, by a built-in constraint or motive for self-regulation; at a time of national struggle and individual self-sacrifice, self-interest had to veil itself decently in a cloak of legitimacy by claiming to be one aspect of the national interest. Since all the participants knew this, and knew each other's bargaining positions well, accumulating experience drew them all towards a set of compromises which never actually outstepped the bounds of the possible. If, on the way to 1945, some of the most intractable questions were buried, the extent of their achievement remains unique.

Because the War Cabinet and the full Cabinet tended to divide on party lines when future policy was opened up, they did not provide a suitable forum for discussing reconstruction, at least in Churchill's eyes: hence his doctrine of 'all for the war and nothing not for the war' laid down, in some exasperation, in October 1943. Churchill had set up a committee on War Aims, early in 1941, with Attlee in the chair and given it a brief to consider post-war problems, but when it produced only cloudy generalities it was put aside.[2] Attlee in turn brushed aside Harold Laski's attempts to raise such issues; and when Laski turned to Churchill instead, the latter answered, 'We ought to win the war first, and then in a free country, the issues of Socialism and Free Enterprise [can] be fought out in a constitutional manner.'[3] A similar caution if not outright hostility to premature policy-making can be found in Churchill's approach to the first Beveridge report; it raised hopes that a war-torn nation might simply not be able to afford. Conservative Ministers were, of course, involved in much post-war planning, but apart from R. A. Butler those who did most were the 'temporary politicians' like Anderson, Woolton and Lyttleton. Their Labour counterparts increasingly kept quiet, waiting for the end of the party truce. Bevin thus found himself at odds with his party – or at least the radical end of it – in his advocacy of continuing the Coalition into peacetime.

This is not to deny Ministerial authority over reconstruction planning. Little was done in the committees of officials without Ministers' knowledge. But knowledge did not convey approval, let alone adoption of the new ideas. As far as Coalition leaders were concerned, it is probably accurate to suggest that they wanted such activity to go on, so that the preliminary stages could be accomplished. Those decisions that were necessary before the Coalition broke up could then be taken, and the rest handed to whatever Administration took office after the post-war election. What they probably did not realise was that the centripetal force of the wartime system would work to create such a ferment on those committees that the original rather vague agendas would be transmuted into a coherent corpus of ideas, which Ministers might subsequently accept, curtail, amend or reject,[4] but which they could not think through again, in order to produce alternatives.

Reconstruction thus bears only the most superficial resemblance to Addison's lonely stand, *contra mundum*, in 1917–18. Delegation of Ministerial authority to civil servants had another very important consequence: it ensured that the questions would be argued out primarily within the committee structures and not outside. The institutions would, therefore, have to contribute and participate through the system, and not campaign in public; and the political party machines would stand apart, waiting for their turn once the Coalition had dissolved. The parties were thus circumvented much more seriously than their leaders who had to react continually to the volumes of paper coming from below and whose personal intellectual graphs can hardly be abstracted from contact with the Civil Service in these four years. New intra-party alignments and divisions were developing, between Churchill and his close colleagues, Cherwell or Beaverbrook, as against Butler and the Tory Reform Group and the Conservative Research Department, or between Attlee and Morrison on one side, and Dalton and the Labour Party radicals on the other. Whereas Attlee reacted to the draft White Paper on Employment Policy in April 1944 by confirming his belief in a mixed economy, distribution of whose rewards would be guaranteed by full employment, Dalton decided that 'the acid test for any industrial system . . . lies in its ability to give those needs [of employment and production] a continuous and effective expression, to provide an ever-widening market for the products of human skill and scientific invention. This the capitalist system has failed to do.'[5]

Ministers' busy remoteness and sporadic involvement in such disputes put the responsibility for advanced thinking on a very heterogeneous body of mandarins and recruits from outside the Civil Service. Their ideas (as opposed to their working practice) ranged from those who clung to traditional concepts to others who imagined that the future would, in every way, be different; within both these very wide categories there were some who tried to use the reconstruction process in a defensive way, others in a creative, even radical one. Age and experience mattered less to their work than very general pragmatic or Hegelian principles: as Sir Thomas Philips put it, they had to make up their minds, depending on 'what is *acceptable* . . . in the public interest'. Almost without exception, however, they kept the process to themselves, a narrow guild who admitted proper influence (that is, proper to the wartime system) but as little as possible the intrusion of prima donnas like

Beveridge (whose exile to the Committee examining welfare provisions was generally welcomed) or of 'revolutionaries' like Harold Laski.

Certain primary limits to reconstruction intruded themselves and could not be baulked. Britain's need to survive had dictated the pattern of wartime finance. As a result, the country was now locked into the sterling area, with its massive holdings by countries some of which, in the post-war world, could not conceivably be expected to share British interests.[6] Shortages of dollars had been endemic from the start; the post-war national debt would be inordinate, and the balance of payments precarious. All had been foreseen by Treasury officials and the Bank, who had handled the sales of dollar assets, and raised the loans from New York in 1940. Lend–Lease, and the February 1942 Mutual Aid programme kept the British war effort alive, and by mid-1942 dollar shortages had ceased to be Keynes' main problem. But capital goods were excluded by the USA from Lend–Lease, in 1943, which was further cut a year later in the interests of the American effort against Japan. Starting in July 1944, Britain began the negotiations with Henry Morgenthau which led on in due course to the Ottawa Conference and Keynes' mission to Washington. Lend–Lease, renewed for the UK's contribution in the Pacific in April 1945, finally ended abruptly that September.

There could be no reasonable doubt, first that Britain would have to export to survive, and secondly that the terms for survival had been worsened in advance by American penetration of former British markets in Asia and Australasia, and by US-inspired exclusion from Latin America. Stringent measures to cope with debt repayment, the balance of payments problem, and high public borrowing became governing principles, barely open to argument. Other departments had little choice but to accept Treasury rulings; they could only argue the level of priority to be attached to physical reconstruction, and expenditure on welfare, health, education or – at the very end of the line – personal consumption. Rather than rebel against harsh logic, the committees either discussed finance couched in terms of capital as against income taxation, or the share of investment funds to be allotted to private industry, or argued, with varying degrees of optimism, about a new economic world order which would permit each nation to reconstruct without suffering balance of payments problems, because of an assumed common interest in freer trade, growth and full employment.

The other main constraints, being rather more under British

control, were more fully blended into the reconstruction debate. But certain aspects of industrial reconstruction and manpower policy proved highly intractable. As Keynes pointed out in Washington, in 1945, the British economy had been debilitated not only by war damage and loss of life, but by unwelcome aspects of industrial concentration; nor had Britain benefited as much from applied research as the United States. There was reason to be deeply worried both about the investment base, and how the investment funds that did exist could be applied to an often backward and ill-coordinated private industry, without perpetuating the large numbers of small and inefficient units and generally restrictive mentality characteristic of the 1930s.[7]

Board of Trade plans looked to regenerated trade associations acting as agencies for modernising and reconstructing industry; but they lacked an institutional answer to remedy patent shortages of scientific and technical manpower, or the lack of equipment, laboratories, research and development facilities, 'which meant, simply, that Britain was inadequately prepared for the international competition in technologically advanced goods which would develop after post-war shortages of primary products were overcome'.[8] Government organisation of science had remained a piecemeal adjunct to war needs (like the Tizard Committee or the hermetic groups at Bletchley Park), without making much impression on the academically-centred outlook of scientists themselves, and without linking scientists as a coherent group in any permanent sense to government. Even the high-level link between Churchill and Cherwell carried no weight beyond the War Cabinet, especially when Cherwell and his contemporaries, Tizard, Bernal or Blackett had so little in common.[9]

Since mobility in wartime reached a remarkable level, and training expanded exponentially to make up for dilution and substitution by women, the main labour constraints occurred in the form of shortages of skilled workers and, rather later, declining productivity. Real scarcities had shown up by mid-1943, which could not easily be remedied. Redeployment and training became a constant preoccupation of the War Cabinet once it appeared from MLNS surveys that manpower budgeting had reached its limits. Whatever plans were made for the future had, therefore, to take account of first the massive wartime distortion of the labour market, and secondly (if controls were simply relaxed) of the danger of a tumultuous surge of wages in a seller's market like 1919–20. The very success of manpower control militated against its quick reversal; yet, paradoxically, the controls which would allow a slow steady restoration of a free system were those likely to be most immediately and widely resented, as intolerable restrictions on post-war liberty.

To this extent, the 'free space' was actually very narrow.. Yet the inner groups, logically and rightly, set themselves to argue from first principles, accepting ruefully enough that constraints existed, without allowing them to dominate discussion. Perhaps memories of missed chances in 1917–18 haunted them for the departmental records are filled with references to the First World War and its aftermath. Survivors confess to having been aware of 'Time's wingèd chariot hurrying near', yet time existed for most of them to change their minds about what was necessary and feasible, along a graph whose bottom line marked a transition from comprehensive gloom in 1941 to qualified optimism by 1943.

The mandarins all agreed, in very general terms, about planning the economy and on the importance of the sterling area; in addition, physical controls were universally seen to be temporary,[10] to be phased out as soon as possible. But they came only slowly to accept demand management or full employment as principles in post-war policy. The highly controversial memorandum put to the Post-War Economic Issues Committee in March 1941 by Professor James Meade[11] (advocating a pragmatic, redistributive policy, based on maintaining a high level of demand, upwards or downwards in relation to the general level of unemployment, rather than one based on specific acts of policy) though it struck sparks, was not widely accepted until 1943–44. From another angle, what MLNS called 'full employment for all those who wish to work' crossed the threshold of acceptance only in the context of world-wide expansionist trading policies which, it was assumed, would be led by the United States.[12] In this sort of progression, all could agree that persuasion emphasising the need for voluntary commitment offered the only hope of public acceptance; this in turn added weight to arguments for demand management (indirect means) rather than direct physical control.

Although some officials and committees misread the lessons of 1917–20, or superimposed them too rigidly (when it came to demobilisation, for example), they do not appear to have become prisoners of the illusion that what individual representatives of labour or industry or banking promised to contribute, at a time of collective altruism, would always bind their successors – certainly not when it came to the hard questions of wages, investment, or productivity. But most seem to have subscribed to an astonishingly pervasive assumption, shared equally by Ministers such as Attlee, Cripps and Butler, that the interests outside government would, as part of a bargain and in return for state assurances of prosperity and full employment, curb their own members' selfish and sectional demands.

Almost from the start, the mandarins agreed among themselves that in peacetime, if there were to be economic management, it should be carried out by the Treasury; if industrial regulation and an export drive, then the Board of Trade; if reform of the labour market, it should be by MLNS. The concept of full employment offered a unique facility for each department to achieve its aims at least cost, provided that a bargain involving reciprocal obligations were made with the institutions whose markets they sponsored. The Treasury would be able to safeguard its prime concerns, sterling and the balance of payments, without the odium of concomitant deflation which had dogged it through the 1920s. Trade could bridge the policy divide between its pursuit of free trade and exports, on one side, and stimulation of efficiency and survival of firms in the home market on the other. Finally, Labour could (with trade unions' responsible help) secure both levels of wages acceptable to industry and an adequate supply of skilled manpower. This at least evolved as the Economic Issues Committee's dream, late in 1941, when it drafted a memorandum of national priorities which reconstruction planning in fact followed remarkably closely.[13]

But behind the face presented to Ministers, some quite fundamental divergences soon appeared. If the economy were to be managed, should it be done via demand or supply? Should the first emphasis be on industrial efficiency or full employment? Was deficit financing permissible and if so for how long? Though these questions came from the economists, they had an inalienable political content, which acted forcefully on the political principles concerned and for the rest of the war habitually separated the War Cabinet Economic Section from the Board of Trade (which could usually count on support from Supply, Production and MAP) and the Treasury (though to a lesser extent, either because its officials grasped their importance rather late on, or because they wanted to play brokers between the others).

Trade officials, ably backed by the former IDAC men[14] now in Supply, and using empirical evidence from Ministry of Production experience, launched their claim to be a future Ministry of Industry, and defined Britain's main problem as one of recapturing export markets and keeping industry competitive.[15] In that sense, the 'sheltered' home-based industries should not be allowed (as they had in the inter-war years) to check 'progress'. Hubert Henderson's strictures about monopoly, cartels and restrictive practices hit hard at management: Board of Trade remedies ranged from managerial reform to technological innovation and investment – what a later generation would call the supply side. But the Board of Trade introduced a new and endlessly disputable element when it argued that it had an additional 'duty to the consumer' which could only be exercised in ensuring lower prices and better products. That of course involved liberal trading policies, and a concern with wages and industrial costs. Industrial efficiency, it was assumed, depended on freer competition; but competition among firms not competition in a sense which would be detrimental to trades unions' collective bargaining power, because BOT had evidently no wish to dismantle the industrial relations system or the ethos of wartime tripartism and left the issue of trade unions' restrictive practices, tacitly, to MLNS. Hence monopolistic and restrictive practices were cast as bad in themselves, permissible only in special circumstances.[16] Such a thoroughgoing assault on the practices endemic in the 1930s implied reform not only at trade associations' level but right down to the individual firm.

Lionel Robbins, speaking for the Economic Section, meanwhile pointed out the contradiction between competitive efficiency and the demand inflationary consequences likely to follow full employment. Combined as it was with Beveridge's own well-founded fears of wage inflation under conditions of trade union monopoly power (forecast by Keynes in *How to Pay for the War* (1940)), this argument amounted to a major spanner in the works; it was never logically resolved, and subsequent discussion could proceed only by a tacit agreement to let it lie, though its substance was written into the cautionary (and little read) small print of the 1944 White Paper.

Robbins had exposed the weakest spot in the assumptions on which planning and indeed the whole wartime system had been instituted. If self-interest were taken to be the guiding principle of human activity then, once external constraints were removed, economic management on the basis of tripartite collaboration would inevitably lead to oligopoly and abuse, accompanied by inflation.[17] Subsequent arguments had, therefore, to assume either a return to a free market which all participants knew had not existed in living memory – and perhaps never had existed, even in the early nineteenth century – or that the external threat from Nazi Germany which had so far enforced good behaviour could somehow be transmuted into a peacetime constraint sufficiently powerful to harness the residual altruism of interests and institutions. For readers of Adam Smith, this implied a profound change in human behaviour. Board of Trade officials at first reacted to Robbins *démarche* by hoping that his predictions would not prove true. Later, they rallied around the idea of a package deal crowned by full employment policies, pleasing to all partners, sufficient to create a permanent consensus.

In between, a great variety of propositions emerged. Some, like BOT's scheme for Regional Boards for particular industries under an overall Industrial Commission, look forward nearly thirty years to NEDC. Being voluntaristic, they did not, however, confront the problem of monopoly power. Trade officials refused to take head-on the question of monopolies (influenced presumably by their practical knowledge of the forces in industry, financial and other services, ranged against them) preferring to define each one, seriatim, as legitimate or as an abuse, according to an ill-defined standard of 'maximum output and efficiency'. Unfortunately, as the Treasury pointed out rather sardonically, civil servants possessed no overall picture of 'industry's' role in the economy as distinct from a (political) conception of the economic system itself, and hence no empirical basis for measurement.

This may have been unjust to Trade men who had gone far in 1943 towards uncovering the long roots of Britain's historically poor industrial performance. But it is clear that even they failed to see, then that the prevalence of small firms in Britain implied an inadequate base for investment in research and development. For most BOT officials (unlike Robbins who had spent his life in academia) the archetypal industrialist was the owner-manager of a small or medium-sized factory, alert to new opportunities for profit, rather than the managerial elite of large corporations who were, officials believed, inherently predisposed to rig markets, regulate production, and evade international competition by concentrating on the easy home market. These images of course derived from the inter-war years (if not from before 1914) even if they remained only too relevant in Britain long after the war. But their prevalence obscured both the vast process of concentration which the war had only interrupted, and the degree to which Britain would in future be subject to the operations of multinational trading.

Cleavages on such central matters might, if pursued with their full theoretical rigour, have stultified the work not only of the Economic Issues Committee but the reconstruction package itself. It is characteristic of British government practice that they failed permanently to split the officials, who seemed unwilling to follow Robbins or Henderson far, being concerned primarily to produce agreed documents for Ministers who had no time to spend on disputation. Already, in 1943, some first principles were being buried by officials' day-to-day realism. But not the question of balanced budgets. The Treasury old guard fought on, even after deficit financing had been accepted in the Budget in April 1942, and ensured that the officials' draft of the 1944 White Paper would argue not only that maintenance of full employment would require more than a high level of demand, but that at the same time deficit financing should be regarded as acceptable only in bad years; surpluses in good times should guarantee balanced budgets over the longer term.

From these complicated interchanges, spread over nearly three years, it can be deduced that the Treasury had in no way given up its claim as 'guardian of the public purse' to the final say, within an ordered budgetary procedure, and to arbitrage between Economic Section and Board of Trade. In the end, it sided with the latter at the price of accepting the idea of a managed economy, despite the logical inconsistencies Robbins had pointed out. The Treasury would accept new principles, so long as it retained traditional practice. Government had to go on; Ministers had to be served. Against that, Robbins and his colleagues could be dismissed as theoretical, idealistic and – worse – temporary. By their standards, it is a tribute to Treasury officials' faith in the new ideas and their capacity to handle them, that the 1944 White Paper reads as lucidly as it does; it is a tribute to Robbins that his predictions remain valid forty years later.

Meanwhile, however large its role in shaping the war effort, which probably peaked in 1943, MLNS took a more lowly part in charting the future. Its officials sought mainly to defend what they had helped to establish through the NJAC/JCC network: the practice of joint consultation, and conscious involvement of unions and the TUC in the state's orbit. They wished to continue wages regulation in order to prevent a disorderly return to collective bargaining; and to maintain price stability to prevent a rush of wage claims, strikes and inflation; in short to preserve good industrial relations, and parity so far as possible between the two sides when it came to replacing arbitration by normal peacetime conciliation. If in conditions of future austerity the standard of living had to fall, they preferred this to happen through inflation, rather than by cutting money wages, for they feared to repeat the industrial strife of the period of wage cutting, in the 1920s.[18] Theirs was a liberalism which blamed the failure of recovery after World War One not on strikers but on economic dislocation and which, at heart, defended the mass of workers, whether or not organised in unions, who as individuals had suffered most, and who, if the Board of Trade and the BEC had their way with wages, would face a second deprivation.

Aware that the window was open and that it was unwise not to edge it wider, the institutions, discreetly, or vociferously, told the committees their views. The financial sector, represented by the Bank, had the great advantage that the officials almost universally accepted that post-war priorities would revert to their peacetime order, with the balance of payments and sterling first, manpower (including health and education) third, 'industry' in between. (Consumption would come a poor fourth.) Montagu Norman and his colleagues, however, took a very strong position on more controversial questions. They imagined that exchange control would be only temporary and that sterling would, in due course, revert to being fully convertible. In the meantime, its status as an international reserve currency would naturally be preserved, together with the sterling area. Treasury officials concurred, as did the Board of Trade. Whether this majority of the inner elite would for choice have gone quite so far as the Bank did in planning for a sterling-based economic zone in which Britain could operate without dollars, and retain a banker-client relationship with the holders of sterling balances, is not so clear.[19]

Until his retirement in April 1944, Norman had had an extraordinary, perhaps unique position. His ease of access to and familiar links with the US Federal Reserve Bank, the Canadian and other Commonwealth Reserve Banks, backed by more than twenty years' experience as Governor, gave him an authority which the Chancellor, Kingsley Wood, and Churchill himself found persuasive. As early as June 1940, Wood took on Catto (who was to become Norman's successor in 1944) as a special advisor when he set up his Consultative Committee to represent industry, banking, commerce and trade unions; subsequently Catto developed a close working understanding with Keynes that complemented the Keynes–Norman *entente*. Continuity between Bank, Treasury and Chancellor was to last, through the Bretton Woods negotiations, down to Keynes' death.

The Bank steadily developed an interest in the idea of a national post-war social and economic settlement. Its team of planners, in the research department, were probably more highly experienced in industrial and manpower problems than their Treasury counterparts, and influenced Treasury submissions to central committees. What Wood called 'those progressive developments which we all desire to achieve and on which we are already engaged', in his 1943 Budget speech, included full employment as well as export trade recovery, price and wage stability, and liberal international currency arrangements. Even the Treasury 'old guard', men like Sir Wilfred Eady, having long since accepted the '3 per cent war' and the operations of the Capital Issues Committee, seem to have found less and less difficulty with the idea of a comprehensive 'settlement'. But some of Norman's direct intrusions, such as his attempts to get his own protégés into the Ministry of Supply, were resented. Norman himself had also too long a history, including the 1931 crisis, to be acceptable to Ministers in a future Labour government. Catto, a former merchant banker, succeeded him in April 1944, much to the pleasure of the new Chancellor, Sir John Anderson, just at the time when the Employment White Paper came to Cabinet. The Bank's dream – shared, in varying degrees by the CLCB, the merchant banks, the Stock Exchange, Lloyd's, and commodity markets – of a sterling area run from London, with bilateral trading arrangements with the sterling balance holders, bolstered by Commonwealth preference schemes operating in Britain's interest, began, however, to look increasingly over-optimistic and anachronistic, particularly once Lend–Lease had been curtailed in 1943. American opinion grew hostile to what was seen in Washington as a plan for neo-colonial domination of a vast trading market. Officially, the United States took the view that the sterling balances should largely be written off, as part of a general settlement of war debts under the Mutual Aid system – a scheme to which Keynes and the British delegation in Washington reacted with horror, for it constituted an assault not only on London's role as banker to the sterling area, but on Britain's political and trading future. Susan Strange argues that the United States, as *de facto* ultimate guarantor of the sterling area, wished to maintain sterling as precursor to a new international monetary order and would, consequently, have accepted some discrimination in favour of Britain, but never pretensions to run the area as a fief of the United Kingdom.[20]

Because of the functional division between FBI and BEC, and rather more because of the inherent differences of outlook between large and smaller enterprise, no 'industry front' existed. The range of views in World War Two still resembled that of the late 1920s, with a liberal wing comprising the most politically prominent industrialists, chairmen and directors of large, often multinational companies, a centre represented by the FBI Council, and including a number of employers' organisations and a wing which ought not to be described as 'right' but rather as insular and preoccupied with the problematic future of smaller firms in home and export markets. The latter was poorly organised but usually grouped itself with the BEC, in political terms, when wages, productivity and union restrictive practices were concerned. Alfred Mond's heirs led discussion with government, and tended to ignore the rest.

FBI and BEC had both benefited from the war in terms of membership, funds and organisation, and access to government. (By 1946, the FBI had, for example, ten policy advisors and 29 Directors of Commodity Divisions in the Ministry of Food alone.) At central and regional level, its leading members had made the acquaintance of civil servants and Ministers; through the Capital Issues Committee and the JCC it had penetrated both the City and the area of 'labour issues' previously guarded by the BEC. The FBI could thus present itself in the post-war economic issues debate as a broker for industry, almost to the exclusion of the BEC.[21] But the FBI's obsessive fear that Britain would face a slump comparable to 1921, meant that its pleas for government assistance made little impression; Board of Trade officials believed that a post-war boom would float industry through the transition period without aid and saw in the FBI's pleas only more evidence of the need to enforce competition.[22]

Like the civil servants, industrialists started gloomily and became slowly less pessimistic. In 1942, the FBI's pamphlet, *Reconstruction*, argued the need to perpetuate wartime association of industry with government predicting that, unless the state ensured a high level of growth, unemployment would return. Any suggestion that this implied protection or a revival of pre-war oligopoly was, however, rejected by the 'liberal' group (whose own *A National Policy for Industry* also appeared in 1942). Two years later, in *The Organisation of Industry*

(1944) the FBI presented a view more congenial to the Board of Trade which rather tardily claimed paternity for the idea of self-regulation: 'the government should confine itself to producing a framework of national economic policy, leaving the details to be filled in by working organisations provided by the industries themselves'.[23] Member firms' and trade associations' reluctance to get sucked into a bureaucratic structure can be seen in its insistence that any peacetime system should be voluntary.

The BEC Council regarded these publications with aloof disfavour. Having dealt for more than twenty years with 'political' matters, it still saw the FBI as 'soft', prone to schemes for feather-bedding; and the authors of *A National Policy for Industry* as union sympathisers.[24] But it responded by broadening its constitution to allow it to deal with purely industrial problems, evidently hoping to bludgeon the FBI into a merger. The BEC's own (by no means reactionary) message, underlined by its strongest member, the Engineering Employers' Federation (EEF), was that the wartime practice should guide Ministry of Labour and employers in post-war Britain. Good Labour relations and a flexible labour market, not state protection for industry, should be the war's lasting monument.

Individual managers and owners, of course, took their cues from the condition of their own firm or trade association rather than from the aggregate opinions of central organisations. As far as can be gauged from FBI and BEC papers, most of them assumed that the wartime bodies like NPACI and NJAC would continue, suitably adapted. Where individuals like Richard Glenday or William Wallace, or like-minded groups brought together, for example, by the Nuffield Foundation at Oxford, or on the Central Committees of Export Groups, expressed distinctive views they followed lines familiar to pre-war 'middle opinion'. Samuel Courtauld alone sought a measure of state corporatism, far beyond what most of his colleagues thought desirable, involving Board of Trade reform of trade associations, state control of investment, state ownership of basic industry, an FBI–BEC merger, workers' participation (so long as unions accepted complementary responsibility) – and controls over wage bargaining.[25] Some of his ideas nevertheless found a place in Beveridge's 'Full Employment in a Free Society' in 1944; in particular (paragraph 241) state direction of industrial investment through a National Investment Board, under a Ministry of Finance assisted by the Bank of England.

The Nuffield conferences had a seminal effect on participants and ultimately on their organisations. Indeed, the proceedings at Oxford may have been more influential than the final report, since they made it possible, informally, for industrialists to accept a measure of future state ownership of energy production and the transport system which few in 1943 would have cared to declare publicly. Their spokesman, Cecil Weir, could also indicate, to government officials attending the conference, that such consent for nationalisation would depend on a future government choosing the directors and chairmen of the new boards from the pool of existing managerial talent.[26] Since the industrial 'liberals', Lord Melchett, Cecil Weir and P. S. Cadbury, evidently shared this FBI 'minimum demand' there could be no doubt in the minds of trades unionists and Labour Party members such as G. D. H. Cole, Thomas Balogh, Nicholas Kaldor, and Evan Durbin, who also attended.

It is hard to assign specific influence on government to any of these declarations, or to the manifesto, *A National Policy for Industry* (1942) signed by 120 of the more 'liberal' industrialists. The latter, evidently, intended to affect Board of Trade policy-making by drumming up industrial and perhaps public opinion. From the FBI's standpoint it was important to carry the BEC, and match if not attract the TUC whose own publications appealed to a rival opinion. Being a much more representative group than Mond's 1927 colleagues, they could take a higher ground in the need to dissociate 'industry' from memories of the thirties' unemployment and oligopoly; their tone was of service to the nation, profit in the cause of investment and high employment. Above all they recognised that the state itself had changed: the era of planning had arrived.

Some of their chosen themes were contested by union leaders, keen not to let industry establish a prescriptive advantage in public conscience. But at the time, what mattered most to trades unionists was industrialists' firm repudiation of unemployment as a weapon to drive wages down and their acceptance of a permanent peacetime extension of the NJAC–NPACI system. BOT officials, however, also noted in their own crucial January 1943 document, *A National Policy* pledged to increase output and efficiency, and to address the question of monopoly by discouraging 'wasteful competition' on one hand, while on the other encouraging competition ('in the public interest') in the labour market. If the 120 industrialists intended to reassure the Board of Trade, and eliminate sanctions against industry from its armoury, they probably succeeded.

But they ran ahead of either the FBI or BEC in asking for reassurances. Even if government were committed to demand management and a liberal international trading policy, the cycle of boom and slump would persist; consequently, industry (they spoke of course, for manufacturing industry) needed to be defended. The 120 therefore set up the National Policy for Industry Committee, with Walter Monckton in the chair, and heavyweight members like Henry McGowan, R. Barlow and W. Pilkington. (Citrine was invited to join but to their chagrin he declined when the FBI/BEC merger failed.) Their first meeting, in October 1943, set out a long-term agenda which, consciously and deliberately, ran parallel to the inner deliberations of the civil servants.[27]

The committee accepted from the start that the commitment to full employment was in industry's interest. Full employment meant high home demand, whatever the competitive situation outside. Secure there, industry could fulfil its export duty and keep the balance of payments in equilibrium, and if wages rose (as in conditions of full employment was inevitable) the home market could bear the cost. (Small wonder that Joan Robinson, the economist, complained on behalf of the public, as consumers.[28]) In return for full employment, the unions would exercise a decent wage restraint; and the financial sector, grateful for London's uninterrupted recovery of world leadership, would play its part (as some of the banks had done, haltingly, in the 1930s) in industrial investment.

It is not clear from the documents whether the Board of Trade took the leading part, ahead of industry in 1942–43, or relied more heavily on the input of leading industrialists than its officials cared to admit on paper. Many of the links were purely personal and have left no record. At the least, enough industrialists were aware of what was going on in the official committees to ensure that their colleagues in the FBI and BEC Councils adapted to the new shape of the economy germinating in Whitehall; and the process culminated with the publication of the FBI's *Organisation of Industry* in 1944. They saw that the pre-war structure of industry could not support what was coming to be the post-war settlement unless they collaborated. They would pay a price, they supposed, in losing some monopolies and restrictive practices, and in accepting state ownership of certain industries, but these concessions might be limited by bargaining. They would not, for example accept Beveridge's National Investment Bank nor a blanket legal prohibition of monopoly, nor the appointment of any but experienced managers on State Boards; as for the labour market, they would accept the survival of collective bargaining, despite their fears that unions' power had increased. 'Making sympathetic strikes illegal should suffice'.[29]

Even more explicitly than the financial sector, the National Policy for Industry Committee proposed a contract with government in which, voluntarily but with a due sense of responsibility to national interests, industry would make itself productive and efficient. In return, they expected government to manage the external economic environment, diminish fluctuations and facilitate exports, and ensure (by legal restraint where necessary) the basis for good industrial relations. As for their own duty as Monckton put it: 'The responsibility for those directing industry is to hold a just balance between the varying interests of the public as consumers, the staff and workmen as employees, and the stockholders as investors; and to make the highest possible contribution to the well-being of the nation as a whole'.[30]

This mellifluous draft was not simply Panglossian. It admitted grave defects: needs for reform, innovation, new technology, new management systems and codes of conduct against profiteering. Deep down, however, the 1930s tone came through: the British economy needed to be defended against an international free-for-all; the export markets were to be recovered through collective, government-aided effort. Such views were unwelcome both to the Economic Section and the Board of Trade.

Whether or not this increasingly centrist (if not social-democratic) group really represented all British manufacturing industry, it accepted a range of social obligations such as collaboration with trades unions over training, the betterment of low-paid groups, some extension of worker participation,[31] and controls on location of industry. To counter Board of Trade accusations, they argued that monopoly was not *necessarily* detrimental; each restrictive practice should be judged on its merits or demerits. Trade associations and cartels, far from being primarily restrictive, 'exercise a stabilising influence against violent fluctuations and dislocating shifts in the currents of world trade and they have an essential role to play in post-war reconstruction, while international economic co-operation . . . will be of the highest importance'.[32] The case they put, however, depended firstly on a close co-operation of FBI and BEC under a Central Council of Industry which was prejudiced when the merger failed; and secondly on continued obedience by member firms to hierarchical organisation which would have no sanctions on behaviour, other than persuasion, once the wartime system of materials and supply allocation had ended. Even Monckton's group could not agree on a model for the Council of Industry, or whether that, or government, should initiate policy.[33] They concurred only on the principle that the state should have no real power to break monopoly. In spite of their prudent fears of being accused of 'corporatism', the Monckton group's intellectual lineage remained that of Alfred Mond, inspired with wartime altruism indeed, but sauced still with the old *schadenfreude*: 'the spirit is lacking on the side of labour and this is partly because workers think that if they work harder only the investor will profit'.[34]

This is not to say that government could not work with such material, only that industry could not regulate itself other than by a mixture of self-interest and altruism filtered through its traditional perceptions of other conflicting interests. 'What you and I originally hoped for', McGowan told Monckton in January 1944, 'was for a committee in which the major employers' organisations would come in on one side and representatives of the TUC on the other'; without that, he believed, even government could not act.[35] Even if Citrine had joined them, it is inherently unlikely that tripartite discussion in 1943 (*before* the full employment package had been put together in government) could have gone much further than it had in 1929–31. Too many hard questions intruded to prevent a distinguished but self-appointed group from performing as an industrial parliament. Nevertheless, by the end of 1943, 'industry' under its various aspects, had clarified its outlook and given government a brief for its version of a post-war settlement; based on a tripartite, voluntary structure, providing access to government, influence on policy and assistance to the state. So long as government gave industry for the first time a substantive *generic* priority it would in return listen to what Ministers wanted; so long as it had a voice in the determination of that interest, at least as powerful as those of unions or the City of London, it would conform to the eventual national interest.

Because of its ideological coherence, and long habituation to dealing with one department (the Ministry of Labour) the TUC could, far more easily than 'industry', address government as a representative body. The world of organised labour, after all, lent itself to straightforward categories, unlike manufacturing industry where even the Monckton group's schema – comprising basic, largely state-owned industry, large companies, and small firms – ignored middle areas, the role of multinationals, and oil and steel companies. TUC officials saw, correctly, that planning for reconstruction would become a continuous process, so that the more links they had with departments other than MLNS, the stronger their voice would be. Because this permeation was essentially informal, the Economic Committee took the lead, rather than the General Council: the smaller group included the 'big six' and senior officials and could report back when necessary.[36]

Lacking the obvious personal advantage of prominent industrialists, the TUC failed to establish a link direct to the War Cabinet. But wartime Ministers did not deliberately disfavour it, and towards the end used the prestige it had built up through the Anglo–Soviet trade union link in their foreign policy. Because the TUC took the government's side against Soviet insistence on the 'second front' and also tried to contain the British Communist Party's advances, Citrine saw much of Churchill and Eden, the Foreign Secretary. Conversely, the TUC could claim to have a peculiar insight into Soviet priorities which increased its value to Ministers. Admittedly, Citrine failed to play broker between the Soviet Union and the American Federation of Labour in 1942–43; but the moves which led in October 1945 to creation of a World Federation of Trade Unions, later on to look like a mini-Comintern, strengthened the link with Eden and the AFL (and in the long run facilitated the part that AFL officials played in the European Reconstruction Programme after 1947).[37]

Well aware that its claim to represent all workers, unionised or not, was not shared by civil service mandarins, the TUC developed some shrewd ploys such as seeking equal representation on the proposed Industrial Boards (where union officials might take part in planning for post-war industry, deconcentration, standardisation, research and development, location, technical education and joint state purchasing and marketing). But Citrine and the Economic Department, bound by the need to carry General Council opinion and that of the movement as a whole, could move only slowly. At factory level, rumblings could be heard from shop stewards in certain industries. Officials had no desire to revive a shop stewards' movement in opposition to any union leadership, and therefore referred back continually to the Resolutions adopted by Congress in 1932. Such caution became even more necessary in 1944–45 as individual unions, in particular the newly-created National Union of Mineworkers, demonstrated a growing radicalism. (Early in 1945, the NUM drafted a much more extensive programme for nationalising industries than the Labour Party was prepared to accept.) As far as Labour Party policy went, they took care to remain uncommitted to any ideal of industrial organisation, but assumed that tripartism would continue, with government supplying 'confidential information concerning government policy and the national economic position'.[38]

Insofar as the Economic Committee thought about the post-war world, in the early stages of the war, it confined itself to production and planning. As the idea of full employment reached a more general threshold of acceptance in 1942–43, in the government committees and Beveridge's preliminary work for his second report, these early priorities were reworked. Thereafter the TUC prepared to use every available lever to facilitate a full employment programme: through its International Committee's links with the AFL and later through American diplomats working at the Economic Co-operation Authority, and with the Anglo-American Productivity Council, it attempted to influence United States' economic policy against a possible return to the Gold Standard, with all that that might have meant in terms of automatic deflation. It is doubtful, however, whether TUC members really understood the implications of full employment as a factor in the sort of economic management which the government committees were discussing.[39] Instead of asking the sorts of questions about inflation which preoccupied Beveridge and Robbins, they sought, not unnaturally, to define full employment in the widest sense, and pressed that on the policy-makers, Beveridge included.

At this point in 1943, the TUC directed its main effort at Beveridge himself, rather than at the official committees, a misperception about where most influence lay that was understandable, given Beveridge's success in publicising his first Report, but nevertheless significant for the future. Beveridge in turn, only too well aware that his inquiry into employment policy had been virtually ostracised by the Civil Service, with Ministers' tacit approval, saw that if he could tempt the TUC into agreement, his second report ('Full Employment in a Free Society') would acquire extra weight. He had no natural affinity with union leaders, nor they with him, but each influenced the other, so that, during the winter of 1943–44, the TUC began to shift its faith, tentatively, from physical controls and nationalisation towards the techniques implied in the comprehensive welfare/full employment/ economic management package which Beveridge offered them.

In turn, the TUC formulated an argument about self-regulation similar to that put by industry but with less direct impact on the policy-makers. They recognised, for example, the dangers that Beveridge argued lay in wage inflation, but replied with apparent total

conviction that they would be curbed by higher productivity and
self-discipline – the stronger since full employment would have
eliminated the ancient threat of the sack. By early 1944, the Economic
Committee could offer the government (or rather Beveridge, whom
they took to be its spokesman) a deal – self-restraint of wages to
match employers' control of prices, on the clear understanding that it
would never be asked to accept compulsory arbitration in wage or
industrial disputes, or legal penalties for failure to conform to
agreements.[40] Bargains first, consensus after, voluntarism
throughout, became their motto. Throughout this process, the TUC
showed itself reactive rather than innovative, and took the war
experience to be the status quo: otherwise it is hard to see how its
members could have taken for granted the survival of price control. To
assume that the historic pattern in which management had habitually
passed on cost increases in higher prices would change so swiftly,
required a remarkable act of faith. Nevertheless, the TUC asserted
that it *could* help to keep wages down in relation to unit costs, provided
the system of national bargaining were retained (a reference to the
unwelcome evolution of a system of plant bargaining in certain car
factories in the Midlands). They claimed not to wish to interfere with
managerial prerogatives and indeed said nothing about the idea of
worker participation.

Citrine pursued his departmental contacts, less for their own sake
than to ensure a permanent presence where the TUC could continue to
argue out this bargain, once the war's end removed their temporary
advantage. But interchanges with the Treasury took place at a fairly
subordinate level.

Although the Economic Committee approved of Keynes' proposals
for a new international monetary system, and stood firm with Bevin in
rejecting anything that smelled of the Gold Standard and automatic
deflation, its members seem to have been unaware either of the
implications for economic management of Britain's sterling debts or
the Bank/Treasury plans for the sterling area. In a wider sense, trades
unionists shied away from 'theory', particularly if it emanated from the
Labour Research Department. Arguments about the 'public interest',
especially the Board of Trade's principle of 'consumer interest',
seemed likely to undermine the TUC's claim to represent all workers
by hand and brain, and were, almost subconsciously, rejected as
divisive. Reconstruction and planning were much safer if kept separate
from unions' primary concern, the return to collective bargaining.[41]

A long transition period was envisaged, in which controls might last four years or more, and in which 'the public' would need to be educated to accept tripartism and 'orderly procedures' in industrial life.

At the same time as defending the gains achieved in war, however, the TUC hoped to achieve a more fundamental change in society than any of the other participants. Slowly, and preferably without inter-regional disruption, planning and wealth redistribution would occur. Since their hope that the government would declare its hand ended in October 1943 with Churchill's prohibition on policy discussion, the TUC put the future in the hands of Labour's National Executive and set out, for the education of its own membership and the wider public, what it wanted. Its report, *Reconstruction* (1944) (prepared partly by Alan Flanders and M. Turner, TUC researchers) was not a presentation to government or the official committees but an attempt to mobilise national opinion to galvanise an inert Coalition. Its declaration that 'the trade union movement will never surrender its bargaining powers or undertake to use them for any purpose other than that of protecting or advancing the interests of workpeople' should not be seen as an aid to Labour in a hypothetical post-war election (since the TUC still presumed the Coalition would continue), but as a warning to a Conservative-dominated Coalition that TUC consent could not be taken for granted, but would have to be renegotiated on more formal terms.

Had the Economic Committee been as aware as the financial or industrial sectors of the package taking shape (that is, if it had dealt as directly with the official committees as with Beveridge), *Reconstruction* might have been phrased differently, and the TUC might conceivably have become a little detached from its reliance on the Labour Party. Churchill's prohibition provided instead the evidence for what the TUC had always suspected – that business and finance were to be restored to power, and organised labour required to resume its subordinate position. As it turned out, the TUC inclined to accept what was offered by the Employment White Paper in 1944, but instead of taking it as the sum of wartime policy-making, bargained for more, putting its faith in the working class public and the Labour Party without ever wholly trusting the officials who had worked the White Paper out.[42]

This absence of trust (which did not apply to MLNS officials[43]) in no way weakened the TUC's urge to associate itself closely and permanently with the state, nor its hope that the Coalition would continue during the transition years. Otherwise, they feared that their gains might easily evaporate in a period of strife unleashed by party warfare. The defensiveness of three-quarters of a century had not dissolved. As MLNS observed, 'the right to strike and the right to choose jobs freely are deeply embedded in the minds of British workmen, whether or not they are members of trade unions. These rights will not be surrendered, even in return for permanence of employment. They are regarded as fundamental; and this view of them will have been strengthened by the consideration that it is for such rights as these that the war has been fought.'[44]

Too much stood between the three institutions for any easy consensus. Lacking combined pressure from those quarters, it is conceivable that Churchill's prohibition might have stopped the inner committees going further if it had not been for momentum in other areas of the British polity. Beveridge's first report, on Social Insurance and Allied Services in 1942, as broadcast and disseminated in the Press, and later expanded and extended through the work of Labour rather than Liberal sympathisers and the Army Bureau of Current Affairs, stimulated so great a public response to the promise of social reform that Conservative Ministers found it hard to ignore. Dissent also built up in the House of Commons (and was reflected in the surprising rise of Common Wealth).

Ministers would have been extremely myopic if they had ignored the turn in public opinion, reflected as it was in all the Home Intelligence Reports for the Ministry of Information after 1943. The Ministry's own handling of the Beveridge Report (which appeared at one of the worst points of the war) had presumed a unity of thought and action in the nation at large, whose war efforts were to be repaid by a state pledge to eventual victory over Beveridge's 'five giants': Want, Ignorance, Squalor, Idleness and Disease. Just as civil servants, sensitive to a longer-term public interest than many politicians, and to public demand filtering up through local offices of MLNS, Health, Pensions, saw the need to make a public commitment,[45] so the public came gradually to accept that the state – not parties nor government – would guarantee the contract.

In presenting this message, however, in and after 1942, the departments and Beveridge himself (who embarked on a personal crusade) played down the more restrictive aspects of the original Report. Their audience wished to hear more about benefits than constraints; it was by no means certain that 'benefit in return for contributions, rather than free allowance from the state, is what the people of Britain desire', as Beveridge originally claimed.[46] Instead, public demand overrode initial Treasury fears of unbearable cost – a result that was then rationalised by the calculation that 'if the scheme was rejected, more would certainly have to be paid out to placate particular interests', and the contributory principle itself might be abrogated.

How to pay for the cost of welfare services subsequently became one element in what can be seen as the 1944 White Paper 'package'. How to persuade the nation at large (and especially the trade union movement which had not guaranteed the co-operation of workers who, the TUC believed, had barely been consulted), to accept the rules of that compromise remained the dilemma of home propaganda down to the late 1940s. Government too attempted to mobilise what it conceived public opinion to be in order to impress the responsibilities spelt out in the package forcibly on unions and industry. This need to carry consent was so acute that it may also have shaped the idea of economic management. As Lionel Robbins had argued even in 1941, 'Public opinion will almost certainly insist that a national policy of the kind needed to diminish unemployment should not be abandoned for the purposes of preserving international commercial and monetary agreements',[47] or, he might have added, for deflationary policy.

If their brand of public education succeeded, Conservative members of the Coalition could hope to prevent demand brimming over while the war was still going on, and perhaps also prevent the radical swing that was only too evident in 1943–44 from benefiting the Labour Party. In this indirect sense, what the political parties did (or in the case of the Conservative Party did not do) also affected reconstruction planning, so that the TUC did not err in its reliance on the National Council of Labour and its own sponsored representatives in the House of Commons.

This is not to say that currents in the Conservative Party were irrelevant. Planning had been discouraged by Churchill, Kingsley Wood and Woolton (whose party brief included reconstruction) in 1940–42; but certain markers had been set down. In July 1940 Sir Robert Hacking the Chairman had asked Butler to study public opinion 'with a view to adjusting the Party's outlook to the radically different trends of thought which prevail at a time like this'. Butler duly set out to modernise the organisation.[48] But the agenda that the reformers set themselves was a fair indication of pre-war priorities: an odd combination of agriculture, education, national security, finance and industry, forestry, reconstruction, electoral reform and 'the constitution'. Much of the discussion that followed was grounded in assumptions from the preceding decade and even on the questions of industry or fiscal policy shows little evidence of consultation with outside interests. Efforts to keep an ideological balance on the main research committee probably delayed matters; as did Butler's departure to become Minister of Education. Sir David Maxwell Fyfe took more interest in party propaganda than research and his views on state intervention remained intransigent.

The initiatives of the Tory Reform Association (which 'fused the old Tory tradition of state interventionism with the more recent ideas of Harold Macmillan and other radical Conservatives of the 1930s'[49]) were, as yet, unacceptable. The Post-War Problems Committee's comment on Beveridge's first report sourly represented the party's centre of gravity: 'provision by the state of complete social security can only be achieved at the expense of personal freedom and by sacrificing the right of an individual to choose what life he wishes to lead and what occupation he wishes to follow'.[50] Full employment was to be seen as an uncovenanted benefit of the return to prosperity *after* reconstruction, not an essential pre-condition. If prosperity did not return, then austerity would follow, with reduced consumption and cuts in these evidently spurious social security concessions. Given such an approach, it is hardly surprising that the Committee members worried about eroding the contributory insurance principle and about 'loss of the will to work' – not only among workers, but also among managers and investors, who it presumed would continue to seek easy returns rather than hazard their wealth in new enterprise.

Butler's return in 1944, and a general realisation that the mood of the public would not welcome such bleak 'realism' if it were couched in an election manifesto, helped to soften the tone. Sir Robert Topping warned, percipiently, of electoral disaster if the party did not choose new, younger candidates, untainted by association with the grey 1930s. Under Henry Brooke, the reconditioned Research Department became 'workshop to the Party', without, however, injecting any real originality or resolving a growing confusion about where the party was actually going. The Tory Reform Association, though vocal, failed to acquire influence in this climate. Brooke pleaded vainly for the 'paramount need for setting forth in modern language and with modern application, a statement of what Conservative philosophy really is'.[51] Gelded without direction from Churchill, the Party failed to evolve an alternative axis of policy-making among its leaders, to remedy the gap left by Churchill, although there was talk of an Eden–Butler–Lyttleton combination.[52] Public demand went without answers that could be printed, and the Conservatives faced an election with few of the insights and rapport with public opinion that buoyed up their opponents. Bland in content, aggressive in expression, their manifesto represented the reverse of what the electorate required.[53]

Labour went through its own bleak years, shorn of leadership as its Ministers accustomed themselves for the first time to running great departments of state. Its Research Department worked in low key through 1941–42 and revived in 1943 almost too late to affect discussion in the inner committees of officials. But in October 1943 a Home Policy Committee, run jointly by Morgan Philips (NEC), J. S. Middleton (PLP) and Citrine (TUC) was set up to co-ordinate planning and reconstruction. It made contact immediately with Beveridge and his entourage of advisors, and with MLNS and BOT officials, while two of its members began to attend the TUC's Economic Committee.

Until this point, policy-making in party headquarters had been restricted to exegesis of past Conference Resolutions, mainly from 1933–35, with a view to a distant election at least two or three years after the war ended. The tradition established by the XYZ Group (founded in 1933 by Nicholas Davenport) whose most gifted members, Evan Durbin, Douglas Jay, Hugh Gaitskell, Nicholas Kaldor and Thomas Balogh were all now in government service, seemed to have run out with the publication in 1940 of Durbin's book *The Case for Democratic Socialism*, even though it gave them the basis on which to review the failures of the inter-war years, incorporating Keynesian principles of demand management and emphasising the state's role in providing social justice, rather than physical planning.

During 1943 this tone changed, almost abruptly, at least in the Research Department and the Home Policy Committee, as Harold Laski, and to a lesser extent Hugh Dalton, tried to use both to prepare and disseminate policies which would ensure a breach in the Coalition, and thus isolate Attlee and his staider colleagues.[54] By 1944, thanks to their views on support for the Soviet Union, both were isolated; yet to a considerable extent their work seems to have carried rank and file opinion in the constituencies. Small groups such as 'Socialist Commentary', though active in asking penetrating questions about technology, competitiveness and the future pattern of work, in comparison lacked impact either on the leadership or the traditional left.

By November 1943, the HPC had prepared a document enshrining the doctrine of full employment in an iconostasis of new post-war controls, including powers to reduce the Bank of England to a department of the Treasury 'subject to the direction of the Chancellor and the Cabinet'. The radicals wavered later only on whether to control industrial investment through a Public Board, the existing Capital Issues Committee, or some new Treasury instrument. In no circumstances was the City of London to regain its predominance or freedom from its 'great creditor', the government.[55] Ideas of almost unlimited planning – for industrial development, imports, exports, scarce raw materials allocation, and the exchange rate – infused the HPC's documents right through 1944 and must be seen as far more than a mere revenge for the 'bankers ramp' of 1931. Wildly unrealistic in its assumptions about United States' attitudes towards the sterling area and Britain's 'dollar gap', such a programme could not but alienate Attlee and Morrison, who were soon taking Keynes' side in the exchanges in Washington.

On the labour side, the HPC adopted a 40-hour week and worker participation in industry – the latter in terms of works councils and workshop self-government.[56] Steering between fears of inflation and deflation, its members fastened on purchasing power as the key to full employment: hence price control bulked large. A figure of 500 000 unemployed (3 per cent) was taken as 'reasonable',[57] (though Beveridge had still not specified his figure). As if this were not heady enough, in an attempt to catch the rising public mood, Laski published a visionary polemic *The Old World and the New Society*, which offended many in the party and those TUC pragmatists who thought more about jobs than socialism. They backed Morrison and the detailed studies which culminated in Labour's *Plan for Reconstruction* (1944). A real fear that deflation might be imposed on Britain, post-war, temporarily brought together Morrison, Bevan and Gaitskell in support of a scheme which envisaged the state as providing finance and stimulus to reorganisation of industry, without broadside public ownership and only a loose measure of supervision of a large private sector.[58] But Bevan remained the critic on most occasions, and only joined the mainstream when elected to the NEC in autumn 1944.

Tough language in Research Department papers ('specious cries for self-government in industry mean in practice the right of the private owners to go their own way, often with the help of the state') belied the party leadership's interest in consensus between industry, finance and labour: 'But if private enterprise co-operated, there would be enough investment funds for all . . . Our policy will have to be one that will make capitalism work.'[59] Dalton found this latter statement quite inadequate, and in a series of redrafts sought to give it a more socialist gloss. Differences over presentation rather than detail dogged further efforts during the first half of 1944.

Briefly, at the end of that year, and in particular at the Party Conference in December, the radicals triumphed. A resolution proposing the nationalisation of land, much of heavy industry, banking, transport and energy, put by Ian Mikardo, was passed and for a time shaped the drafting of Labour's election manifesto.

But the challenge subsided. Attlee and Morrison had always tried to ensure that party policy matched public demand and since by 1945 it appeared that the electorate was more concerned to have a limited but guaranteed social reform rather than gamble on greater change, *Let Us Face the Future* was tailored so that in the end it amounted to little more than *Labour's Immediate Programme* (1937). The actual balance between public and private industry (with the steel industry as the most contentious point) remained undecided into 1945, by which time, under the influence of Michael Kalecki, the party's economists had begun to fear the power of pent-up demand and a possible inflationary boom.[60]

Reconstruction, and that very large, fundamental part of the post-war settlement which rested on principles established before 1945 thus owed relatively little to the political parties; even the 'great originators' Keynes and Beveridge figure, in a general assessment, less prominently in the matrix of policy-making than their biographers have claimed. Some common ground existed from an early stage of the war between the competing industrial and union interests, on which the inner government committees capitalised. But consensus did not simply emerge: it had to be fought for, and at crucial points, Ministers of both parties adjudicated or intervened, as the narrative of certain crucial policy decisions (see Chapter 3) shows. Nor did this competition occur only in smoke-filled corridors and committee rooms; each interest appealed, in a variety of ways, to public opinion, knowing that government was in a position to measure that opinion and highly interested in maintaining it in equilibrium. In a deep, if unquantifiable way the electorate made its inchoate wishes known, without benefit of elections.

The common ground contained four organising principles: first that elements of wartime tripartite, voluntary organisation would survive, staffed by some of those who had managed the system; second, that reconstruction and its aftermath would be planned, though only transiently by the use of physical controls; third, that each institution, and the departments to whom they were now affiliated, would bulk much larger in the extended state, and government policy-making, than had previously been the case; fourth, that a political contract between them was *possible*, in which rewards and obligations might balance the demands of self-interest – a conundrum to which full employment provided the key.

In the beginning, in 1940–42, each had its own understanding of the 'shape' of the economy, and its potential in the future, should Britain survive. Here there existed the greatest gulfs; here what can only be described as government brokerage mattered most. 'It may be thought it would be impossible for trade union leaders to accept and act upon these assurances under any system of private enterprise and free competition,' an MLNS official wrote in mid-1942. 'There might, however, be hope of success if the principle were put forward by the state as part of an orderly system of *post-war* planning, designed to promote social security and to remove the danger of industrial depression; and agreed after full consultation with General Council and BEC.'[61] Only government could hammer heads together and offer sufficient blandishments when, as one industrialist put it later, 'the truth is that, human nature being what it is, fear is the only thing to spur labour to greater efforts. It was fear of invasion, not only abstract patriotism, which caused the spurt in the Dunkirk days.'[62]

Labour Ministers in the 1945–50 government certainly believed that fundamental quarrels *had* been harmonised. Attlee's and Cripps' vision of co-operation between government, industry, commerce and labour would otherwise have been mere folly.[63] Opinion in Whitehall may have been more sceptical, since the real battles had been fought there, slowly to accommodate clashes of principle and interest at all levels. To the end, the Treasury and Board of Trade stood out against giving parity with finance and industry to organised labour, and conceived of industry itself in terms different from those of MLNS. For both of them, the industrial and labour markets could be managed indirectly, from above, in the national interest, without benefit of assistance from the institutions.[64]

From that standpoint, MLNS ranked as a sponsor department which had allowed itself to become a lobby for its special interest. Yet MLNS judged accurately the importance of full employment, as the major public aspect of management of the economy (for which the ground rules did not then exist) designed to prevent slump, by stabilising demand at a permanently high level. Caught already by the attractions of that proposition, Treasury and Trade had, perforce, also to concern themselves with the dilemma of wage inflation, and ask whether to accept MLNS assurances of union good behaviour in return,[65] or whether to work into the new policies other, more subtle means of indirect control.

There is a certain serendipity about this conjuncture in 1943, absent from the politics of other belligerents. Britain was, in fact, the only major participant in World War Two which went through this sort of process, perhaps the only one in which it would have been feasible. Forty years of experience in competition between conflicting institutions and interests, and a far denser pluralistic habit of determining issues, allowed to emerge, in wartime, an unlikely thing: a gamble on the future which in turn influenced all the victor powers and shaped politics in Britain for two generations.

3 Bargaining for Reconstruction

Reconstruction did not follow a natural progression leading easily and directly to the post-war haven of welfare state and full employment. At times, especially in 1941–42, it seemed as if the planners were still trying to solve 1930s problems. Their inter-war experience continued to infuse discussion on the inner government committees so that the main product, the 1944 White Paper on employment policy, became a palimpsest whose original ink and pigments occasionally showed through. No simple lifting of old constraints occurred, allowing pre-war 'middle opinion' to dominate the agenda – indeed whatever new ideas or principles emerged, traditional governing practice was very largely restored. The picture given in most accounts written after the war, with Whiggish overtones of evolutionary improvement based on an assumed alliance between Ministers of both parties, bureaucrats and outsiders, drew its colour from ideas about the role of government which at the time participants did not share. Instead, they competed to write the future's agenda in all areas where their substantive interests were concerned. Striving for advantage, each department or institution tried to influence the plans, thus ensuring, first, that what emerged was not what had originally been imagined, and second that the many different plans for reform, ranging from policies on trade to budgetary balance, monopolies to the labour market, would finally be amalgamated into a single scheme, as the best if not the only way to win general agreement.

In this process, questions of status and tradition in government helped to determine how things were done. The committees slipped naturally into a hierarchy of importance, depending on subject matter, chronology of appointment and seniority of personnel. Machinery of Government (MOG) determined the pattern of future Cabinet and departmental organisation, sponsorship and the geography of planning; Post-War Economic Problems first defined the problems, then Post-War Employment argued out the interdependent package on which the 1944 White Paper was based. In the end all of them accepted full employment (as yet imprecisely defined) as crucial in terms of reward for the electorate and obtaining consensus among the 'governing institutions'. By the end of 1943, it appeared achievable, so long as the various incompatible demands could be harmonised. Thus Treasury opposition to deficit financing in years of slump (necessary to help bolster demand and prevent automatic deflation) could be offset by a commitment in the White Paper to surpluses in good years providing for general equilibrium. Some deeper contradictions, however, only made themselves obvious after the package had been agreed: such as what level of unemployment actually constituted 'full employment' for the purposes of demand management. Even harder questions were buried since they could not be resolved – only to surface again many years later.

Limited aspects of a vast canvas matter here: machinery of government, industry and trade, finance (domestic and international). All of them overlapped, being as interdependent as the officials who staffed the committees, but separation is not anhistorical since the sense of interdependence did not come at once and was still imperfect in 1944. Machinery of Government (MOG) took priority, its object being the shape of government, how it would work and what the state wished to be.

MOG began in November 1942 with questions not unlike Lord Haldane's 1917 brief: what should be the role of and functional division between Ministers? What should be the type of Ministerial body – large Cabinet, small War Cabinet, or hybrid? How should this body be staffed and advised and by whom – should independent (academic) economists appear, for example? But unlike Haldane's wide-ranging inquiry, the committee accepted the status quo of 1939 and under Treasury influence eschewed Hegelian first principles. There would be no Ministry of the Plan nor the Interior. Wartime experience was taken to be transient and there seemed no point in discussing the relative merits of either a command economy or the sort of market economy they imagined to have existed before 1914.

To eliminate 'theoreticians', as much as to ensure party balance Churchill and Edward Bridges took great care in selecting both the Ministerial and official committees. MOG let it be known that it welcomed evidence but only from within government.[1] In practice, the Treasury dominated by sheer volume of its presentations on 'Treasury control', management of the Civil Service, function of the Cabinet Office and the future role of scientists and economists. Formally, MOG asked itself, should the pre-war practices of ministerial responsibility to parliament and Treasury control of public expenditure be restored? Behind, of course, lay these questions: which should be the controlling department in Whitehall? Where should the centre of gravity be? Should there be an 'expert overview' and if so, should it be prepared (and by whom) to help the Cabinet or the Chancellor, or the Prime Minister?

Throughout the proceedings, Treasury witnesses argued a 'constitutional' case, based on a classical interpretation that had varied little since before 1914. Only within this given framework would they argue about any of the new techniques and government aims. As a *non possumus* tactic it succeeded in blunting the criticisms put forward by Robbins, Beveridge and academic radicals such as Norman Chester. As a result, apart from debates on the role of non-governmental organisations (subject of a separate enquiry under Sir Cyril Hurcombe) and the part to be played by independent economists, where Robbins and Beveridge concentrated their efforts, the official MOG committee (and to a very great extent the Ministerial Committee) worked from an assumption about what was already 'known' and excluded altogether analysis of alternative methods of government. Their *outillage mental* would have been instantly recognisable to Warren Fisher, Hankey, or even the 1912 Macdonell Commission on the Civil Service. Conditions for Treasury peacetime primacy and the position in Cabinet of the Chancellor of the Exchequer were laid down even in the high days of wartime manpower budgeting. No one questioned the Treasury's responsibility for the Civil Service as a whole. Some witnesses went further, arguing that the Treasury should be seen as a training ground for top men who would then staff other Ministries but this view was so unwelcome to spending departments that it was not seriously considered.

The MOG committee also agreed that it would be desirable to keep future Cabinets small and manageable (it was assumed that one followed the other) and to lay down clearly demarcated Ministerial responsibilities.[2] Old departmental rivalries embodied themselves in new arguments. The Treasury asked for a Minister of Economic Affairs, not to meet the need for which Harold Wilson created the DEA in 1964, but to cut off the Board of Trade from international economic policy. Building rather factiously on BOT's unresolved contradiction that it spanned both trade and industry, the Treasury tried to subordinate it in order more easily to manage Britain's whole external account.[3] Hugh Dalton fought back vigorously, contending that his department should represent both industry and trade. Fortified with an 'industrial budget for economic planning' and powers over price-fixing and monopolies it should rank equal to the Treasury, 'a solid and habitable modern half-way house between old-fashioned private enterprise and old-fashioned nationalisation'.[4]

Sir Cyril Hurcombe's sub-committee examined the part that corporate and non-governmental bodies would take in government. That tripartite consultation should continue was never doubted: Treasury, BOT and MLNS had already committed themselves so far to their sponsored sectors that the various pyramidal networks, from NPACI, NJAC and Production Committee downwards to trade associations and individual firms, were guaranteed to continue. In all their discussions it is clear that, conceptually and in practice, Ministers and officials held images of 'industry' and 'labour' as collective entities threatened with fragmentation if sectional interests were allowed to operate unrestrainedly. Existing networks should not be allowed to ossify or become regulatory agencies, they believed, but should remain dynamic links between government and industry and labour markets.

MLNS advocated a system of tripartite Trade Boards, whose primary purpose should be to achieve good industrial relations and moderation and stability in wage bargaining. They qualified this by arguing that although these aims could not be gained without state intervention it must bear not on collective bargaining, but indirectly through encouragement of responsible self-regulation.[5] BOT looked to similar Industrial Boards under the general direction of an Industrial Commission whose aim would be to encourage industrial efficiency; which 'would deal with all questions other than those involving high policy, in such a way as to secure the confidence of opposing interests, producers and traders for example'.[6] BOT wanted no powers to control output or prices, but a means to foster strong trade associations with whom to deal or, alternatively, even stronger Boards to replace them altogether and concert what was seen as industry's main post-war task in the export trade. This intermediate mechanism would of course be 'neutral' – that is, outside party politics.

Although the MOG committee argued the precise form in which the institutions' corporate bias would be embodied, there is no evidence of any desire to abandon – or even modify – the wartime system. But on the two contentious issues of an economic overview and the role of economic advisors there could be no such consensus. In the complete absence of a command structure headed by a Minister of the Plan, the first choice lay between a single body to make central analytical assessments for Ministers and pluralist bargaining – in effect a reversion to the hallowed practice of departmental brokerage with the Treasury over scarce financial resources. In the end, this choice turned out to be less important than the second question of whether Treasury or independent economists should make the analysis, since the idea of a central assessment would have been of small value if it had merely led to better-informed inter-departmental warfare. From the start, the Treasury argued that 'given the problem of rational and consistent disposition of resources, there can be no pluralistic solution here' – the answer should be in the hands of Ministers responsible for 'policy'.[7]

Inter-war experience gave no pointer to whether the job could be done on 'neutral territory', abstracted from party politics, nor whether the assessment should be for the Chancellor alone, or in conjunction with the Prime Minister. Sir Donald Fergusson (from Agriculture, one of only two Ministries with a long sponsorship tradition) complained caustically that pluralism under Treasury scrutiny resembled 'the hostile scrutiny of rival companies' shareholders'. While his colleagues expatiated on the supposed failure of the old Economic Advisory Council, he argued for semi-independent Commissions, with statutory duties (responsible to parliament like the 1934 Unemployment Insurance Commission) who would give the Prime Minister the means to evaluate and decide all Ministerial proposals, including those from the Treasury. What amounted to institution of a presidential system proved completely unacceptable; and the other officials decided that, whatever shape assessment took, it would remain under Treasury aegis.[8]

At this point, Beveridge put in his proposal for an Economic General staff, a body of gifted, primarily academic economists who, as Hubert Henderson pointed out, would not be endowed with the 'marvellous chameleon-like adaptability of the civil servant' and could, consequently, be relied upon to argue a dispassionate, non-departmental case. In Beveridge's opinion, without such outsiders, the system would soon revert to peacetime inefficiency, while the economy as a whole would fall under permanent state management. He wanted to include a sort of political market mechanism to balance the Chancellor's concern with national income, demand, and full employment; its reports on all major economic problems would go direct to Cabinet. But as Barlow pointed out, this 'planning and intelligence staff of economic experts' was neither an Economic General Staff nor an autonomous advisory body.

Robbins did not go so far, confining himself to extolling the value of academic, non-partisan opinion such as he believed the Economic Section had so far provided. Bridges, who concurred, wished to keep it in the Cabinet Office. Others wanted it given to the Treasury to help in the new work of predicting national income and fluctuations in demand.[9] Final location of the Economic Section was only settled in 1947 (see page 137). Beveridge's wider-ranging formulation proved too fundamental, too philosophically intractable, and was buried, leaving the Treasury to concentrate the MOG Committee's attention on the antithesis between 'Treasury control' and 'pluralism'. 'Orderly government' it declared, in response to criticisms of its pre-war practice, 'requires that demands and projects shall be examined together in one place so that they may be seen in relation to one another and to the general situation, so that priorities and orders of importance may be established'.[10] Using the doctrine of parliamentary sovereignty, the Treasury in practice asserted its claim to powers of determination by control of public expenditure; which, in terms of the vast new essay in economic management, implied an extension of real power far beyond any inter-war experience.

Throughout, Treasury memoranda disingenuously presented this power as exercisable by the Chancellor on behalf of his Cabinet colleagues, a sort of general will of which he served as mere custodian. Surprisingly, the other members allowed this somewhat specious formulation to pass (only Sir Ernest Gower being bold enough even to point it out) and focused, as was intended, on the manner of control, not the principle. In terms of which Dicey would have approved, they discussed control of expenditure not management of national income aggregates. It is true that the rules of economic management still had to be learned: officials in 1943 stood no further forward than Balboa on his peak in Darien, looking at an ocean of whose currents and storms they knew nothing. Nevertheless the subsequent Cabinet decision on 29 November 1944 that for all practical purposes the Treasury would constitute the economic planning and management centre, went far to determine the nature of what was to follow and the way the economy would be understood.

As a corollary, the Ministry of Labour reverted to its former concern with industrial relations, conciliation, training and labour law, with the addition of health, safety and welfare at work. The Board of Trade was confirmed as residuary legatee of Supply, MAP and Production but not as a full-blown Ministry of Industry. Fortified by Cabinet decisions which were direct consequences of MOG Committee recommendations, the Treasury could then concede on many other matters, such as budgetary deficits in years of slump. What had existed before 1939 was restored: the traditional Cabinet, with individual Ministers responsible for major departments; and continuation of existing patterns of sponsorship. Apart from the delicate matter of consumer interests (soon to be assigned to quasi-governmental organisations such as the Monopolies Commission) lines of responsibility reflected existing institutions' interests in government. The fundamental question of the state and its interest never came into focus at all but was perceived only obliquely in these committees, as a sort of ultimate sanction to ensure consensus, once the package on which the post war settlement was to be based had been agreed.

Before that could be composed, Ministers and their officials had to decide in the autumn of 1943 how far planning and economic management would extend and by what means they would be implemented. Decisions here, inevitably, had a binding effect on whatever government took office in 1945.

Since it was assumed that the Coalition would carry on, there was no conscious effort to forestall a possible Labour administration. Nevertheless, as Tawney and Laski (from different points of view) realised, that would be the effect if physical controls, other than over capital movements and building licences, were given purely temporary status in a transition period. But it is hard to be sure whether Labour Ministers (most of whom later seem to have imagined physical controls to mean the activities of the Ministry of Town and Country Planning) appreciated as clearly the cumulative effect of separate decisions taken in 1943–44, even when they related to industries soon to be nationalised (see page 117). (Cripps stands as an exception: in a speech as early as 9 March 1943 he declared that a department's intervention in an industry (in this case aircraft production) should be guided by its technical and commercial expertise: in post-war planning, departments should also be guided by the companies they sponsored in all matters of research and development and production. He alone looked forward to the 1949–50 debate in the Labour Cabinet on the state and private industry.)

The main doubts of the newly-appointed Employment Committee (which in October 1943 took over the principal functions of the PWIEC) about economic management centred on the likely countervailing effect of monopolies and restrictive practices – among industrial firms even more than unions – and on whether the Treasury would actually be competent to conduct such an elaborate and unprecedented exercise. Robbins, by now more than half-way towards accepting state intervention, put the charge bluntly: the Treasury would be too passive and pusillanimous to run the economy efficiently, without a barrage of new devices (such as variable social security payments, direct intervention in industrial investment via public finance corporations, and tax allowances for capital equipment) to make it feasible for them to stabilise demand and consumption.[11]

Having had its own internal discussions about how far to use exceptional measures early in October 1943 (in response to Beveridge's proposals for the Economic General Staff), the Treasury argued in a crucial interdepartmental confrontation with its rivals, who were still trying to hold onto some fiscal independence, that economic management would not be based on abstract general principles (other than that of balancing budgetary deficits by surpluses in other years[12]) but on actual, and as yet unknown conditions. This amounted to a request: trust in our judgment to use the budgetary armoury when the time comes. Given the Treasury's rather naïve assumption that production could easily or quickly be diverted from capital to consumer goods and back, it was dangerous ground for the Economic Section to concede, but neither the Board of Trade's pessimistic analysis of British industry's backwardness, in terms of peacetime international competition and poor investment prospects, nor Robbins' own feelings about managerial incompetence seem to have made much impact. The Treasury indeed conceived of policy in fiscal and monetary terms as if investment were barely a government concern. That cheap money would provide it was established doctrine, based on a highly optimistic reading of recovery in 1932–35, which later transmitted itself with remarkable force to Dalton, Chancellor from 1945–47.

Of course, Treasury officials agreed with BOT and Robbins about the need to diminish monopolistic and other restrictive practices (though they equivocated about resale price maintenance, hoping its retention would stabilise prices, wages and full employment). They had come to believe by the end of 1943 that industrial change could in future be achieved *pari passu* with demand management, leaving adjustment in the labour market to MLNS. They judged that the Board of Trade's Industrial Boards and tripartite Industrial Commission would suffice to promote rationalisation, mergers, capital investment, research and new managerial techniques; in return for this implied demarcation, trade officials accepted that the great bogys of inflation and money supply could be controlled by the Treasury, and that it was BOT responsibility to assist by trying to remove domestic restraints on production, together with tariffs and other obstacles to international trade (see page 97).[13]

This alliance led to a common set of principles which subsequently moulded the whole debate on state control of public industry, and the balance between public and private sectors; even if in the end it by-passed Robbins' criticism of British management. A judgement on whether Labour Ministers fully understood the implications depends on how one reads what they said to sympathetic businessmen, rather than to their party Conference: 'there can be no doubt that regulated private enterprise will continue to make, in appropriate fields, a large and indispensable contribution to national prosperity'.[14] They were certainly aware of the views of industry (expressed at the Nuffield Conference) that a measure of state ownership could be accepted provided the managerial elite continued to run the new public boards, and they concurred with officials' opinion that 'the principle of representation of sectional interest was to be deprecated', whatever earlier talk had taken place about worker participation.[15] By the end of 1943 substantial agreement existed in government as a whole about the principles which any further state control were intended to implement: efficiency in notoriously inefficient or unprofitable but essential infra-structure industries; good management and industrial relations; self-generated investment, and corporate independence of government. A state sector figure of 20 per cent of the industrial base seems to have become widely acceptable.[16] Organisation and the principle of Ministerial responsibility followed the examples of the

CEB, the BBC or BOAC, state corporations of the 1930s, abstracted from party politics. So close were these to the aims of Herbert Morrison's 1934 model of a nationalised industry that Labour Ministers did not dissent.

In the debate about Industrial Boards and the nature of the post-war transition period, nationalisation did not become a distinct issue until the Labour Government came in and set up its Committee on the Socialisation of Industry. In 1943–44, under the Board of Trade's aegis, Ministers and officials assumed the need for state controls over much of private industry during the transition, to prevent it from lapsing into restrictive habits, and to defend consumer interests against any combination between management and labour to raise wages and prices. But thereafter government's part would consist merely in providing support and advice, with intervention restricted to cases where industries asked sponsor departments for assistance, or where the national interest was in jeopardy. Positive planning would, indeed, serve to modernise public industries, but reform of private industry would come from competition and emphasis on the contribution to be made by small business.[17]

During the same transition period, controls over prices (essential to keep the cost of living down and stabilise wages) would continue; so would the Essential Work Orders. MLNS officials imagined at first that compulsory arbitration would have to go at once; instead it was extended by agreement with both sides of industry in March 1944. But the watchful Treasury, afraid trade union co-operation might be bought at too high a price, put forward a claim to vet wage settlements in all public industries; this was accompanied by an admission that it would be anomalous to interfere with 'management policy'. Officials generally seem to have imagined that newly-nationalised industries would resemble the state corporations of the inter-war years; while ensuring parliamentary accountability, they should take care not to let an 'independent board' be submerged in political issues and Ministerial interference.[18] Ministers, as the Treasury argued, should not fix prices, for that would subject them to endless pressures from wage-earners in the industry on one hand and consumers on the other; and whatever the theoretical argument for making a profit, debt service should have priority, even over capital investment. Wages could then be left, as MLNS had always hoped, to collective bargaining, as in any private industry.

Such arguments might have gone on indefinitely until they were overtaken by practice. It is nevertheless remarkable that in a short period in the autumn of 1943 a handful of officials – admittedly briefed by industry, unions and the banks through sponsor departments – could define so many of the fundamentals about the state and industrial organisation. There is little here that was not still at issue, forty muddled years later.

Since full employment became the keystone of the arch, holding together in equilibrium what otherwise would have been incompatible and politically unachievable demands, its genesis needs to be analysed. Few in public life would have disagreed with Beveridge's inclusion of 'idleness' among his five evil giants, and most, in tune with Seebohm Rowntree, would have made unemployment a contributory cause of all the rest. But the first to make remedies for unemployment the pivot for reconstruction was probably James Meade of the War Cabinet's Economic Section who wrote the seminal paper, early in 1941.[19]

He divided unemployment, as Keynes and others had often done, into cyclical, structural and temporary categories, and addressed the first. Government should maintain the general level of demand 'at a height sufficient to absorb the unemployed into new occupations as quickly as they can be transferred to them'; public works, now under the guise of 'reconstruction', together with appropriate external financial and trade policies, should be complementary. Unlike much of the market support practices of the 1930s, this assumed that government would consciously resist business and union tendencies to form cartels and monopolies, in order not to restrict employment arbitrarily. A brief post-war boom followed by a slump on the 1918–21 pattern was assumed; counter-cyclical activity should therefore occur at once.

To sustain general demand for labour, the banking and financial system should encourage or discourage capital construction and raise or lower interest rates depending on the stage of the business cycle. Government spending, including that of local authorities and public utilities, would follow suit, while fiscal controls on consumption – hire purchase restrictions, indirect tax rates, and social security insurance – would be varied accordingly, through the budget. Deficits would be legitimate in depressed years, as would be government borrowing for physical reconstruction. Government would avoid deflation but not a moderate rise in prices and money incomes (which were impossible, so Meade thought, to control except by means of a capital levy). A policy of continuous debt redemption should be followed, provided that it

could be financed without restricting consumer expenditure. Wage
stabilisation would give protection against both inflation and cost-
induced unemployment.

In a covering note, the secretary, A. J. Baxter minuted:
'undoubtedly the government will wish to provide after the war for full
employment for all who wish to work'. But the Economic Section
made no attempt then to specify what constituted 'full employment',
leaving that to the departments, or interested bodies like Political and
Economic Planning (PEP), the Nuffield conferences, or later
Beveridge himself.

At this time, the department supposedly most concerned, MLNS,
was still busying itself considering measures of some antiquity, such as
lowering the retiring age, raising the school-leaving age, and (the
TUC's old staple) reducing hours of work. Its officials tended to
concentrate more on shortages of skilled labour, the grave problems of
post-war female unemployment, rigidities of the labour market, and
lack of mobility and training schemes. But by 1942 they were talking of
the possibility of rising living standards, provided wages could be held
and the export industries prevented from again becoming 'the
Cinderella of British industry, offering the lowest wages'.[20]

A sort of hierarchy of immediate labour priorities began to emerge,
beginning with demobilisation, going on to retraining and assisted
transfer, wages policy, and then long-term or structural
unemployment. By the end of 1943, when Beveridge began to put
together his report on employment policy, levels of wages, prices,
efficiency of industry and productivity had become commonplaces of
official and Ministerial conversations. From then on, all the various
reconstruction aims were increasingly centred on the attempt to cure
the greatest evil of the inter-war years.

The dilemma, which Beveridge soon made public, was that to
combine all aims in a single package involved a vast effort of trust in the
will and capacity of British industry, banks and unions to submerge
sectional advantage and outright greed for a greater public good.
Whatever assurances of behaviour each sponsor might give (and
MLNS on behalf of the TUC were, perhaps, the most prolific) a
profound scepticism remained: hence the various conflicts over
supplementary checks and balances which embroiled, variously, the
Economic Section and Board of Trade, Treasury and MLNS. In this
sense, the ultimate victory for Treasury economic management
exercised primarily by the use of fiscal levers, represented an
admission that the state could not alter the pattern of human

behaviour, nor rely on institutions' altruism where their members' interests were concerned.

In this two-year process, outside interventions were of secondary importance. A whole history could be written, pointing up the contributions of the Nuffield Group, E. F. Schumacher and Beveridge's other assistants, G. D. H. Cole, the 120 industrialists, PEP, and of course Beveridge himself, prevented by the Cabinet Office from letting civil servants sign his Second Report for fear that that might prejudge the interdepartmental debate.[21] In the dimension of public opinion their work mattered greatly: Beveridge's celebrated definition in his broadcast on 14 October 1943, that full employment meant more jobs than workers, stimulated wide interest. But it was his preoccupation with the danger of wage inflation, in conditions of trade union monopoly power, that carried most weight with government which was never so disposed as MLNS to accept TUC professions of good behaviour at their face value.[22]

In its negotiations with Beveridge, which began shortly after this broadcast, and were intended to influence his recommendations, the TUC argued vigorously that full employment should not imply any downgrading of wages or expectations. Whilst their attitude reinforced some of the misgivings, the TUC had some success, as can be seen from the formula 'Full employment at rising living standards in a free society' which they agreed with Beveridge in March 1944.[23] But as has been pointed out, this had only a small impact on government planning.

The Post-War Employment Committee (set up in October 1943) brought all these strands together, with the emphasis on departmental points of view. What Beveridge said in public and to the TUC must be seen as an extension of this activity, not as central to the Treasury–Board of Trade misgivings about restrictive practices and wage inflation that delayed into 1944 final acceptance of full employment as a post-war target – in spite of the Cabinet's desire to get in ahead of Beveridge's second report. However much MLNS interpreted the TUC favourably when discussing the prospects for wage stability, Committee officials and the Ministers they advised could not avoid the dilemma that, on the basis of what they knew, full employment, stable wages and industrial efficiency appeared to be incompatible.

MLNS rather vainly countered by suggesting that economic management could not operate without trade union compliance, and that co-operation and support would not be forthcoming without a deliberate policy of high, continuous employment, sustained over many years.[24] To the argument about negative power, BOT replied curtly: 'We would not achieve full employment unless industry was efficient and could stand up to foreign competition'. Yet so far had the idea of a package gone, by the end of October 1943, that BOT found itself induced to circumvent its own logic. To accommodate the various defences of restrictive practices put up by MLNS, the TUC and FBI, the Board took refuge in hopes for more liberal international trade which would produce such prosperity that they would not seriously inhibit efficiency.

The Treasury's answer was to redefine the problem by defining full employment at a low enough level for unemployment not to lose its ancient deterrence in the labour market. Although no figure was given, formally, in this highly sensitive area (where in TUC eyes 3 per cent unemployment was becoming a reasonable target) something between 7.5 per cent and 9 per cent was assumed. Beveridge's talk of 3 per cent made no discernible impact on deductions evidently drawn from inter-war experience. In June 1944 the Chancellor suggested 8.5 per cent as a working assumption for the Government Actuary's benefit.[25] If this sort of figure had been maintained, of course, economic management in the 1950s and '60s would have been wholly different and post-war economic history might have suffered far fewer fluctuations.

In the end, at a remarkably candid meeting on 26 October 1943, the Post-War Employment Committee admitted that, in a world of giant industrial companies and trade agreements fostered by governments, the very nature of markets had changed: it was simply impossible 'to put the clock back and achieve the competitive conditions which prevailed before 1914'.[26] Was efficiency then even relevant to their deliberations? No, said the Economic Section; yes, said the Board of Trade. 'Measures to maintain aggregate demand and to control structural dislocation [Robbins' case] could not be fully successful unless industry was sufficiently efficient and well-equipped to stand up against foreign competition in both home and foreign markets'. Argument therefore rolled on, to address wages, restrictive practices and investment.

Much progress had been made by the end of 1943. The Ministerial Committee on Employment now fully accepted that some sort of economic management was necessary – 'experience has shown that the process of absorbing unemployment through deflation, if effective at all, may be very long drawn-out and accompanied by widespread misery'[27] – and had committed future Cabinets to maintaining national expenditure and income at high levels. Special provisions would be needed to cope with structural unemployment, during the transition period. Sections of their report suggest that Beveridge's public crusade may not have been wasted; but it still contained huge ambiguities. The majority of Ministers thought it impossible to control the volume of investment in the private sector, so that to effect its aims government would have to rely on the provision of cheap money, and its limited control in its own sphere of public utilities, nationalised industries, and local authority capital projects. As for wages in this state sector, they piously hoped for the best: 'our national capacity for combining liberty with an absence of licence will help us steer our way through'.[28]

On a wing and a prayer, policy moved through various drafts towards the White Paper which was published in May 1944. As always, at this stage, under Cabinet Office influence, the departments rallied round and played down their differences. But they had an extra stimulus, to issue the White Paper if possible before Beveridge published his report with its more radical targets. Given the popularity he had won with his first report, and the dangers of public enthusiasm for full employment unfettered by their own misgivings, they looked to Cabinet to provide political education: 'in view of the experience after the last war, there were advantages in making clear the dangers which would arise if the economic situation were allowed to get out of control during this [transition] period'. More and more, officials emphasised (as MLNS had always done) the interdependence of all the desired benefits and rising living standards with the duties that would be owed in return for full employment: stable wages, rising productivity, competitiveness and the dedication required from each contracting party, management, workers, the City and the public.

Thus a political and economic contract was proposed. In its final version, the White Paper (Cmd 6527) comprised 'a declaration of purpose by the Coalition Government, as well as a blueprint of the method' (according to a later MLNS summary). The White Paper laid down two conditions for a 'high and stable level of employment': first, an export trade substantial enough to balance imports and overseas investment; second, stability of prices and wages, through the predicted post-war depression and into the cost-competitive era afterwards. Parts of it, as Cherwell put it, 'read like an antiphon by Keynes and Eady', for the whole document represented a masterly combination of traditional orthodoxy and Keynesian technique.

Critics might point to the likelihood of far more serious balance of payments problems than Ministers or officials had dreamed of, yet it

was still possible then to be optimistic about stabilising world prices of
primary products under a liberal, expansionist trade regime. Cynics
could argue that the whole issue of restrictive practices had been
fudged, and that self-interest, greed and fear would undermine the
balance of duties and rewards at home, and soon shatter the mood of
individual dedication, self-reliance and enterprise reiterated in
paragraphs 53, 54 and 56 of the White Paper. Only experience could
decide whether the whole thing was a gamble or a shrewd judgment
about the deeper interests of each.

The White Paper proposed but did not contain, a contract. The Labour
Party had already put forward its own contribution, emphasising the
importance of price control and high level public expenditure: to
Treasury annoyance, its research papers pointed up the fact that 'the
Budget need not be balanced each year'.[29] The left of the party had few
good words to say. Bevan attacked it in his polemic, *Why Not Trust the
Tories?* (1944) written under the pseudonym of Celticus, for its
supposed surrender to commercial market forces. The TUC, irked
perhaps at not having made more impression on the White Paper, after
its success with Beveridge, openly criticised the definition of full
employment. To the Economic Committee it implied the continuance
of capitalism in a newly stable form, with none of the dynamic social
justice promised by Beveridge[30] (though a few individual unions took
more notice of the government document than they did of Beveridge's
report).[31] Some of the TUC's reservations were aimed at mobilising
public opinion but there can be no doubt that a real dissatisfaction
existed, which worked itself out during the next year, first in the
Post-War Reconstruction Report, which set out the TUC's alternative
aims (public control of industry, protection of workers' living
standards, control of and participation in private industry) and
secondly in the formulation of an even more comprehensive definition
of full employment than they had put to Beveridge.[32] More, the TUC
claimed a share in wider policy; to have a say on land use, the supply of
money and credit, the location of industry, the rate of investment and
foreign trade.[33] A feeling of having been let down, fobbed off with
meeting Beveridge as surrogate for government, as well as pressure
from below at the height of the radical wave, may explain the tone; but
as MLNS had long realised there could be no going back to the
humbler position of 1939.

Industrialists had their own worries, though the FBI congratulated itself that the White Paper made no mention of Beveridge's loathed National Investment Board. Most seem to have been reassured by the primacy given to the Treasury, and the contingent assurances against prolonged deficit financing and government competition with private industry for scarce investment; but they jibbed at interference in the market place by state bulk purchase and sales. In the end, the FBI endorsed the main themes because of what it would do for them, by creating a labour force whose high and steady purchasing power would sustain a prosperous home market and long-term investment plans.

The BEC showed greater caution, being as preoccupied as ever with the danger of rising wages unaccompanied by higher productivity. If they had known that the compromises made in drafting the White Paper embodied the unspoken assumption that a mild rate of wage inflation was to be expected, their opposition might have been much more vocal. Unlike the FBI, they had rarely lost the chance to put unpopular views and they had less reason in 1944–45 to seek political acceptability.

The main criticism, however, had already been dealt with before publication. The financial sector had tried to influence government first to defer Beveridge's initial report in 1942 and then to cripple the full employment package in autumn 1943 on the grounds that Britain's external situation after the war would be so critical that the nation simply could not afford this proposed generosity.[34] The City failed against the centripetal forces at the centre of government, but it is possible that its reservations may have influenced Treasury officials in laying down their definition of 8.5 per cent unemployment as the level at which to manage the economy.

The further range of rejection of the whole concept of state intervention implied in Friedrich von Hayek's *The Road to Serfdom* (1944) had very little impact on contemporary British policy-making[35] although that strand in European and American intellectual history can be traced in the biographies of individuals like Milton Friedman, then an official in the US Treasury. (But it is worth noting that in his 1948 paper, 'A Monetary and Fiscal Framework for Economic Stability', in *American Economic Review*, Freidman argued that a nation's budget should balance in the medium term, and in the short term could fluctuate between deficit and surplus according to the national interest, just as the 1944 White Paper had stated.) Fears of the resurgent state were widely shared however in the mid-1940s as George Orwell's *1984*, published in 1948, suggests. They influenced Beveridge's concern with inflation, excessive dependence on the state and the loss of liberty, even if in other respects he wished to give the state greater power – over investment and central economic decisions – and they contributed to an attitude deeply suspicious of group interests masquerading as the public interest that can be found in each of the institutions' views about others' activities, though never of its own.

Of greater significance for Britain, three crucial issues had been laid aside, wrapped in platitudes to enable the White Paper to appear at all. The attack on restrictive practices mounted by the Board of Trade since November 1942 had never really been pressed home in Ministerial Committees, largely because several Ministers had convinced themselves – or been convinced by lobbyists for industry and unions – that restrictive practices on both sides of industry had contributed much to maintaining employment and wages in the 1930s. In particular, 'unregulated competition, especially in the field of international trade, was recognised by trade unions as liable to produce most undesirable consequences'.[36] This was Bevin's view, trenchantly put by Dalton; but shared also by some Conservatives with agricultural interests who cited the world of pre-war Agricultural Marketing Boards. Reflecting the vision of many industrialists, the Ministers of Production and Aircraft Production concurred: 'some measure of restriction and regulation was an essential part of any planned economy'. Anti-monopoly legislation would be hard to apply to a diverse economy like Britain's. Nor should government seek to prevent a high rate of profit because that would inhibit confidence 'and so prevent an expansion of employment'.

Industry's lobbying was predictable enough. Because wartime price control had been based on average costs, many less efficient firms had remained technically profitable. All these firms and their unions now had a vested interest in restricting or even eliminating future competition. The BEC Council worried about a future in which its members would have to recoup any higher wages from increased productivity at a time when production could be expected to be in decline – a matter which, they claimed disingenuously, 'called for active collaboration, not only of trade unions, but of individual workers'.[37] Treasury Ministers and Board of Trade officials who did not share their Minister's partial opinion may have had little taste for arguing with Bevin and Dalton in dogmatic mood. They contented themselves with discussing the interest of the public as consumers, rather than the effect of restrictive practices on competitiveness. Even BOT's Industry Commission came to be interpreted in a wishy-washy way, so as not to arouse hostility or 'uncertainty' in industry. Robbins' warning that the United States would insist on freer trade and the break-up of cartels, including Imperial Preferences, should have alerted them – yet even by the time of Keynes' mission to Washington the Cabinet had advanced no further than a proposal to investigate cartels in the light of their effects, *after* a complaint had been made.[38] Specious reasoning swamped the debate and the Board of Trade itself supinely chose, not legislation, but a register of restrictive practices, supervised by itself. The Committee on Reconstruction compounded this evasion, with Morrison's approval: some degree of monopoly was, they believed, actually beneficial, so long as the state had some surveillance. Government should not 'be negative or interfere unnecessarily with the natural growth of business organisation, or seek merely to get back to 19th century *laisser-faire*, but rather to promote, by positive action, an increasing volume of employment and consumption'.[39]

In the apparently overriding interest of consensus about the full employment package, a vast question had been buried, which would not be resurrected until the early 1960s. A central element of 1930s oligopoly had not only been admitted as being too massive for the state to control, but positively justified. Thus the post-war shape of the economy was tailored to the existing mentalities and practices of industry and labour.

Something similar occurred with wages. In the October 1943 discussions, the Economic Section had wanted to be able to vary wages, as well as social security payments, to assist depressed areas by attracting new enterprises. This ran clean counter to the established concept of a national wage for each union in different industries and was abandoned. Although MLNS officials had talked in 1942 about 'co-ordinated consideration of wages' to prevent a spiral like that seen in 1918–20,[40] later they took a more detached view, unlike the hawkish officials of BOT who wanted to set up quasi-independent Commissions to bring 'general economic facts' to bear on wage bargaining. MLNS never imagined anything but a return to normal collective bargaining: restoration of the pre-war system of industrial relations was to be made conditional only in the sense that unions would be expected to behave responsibly where their restrictive practices were concerned. Recognising that Beveridge's nightmare of inflation existed, MLNS saw no escape in wages policy or compulsory arbitration. Their answer was to incorporate the unions, by continual 'education', politically and ideologically into the polity precisely as envisaged in the 1944 White Paper.[41]

The Committee of officials shied away from discussion of wages' control even when formulated in terms of the 'community interest'. The PWIEC often referred to the TUC's conciliatory attitude on the NJAC. It would have been hard on this issue not to have been aware of what Labour Ministers felt: in particular, although Bevin accepted some of the strictures levelled by BOT and Robbins, he defended union restrictive practices as robustly as any interested party. For him wages could be too low, but never too high. Other departments such as Aircraft Production took the same line, on the grounds that cartelised wage arrangements might be the only way to sustain a post-war export trade.

The TUC never actually committed itself to wage restraint, beyond what price controls could achieve; and its assurances to Beveridge were qualified insofar as it had limited authority over member unions and the movement.[42] Unions would not be agents, as they had been in wartime. Government would have to convince the mass membership that it shared their objectives if it wanted good behaviour in return. A careful reading of the TUC's debates and public statements suggests that Citrine and his colleagues were steering with some care between the accelerating demands of shopfloor workers, now determined to ensure the rewards their wartime sacrifices had earned, and the General Council's own perception of what government could actually accept. Prudence dictated a certain ambiguity, especially once it became clear that the coalition would dissolve and an election would follow, soon after victory in Europe. Defensive, slightly standoffish, aware of having been finessed by the White Paper, yet afraid that deflation and orthodox monetary policy were still on the post-war agenda, the TUC set out a series of bargaining positions on state controls and economic policy, perhaps without realising that, from the Coalition government's point of view, bargaining had already ceased when the White Paper was published. This may explain why it exercised less influence on Labour Ministers in 1944–45 than it did on the Party's manifesto.

After monopolies and mergers, the third area that the White Paper evaded comprised managerial direction, investment and related industrial problems such as location policy. Once again, discussion of organisation and methods, in particular of BOT's proposals for Industrial Boards and a tripartite Reconstruction Finance Committee and Location Board, set the departments at loggerheads. One side headed by Robbins, with Beveridge taking an extreme position, called for positive intervention; the other (BOT, Treasury and MLNS, and of course the FBI) talked in terms of persuasion and education, as if these new Boards were to be no more than mild extensions of the old Balfour Committee.

In their major investigations into industrial efficiency in October 1943, Trade officials had tried to identify areas such as aircraft production, steel, cotton, electrical goods and textiles which seemed ripe for improvement; whose size could be extended, plant renewed, and which could be offered short-term export credits or assisted into new markets such as Russia and China.[43] In the engineering sector in particular it soon discovered resistance, deeply rooted in the mentality of the depressed 1930s which showed itself in a preoccupation with reserves rather than investment, a suspicion of new machinery and product design, and a reliance on sheltered home and imperial markets.

Given such evidence, BOT set itself to assault bad management practice, hidebound attitudes and wasteful expenditure. Reasonably enough, its reports emphasised the lessons of war; the need for standardisation, use of technology, appointment of scientifically trained personnel.[44] As Keynes was soon to point out in the United States, much of Britain's plant had been worn out through overuse, for Britain had been more totally committed to the war effort than other Allied nations. At a fundamental level, BOT thinking assumed, first, that the British economy would continue to be as balanced and varied as it had been before the war, and based on manufacturing industry; second, that it would be possible to overcome the problem that small-scale business could not support research and development programmes adequate to meet American competition; and third, that the home market could survive a multilateral trading environment without protection or exchange rate manipulation. These opinions took for granted solution of the sterling balances and sterling area difficulties and the arrival, under US auspices, of a liberal regime of international trade. In domestic policy, they assumed the start of a process of industrial regeneration, in which the prime mover would be government, working through a tripartite structure.

But the Board hampered its own work, not least because of its decision, taken at the start, that legal remedies (on the lines of American trust-busting legislation) would not work, and that persuasion would suffice, exercised through the Industrial Commission and Boards. Equally seriously, their underlying premises differed quite profoundly from the sort of fiscal policies advocated by the Treasury. In short, supply-side policy ranged itself against demand management, across nearly every sector from agriculture to scientific instruments.[45]

An open clash was averted by a process of grinding down the Board of Trade's momentum. By mid-1945, the proposed managing instrument of Industry Boards and the Commission had been abandoned and replaced by much weaker Development Councils. But the Board's resistance rumbled on, in other areas of policy such as restrictive practices, investment and location of industry, since the Minister, Dalton, continually emphasised the need for a tougher state role: 'my view is that you should have either really free, profit-seeking competition, or else a centrally-planned public enterprise'.[46]

Part of the problem of transition lay in how to allocate investment funds after the war. The Treasury, Bank of England and City institutions assumed that the Capital Issues Committee's total control would shortly be abrogated, but that government would hold on to considerable powers, to ensure a distribution favouring export-orientated industry and rationing of less essential requests. In 1943–44, most participants believed there would be a post-war recession but that the United States would take the main part in fighting Japan without ending its support for Britain so that industry need not face up immediately to world competition nor rely wholly on internally-generated profits.[47] But arguments developed between those, like Keynes, who believed that banks should be the principal source of investment capital and the FBI, avid for tax concessions, which advocated investment from retained profits. Free discussion on the merits of either case was inhibited because it became caught up on other fronts and in extraneous prejudices. The Treasury was not prepared to allow concessions or tax inducements (such as the FBI asked for) except in specific areas of need such as research or aid to small business; and put its faith, quite simply, in cheap money.[48] The various cleavages about priorities, such as Robbins' claim for industry as against the Ministry of Housing's claim for 'social capital', or disputes between what amounted to competing methodologies, matter less here than the fact that the conclusion came about between October 1943 and the 1944 White Paper final draft, after parties had exhausted themselves, and as the lowest common denominator of agreement.

These months showed that it was impossible to reach agreement on what was desirable: whether the promotion of small firms or large units, decentralisation or mergers, internally generated investment or banking provision, state action at the level of a single industry or the use of public investment as a general balancing factor. In the end it was accepted that the creation of FFI and ICFC, together with government support for research through the Department of Scientific and Industrial Research, would be enough to satisfy the small firm's needs. On the main issue, the Treasury won with its insistence that the prime aim of economic management was to get the timing of investment right in relation to full employment policy, rather than to regulate the competitiveness of industrial firms as BOT had originally intended.[49] This also meant rejecting any suggestion of Beveridge's National Investment Board which pleased the banks which would, henceforth, ration capital to industry. There is some evidence that the Treasury understood that the reformers' contention about 'the national tendency to "make do" with equipment that was out of date' was accurate but would not act for other (to them more important) reasons, to do with control of the difficult process of harmonising government fiscal action with events in the economy at large. But they actually argued that the 1944 White Paper's proposals for grants or subsidies would be adequate, once the initial peak of demand for re-equipment purposes had passed.[50]

The question was postponed, rather than buried. For many officials and Ministers it had barely been a matter for government at all, but for the financial institutions. Reintroduction of a five-day week, regular overtime, and a temporary fall in the real cost of labour after 1945 subsequently made it cheaper for management to invest in workers rather than machinery, so that firms' inefficiency and inadequacy of plant perpetuated itself. In due course, BOT's 1943 prediction that they could 'only expect a widening of the considerable gap between the productivity of Britain and US industry' came true.

The issue of post-war location of industry, originally raised in the mid-1930s, merged into the debate about controls over town and country planning and land usage at regional as opposed to national levels. BOT 'radicals' such as Alexander Meynell wanted to use Industry Boards to implement a micro-economic policy to diminish regional imbalances, and solve the long problem of the depressed areas. Preferring to rely only on general, macroeconomic levers, and concerned at the likely cost of so much state planning, the Treasury (though not the Economic Section) objected. Prematurely discouraged, the Board fell back on the recommendations of the Barlow Report (1941) and the much more limited project of using location policy to site new factories so as to draw employment and prosperity away from the magnets of London and Birmingham.[51] Dalton made this his main work at the Board, the end product being the 1945 Redistribution of Industry Act.

Even that drew criticism not for intrinsic demerits but because doubters wondered whether location policy *could* be part of demand management, just as they questioned whether it was possible to attack cyclical and structural unemployment together. Robbins thought not: 'the essential test in a depression is to avoid deflation, not to attempt permanent shifts of resources'. The old battle lines renewed themselves in this different setting; this time Supply, Aircraft Production and the FBI backed the Economic Section, on the grounds that it was better to revitalise old staple industries than to bring in new ones which might fail either to take over or to provide the same quantity of employment. What markets the old staples could recover, they failed to specify, but they did point out that they stood to provide more employment than any conceivable alternative.[52]

Industry tended to lose both ways in these conflicts, gaining neither the stimulus which BOT believed Industrial Boards could provide nor the survival of the Ministry of Production's Regional Boards, which the FBI believed had galvanised specific industries with a sense of national priorities. (Being industry-based, with private-sector chairmen, they ran counter to Dalton's dreams of wider planning and were abolished in 1945.) In the field of training, MLNS and TUC lost similar battles. In such by-ways, the pursuit of full employment, core of the political contract government and officials so much desired, worked to the lasting detriment of the industrial base as detailed case histories of industries such as coal and steel show.[53] Heavy steel manufacturers, long depressed, looked to economic management for a stable level of demand and profits, in monopoly conditions, whereas more competitive firms, like United Steel and Stewart and Lloyds, had been prepared to co-operate with measures designed to increase efficiency. The aircraft companies and construction firms, who had learned in the 1930s to ride the trade cycle, now looked to secure home demand and protected semi-imperial markets such as the Middle East.[54]

Short-term victories over cyclical unemployment were seen as ultimately more important to continued good government than a long-term investment in international competitiveness. How far the decision-makers can be blamed for shortsightedness depends on what weight is given to the priorities of 1944–45. *At the time*, given the aims of the 1944 White Paper, what the advocates of the economic management package said was reasonable. At least they reached a final decision that was internally coherent, no matter to which policy area it applied; in summing up, it must be remembered that the Machinery of Government Committee had laid down that, in the last resort, it was preferable for one department to predominate, rather for the state to permit pluralistic confusion. Yet the political system remained pluralistic, in a very broad but intricate sense, and simply because things went this way does not mean that a Ministry of Industry, fully constituted as Meynell and others wanted, could not have coexisted with the Treasury, as a later generation discovered that micro and macroeconomic policies could coexist.

In the estimate of all the participants, the 1944 package could not stand without an agreed counterpart covering external trade and international financial policy.[55] In this field, however, the government had far less freedom to plan; and the Treasury had to admit the existence of a parity of authority with the Board of Trade and Bank of England which it denied over home policy.

Back in 1941, the Board had placed recovery of export markets among the most urgent post-war priorities, to which the Economic Section added a rider that trade cycles, being beyond Britain's control, required international co-operative action, by *every* major country.[56] Officials and Ministers, in general, believed until at least 1943 that industrial trade negotiations would be conducted on the basis of equality with the United States, and that all the victor powers would, in fact, commit themselves to liberal, expansionist trade policies. War with Japan would, they imagined, tie up the United States and leave Britain free, inside the sterling area, to reconstruct or re-establish former trading patterns. This was the tenor of the occasional weekend meetings in 1942 at King's College attended by Hopkins, Henry Clay, Dennis Robertson, Cobbold, George Bolton and Keynes himself, and occasionally a representative of the Bank of Canada. But the implied concert between leading economists in the Treasury and the Bank, with support from Robbins and the Economic Section, could not entirely decide the balance in government between external and domestic factors – it remained a political balance, even if the constraints were usually discussed in purely economic terms.

Dalton and his officials at Trade hoped that the Western Allies' liberal policy, embodied in what eventually became the General Agreement on Tariffs and Trade, would facilitate the British full employment package and non-industrial capital spending (on housing or hospitals) as well as assist in the export drive and the pursuit of industrial competitiveness. Once again, the fundamental question raised itself in a different form: would industrial efficiency and the national interest be served better by free trade or through bilateral trade within the sterling area? Because the bilateralists habitually overstated their case, it was not certain that the two were mutually exclusive; but their advocates certainly distinguished themselves from the radical (usually Labour) critics who favoured physical planning and import controls. Not all choices were open. As Keynes was to find, in 1944–45, the USA espoused free trade but discriminated against Britain, prohibiting, for example, access to dollar earnings in shipping and insurance on the Atlantic seaboard and in South and Central America.

The story of Anglo-American disputes over trade is familiar. Two differing interpretations had been at issue even in August 1941 when Roosevelt and Churchill discussed Article IV of the Atlantic Charter (Roosevelt trying to prevent any return to the closed economic systems of the thirties, Churchill insisting on the UK's 'present obligations', that is the 1932 Ottawa agreements and Imperial Preferences). Thereafter, Secretary of State Cordell Hull and his Assistant Secretary Sumner Welles defined free trade doctrine in a way which allowed American companies to utilise world-wide the vast surplus capacity they had built up in wartime. US foreign policy turned against the sort of use of sterling area that the Bank and Treasury had planned since 1942. There were those – the bilateralists – who argued that, in this confrontation, Britain need not concede Imperial Preferences, nor the use of the area as a trading bloc; sterling need not be made convertible, and bilateral agreements (which the Bank had already prepared in association with the Treasury Overseas Finance Division) might be offered to Argentina, Egypt, India and the Dominions. Reconstruction could then proceed, uninterrupted at home and insulated from the United States, in order to meet both the public's politically-invincible demands for consumption and industry's need gradually to adjust. A short-term loss in competitiveness, they argued, could be regained later.[57]

The aspirations proved to be by no mean uncongenial to Labour Ministers such as Attlee and Bevin, whose plans for social expenditure stood at risk from the deflation that seemed inevitable if Britain entered a multilateral trading system; though of course the Labour Party took a different view from Conservatives of what the future of the

Empire should be. As the United States' position became clear, the bilateralists attracted support from Beaverbrook and Churchill himself. Nevertheless in Spring 1943, the Cabinet decided to fall in with American requirements. Their attempt to retain existing rights formed the basis of Keynes' negotiations in September. The main factor in this was not choice but the fact that holders of the sterling debts had made it obvious that their interests did not include assisting Britain to finance reconstruction at the expense of their own capacity to earn dollars.[58]

Keynes' plan, fully backed by the Treasury, provided for a Clearing Union, a proto-International Monetary Fund, to resolve the problems of creditor countries with large surpluses without impairing world demand. For the present, however (and until 1947 and Marshall Aid), the United States saw no reason to pay so that Britain could shelter behind an artificial barrier and indulge in what many Congressmen and US Treasury officials saw as unjustified domestic expenditure. White's stance in the negotiations was so harsh that it gave a last stimulus to the bilateralists, inspiring Leo Amery's 'alternative policy' which would, to put it crudely, have compelled Britain's sterling creditors to buy British exports and tailor their economies to her needs.[59]

At the back of this can be seen a combination of City institutions (rather less realistic than the Bank), Beaverbrook (who had not forgotten his 1929 Empire Free Trade campaign) and R. H. Hudson at Agriculture together with the NFU and the FBI, who were concerned in various ways with stabilising London as the foremost money market in sterling, increasing invisible earnings, and the safeguarding of existing markets.[60] None of these aims, incidentally, benefited the Dominions, who had already effectively been relegated in government eyes by the Anglo-US Trade Treaty in 1938. They were routed in Cabinet in December 1943, by Richard Law, speaking for BOT: 'there is no mechanical device by which we can ensure that the rest of the world will maintain the population of these islands at a standard of living higher than that which it is entitled to by its activity. That would depend on the energy and skill of its people.'

The BOT's case left no doubt that a return to the trading patterns of the inter-war years was impossible, even if sterling creditors had been willing. Britain could not take the risk of being locked into production tailored to markets like Argentina. That lesson had been learned by Lancashire in the inter-war years over the Indian cotton trade. In any case, the creditors would not play, even to the limited extent proposed by Cobbold in his 1945 negotiations with Egypt and the Argentine. It was too easy for such countries to threaten to convert into another currency, and force the pound off its level of $4.06 – with no safety net beneath.

Sir Wilfred Eady and some Treasury OFD colleagues sided briefly with the bilateralists but the Treasury majority and the Bank lined up with BOT and Sir John Anderson. Lord Cherwell used his influence with Churchill and may have prevented him listening too eagerly to Beaverbrook.[61] Churchill tried for a time to compromise, to keep the Labour members of his Cabinet happy by rejecting a gold standard, while clinging on to Imperial Preferences, 'unless or until we are in the presence of a vast scheme of reducing trade barriers in which the US is taking the lead'.[62] At the time, this tactic seemed the best way of getting Lend–Lease written off and obtaining Keynes' loan; and it is possible that such bargining won more concessions than would otherwise have been the case. Early in 1944, however, Keynes decided that there was no choice but to play along with the United States, and if Lend–Lease ran out, to borrow even though the terms would be tough.

At home, though bilateralists had been silenced, the argument took a new form as the Treasury investigated the confused area between 'trade' and 'industry'. BOT had believed in free trade as the ark of covenant since the mid-nineteenth century, and Dalton was as committed as his officials to liberalising. But this implicitly put the 1944 package at the mercy of foreign governments and trading partners. If they chose not to follow similar policies, full employment in the UK would be that much harder to achieve. This risk the Treasury proposed to eliminate, by retaining some control over imports and exports, and taking powers to decide 'what we can afford to pay for'.[63]

In Washington in 1944 Keynes argued consistently for a return to the status quo of 1940, Britain having borne the worst burden.[64] Facing what was expected to be another two years' war in the Pacific, the United States negotiators were prepared to write off the debt, but not to extend Lend–Lease. When Japan surrendered abruptly, in September 1945, Keynes had no choice but to accept these terms and negotiate for a loan on the best terms he could. Almost before the domestic side of trade policy had given the British public more than a taste of future benefits, Attlee's Ministers had to ask themselves how it would have to be amended, and whether the terms of the loan, and the institution of a new international monetary order would limit their capacity to manage the economy as they had envisaged.

Meanwhile, the bilateralists argued that Keynes had given too much away. Keynes certainly believed he could make the argument that

Britain had deranged its economy in order to survive stick more than turned out to be the case. But he did win concessions, most of all in delaying the agreement of specific proposals until Americans like Henry Morgenthau, Secretary of the Treasury and Federal Reserve Bank officials reached a more sympathetic frame of mind about the sterling balances. But his candour in his Press Conference in mid-September 1944 went too far for the bilateralists because it exposed the innate weakness of their case: 'it may well be wholesome for us to be brought up sharp against the necessities of our post-war options, instead of being deceived, as well as comforted, by temporary expedients which would do little or nothing to solve the real problems of the transition'.[65] To an American audience that made sense, but to TUC, Labour Party or, for different reasons, the FBI (who blamed him for letting the United States dominate the new IMF, and for losing British freedom to manage its currency) it did not.

Those like Richard Glenday, the FBI secretary, who had hoped that Britain could recover inside the sterling area behind import quotas and export subsidies were furious. Privately, some Bank officials complained that Keynes should not have conceded the commitment to convertibility of sterling as early as 1947. Realising the futility of fighting a battle that could not be won, however, the FBI grumbled but held its fire until the first GATT negotiations. In the end, Britain retained protectionist defences and the substance of its Imperial Preferences, even after GATT began in 1947. British firms also fell back thankfully on Commonwealth and Middle Eastern markets, as alternatives to the hard task of breaking into American or European ones. But even if it turned out to be less harsh than expected, the enforced external settlement did put in question many of the assumptions which had buoyed up the making of the White Paper in 1943–44; and since the post-war external situation made it imperative to export at once, industrial output was geared up to short-term production at the expense of long-term modernisation. For nearly twenty years until the easy, traditional markets changed, the questions put by the Board of Trade lay dormant, as industry made its own adjustments more or less free of government discipline. On the other hand, a sheltered sterling-area trading bloc would probably have had an even more deleterious effect on industrial competitiveness

Industry, and its spokesman the FBI, was not of course the only sector interested in safe export markets and a secure home base. The 'thirties mentality' edged back out of the shadows where the war emergency had exiled it, to infiltrate all the bargaining of 1943–44 and thus irrevocably to condition the way the 1944 package was later implemented. City institutions set themselves to restore rather than reconstruct – except insofar as the Bank of England prepared itself to operate as a peacetime Central Bank. Through the 1943–44 discussions, they backed the Treasury and there is no evidence of their taking a separate line, for example, over money supply, once their objections to the full employment package had been set aside. Instead, severally, they discussed the future of the capital market, industrial and local authority needs, and the organisation of the Stock Exchange.

Their discussions centred on controls over investment funds and industry's requirements in the transition period before it became 'self-sufficient' (as everyone imagined it would). Government departments and Ministers assumed that the banks, stock market, and insurance companies would continue to abide by existing and future controls. City institutions did not disillusion them, and in turn assumed that government would, as in 1918–26, assist London again to become a world financial centre and a major earner of foreign exchange, chiefly in dollars. The shock at the war's end of being shut out of many American shipping and insurance markets was, therefore, considerable. That, and the way the construction of the IMF appeared to threaten the sterling bloc, may explain firstly why in 1944 the Bank of England attempted to influence the Treasury into rewriting those parts of the White Paper which permitted deficit financing in bad years, and secondly why it raised no opposition to continuing existing controls on bank lending and capital issues under Treasury instructions.[66] The City desired government to behave correctly, especially if the post-war government should be a Labour one.

This alternation between direct opposition and wounding scepticism about the economic management package suggests that the old clash of interests between financial and industrial institutions had not evaporated; nor had the banks lost their fear that all politicians would, if they could, forget the rules of sound finance in the pursuit of consumption and electoral popularity. Catto, as Governor, and his officials could take a wider view, but in most of the banks, as in the industries they lent to, chairmen were still men trained in the 1920s, who had reached the top in the mid or late 1930s. Heads of the big eleven clearing banks for another twenty years would still assume that branch managers would deal with the same pre-war clients on the basis that firms generated their own investment, or guarantee their overdrafts with prudent reserve policies. The vast sums needed for export finance, they imagined, would be provided by the merchant banks. (Not until the early 1950s were clearing banks' reserves channelled this way.) In justifying a return to past patterns, each institution argued that it would make a substantial contribution to dollar and foreign exchange reserves at a time when the horrific pattern of debt outweighed all other considerations. Each should, therefore, in its overseas dimension, be treated with exceptional privilege. In extreme forms, this cast of mind argued that industry, apart from certain advanced and internationally competitive sectors, should take second place in reconstruction: in short that Britain did not *need* a 'balanced' economy of the classical, late-nineteenth-century type and should concentrate only on those industries and firms which could survive in the new environment. As yet this was far too radical a view of 'efficiency' even for Board of Trade tastes.

Trade, in any case, had directed its November 1942 enquiry to those industries most likely to revert to what it regarded as the bad practices of the inter-war years: cartels and restrictions, concentration on the home market rather than the risky export one, building up reserves rather than investing, settling into cosy relationships with unions, and passing on the cost to a public whose pent-up demand would prevent it from either discriminating or complaining. It never pursued its case for efficiency beyond manufacturing industry and left untouched those sectors, banking, insurance and agriculture, which, it can be argued, became the most efficient of all during the next forty years.

In the immensely complex geography of British industry at the end of the war, energy, efficiency and vision coexisted with innumerable legacies of pre-war mentality at the same time, in the same industries, and often in the same firms. The evidence of its surveys did not lead the Board of Trade necessarily to predict prolonged relative decline; and Britain's actual decline clearly owes much to developments in the 1950s and 1960s. But from the various investigations the Board made in 1942–44, it does seem that, even at the peak when industry had become producer for total war, there was cause to worry – and not only because of the distortions Keynes had patiently explained in the United States. Steel, engineering, shipbuilding, chemicals, cotton and textiles seemed particularly at risk.[67] British managers could have argued that in seeking to restore their dominance over safe markets they differed hardly at all from many American companies who were preparing to do the same, while German, Italian, French or Belgian companies could not, for obvious reasons, yet be competitors. But this ignored the context in which the Americans operated. To be fair, most British industrialists accepted the package of ideas contained in the 1944 White Paper; if aspects of the pre-war trading system were to be restored, mass unemployment was not. War had taught them about how demand could be manipulated and how it could ensure profitability. In taking their model of how things should work from pre-war, they merely repeated what their predecessors had done in 1917–19. Even Keynes, in the first chapter of his *Economic Consequences of the Peace* (1918) had lauded the pre-1914 world. Shorn of the unpleasant side-effects of the thirties, the models were, perhaps, more practical than those of 1914. Industrialists wanted the bright dawn the White Paper promised; but they could not yet trust it, and so approached it in the spirit of the just centurion, with their old intellectual baggage intact.

Ministers and civil servants, bankers and trade union leaders had gone down the same path of experience, and it may be that those who seemed most radical were only those with least to lose. Unfortunately, the survival of so much formative experience, like the survival of debilitated but still working machinery, inhibited change and adaptation in ways from which other war-devastated European countries were necessarily exempt. The production and exports drive, for example, was seen as an immediate goal, in order to sustain both reconstruction *and* consumption at home; acceleration in both was to be achieved by sheer volume, using existing plant, and reducing labour costs. That such remedies had worked, for a time in the late 1920s in the rationalisation era, served as a guide to what was done in the late 1940s but not in the longer term.

Even if it had been practicable to enforce modernisation and to finance renewal of plant (which was not the case in the conditions of 1946–49) it would have been hard to do so using the political system in which the 1944 package had been developed. The practice of pluralistic bargaining, inside a war-extended state, survived. Sectional opinions and interests continued to flow in from each governing institution (themselves a compound of a thousand lesser and often more backward-looking interests). As a victor power, Britain could not easily foreclose on any of these, for each group had made sacrifices, all had a right to join in celebration. That all could not be satisfied was not yet clear in 1944–45. The hard questions which would have produced conflict over substantive interests like profits and wages, at a time when politicians and officials believed that the country could not have faced political infighting, had been pushed aside.

Indeed, the 1944 White Paper's promises may have prolonged an illusion about the price of political harmony and handed on, at a deeper level, a dangerous ambiguity to the Attlee administration.

The 1944 package was never free from criticism. Its inception caused one of the most wide-ranging, intellectually stimulating and perceptive arguments ever to take place in Whitehall. But its completion involved a set of compromises whose validity depended on acceptance by every group concerned of a continuing interest in the original aims and obligations. Months of hard bargaining produced an agreed document of great significance for the future, but the various conflicts of ethos, even ideologies, within government and governing institutions (for example about liberal trade in relation to the sterling area or exposure of industry to world competition) remained. Yet the concept was so all-embracing, so compelling in its harmonious balancing of rights and duties, that it did inspire genuine enthusiasm. Some of the most ardent critics, like Robbins, were partially converted. Others – probably the majority – had temporised, and would continue to do so until implementation of economic management put their real interests at risk.

Though the Coalition did to a very large extent bind its successors, simply because in 1945 there was neither time nor willpower to think up an alternative, and because Labour's own leaders lacked faith in a 'socialist alternative', it could not bind the public not to expect its rewards, however much departments or Ministers appealed to it as the 'consumer interest'. On the other hand, major issues had been largely predetermined: the choices between physical and fiscal controls, between an interventionist policy for industry and aggregate demand management. The rules of the game had yet to be learned, but the participants knew that they were to play on the same board. The nature of the state, its departmental hierarchy and scope, had been laid down. The numbers and status of those entitled to play in the game had been accepted. If this had not been done in wartime and by these committees acting vicariously for overburdened Ministers, it is hard to see how it could have been done so comprehensively later in the turbulent conditions of 1945–47.

That so many issues could come together in the nine months leading up to May 1944 is not surprising. The war could now no longer be lost; and by early 1944, planning for D-Day made it certain that, with American aid, it would be won. The Coalition's precarious commonalty began to disintegrate soon afterwards, limiting the scope for any agreed extrapolation from the White Paper which stood, therefore, like a gospel binding whichever party would form the next administration. 'Outside', the public avidly listened to a press and BBC counterpoint between it and Beveridge's more dramatic prose. But whatever the polemicists said, either political party's freedom of action radically to change the White Paper's formulation was rapidly reduced. Much of the history of 1945–51 represents Labour's discovery of how narrow that margin was.

Counterfactual questions can be put about whether the buried questions could, or would have been argued out and resolved if the Coalition had survived and an election been postponed to 1947 or 1948, after a supposed 'period of transition'. Given the centrifugal tendencies among members of the institutions, on the shop floor, among companies suspiciously looking forward to a highly competitive and hostile future, what was gained in 1941–44, in the interstices of fighting total war, stands as a remarkable achievement.

That its authors failed to argue out the details can be blamed as much on Ministers' increased sensitivity to party-political stresses as on the intrinsic difficulties of problems like investment, productivity, and the future of the capital market.[68] At this level, the 1944 White Paper represented a work-in-progress report, over which it was expected the participants would argue. The TUC wanted more, the City of London less. Industry divided on many lines between large and small business, export-orientated traders and domestic-market suppliers, the lukewarm and the enthusiasts.

In supporting it, to the extent they did, the institutions may dimly have been aware, not only that they were submerging their immediate self-interest in a higher national interest and taking on moral obligations, but also that the desired result could be self-fulfilling because no one party to the contract would be seen by the others to be first to back out. The War Cabinet admitted to being 'impressed by [its] past psychological value in bringing home to the mass of the public exactly what a policy of maintaining employment demands; a conscious attempt by the whole community not to drift with the ebb and flow of the economic tide, as in the past, but to set itself to reduce such fluctuations to a minimum'.[69]

But at the level of the machinery of government, the questions of how decisions would be made and by whom had ceased to be a matter for discussion. Protests could still be made, for example by the TUC, but an opportunity to reopen them would not occur until all the participants had been convinced that the system was in disarray – at the very end of the 1950s. The state apparatus bequeathed to the Labour government of 1945–51 was not only not susceptible to amendment; it contained within itself a blueprint for economic management intrinsically hostile to the decisions of the 1944 Labour Party conference and to the spirit if not the letter of *Let Us Face the Future*.

4 Managing Austerity 1945–47

The Coalition started to break up in mid-1945; even Bevin, who had previously argued for its continuation, rebuffed an overture that Churchill made to the Labour Party during the Conservative Conference in April. At a crucial National Executive Council meeting on 18–20 May, Attlee, Bevin and Dalton found themselves in a minority in wishing even to prolong its life a little and Labour Ministers immediately resigned. The General Election gave Labour the second overwhelming majority of the century: 393 seats, with 47.8 per cent of the vote, as against the Conservatives' 210 seats and 39.6 per cent. The results showed a switch of perhaps two million middle-class votes and confirmed that a complete change had taken place in the geography of Labour's electorate. Change at the top, however, proved far less dramatic.

The new government inherited a form of state organisation in which Coalition Ministers and their civil servants had had almost total confidence. Labour Ministers continued to believe in office that this would channel the divergent wills of interest groups and institutions and hold them and the public to the political and moral obligations attached to the central, desirable aim of full employment. In making a conscious expiation for the failure of 1917–19, they and their Conservative Coalition colleagues had, by implication, also accepted a political conclusion about inter-war governments' experience. In trying, for example, to hold FBI and BEC together after their proposed merger failed, or in taking advantage of Beveridge's negotiations with the TUC, they had recognised that government's ability to plan would decrease in peacetime, once physical external threats had vanished. The state would need the institutions as much as they wanted to be involved with it.

The existence of corporate bias thus offered itself as a continuing way to sort out the hard questions, an insurance against a relapse

112

into the sorts of conflicts which had scarred Britain in 1919–21 and 1926. Institutions as well as the public would however have to be educated, in order to keep them sensible of their duties in the future once collective wage bargaining and the pursuit of profit had been restored.[1] Political propaganda would play a large part; hence the publicity given after 1946 to the *Economic Surveys*. Stultified by disintegration of the Coalition in 1944–45, departments were at least still able to plan for the better incorporation of industry through the sponsorship system and reform of trade associations. The whittling down of Industrial Boards' intended powers can be seen as a form of accommodation by the Board to Trade to what management was actually prepared to concede.[2]

Managers prepared themselves, without too much heart-burning, to coexist so long as government expectations did not involve any sacrifice to trade unions of their authority.[3] Most were content to accept the hierarchic pattern of sponsorship, realising that in peacetime they might still find it valuable, as the aircraft manufacturers and farmers had in the 1930s. The fact that many of their members left the Ministries of Supply or Aircraft Production straight for the boardroom (or like Norman Kipping, the FBI) made for continuity of ethos and practice. The new government soon perpetuated the system by reconstituting the NPACI on the basis of parity between employers and trades union representatives (with two members from nationalised industries) like the NJAC. Later, the Economic Planning Board and the Dollar Export Council were given similar tripartite foundations, as were non-government bodies such as the Anglo-American Production Council.

Although it had long desired parity, the TUC's wider ambitions were frustrated. Citrine had not misinterpreted his colleagues' intentions in stating that TUC co-operation would be essential on all labour questions. Disconcerted by the external economic crisis in 1945, and profoundly worried by the possibility of deflation, the TUC committed itself to an unprecedented · involvement in consultation and planning. There is really very little substance in the old charge that the unions forced the Labour government to abandon physical planning in order to safeguard their aggressive wage claims: if anything, the reverse is true, for most union leaders (even, perhaps, Citrine) had come to admire the Soviet Union *because* it was a planned economy. What they sought was to strengthen the machinery of government to permit such incorporation: to convert Joint Production Councils (which had, by common consent, worked well) into 'full employment councils', and to use Trades Councils as management used trade associations as agents for government in the production drive. Behind this can be seen an attempt to create a vast series of closed shops, apt to dominate the labour market and imprint on industry as well as government of the TUC's fuller definition of what full employment meant.

Attlee's Ministry showed itself strictly disinclined to accept such claims. (Dalton, ever-suspicious of the TUC barons, made a practice of seeing union delegations himself to prevent contact between them and his Trade officials.) But a reassertion of Arthur Henderson's old dictum that the party had responsibility for all political matters, the TUC only for industrial ones, did not mean that the government did not fully accept the doctrine as well as the structure of an extended state, incorporating a community of interests complementary to the party-parliamentary system. The state, they believed, should be sensitive to these interests, without favouring any one of them. Thus the Second World War experience encouraged a somewhat complacent and very insular belief in the value of British institutions and recent traditions, especially when these were compared with those of other European nations. The system was, however, to an extent that few fully understood, also partly a creation of the very interests whose rights *vis-à-vis* government they disparaged, shaped by the brokerage that had occurred continuously inside government. Permeation of the state by institutional values may explain why debates about the public interest in 1943–45 had been so opaque, and why the idea of the public as consumers, with an interest in lower prices, better distribution and efficiency that cut across the vested interests of organised industry and labour, caused trouble – from which electoral victory did not free the incoming government. Ministers may have imagined that they would continue to enunciate the national interest, and would find it accepted freely and in common by institutions and public. Only with hindsight, after the 1947 crisis, when the institutions ceased more quickly than departments had imagined to be able to bind their members as government wished, was it obvious that the national interest had already become the basis for – and indeed the product of – competition.

The Labour governments seemed to be, more than any since 1925 and perhaps since 1906, ministries of all the talents. Unfortunately, many of those talents had grown tired after five years of Coalition service. Ministers were short of ideas, at loggerheads with each other, and out of touch with the party machinery and the constituencies that gave them their astonishing parliamentary majority. Yet their early record shows no lack of the leadership and political willpower necessary to carry out their aims in conditions much more difficult than any of them could have imagined when *Let Us Face the Future* had been drafted.[4]

Attlee has always been seen as the great co-ordinator, archetypal broker, conciliator and chairman of committees. His was not a deep mind, nor even a decisive one like Bevin's. Integrity, efficiency, courage, loyalty to traditional institutions made up the national virtues which he saw himself representing and which he had, himself, always displayed. In his use of the imagery of consensus he played on national effort, common duty, fair shares for all. He had not, as Kenneth Harris shows, been subordinate to Churchill and had acquired an exceptionally clear grasp of Cabinet work and of how to use the departmental machine. His concept of what needed to be done applied as much to foreign affairs as to the health service. Like all good chairmen of the Cabinet, he had the gift of separating the essential from the important (shown, for example, in his decision to proceed with development of the atomic bomb once the Truman government had withdrawn the United States from the Quebec Agreement). Unlike the majority of modern Prime Ministers he was ready to pay the price for making the distinction, even when some of his colleagues would not.

With his simple, almost military attitude to authority and responsibility, he would not tolerate any claim by subordinate Ministers to sabotage the grand design by scheming or disloyalty; nor any overriding right of the Party Conference, nor the TUC to tell Ministers their business. Although the Cabinet had probably for the last time a majority of members of working-class origin, it was not in any egalitarian sense a working-class administration. Radicalism and its largely middle-class exponents lay dormant during the first two years. As Paul Addison puts it, 'The Labour Party of 1945 was led by an alliance of Oxbridge intellectuals and TUC oligarchs. Committed as they were to working-class welfare, they had no interest in redistributing authority . . . the ethos of the time was managerial, with orders and injunctions flowing down from on high; and Labour leaders expected the people to respond.'[5]

Attlee's strong sense of duty and reciprocal obligations meant that he could order striking dockers to return to work because of what government had done for them;[6] and he told Cabinet, in 1949, that National Service constituted a reasonable request in return for the Welfare State.

In making his broadcasts and appeals, the Prime Minister saw himself as spokesman for the nation, in the MacDonald tradition, rather than as advocate of one class in a struggle with others. He took care for example to avoid any semblance of disfavouring the managerial elite on ideological grounds and argued that employers should accept controls because government, with their interests also in mind, had reduced them to a minimum. In some trade unionists' eyes, this amounted to partiality: 'It is the *duty* of every employer,' Attlee told the National Union of Manufacturers in November 1946, 'in all the areas where full employment is already established, to see that he does not use more workers than are really needed for the work in hand, and that he does not take labour for less essential purposes. . . .'[7] Here he drew out lines for a legitimate co-operation between government and private enterprise, 'inevitable if the aims which the country has set before it of maintaining full employment, and balancing our international payments, are to be achieved'. Only if industrialists evaded their obligations, would government assume 'the power to take such action as seems expedient, and is desired by all'.

Christian, contractual and certain, his language's bleak realism reflected the traditional English public school concept of duty. The aims he extolled, full employment, a decent standard of living, health and housing, like the demons of depression, unemployment, poverty and misery, derived from his personal experience in the inter-war years. His faith in popular altruism to pay for reform with self-abnegation may have been misplaced but it was not naïve. As Attlee understood, labour had made its gains already and should not ask for more – the government's duty was to defend its constituents, not so much against a counter-revolution as against blind, inexorable shifts in the international economy.

In applying these principles, Ministers found themselves trapped in the machinery of government in whose form they had already acquiesced. As Lord President, with responsibility for planning, Morrison confronted Dalton, at the Treasury, who saw himself as the bringer of cheap money, latest in a long line of innovating Chancellors. At the Foreign Office, wrapped up in dealing with the

Soviet threat, the danger that the United States might drift into isolation, and the chaos in post-war Europe, Bevin had little scope to stand as champion for the TUC as he had done when Minister of Labour. Like the Prime Minister, most members of the Cabinet took trade union responses so much for granted that they also came to seem partial in their efforts to persuade rather than coerce management. The left chose, for the time being, not to represent themselves as advocates of the full party programme because they had really no leverage over the Cabinet as a whole and were, in any case, too busy to do other than manage their departments. Some who might have done (like Isaacs at the Ministry of Labour who had a reputation as a radical) were as yet junior and inexperienced. Policy at the centre – that is, the Treasury, Lord President's Office, Foreign Office and Board of Trade – followed closely the Coalition's full employment package therefore, gilding it with the language of fair shares and social justice and identifying it with the national interest and the economic aims of social democracy. None of this was very original and some was mere hyperbole, with Morrison as fugleman for what he called 'something new and revolutionary which will be regarded in time to come as a contribution to civilisation as vital and distinctively British as parliamentary democracy or the rule of law'.[8]

Labour Ministers understood that planning would differ from wartime. They would have to argue their case with the public, not dictate. As Stafford Cripps put it, they would '*guide* production into the necessary channels, according to the plans which we have formulated'.[9] More crisply, apropos of French methods of planning, Bevin declared: 'we don't do things like that in our country; we don't *have* plans, we work things out practically'.[10] Planning meant allocating scarce resources, budgeting for manpower and raw materials, using the annual budget as regulator to manage national income and expenditure. Physical controls were intended to survive only for a limited period – though in fact they did rather longer than predicted in 1945. The principles were set out in a draft for the (unpublished) 'Economic Survey for 1946', which suggests that, with the exception of Morrison who wanted to go further and enlist the support of public opinion, the Ministerial Committee on Economic Planning was content to accept the limitations. In contrast to Morrison, Dalton and Cripps, sceptical of the response from a war-weary electorate, preferred the veiled anonymity of managing the economy to the risk of spelling out what austerity in 1946 actually meant.[11] Dalton's period at the Treasury was not one of physical planning although he welcomed the retention of manpower controls to ensure an adequate supply of labour. The dramatic shift to fiscal budgeting under Cripps in 1947–48 depicted by Samuel Beer in *Modern British Politics* (1965) was actually no more than a shift of emphasis within a longer continuity from Kingsley Wood's 1942 Budget.

Of the leaders, only Cripps had a clear and comprehensive idea of how the issues raised in government in 1943–44 should be composed in a distinctively Labour way. Attlee and Morrison lacked his economic understanding: for all his talk, Morrison the skilled bureaucrat failed to use the apparatus of planning he so busily accumulated or the men who remained on his Lord President's Committee and in the Economic Section. Much of what the government did in 1945–47 (in areas other than welfare, education and health insurance) was intended simply to maintain full employment, achieve economic recovery and keep the participants to the 1944 political contract together. The main threat as they saw it was inflation impairing the export drive, for wages rose by 9 per cent in 1945–46. It is therefore hardly surprising that they did not deliberately raise the hard questions in whose burials they themselves had acquiesced in 1943–44.

Accepting what had become the Treasury's instant tradition, Ministers preferred to avoid the sort of stringent exposure to international competition, backed by anti-monopoly legislation, which Dalton and his officials had pushed only two years earlier. At the Board of Trade in 1945–47, Cripps concerned himself mainly with the revival of decayed regions using the Distribution of Industry Act. As the FBI desired, trades associations not Industry Boards became his lever. Only in the export sectors, where production mattered most, did Cripps go further, by setting up working parties with Trade officials having equal membership with unions and employers. Seventeen of these were planned but only three existed by 1947; they had no powers but exhortation and once-suspicious industrialists accepted them with equanimity. Despite regular complaints about 'creeping socialism', very little actual control took place: men like Edwin Plowden and Lord Hyndley among the officials realised that most Labour ministers shared their belief that planning had limits dictated by industry's voluntary response on one hand, public tolerance on the other.

From Attlee downwards, Ministers accepted that economic

planning for industry would have a tripartite dimension in which government would consult, not bargain. Instead of trying to dictate, they sought to safeguard political authority. According to Attlee, reconstitution of the NJAC was intended to perpetuate the climate of harmonious industrial relations without giving industry or unions leverage over government policy. He continued to assume that both sides, grateful for full employment (or the loan negotiated from America) had their duties; it was for government 'to get our vast industrial machine into gear'.[12]

A similar simplicity applied to the question of nationalisation. Finding it difficult to choose between its debt to the moral legacy of R. H. Tawney's *Acquisitive Society* and the detail of 1930s Labour Party Conference resolutions, the government emphasised, variously, the ethic of state ownership and the hope of achieving practical efficiency without advancing far the more complicated debate about whether to substitute (or even define) social needs and priorities in the industries it chose.[13] Ministers on the Socialisation of Industries Committee were introduced to the morasses of administrative practice by their officials who asked questions they found hard to answer: whether government should be involved in wages-bargaining, or leave so crucial a part of public industry's costs to their Boards; whether they should limit the right to strike in essential industry; whether they should make a profit for the state (assuming that they could even cover debt servicing and investment); and whether they should look at what was delicately termed 'workers' assistance in management'.[14]

In 1942–44, permanent officials and 'outsiders' had served the Coalition well by arguing out such issues from first principles. Now the latter had gone back to academic life, industry or banking. Keynes died in 1946 and only a few of the gifted Economic Section team, like James Meade, remained. Instead, the departmental officials, steeped in older traditions, based their advice on both wartime consensus and pre-war experience. They enhanced the tendency of senior members of the Cabinet to interfere as little as possible with the way management and unions conducted their business at any level below that of central organisations. When it came to setting up and giving commercial terms of reference, officials in all the departments conceived of the new State Boards in the mould of the old state corporations, with union consultation grafted on. The result came close enough to Morrison's model: Ministers, aware of the TUC's own unease about dual allegiance, seemed content to accept officials' recommendations about 'workers' assistance'.[15] It is inept to make workers' control a test of 'reformism' when government, TUC and the majority of party workers imagined that the new Boards would extend good practice, not promote social revolution.

A more substantive criticism is that the government's benign attitude to management allowed the moment for real reform of industry to pass, almost unnoticed. Its leaders' emphasis on the role of industrial policy not as a progenitor of change, but as 'the custodian of the public interest, specifically aimed to ensure continuity and prevent fluctuations from one government to another',[16] (a view put by senior Ministers to the 1944 Association, 'a businessmen's group which sought to bridge the gap between industry and the Labour Government'), was indeed, more accommodating than the party as a whole would have liked. Quite deliberately, the government had set itself to preserve social priorities, working class gains and continued domestic consumption, knowing that the United States' negotiators counselled greater caution, if not actual deflation. To survive in the lowering international situation, it needed the co-operation of industry and the financial sector more than that of the TUC in the years to come and simply could not afford, arbitrarily and unnecessarily, to alienate either.

What is odd, and rather touchingly naïve, is Ministers' reluctance at first to go beyond persuasion of the public into propaganda, as if the base art (whose machinery they had inherited intact) were unnecessary and might taint what they sought to do. This delicacy was confined to the older men,[17] and distinguished them from Richard Crossman, Evan Durbin, Patrick Gordon Walker or Kenneth Younger, a generation who tended to equate democratic planning with the public interest and did not baulk at the conclusion that if they could not persuade, they must compel. The former saw in persuasion the language of realism, a declaration that the long-suffering public should neither be exploited nor manipulated. At least until 1947, the low level of strikes and interruptions vindicated their judgment and suggested that the imagery of shared sacrifice retained its freshness.

Dealing indifferently with both sides of industry had another advantage that the government continued to see eye to eye with senior civil servants on how the full employment–economic management package should be implemented. Attlee's administration relied on the same dense web of official committees, and on a community of interest that can only fully be explained by its leaders' concept of public service. Class background seems irrelevant when looking at the relations of Bevin and his Foreign Office mandarins, or of Bridges and

Attlee.[18] There is talk in Dalton's diaries of civil service reform, but nothing in the papers of Cripps, Morrison or Attlee. Ministers seem to have relied on their officials without fear of leaks (for which Attlee had a particular aversion) or defection to a future Conservative administration.

The committee structure and the individual excellence of officials like Norman Brook made it possible for Ministers to focus without becoming detail-obsessed on the intricacies of governing Germany, the sterling area, or the inception of OEEC. The transition to peace under machinery of government priorities agreed in wartime, virtually eliminated conflicts like those of 1918–19 between No. 10 and the Treasury: the concept of a decision-making 'centre' emerged as something essential yet uncontentious, blending in reasonable harmony nineteenth-century theory and mid-twentieth-century practice. In what became a turbid and contumacious Cabinet after 1947, Attlee could hardly have survived without the Cabinet Office, the mechanism which helped him to prevent friction and ensured that the key ministers were more or less in tune.

In the Ministry of Labour (now MOL) the transition from central planning to decontrol of manpower and wages occurred with the same lack of innovation or conflict as elsewhere. Under Bevin's tutelage, Isaacs eschewed Bridges' far-sighted suggestion of a national planning centre for public industries, and contented himself with approaching each case under the Control of Engagements Order on its merits. MOL dared not entertain a policy of direct intervention in the labour market – though the result was put to the House of Commons in more high-flown terms as a compromise between national needs and individual freedom.[19] In the labour market, as in industry, a body with over-arching powers would not have been acceptable to industries, unions or the banks. There was, in short, no 'failure of planning' because planning in any sense other than the management of scarcity was not on the agenda.

Already in 1945–46, patterns of pluralism returned to the centre of government as the history of manpower planning for the armed forces indicates – accompanied, however, by a rather surprising degree of authoritarian behaviour where minority dissent could be blamed on political agitation. Deakin turned the full force of the TGWU on Trotskyists as Bevin had done on Communists before June 1941 and as both were to do again after the Cold War began in 1947. Troops were used to help clear the docks of perishable goods as early as October 1945. But although the use of emergency powers against strikers

threatened to divide Attlee and Morrison from Cripps and Bevin, and
to revive civil servants' mistrust of the trade union movement, no
serious tremors occurred in public opinion during the first eighteen
months – that is, until the fuel crisis of the 1946–47 winter and the
political and economic troubles that followed.

Senior ministers did make a set of judgements about the relative
importance of external issues, notably defence, the Soviet Union and
the future of Germany which, long before the decision to take part in
the Korean War, made foreign policy immensely costly in terms of
hard currency, manpower and industrial production, to the detriment
of the economic management package. But in dealing with the
international economic environment, the government did not have
much freedom of action, and probably rather less than they had
imagined – though Attlee tended to deny (in public) that domestic
policy was largely governed by external constraints. They knew from
Treasury advice and Keynes' reports before they took office that the
balance of payments would be a serious problem, but thought it not
insuperable, so long as production and exports rose sufficiently. This
assumption could not survive the appreciation Keynes made in a
despairing memorandum, 'Our overseas financial prospects' in mid-
August.[20] Lend–Lease ended abruptly after Japan's surrender,
removing the facility which had allowed the UK to finance two-thirds
of its £10 000 million debt in wartime. Thereafter the debt could only
grow larger. Keynes estimated a shortfall on the balance of payments
of nearly £1 000 million for 1946, tapering only slowly in later years. In
default of an export recovery almost beyond imagination, there
seemed no alternative to heavy deflation and reduction of imports to
a level which would mean a devastating fall in the standard of living
and in basic nutrition.

This the Attlee government with firm political willpower and a
sharp understanding of the electorate's mood would not permit. They
had perhaps been misled, in their estimate of American attitudes, by
the admiration for Roosevelt and the New Deal prevalent in the
Labour Party; they had not worried, for obvious reasons, about
American antipathy towards the imperial legacy (until they began to
understand its economic dimension); and they continued to believe in
the United States' role as leader of a new world order, even when they
saw its agencies establishing what amounted to economic hegemony in
Italy and to lesser extent in France. This sympathetic myopia survived

the ending of Lend–Lease and the crude lack of understanding shown by the American negotiators in 1945. It predisposed the Government to work with the Truman administration if for no other reason than that in the long run Britain stood to gain by being part of that new world order of liberal trade and western defence and could only lose if (as the Foreign Office and Bevin himself feared) the United States withdrew into isolation as it had after World War One.

Reports from the negotiators sent to the USA in September 1945 were disappointing from the start: not only did the American team led by Fred Vinson, Secretary of the Treasury, and Will Clayton of the Department of Economic Affairs seem hostile but they were emphatic about retaining subsidies to benefit their own depressed industries while insisting on British commitments to multilateral trade. (Officials in the State Department proved no less intransigent: it is hard to evaluate, for example, the way Britain was cut out of the Manhattan project without concluding that America feared that Britain would gain advantage in atomic energy development from US work.) Pressed from behind by the US Chamber of Commerce and the National Association of Manufacturers, Vinson and Clayton gave the impression of not wishing to understand the problems of the sterling area, even if they did not actually follow the wilder men in Congress in claiming that Britain had already lapsed into socialism at home, while renewing imperialism abroad.

Keynes had called it a 'financial Dunkirk' before the dealings began, for the USA held all the high cards.[21] Recognising the need to co-operate closely with the Americans, Keynes wanted to move quickly towards convertibility with the dollar and to write off part of the sterling balances, preferably before 1947. The Bank of England and the Treasury OFD disagreed, being less certain that British production capacity could expand to meet the challenge of competition, and hoping still for an autonomous role for the sterling area. The wrangling dragged on, while the hoped-for loan on which the government's social welfare programme largely depended fell from the $5 billion at a nominal rate of interest originally mooted to $3.75 billion at a commercial rate of 2 per cent repayable over 50 years. Keynes, out of sympathy with both the Americans and his Chancellor, Dalton, settled the terms of the loan and accepted convertibility of sterling for July 1947. At the time, early in December 1945, the Bank and OFD seem to have been less worried about the strain posed by the latter than the effect of what they saw as anti-British feeling focused on their trading aims in the sterling area and on the establishment of

European Monetary agreements (EMAs) favourable to Britain's bilateral trade which, they insisted, were 'an essential substructure of Bretton Woods'.[22]

The dispute between Keynes, who accepted a liberal internationalism, and the bilateralists could not be resolved so long as the Bank and OFD hoped their negotiations with the sterling balance holders, and with reviving European countries, could provide an alternative trading network. At this stage, in 1945–46, the bilateralists wanted government to institute detailed planning of British trade to ensure that the export industries became competitive, and to build up import substitution and barter deals.[23] The anti-bilateralists of course took a much wider-ranging position with which in the end both the Treasury OFD and Bank of England had to sympathise. Complex and technical as the whole subject was, it came down to a fundamental difference of opinion about Britain's position in the world: was it a weakened but still worthy collaborator with the United States in building a new world system, backed by the IMF, or was it a battered but autonomous power, standing equally in Europe and the sterling area?

The Cabinet did not decide on the loan settlement, in the main debate on 5 December, in these terms, partly because they were railroaded by the urgency of the case and partly because Dalton chose to present acceptance as the only alternative to severe deflation. An almost united Cabinet backed Keynes – correctly, because the Bank's negotiations with Egypt and Argentina showed, by the middle of 1946, that there *was* no alternative. This left the Bank and Treasury to try and retain what benefits they could from the sterling area while rationing the hard-won dollars in the hope that the pound could stand convertibility in a mere eighteen months. When India also brushed off their negotiating team, in February 1947, it became clear that speculators against the pound had an enormous advantage. Given the unpopularity of EMAs with European countries seeking to break into dollar markets, all concerned began to worry about the date that Keynes had had to set.

Dalton wrote as early as December 1945: 'my cynical reflection on the American loan is that we shall be able to make good use of the dollars – though we wish there were more – but that it is quite certain that the conditions will have to be revised before AD2000 and that even in the next year or two, it may well be that circumstances will require a considerable variation, which might even be unilateral'.[24] His less cynical, more complacent colleagues woke up very slowly to the implications. By January 1947, Dalton probably realised that convertibility – then only six months ahead – would fail; but his Treasury officials advised him not to ask for another loan from a still-hostile United States. Instead, he addressed a memorandum to the Cabinet, already reeling from the effects of the harsh winter, recommending very severe cuts in imports and expenditure (see page 131). The crisis had begun.

In some American accounts, particularly those of the 'new right', Britain's slippery path had begun in wartime with the 1944 package itself, but degeneration had really become dangerous only with the government's attempt to provide social welfare and public consumption before it had earned the money to do so. British left wing critics have emphasised the burden of overseas commitments, defence and armaments including development of the atomic bomb. Keynes himself talked about 'a vast overplaying of our hand' before the export trade had been built up. Critics in the financial sector argued simply that British could not afford cheap money, wages – inflation and a consumption boom.

The problem was that the liberal trading pattern did not develop at once and, during the transition, down to 1947 when GATT began, Britain became heavily dependent on the sterling area, and what it could achieve in Europe. As the dollar loan ran out, EMAs and the sterling area failed to fill the gap. The Cabinet remained complacent insofar as it treated 'exports' as a separate sphere, one that bore no relation to the actual state of industry, its investment costs and labour productivity, but which could be expanded by simple incentives and exhortation. By putting sterling itself at issue, convertibility in July 1947 was bound to force the government either into deflation (which it had renounced in advance) or austerity – for which the public was almost unprepared.

In the Cabinet's defence, it can be argued that, when the terms of the American loan were accepted, a great temptation existed to hold the alliance of industry and unions around the 1944 package and hope that the targets could still be reached. A more political temptation, to which Dalton evidently gave way, was to go ahead anyway, despite the American terms, and find out what had to be done when the night actually fell.[25] A Labour government did not have an 'alternative' to reconstruction; nor, in terms of the opinion of electorate, unions, and management, could it turn towards a command economy (though Keynes evidently feared that possibility and tried to prevent it). Labour's key economic ministers in fact gave Keynes the best help they could and accepted the result, fatalistically, so long as the denouement did not *compel* them to deflate at a time of high unemployment.[26]

In December 1945 a minority of the Cabinet, Bevan, Shinwell and Alexander, tried to argue against acceptance of the loan terms, on principle, and in defence of what they took to be Labour's political mandate. They were silenced by their seniors, headed by Bevin, who seems to have accepted the assurances of the FBI and TUC that the dollar gap could be bridged without imposing intolerable strains on firms or their workforces.[27] In retrospect, it was clearly an illusion to imagine that the export trade could sustain the government's commitments to social security, the housing programme, existing levels of rations, and increased spending as well as to the level of investment and imports required for reconstruction. The fact that the targets were met for a time does not justify Ministers' over-optimism or wilful blindness, only their political nerve.

It is possible that careful planning in 1946–47 could have averted the worst of the 1947 crisis, as Sir Alec Caincross has argued. Dalton's refusal to abandon cheap money in his 1947 Budget, and his reliance on Treasury officials who underestimated the chain reaction which, judging from his diary entries, he foresaw made that unlikely. Until well on in 1947 the majority of Ministers probably believed that the gamble could work. In February, for example, Attlee and Bevin refused Dalton's request to postpone construction of new power stations because of the forecast deficit of £400 million. Cabinet discussion indicates that they regarded their political contract with the electorate as something that overrode external necessity.[28] But the care they took not to alienate United States' opinion in 1946–47, and the narrow way in which they presented the issues to parliament and public, helped to disguise the acute seriousness of Britain's position from management and workers in manufacturing industry on whose efforts survival depended.

British industry suffered from two long-term and profound disadvantages which the late 1940s enhanced rather than diminished. Firstly, production in small units in small batches, with uniformity of production the exception, predominated until the 1960s. This pattern was confirmed by several factors. Controls retained in the post-war Production Authority system were designed to increase volume rather than affect its content. A steady home market, buoyed up by full employment and the beginnings of the rise of mass consumer demand, encouraged tendencies towards proliferation; while the retention of resale price maintenance and other restrictive practices meant that plant that was inefficient (in terms of international competitiveness) became profitable again and remained so. It was, in any case, hard to buy new plant from the dollar area and the British machine tool industry significantly failed to fill the gap.

Secondly, investment and the intake of new technology lagged far behind America, except in a few cases such as civil aviation, where for a time Britain held a world lead. The cost of wages relative to the price of manufactured goods rose, higher even than in the inter-war years, partly because of full employment policies, partly because unions concentrated, in their bargaining, on money wages bearing in mind the cost of living, partly because it suited employers, particularly in the car industry, to settle and pass the cost on to the domestic consumer rather than face strikes and lose to their competitors. Thus campaigns to increase production almost inevitably involved an increase in the intensity or volume of labour, rendering Britain yet more backward when compared with the United States. Britain had lost through over-commitment in wartime when the American economy had attained an almost invulnerable lead. Re-equipment had for lack of dollars become more difficult than in any previous generation. But that alone does not explain the discrepancy in competitiveness (though Keynes tried to put the blame there, in his negotiations).

The Production Campaign, renamed the Prosperity Campaign early in 1946, marked the start of a series of annual exhortations to intensify output per man (as productivity was then defined). Given the insistence of Cripps, Morrison and Attlee on persuasion rather than coercion, the government had to rely in its propaganda on reviving popular altruism with the concept of the nation in danger, in a peacetime mode. Common sense and FBI and BEC advice enjoined them to keep wages stable, so as to hold costs down and export: this, in terms of the 1944 package, meant keeping prices and the cost of living down. For such a strategy, union and management co-operation was required.

Both sides contributed to the bargain, according to their lights. The TUC accepted that its members must work harder; it agreed to give direct support to government by furthering the Prosperity Campaign, and by galvanising individual unions into forming 'efficiency departments'.[29] In industries like coalmining, which could not attract workers because of bad conditions, the TUC could recommend shift working; it also backed the British Institute of Management in a long campaign to introduce 'scientific management'; and even sent joint delegations with employers to the United States to study American production methods, including sophisticated forms of Taylorism.[30] In return, it raised with government the issue of the 40-hour week, on the reasonable grounds that after five-and-a-half years of war, union members needed to relax – a claim which, when associated with the return of regular overtime, had the unpleasant by-product of increasing employers' and Ministers' awareness of the problem of wage-inflation.

For their part, the FBI and BEC conceded that the government had a right to interfere in industry – by demanding information, setting up investigations, and by legislation such as the Trade Organisation Bill. The FBI took part in the censuses of production which formed the basis for Production Authority planning, and joined trade unions on the Anglo-American Production Council with a vigour that went some way towards overcoming the congenital mutual suspicion and secrecy of its member firms and trade associations. But where the Board of Trade attempted to go further and set up Industry Boards in areas where trade associations did not exist, the FBI's tone became resigned rather than enthusiastic.

From the government's side, the Board having been baulked in 1944 in its offensive against RPM and restrictive practices, now turned out to be a less than precise instrument for eliminating inefficiency. Caught off-balance by the revival of consumer demand, and by the fact that full employment came about in peacetime almost without conscious effort, BOT concentrated on achieving volume production at a time when severe cases of inefficiency were developing, notably in engineering, machine tools and scientific instruments. Ministers and civil servants at the time seem to have forgotten how to encourage efficiency – maybe, even in wartime, they had never done more than touch the surface of that complex of problems – and turned their attention to restraining the recovery of German industry instead, as if that were some sort of alternative.

They made better progress in the fields of science and technology particularly in defence-related industries by bringing customers and contractors more closely to Research Councils and, through sponsorship, to each departmental chief scientist. But these disaggregated links failed to impress central government: the newly-founded Advisory Council on Scientific Policy sat in the wings, able only to affect the educational output, rather than the direction or promotion, of scientific manpower. Once again, those industries most tied in with sponsor departments, such as aerospace and agriculture, benefited most.

Government could have utilised its newly-acquired public interests more. (This had, after all, been the substance of much discussion in 1943–44.) But the aims of 'best-practice' development in newly-nationalised industries conflicted with decisions not to take over more than 20 per cent of the industrial base, and to compel each public industry to be self-supporting in its capital spending. Furthermore, in order to prolong the parliamentary truce, Ministers were careful about using the bulk purchasing and supply levers that now became available. Worse, Morrison and Attlee turned out to be bad judges of managerial ability when it came to nominating the Boards for coal, transport, or energy, arbitrarily restricting their choice to a narrow list of the 'great and good',[31] and tying salaries down well below industrial levels, thus beginning a malign tradition that lasted for more than twenty years. For senior Labour (and later, Conservative) Ministers, state industry Boards required managerial brokerage on the fringes of the state, in the hands of *administrative* experts; they were not conceived of as entrepreneurial examples to industry at large nor, in the French sense, as the state's weapons in economic management.

Employers reacted favourably to a policy which appeared to confirm the bargain sketched out in 1944. Over time, however, the FBI and BEC began to realise that low salaries attracted hidebound or second-rate managers and that this reinforced the inbuilt pattern of conflicting objectives dating from the government's initial failure to lay down clear priorities, other than for debt servicing. Government got the worst of both worlds for, by 1947, public industries had come to be seen as state instruments, albeit inefficient ones, determining the prices of energy and transport in an arbitrary way while soaking up large quantities of scarce capital.

Government could perhaps have used its control of investment funds in such a way as to contribute to industrial efficiency, had it been less committed to maintaining full employment with the minimum of transfer and retraining, or had it not left allocation to the Capital Issues Committee which was, in effect, a City institution, more concerned to emphasise the balanced budget provisions of the 1944 White Paper than those which permitted deficit. Down to the end of his Chancellorship in the autumn of 1947, Dalton regarded the provision of cheap money as a sufficient facility on its own. But this encouraged consumption by the public as well as industrial investment; restraint of consumption then became a major concomitant of economic management, impelled by Treasury, Bank of England and Stock Exchange fears of an inflationary cycle at a time of enormous balance of payments deficit.

Although Dalton did distinguish capital from current expenditure in his Budgets, the City authorities became preoccupied with restraint and never offered more than marginal inducements to management to invest nor to discriminate between one area and another. On the basis of the long discussions before 1945, Labour Ministers (and the Treasury) assumed that investment in public industries would, *tout court*, lead to reduced prices generally and hence to wages stability; private industry would generate its own. As a result, the capital market failed to work necessarily to the advantage of export industries but benefited rather the heterogeneous mass of smaller companies competing on the domestic side. Not until Harold Wilson's BOT paper 'The State and Private Industry' (1949) did government attempt to use investment as a form of beneficent intervention, though that had been the Board's original intention, back in 1943.

Other ideas aired in those early debates lay dormant. Having presented restrictive practices to the American loan negotiators as something which could be justified as defensive measures in a depression, the government wrote BOT out of the original war against monopoly and cartels and convinced itself, apparently, contrary to historic experience, that the British export industry was naturally competitive (the 1930s being an aberration) and would take advantage of the liberal trading pattern soon to be created under GATT.[32] Given industries' dependance on sterling area and other sheltered, Middle East markets, this was highly unrealistic. In political terms it can be explained, however, since they found themselves confronted, after 1945, by a tacit alliance of unions and management in favour of restrictive practices, cartels, and the closed shop.

Ministers and civil servants, with the exception of those at the Board of Trade, compromised. Such restrictions would only be temporary, so the argument ran, until recovery had burst through the 'transition period'. Britain was not unique in this recidivism. Older habits of mind and national bureaucratic methods dogged all European countries during the first years of recovery, until the 1947 crisis debilitated hopes of restoring life inside old ideological frameworks, and at the same time brought a *deus ex machina* in the shape of Marshall Aid.[33]

Scarcity of labour, first as a general problem, then as particular shortages of skilled workers in unattractive industries and in the export sector, bore much more immediately on government thinking, and

became the Ministry of Labour's chief obsession down to the 1970s.
Despite demobilisation and curtailing of Services' manpower demands
in 1946, government had to resort to offering inducements to workers
to take up these jobs since Ministers would not entertain direction by
means of Essential Workers Orders and the Control of Engagements
Order. Shinwell (whose lack of foresight as Minister of Fuel and Power
was partly responsible for the degree of chaos caused in the
exceptionally severe 1946–47 winter) did at least try to obtain directive
powers over manpower and wages in November 1946. He was
defeated in Cabinet by the usual combination of Bevin and Isaacs (an
ineffective Minister whose retention at MOL until 1950 may be
explained as a means to allow Bevin to retain influence over his old
department). Civil servants expressed much scepticism about setting
precise targets,[34] and that appalling winter merely brought to a head a
crisis that already existed. According to Dalton and Cripps, who put a
range of proposals to Cabinet in an angry meeting, 16–17 January
1947, they could postpone raising the school-leaving age, institute
National Service for young women, or reduce the Armed Services in
size. The spending departments ganged up and defeated all three
choices, for there was by now even in times of crisis no real willpower
at the centre radically to look at the way the labour market had already
developed.[35] Short-term solutions, like using foreign labour or 'Bevin
boys' in the pits, were adopted instead of the politically dangerous
reintroduction of controls, and the Cabinet settled for a policy of crisis
avoidance, phrased for public consumption as a productivity
campaign.

Some of Keynes' comments, shortly before he died in 1946, suggest
that while he did not greatly care for the Treasury's policy of 'fine
tuning', 'he was a believer in financial devices for regulating the level
of employment from the demand side rather than by efforts to do so
through detailed intervention, operating directly on supply'.[36] Insofar
as the 1944 package laid down a guiding principle, it was, of course, full
employment. But what was full employment? For officials it had never
been more specific than the 'high and stable level' of the White Paper.
Kingsley Wood had given the unofficial figure of 8.5 per cent in 1944:
many civil servants assumed 8 per cent as a rough guide. Only the
outsiders, like Beveridge or the TUC, dared to guess at anything as low
as 3 per cent.

The TUC's 1944 Report on Reconstruction gave it no special
standing to bargain with a newly elected Labour government and they
wisely adopted a policy aimed to convert Ministers to their target

rather than preach at them for backsliding. Union leaders took for granted that wage and price stabilisation would continue and that, within the 1944 package, it was open for them to try and get adopted as low a level of unemployment as the Treasury and employers' organisations would admit. Labour shortages in the years 1945–47, however, gave unions an advantage in wage bargaining which led in due course to excessive demand – checked by Dalton's second crisis Budget in 1947. Conscious as they were from the start of the dangers of wage inflation, it is hardly surprising that Treasury Ministers resisted specifying any figure for full employment. They did, of course, learn how to manage demand (often, as Robert Hall of the Economic Section pointed out, making up many of the rules as they proceeded) and they deliberately sought to keep unemployment as low as possible. By mid-1946, a complicated body of practice in running the economy existed, categorised by assumptions about what was 'acceptable' and what constituted 'overload'. The fact that full employment came easily in world-wide conditions of scarcity meant that fairly simple indicators such as gross unemployment figures, the index of industrial production, and the balance of visible trade, sufficed.

The TUC soon realised that they had not converted government to their wider definition, though they never accepted the Treasury view that targets had to be set within empirically-determined limits of the economy as it existed; but since actual unemployment stood at 2.4 per cent in February 1946 they concurred with the government's definition in the 1946 White Paper (Cmd 6709). Under pressure from officials on the Ministerial Economic Planning Committee who needed a target in order to draw up a manpower budget, the Cabinet finally assented to a range of 3–5 per cent (which they thought might shock the public but which allowed for 'natural elasticity of the economy')[37] in the 1947 *Economic Survey*. Ministers thus set themselves an easy target.

If the TUC felt ill-requited at first, the General Council did not show its anger in public. Yet the cards were slowly being stacked against them, on the grounds that their members were taking easy pickings. As early as November 1945, Beveridge set a new tone, warning that unions must increase production.[38] Writing in the *Star* in April 1947, he declared, 'We have not since the war had the best possible leadership, politically from the government, or industrially from the trade unions. The man who thinks we can all become happy and rich by doing less and less each week for higher money wages is a fool.' Caught asking for something they already had, while failing to control wages (which they regarded as inherently uncontrollable), union officials found themselves unpopular with government and the Press, a process some employers noted with unconcealed *schadenfreude*.

Until the early part of 1946, when manpower shortages became acute, no one in government or on the NJAC appears to have been worried by the way wages began to move upwards once controls had been lightened. Order 1305 still prohibited strikes (though it did not prevent them) and the Treasury, working on the 8 per cent target, assumed that unemployment would still exercise some disciplinary effect. Herbert Morrison's industrial sub-committee had, however, already put down a marker in October 1945: 'In the long run, a proper relationship between the nation's needs and the distribution of the labour force can only be secured by a rational and effective wages policy'.[39] Although the idea was scouted by Bevin and Attlee under the aegis of Morrison and Edward Bridges (who still hankered after a central policy body to succeed the Economic Section) a working party took it up.

Substantial wage increases in the engineering industry, and the difficulty of getting men into coal-mining or agriculture soon sharpened the discussion. By April 1946 the working party, chaired by Max Nicholson, had a national wages policy ready. With general support from officials in the Treasury, BOT and Cabinet Office, it proposed a National Incomes Commission on which government, industry and unions would argue out national rates, without compulsion.[40] Morrison confronted Bevin and Isaacs whose view that 'the unions are, under their own rules, the responsible negotiating authority', and that to abandon collective bargaining with employers alone would be to destroy union leaders' authority, drew strength from the spread of shop stewards' activism and plant bargaining in the Midlands.

To use Bevin's celebrated phrase, the working party had opened a Pandora's box and found it full of Trojan horses. Themes relevant thirty years later were raised: that wages were driven up by powerful groups of workers, whose gains others compared with their own differentials; that full employment called for great restraint; that some workers preferred job security to high wages; that restraint (which in 1946 still meant no wage demands at all) should apply to some industries but not to others where there was a shortage of workers, that the rate of turnover could serve as an index of labour mobility; and that in a naturally immobile market, it was necessary to wean workers away from concentrating on the money wage.[41]

Such propositions, many of some antiquity, set Ministers and their officials against each other on basic economic issues of what wages were and how they affected inflation and above all, how they could be controlled. Treasury, Labour, Trade and Economic Section finally constructed a compromise, in October 1946, adequate to prevent the conflict splitting Cabinet. 'Full employment', the Ministerial Economic Planning Committee wrote, 'calls for great restraint. Before the war, endemic mass unemployment with all its evils did provide a reserve of labour to meet fresh demands and also afforded an automatic safeguard against inflationary pressures resulting from increases of wages unsupported by higher productivity. During the war, as labour shortages developed, the sense of national unity and danger provided a powerful safeguard against sectional pressures. It is now necessary, by the conscious statemanship and effective leadership of employers and workers to create an even wider sense of responsibility and a fuller understanding of the economics of full employment and of rising standards of life. Competitive scrambling for advantage will injure all. . . .'[42]

Although in one sense only a gloss on the 1944 White Paper, this language carried rather different overtones. Morrison had wanted to use the government's power in the public sector to plan wages generally and because of this planning element, Cripps and Dalton had joined him, independently of their officials' views. Attlee, Bevin and Isaacs refused to accept such intervention. In the end, Cabinet decided merely to appeal to the TUC, and wrote the terms into the 1947 White Paper, 'Economic Considerations affecting relations between workers and employers' (Cmd 7018). Having pledged themselves against a compulsory freeze, Ministers conceded the 3 per cent target for unemployment and in due course in 1948 sought to negotiate a voluntary freeze through the tripartite forum of the NJAC.

This complicated manoeuvre preserved the co-operative framework of Ministers' and officials' relationships with the TUC. But the reality had changed. Members of the Economic Planning Committee had been convinced that the labour market had become immobile; they believed that something more definite than the 1944 White Paper's sense of mutual responsibility would be required if inflation were not to undermine the government's overall aim of balance of payments equilibrium and rising living standards at home. They could hardly have told Attlee that the aim in itself was unrealistic; instead, and in spite of all that had been said in 1943–44 about managerial efficiency, the onus was fastened on labour.[43]

Nevertheless the TUC's seat at the top table was confirmed, for the

1947 White Paper recognised it as an equivalent partner to the BEC and FBI and praised the merits of voluntary wage determination.[44] In its public language, government assumed that the TUC could and would deliver, because of its sense of national responsibility and its capacity to influence if not control its members. Harmony was taken to be the natural state of industrial relations, interrupted by secondary conflicts within limits which neither side had an interest in exceeding. In this way, the Attlee government set out to do what Lloyd George before had failed: to use corporate bias to institute machinery to fulfil the government's long-term aims. Unions as well as management perhaps appreciated the White Paper's reservations; and the FBI and BEC certainly pointed up their welcome for the TUC's realism.[45] But what the Press and public learned was that wages mattered more than prices.

For this, the TUC's faith in a Labour government was partly to blame. Influenced by the desire of Vincent Tewson (the General Secretary) and his deputy George Woodcock to help the government after the 1947 winter crisis, the TUC's Economic Committee accepted not only that the government's definition of full employment was the most that could be got, given the range of external constraints, but also that wages played a significant part in competitiveness and exporting success.[46] In the long run, as unemployment held below 2.5 per cent and in return for co-operation in the wages policy in 1948, the government gave it its reward – the 3 per cent target enshrined by Hugh Gaitskell in a speech at the United Nations on 17 July 1950. But in gaining this, the TUC allowed itself to be tied down in a way which would have been unthinkable in the heady days of 1944 to the proposition that wage restraint would be the price for full employment and that wages should not exceed increases in output.

The concession can be explained in absolute terms, insofar as the 3 per cent target amounted to a guarantee that no future government would resort to deflation until all other remedies had been tried; also in relative terms, since the Economic Committee had no wish to upset a sympathetic government in a grave crisis. But the long slow loss of trade unions' undoubted post-war popularity may have begun here, in the preliminary formation (or recreation, for it had been endemic in the 1920s) of a different order of sympathies. Denied their full 'period of transition', the politicians were trying to preserve the 1944 balance in altered circumstances, without either abandoning their electoral mandate or opening an internal division between socialists and social-democrats in the Cabinet. Departmental officials hoped also to preserve it, but without betraying other, greater interests for the sake of full employment. A stable currency, balance of payments equilibrium and the export drive inevitably weighed more in this political balance than wages and consumption. A new (but also very old) line was thus superimposed on the traditional faultline between Treasury and spending departments, which ran within the Treasury between the Overseas Finance Division's concentration on traditional sound finance and the Home Economic Division's increasing concern with effective demand. Mandarins collectively remained loyal, and sought only to warn Ministers that some paths in demand management were more dangerous than others. Their cumulative influence, however, tended towards compromises favouring the financial and industrial institutions, rather than the trade unions and wage-earners.

Arguments about control of wages raised the question of how far planning should go and what indeed planning was for, other than regulating scarce resources. Despite his physical decline, Morrison retained overall charge of it through the Lord President's Committee until the autumn of 1947. He conducted a reorganisation of the planning empire in mid-1946 whose complexity barely disguised the fact that its status depended on his political weight and not on any formal parity with Treasury or Cabinet Office. The new system proved to be both cumbersome and amateurish (for Morrison relied on individuals) and worked only because the officials made it work. The official Committee on Economic Planning however, chaired by Edward Bridges, did analyse what planning meant, in a manner worthy of their wartime performance.[47] Harking back to Balfour and Haldane, they defined planning as the accumulation of knowledge as a preliminary to skilled management of national resources, carried out in a way best calculated to maximise government aims without eroding democratic freedom, social justice or a fair standard of living.

Such language showed that the mandarins respected the 1944 package but were, to say the least, unsympathetic either to socialism or the few remaining advocates of a free market. Its apparent liberalism contained a strong statist element: if bargains were not kept, the state should intervene, for full employment was seen as a benefit, not a right. But that formula assumed that the state was strong, when experience showed the opposite. Bridges and his colleagues had, therefore, in the long term to keep Ministers aware of what constituted backsliding, and to ensure that they did not forget the arts of opinion management; public opinion remained in reserve as the counterweight to institutions' arrogance of power. In the short-term (which meant to meet the post-mortem after the winter crisis censure debate in the Commons on 10–12 March 1947), they proposed to set up a new, high-powered Treasury-based planning body – by implication challenging Morrison's shaky edifice. In July, this emerged as the Economic Planning Board (EPB).

Attlee and his colleagues, who had only witnessed the book-keeping side of the Treasury in wartime, may well have underestimated the potential of its re-established strength. Morrison's failure to come to terms with, or subordinate Dalton, at a time when the Treasury was still uncertain how to manage the economy, meant that machinery of government which had seemed balanced in 1945, had by 1947 become unstable. Who would have final authority over planning was not, however, resolved in one simple stage, but in three: first the institution of a Central Economic Planning staff (CEPS) and the EPB (with tripartite representation) in Morrison's name; then the appointment of Cripps as Minister of Economic Affairs to succeed in Morrison in September 1947; finally in November after Dalton's fall, the move of Cripps, with the full apparatus, to the Treasury. The end came about fortuitously, as much a result of political squabbles in which Cripps, with Dalton's help, tried to oust Attlee in favour of Bevin, as of reasoned argument about which department should actually run the economy.

The industrialists and union leaders had no wish to attend another talking shop nor to pledge their authority to schemes undertaken without full consultation.[48] Yet this was exactly how EPB began. The Office of Chief Planner, held by Edwin Plowden, and the Economic Information Unit, headed by Clem Leslie, existed respectively for forecasting and setting the scene for demand management, and for preparing the public using the *Economic Surveys* and the newly-formed Central Office of Information.[49] EPB existed chiefly to keep the central institutions of FBI, BEC and TUC (and through them industry and the unions) informed of what government intended to do: it was never intended to take part in the bargaining that habitually went on in NPACI or NJAC. CEPS on the other hand, emerged as an early think-tank, serving No. 10 at times of crises.[50]

In the brief second stage, these disparate groups had no time to do more than discover a joint admiration for Cripps before Dalton's injudicious tongue brought Cripps to the Exchequer. In the third stage, which lasted down to 1951, the Economic Policy Committee, chaired by Attlee, was at last able to take an overview. This remained the supreme planning body down to 1951, but the Chancellor usually laid down the agenda. Treasury arbitrage had definitely not been desired in 1945, but became inevitable once Morrison's alternative failed – an occurrence that might have provided a useful lesson to the Wilson government in 1964. Planning of industry and labour supply, as Kenneth Morgan argues, was 'half-hearted, indirect and in many ways unsuccessful', even in 1945–47.[51] If such a demonstration had been required, its inadequacy showed that planning in any other sense would not have been acceptable; Plowden and Cripps found themselves in agreement that, whatever the crisis, unless there were literally enemies at the gate, Britain would not tolerate a reversion to physical controls.[52]

Concentration of planning in the Treasury after 1947 had a subsidiary effect, for Bridges and Norman Brook could now relax and let Plowden and Robert Hall of the Economic Section serve the Treasury, thus bridging the gap between Cabinet Office and economic departments and between the worlds of mandarins and special advisors – but for the Chancellor and not the Cabinet as Robbins had originally desired. Apart from Shinwell and Bevan on the left, who complained that real planning had somehow been lost, Ministers found the new system efficient and congenial, headed as it was by an impressive team of Cripps, Jay and Gaitskell. But from then on, and long before Harold Wilson's 'bonfire of controls', it became natural that controls should die away, as circumstances allowed. Trade unionists like Vincent Tewson and Jack Tanner on the EPB welcomed the new organisation and set a pattern of responding to what the Treasury proposed, rather than originating ideas of their own. It was not, as Cripps had imagined in an earlier phase at the Board of Trade, an Office of the Plan, in the style of Jean Monnet; but it was not Bridges' central powerhouse either and it suffered severely after Cripps' own Waterloo in 1949.

The fact that the FBI, BEC and TUC all consented to join EPB, indicates that in 1947 the idea of tripartism retained its attraction. Sponsorship survived in peacetime. Some of the direct links disappeared, or gradually became redundant as the massive apparatus of state purchasing and supply ran down. Much more would go over the next five years with the winding-down of the Ministries of Supply and Production. But the habit of belief that tripartite organisation led to closer co-operation between management and workers had become so deeply rooted that, even in 1951, there was no indication that it would not be continued in the machinery of government, as it had already shaped the EPB in 1947.

Attlee's government turned naturally to the tripartite network to propagate its Production Campaigns, and the FBI and BEC led by the wartime 'outsiders' such as Kipping or James Turner, used it to present their requests to government. Obviously some sectors had better access than others: whereas Agriculture under the 'farmers' friend' Tom Williams achieved even closer relations with the NFU than in the 1930s (becoming, after the demise of the Ministry of Food, a farmers' rather than a consumers' department), industry in general had a much more tenuous, unco-ordinated set of links with Trade. Those between City and Treasury, or aircraft industry and Air Ministry, matched agriculture, to the extent of being almost 'above politics'.

How effective sponsorship could still be can be seen when rearmament and war production were brought back in 1950 to cope with the Korean War (see Chapter 5). After about 1952, however, its significance slowly declined. Officials no longer looked to the network as an effective means of changing attitudes. The Cripps–Plowden planning axis soon undermined the NPACI, since FBI and TUC reacted by seeking closer links with the Treasury – which is what interested them about the Economic Planning Board. Eventually, the Ministry of Labour was left as its main champion, proclaiming through NJAC the wartime efficacy of Joint Production Committees to a world that had begun to forget. The NJAC constituted MOL's primary mode of contact with the TUC; but Phillips and Emmerson championed joint bodies all the way down to Trade Boards and Wages Councils, as means to harmonise industrial relations. The NJAC itself clearly did useful work on labour controls, and in modifying Order 1305, and for some years both BEC and TUC accepted it at these officials' value.[53]

Tripartism still did not mean automatic appointment of union nominees, however, nor did it mean that government abrogated sovereignty to the institutions. As Bridges put it, writing of the 1947 White Paper, 'Like the Monnet Plan [it] relies on co-operation between government, industry and the people'.[54] It prefigured NEDC rather than a revival of the old Industrial Parliament project once espoused by Churchill and Arthur Henderson. The TUC had no lien on the Attlee government and industry's influence was seriously restricted by the FBI/BEC division. Indeed, as in 1917, government encouraged more effective representation: Bridges among many others favoured the merger. It was the Conservatives, during the censure debate in March 1947, who wanted to go further in associating the institutions with planning, and Attlee who rejected it on the grounds that to do so would put the democratic state in pawn.

There is enough scattered evidence to hint that some senior civil servants' concepts of the state were beginning to differ from those of Labour Ministers, on the issue of authority and control of planning. Even in World War One, officials had tended to emphasise the importance of organisations rather than the managing arts of politics; it was their function to do so. But they still agreed that tripartism, that is representation inside the extended state on politically equal terms of bodies which were not, in the markets outside, equal remained fundamental to implementing the 1944 package. The privileges of representation, for both sides of industry, carried equal responsibility for success. As Attlee told the TUC General Council in November 1946, 'The government are building up a system of rights for the people in which the main industries are going to belong to the people. The government are entitled to stress the responsibilities which go with these rights.'[55]

Ministers assumed that they could use this network to further their policy, but until the 1947 crisis they did not expect to have to bargain with either side to reach consensus. The state's scope might be contracting, but government retained its popular mandate and clearly did not expect to have to depend on the institutions' support. But the crises of 1947 and 1949 taught them that sovereignty did not imply power over the external world. It is odd that after this discovery the Attlee government failed to discriminate in favour of the intrinsically weaker TUC: rather the reverse, for it expected unions to conform to its own definition of 'responsibility', even if wages were put at issue long before employer restrictive practices. Later on, in the years of voluntary freeze, 1948–50, price control hit industrialists less harshly than wages control. It is hardly surprising that EPB never became the means to achieve the formal equality Cripps desired.

Whether or not they realised that the state was actually weak, Ministers had believed from the beginning that its strength lay in persuasion rather than command. Hence, as soon as it encountered major difficulties in 1947, they began to cash in on the responsibilities the 1944 White Paper had laid on the institutions, exhausting the language of obligation before they as government had actually ensured that the promised rewards would arrive. Because employers and unions were in fact quite hard put to deliver on wages and prices when the crisis came, given the competing aims of their members, freed from wartime restraints, Ministers had to appeal not only to central institutions but directly to their members, unions and trade associations, and to the public as a whole, thus by-passing and therefore debilitating the instruments in which they still professed to believe.

The government's public assumption that industry, unions and the City would co-operate in the reconstruction programme was accompanied in private by a substantial accommodation of their policy to the reality of what each sector was willing to accept. This may explain why no major cleavage developed. For all the Labour research plans in wartime, as Chancellor, Dalton sought neither a National Investment Bank nor more control over investment than the government already possessed through the Capital Issues Committee. Conflict might have come over shareholders' compensation with government stock in those industries to be nationalised; but care was taken to offset City opposition by calculating the terms more generously than left-wing members of the government intended. Despite the party's plans to nationalise banks and control credit as well as investment, they went no further than to nationalise the Bank of England in 1946 – something for which Norman had long prepared and which Thomas Catto and his staff welcomed. Catto and Eady, in fact, drafted much of the 1946 Bill. Bridges and the Treasury, who believed it should have a measure of autonomy in the pluralist process, helped Catto defend the Bank's rights,[56] in particular to appoint and promote its expert staff and use their work as a corrective to Treasury expertise, against Dalton who envisaged it becoming merely an arm of the government machine. Dalton bullied, and afterwards, resented Catto's victory[57] which for perhaps twenty years retained for the Bank a role as powerful guardian of the currency and the sterling area that materially affected the financial crises of 1947, 1949, 1951 and 1964.

The Chancellor did acquire power to direct the Governor, but 'with care' and only after consulting him. By safeguarding the Bank's internal affairs, the 1946 Act legitimated its authority over City institutions, and confirmed its role as mentor and regulator. Cut off from direct contact, government could not, for example, formally issue directions to the clearing banks without the Governor's approval. The choice of Governor became, therefore, almost as politically sensitive as in the interwar years – yet when it came to choosing Catto's

successor, in 1949, Cripps accepted Bridges' opinion that there could
be no question of a Labour nominee, and picked his deputy, Cameron
Cobbold, thus continuing until 1961 Norman's apostolic succession.

The Bank continued to try to create a trading bloc out of the sterling
area, without great success, and assisted Treasury and Foreign Office
in their negotiations with European countries for EMAs. In domestic
markets it brought about the birth of ICFC and FFI and the start of
reconstruction of the long-term capital market. These represented the
end of a tradition started in the late 1920s, not the start of a new
concern with industrial efficiency. City institutions and markets, like
most of British industry, hoped simply to take up where they had left
off in 1939; most did so, their pre-war mentality almost intact like that
of the rural vicar, who in 1660 after the Commonwealth, 'began again
to use the Book of Common Prayer'.

As a principal earner of foreign exchange, the City had a powerful
claim to freedom from controls but accepted the renewal of exchange
control in 1947. Few if any advances in techniques occurred in these
years. City voices predominated on the Capital Issues Committee, and
the Treasury never proposed an efficiency campaign, as the Board of
Trade did for industry. A handful of clearing banks, led by Glyn Mills,
joined with some of the merchant banks in trying to harness the
lending power of the 'big eleven', to compose syndicated financial
deals. Together with more radical ideas, like creating an Export
Finance Corporation, drawing on the insurance companies which were
then the principal source of domestic savings, it foundered for lack of
institutional support.

Industry took care not to oppose the new government directly.
Insofar as industrialists had a single mind, it appears to have been
directed, in tune with what Cecil Weir had told the Nuffield
Conference in 1943, towards establishing, or re-establishing, the
position of the managerial elite and its right to manage, rather than the
rights of owners or shareholders over their enterprises. In 1945 the FBI
has assured Labour it would look at its policies on their merits, not
their political principles.[58] In the form chosen in 1946–47
nationalisation presented no fundamental threat. The takeover of
steel obviously did; but the government delayed its legislation until
1949, hoping to win industry round, and when it did go ahead, the
FBI prudently left the campaign against steel nationalisation to the
industry itself. The measures taken to meet the 1947 crisis also aliented
FBI opinion for a time. Their responses showed government that it
could not automatically rely on industrial good favour, even though

until then relations had probably been better than with inter-war Conservative administrations.

These were early hints that the 1944 obligations had already receded into a rapidly distanced past. Whatever their differences, FBI and BEC always agreed that tripartism carried with it recognition of their claim to voluntary self-regulation: somewhat arrogantly, in view of the benefits they still drew from it, they argued that sponsorship should not make them into Leninist transmission belts. With 87 representatives in 37 committees in 10 ministries in 1946, the FBI had plenty of channels to express such views.

Although they still concerted tactics with the BEC in opposing wilder variants of nationalisation, the FBI had now been the dominant partner for five years,[59] which may explain why the second merger attempt in 1947 failed. Director for twenty years after 1946, Norman Kipping created a very able team organisation, run by men like Roy Glenday with pre-war experience, and wartime newcomers like D. H. Walker. Their contacts with departments and regional production authorities were, on the whole, much better and their access to knowledge about government more detailed than that of the TUC. A succession of Presidents who were themselves well-known industrialists with prestige to command the Grand Council of 500 members followed Sir Clive Baillieu. From these representatives of individual firms, rather than from trade associations, Kipping built up the membership of expert Committees. As a political–industrial mechanism, the FBI adapted itself to the post-war world more quickly and efficiently than the BEC, and it provided a range of services to members in overseas markets which would have been inconceivable in 1939.

Kipping did not, however, control this massive organisation any more than Citrine, or his successor Vincent Tewson controlled the TUC. Even if committees did most of the work, they had to carry the Grand Council and wait upon minority opinion because the FBI had always tended to avoid contentious matters and to postpone its decisions rather than come to a vote – what Mathias calls 'the transcendent necessity of carrying the membership as a whole'. This tradition dictated delicacy in transactions with a Labour government and a strategy of opposition by detailed amendment[60] rather than outright confrontation. But the FBI soon woke up to the importance of favourable public opinion and held its first 'Next Five Years' conference in 1950 – an irrevocable break from the secretiveness of the 1930s.

In contrast, the BEC's wartime isolation and inactivity continued, even when their favourite issue of wage inflation came back to the agenda in 1946–47. Papers of this period are full of grumbling about the effects of high taxation on managerial initiative, and protests that high consumption and government spending created inflation. These ancient rituals would continue for another twenty years until the merger with the FBI in 1965. Forbes Watson the Director and Andrew McCosh the President found only Morrison sensitive to their obsession with wages and the need to educate unions about unit costs and gaps in manpower supply. Other Ministers found the tone reactionary: it was not for employers in 1946 to call for harder work and longer hours.

Individual BEC members tried to get on with the TUC's big six by talking of a 'community of interests' but such overtures ended fairly abruptly in 1947. The BEC's comments on that year's *Economic Survey*, indeed verged on the apocalyptic: 'the fate of our country will be settled in the next eighteen months. Our conduct now will decide whether our place in the world, our hard-won right to live as free men, and our steady gains in social standards, are to be maintained, or whether we are to sink into unemployment, poverty or distress.'[61]

Exaggerated private language like this devalued itself quickly, and the BEC, wisely, tended to take its lead in public from the FBI. But unlike them, they kept in contact with Conservative headquarters and Butler's Industrial Committee, hoping to instil some of their ideas into future policy. During the March 1947 censure debate they openly took the Tory side, and this political bias increasingly affected the tenor of the NJAC, reducing the influence of what was said there, to the BEC's dismay.[62] Not until the Ministry of Labour was forced into reimposing longer hours and the Control of Engagements Order in the wake of the Korean War did the BEC recapture its old position.

Cossetting public opinion involved government in support schemes for ailing industries such as films, watches and cotton textiles, in providing tax allowances, schemes for investment, and indirect subsidies, to say nothing of direct grants to cotton or British Aluminium and lump sum allocations to ICFC and FCI. In the years of relatively high tariffs before GATT came into effect those mostly favoured short-term capital accumulation by retained profits, and did not tax capital gains.[63] Shareholders' dividends rather than executives' salaries suffered, which fitted in well enough with Labour's philosophy and the government's short-term benefit. This long flirtation with business (which can be read clearly in the papers of Labour's '1944 Association') reached its peak in the paragraphs of the

1947 Economic Survey in praise of management. As Arnold Rogow commented, ten years later, 'Labour leaders were increasingly persuaded that the objectives of private industry harmonised rather than conflicted with the aims of the Labour government.'[64]

Since Cripps, even when at the Board of Trade, showed himself sympathetic to industry's complaints, and since the Ministerial Economic Planning Committee believed it essential to carry rather than coerce the private sector,[65] the FBI found it fairly easy to defend itself against the schemes for Industrial Boards, even though these had been an integral part of the 1944 White Paper package. Consistent opposition by its Trade Organisation Committee to any government organisation with executive authority obviously influenced Cripps' decision, in the 1947 Industrial Organisation and Development Act, to go for more limited Development Councils, and then only in seventeen mainly export industries where his working parties had done the diplomatic groundwork. The Councils were to be tripartite and advisory, a powerless means of communication on questions of training, technology, and research, in no way suitable for 'backdoor nationalisation' nor for the Board of Trade's original 1943 aims of instituting efficiency.

Throughout this transaction, the FBI shrewdly insured that the TUC should not be able to increase its power by using the Councils to restrict managerial prerogatives, while protesting its loyalty to Cripps' intentions.[66] Over the next few years, Development Councils failed either to increase production or reactivate moribund trade associations, except in the negative sense of galvanising them into opposition. Only three came into operation before Harold Wilson became President of the Board in 1949. He proceeded as carefully as Cripps and in consultation with both sides. The TUC failed altogether in what they wanted most from the Councils, to gain access to companies' information and to employers, themselves; instead they had to wait almost twenty years until NEDC's Economic Development Councils came into being.

The Labour government needed industry, and if it could not compel, it needed strong central organisations like the FBI with which to deal. The FBI took its advantage without giving offence. 'A frontal attack on controls will not be successful,' its President, Sir Frederick Bain, told the 1948 AGM, 'but if we can prove that industry is sufficiently responsibly-minded to be trusted to control itself within broad limits laid down by the Government, we may be able to shift the basis from detailed Government controls to internal industrial administration.' Within a year, Wilson had his first bonfire of controls. In the name of self-regulation, corporate bias provided a centripetal force to hold together government and industry, despite the contrary forces of self-interest and conflicting ideology; the result demonstrated the overriding urgency of the external threat and the weakness of government to do anything else.

———————————

Records of the TUC's headquarters committees and Congresses show it wedded to the idea of a planned economy, in terms of controls, Industrial Boards, directed investment, and redistribution of wealth. Although, as it discovered, the TUC did not have as much influence with Labour Party leaders as it had in the mid-1930s, its Economic Committee could reasonably claim to have influence over important matters such as taxation policy (in the October 1945 Budget). Apart from regular interchanges with the Ministry of Labour, monthly meetings took place with BOT so long as Cripps was President, to discuss long-term reconstruction of industry. This harmony extended even to collective bargaining: the TUC agreed, in the interests of all workers, to retain Order 1305: 'unless there was a curb on extravagant and unreasonable claims, sponsored by new elements with the least degree of protective machinery [a reference to shop stewards], sporadic and abortive strikes might result, which would be beneficial to nobody'.[67]

From the beginning, the TUC feared to jeopardise its wartime gains and the promise of full employment by making the Labour government's job harder. It argued the case in favour of controls on prices, for example, on the grounds that to do otherwise would fuel wage claims or erode the value of pensions and welfare benefits. The TUC could be downright when explaining the fall-off in production in 1946: workers needed to relax after their wartime performance and would not necessarily show themselves grateful for full employment. Hence 'some order and discipline on both sides of industry' might be necessary, such as 'creation of an atmosphere of mutual confidence throughout the factories and workshops of this country'. Plain, sensible, downright statements of this order could be heard at the 1946 Congress, and won praise from the BEC. The search for a peacetime equivalent to the golden age of Joint Production Committees soon led leaders and headquarters staff to identify potential discord in the movement – 'workers in some instances see no reason why they should produce more in order to "swell the profits of the boss". It was quite different during the war when production was for the government . . .

Now . . . in some cases the old attitude of "beating the boss" has not lost its attraction.'[68]

Usage of war memory in this way served to reinforce the powers of the 'big six' General Secretaries.[69] The TUC's closeness to government (shown in the way that MOL and Isaacs relied heavily on their support during the 1946 manpower crisis, in the subsequent fuel shortage in 1947, and when implementing the Prosperity Campaign) validated its claim to give a lead to individual unions and their membership. But it did not make the oligarchs loved. Complaints from individual executives, especially their fears about a return to industrial conscription, were either turned down or simply not minuted, for Tewson and his colleagues took no chances where the government's survival was at risk.[70]

If it wished to keep its place at the top table, the TUC had to conform: the difficulty was how to bring criticism, say of the Prosperity Campaign, to bear without being accused of disloyalty. They achieved this by transposing the onus on to the employers, often with lessons drawn by their own delegates from American industrial psychology showing for example without much difficulty that the Prosperity Campaign bore more harshly on the individual worker than on the employer. Productivity, they argued, should be wrung from new machinery as well as higher output per man; management should reform itself as well as expecting unions to do so. More bluntly, Deakin and his colleagues simply 'wished the adversarial character of labour–management relations to continue'.[71]

Beyond TUC headquarters, unions, like the majority of employers, busied themselves solving the problems their leaders had grown up with, building up massive memberships as the TGWU had done in the 1930s. Generally, they failed to concentrate on the key industries of the future, motor cars, and electrical and consumer goods, until the boom years of the 1950s had already begun. Though this bolstered the oligarchs' authority, it led to a form of arteriosclerosis which Tewson's uninspired leadership did little to check. From 1947 onwards the TUC's most vigorous political activity focused on anti-Communism and opposition to the growth of WFTU worldwide; during the height of the Cold War, Victor Feather carried on the attack against individual Communists in members' unions that Citrine had begun with the 'Black Circular' in 1934. Because the Communist Party capitalised on residual admiration for the Soviet Union among a surprisingly large number of workers, this produced a debilitating series of conflicts, notably in the TGWU.

Compliance with government requests, and low-key protest when Ministers failed adequately to consult the TUC, produced a deeper and more general rift between leaders and their more militant members (particularly in the newer industries) than appeared at the time. In subdued but often angry dissent among shop stewards, who were later to rise in their union hierarchies, can be seen some causes of the dramatic changes in the late 1950s and early 1960s, and the emergence of a new 'big six' of an almost totally different persuasion. As in 1931, delivery to a Labour government demanded more of the TUC than co-operation with a Coalition or a Conservative one; and in this sense Bevin's attempt to prolong the Coalition appeared wise. The TUC's problem, in defending its members' interests, was not that they lacked access to government, but that they could not convert access into continuous influence without the sort of struggle that loyalty precluded.

In spite of all the efforts of Bevin to help poorly unionised workers (in agriculture for example) and of Citrine to get formal parity in the machinery of government, the trade union movement had achieved its near-parity with management after 1940 because the war was organised primarily in terms of manpower budgeting. The TUC's relative power had increased vastly by 1945, the more so since BEC and FBI stayed divided, but the solidarity of the movement could not, in the nature of things, give them equality at least while the right to strike remained restricted. This did not become clear at first because of the 1944 guarantee of full employment, and the Ministry of Labour's efforts; but before 1947, the TUC could see that many more industrialists than trade unionists retained their personal wartime links with government, and that the Attlee administration had capitalised on union loyalty while negotiating with the 'other side'.[72] Only Citrine found a place as chairman of one of the new public industries: otherwise trade unionists were swamped by professional managers.

In these circumstances it is hardly surprising that the TUC did not seek consciously to change the action-orientated outlook based on collective bargaining that had served it for nearly a hundred years. Headquarters' staff and a handful of younger union leaders might dream about permeating departmental thinking, using research to substantiate their influence, but for the great majority influence meant deputations and measurable results. The instauration of full employment offered the TUC the opportunity to develop a new mode (just as it did later in Germany and Sweden), a means to participate in the process of economic management. But at the same time it brought a temptation to the shop floor membership in industries where full employment came easily to break out of the wage restraint obligation imposed by the 1944 White Paper. Over the next three decades, this greatly diminished the TUC's chances of success.

Down to 1947 the TUC set itself fairly limited aims where working conditions and wage rates were concerned. They tried to shape the new public industries and find in them a place for industrial democracy, but rarely ventured beyond the 1944 *Reconstruction* document. Preferring to work slowly towards an erosion of managerial prerogatives, the Economic Committee rebuffed more radical proposals for worker participation from railwaymen, miners, and Post Office unions early in 1947. In the end, even a modest proposal for an independent survey of public industries' practice, though accepted by Morrison's Socialisation of Industries Committee, fell to Attlee's veto in 1948. TUC staff pushed their inquiries into new areas such as finance for industry and the workings of the capital market. But though this fell short of the National Investment Board they had dreamed of in 1944, they dropped it once Dalton had pleaded 'practical problems' of investment control. As yet the TUC did not have answers to the questions buried in 1943–44, only statements which civil servants who had spent six or seven years operating controls could easily disprove. On other matters such as sterling they accepted, almost without question, Treasury or Bank doctrine: it was 'in Britain's interest to keep sterling as strong and stable as we can, because the present hope of any substantial degree of multilateral trading depends upon [it] so long as the acute dollar shortage lasts'.[73]

Jealous of any infringement of their now established rights on tripartite bodies TUC officials spent more time trying to retain formal links with the Board of Trade than on establishing them with the Treasury, or with individual civil servants informally, as the FBI did. Ministry of Labour officials remained their primary source of information even about the state of the economy. (The Treasury seems to have provided a certain amount of confidential detail this way, or via EPB, in order to prevent the TUC trying to find a bargaining place on the NPACI.) In such ways, the TUC let itself be conditioned into providing the production and discipline that Labour Ministers asked of it. 'The government,' Attlee declared 'cannot in any way recognise or deal with those who are leading an unofficial strike. To do so, would be to cut at the whole basis of collective bargaining.'[74] Unions accepted delay in repealing the 1927 Trades Disputes Act, and the institution of National Service in November 1946, if not without question, then without complaint. Deakin, the most loyal servitor, had after all ended the war with a picture of an orderly, strike-free society: 'it is the duty and responsibility of all members of the unions, in their own interests and in the interests of the nation as a whole, to preserve a well-balanced outlook and to oppose with the utmost vigour the irresponsible persons whose policies, if followed, would lead not to peace in industry . . . but to national chaos and disaster'.[75]

If such language sounds like the conformity of Orwell's *1984* or Chinese Cultural Revolution slogans, it has to be remembered that Labour's was the best government the TUC could expect. Caught in 1947 between new demands from below and government's recourse to austerity, the oligarchs sought refuge in the 1944 package by responding to the Production Campaign and the urgings of the Anglo-American Productivity Council. Meanwhile, government realised that it could, indeed, count on the TUC, utilised it, and spent its bargaining time with the other side.

In welcoming union leaders' co-operation, Morrison always took care to contrast it with shop floor militancy, where the government would need to use education and propaganda.[76] Public opinion management acquired a high priority during the 1947 crisis, not with a future election in mind, but in order to bring what Ministers regarded as the reciprocal obligations of the 1944 package to bear on personal behaviour. Until then, government had rather scorned to use the propaganda machinery they had inherited, and the tone of the 1946 Prosperity Campaign had been offhand, even defensive. After the fuel crisis and the imposition of peacetime austerity, more effective means of winning support became essential. The old Ministry of Information had been transformed in 1946 into the bland, apparently neutral Central Office of Information (COI) whose Social Survey, initially intended simply to research public opinion, was linked with the Economic Intelligence Unit early in 1947 to study public perception of what the government was trying to do. Backed by the co-ordinating organisation, Home Information Service, this offered a country-wide framework for propagating public policy: some Ministers actively shunned the idea, but Morrison saw it as an arm of the state.[77]

What government sought to disseminate can be read in the *Economic Surveys*, the second of which was published in 1947, in the context of the fuel crisis, and after the battering government took in the March censure debate.[78] It was intended to refute accusations of incompetence, to revive public confidence in the administration, and to engage public support for austerity, however unwelcome. Attlee saw it as the means of taking the nation into his confidence: 'It is essential that all should understand that the maintenance and raising of the standard of life of the people depends upon the extent to which every individual plays his part'.[79] The language of 1945 rang harsher now, and the message was directed at the *public*: unions and management – praised here – could read their duties elsewhere in the 1947 White Paper on wages and industrial relations.

In that gloomy year, the *Economic Survey* sold 200 000 copies and the next one in 1948 sold 440 000. Other campaigns followed, aimed to remedy whatever was the most serious deficiency – exports, manpower or productivity. To get men into the pits, the COI mobilised the Press, the BBC, and even (through the good offices of Arthur Horner) the Communist Party. But it is clear in the drafting, that Treasury officials intended to reinforce government's directive authority, after a period they saw as one of excessive complacency in which unemployment had been allowed to fall too low (to 2.5 per cent), 'a symptom of the highly inflationary pressure of demand'.[80] Rather than curtail demand by deflation, they preferred to gear up production and exports, and cut not only defence spending and oil imports if possible, but also individual consumption. Public expectations, fostered by full employment, were becoming a Frankenstein monster.

It would have been too hard, and invited too much political retribution to have said publicly that after only two years the price of full employment had been too high. Instead, the 1947 *Survey* redefined the problem, The 1944 package was not intrinsically at fault (as later historians of the 'new right' were to allege); it was the obligations that had not been fulfilled. Instead of instituting the harsh controls which they actually discussed in January 1947 (see page 131), the Cabinet decided to persuade, and used the new apparatus very effectively, despite the over-optimistic targets and inherent contradictions of the 1947 *Economic Survey*. Deeper issues of the state's right to expect, and enforce compliance, though clear enough to the originators in the discussions about emergency organisation, were buried in the inner committees and not raised in public at all.

5 Crisis and Austerity 1947–49

An accumulation of troubles, beginning with the fuel shortage during one of the worst winters of the century, hit the unprepared Attlee administration during 1947, putting Attlee's own leadership at risk for months on end. Bright morning never returned after this dismal period. But Attlee survived and the government salvaged what it regarded as its domestic post-war achievements: the universal provision of health and welfare services, and a decent minimum standard of living. Whether this achievement was worth the price paid in industrial disruption and damage to Britain's external position was still a matter of the sharpest debate fifteen years later, when the Treasury's internal history of that disastrous year was written.

Until January 1947, so far as the public was concerned, the government had done remarkably little wrong. In comparison with other European countries, Britain had enjoyed low inflation, a balanced budget, industrial recovery, an improvement in the balance of payments and a high level of political harmony. Few wanted to ask how much of this had been achieved on the back of the American loan. The government itself chose to ignore the fact that the 1946 export targets had barely been met. The fuel crisis and the subsequent disastrous fall in industrial production, exports and construction, accompanied by high, though temporary unemployment,[1] profoundly shocked public opinion and impaired the government's own self-confidence. Working-class morale suffered as supplies of food were cut short, and the Press, not unnaturally, blamed the authorities.

The government had undoubtedly been complacent and now had to fall back on the hope that the electorate, grateful for tangible gains, would stand by it in adversity. Recognition of the emergency, in the shape of conflict over whether or not to bring back manpower controls, brought the first of many angry scenes in Cabinet in

January 1947. Later, on 10 February in a BBC broadcast, Attlee blamed it all on the weather. *The Economist* and the Conservatives blamed him or Shinwell. Great care had to be taken with the Prime Minister's reply in the parliamentary vote of censure on 10–12 March, for he had to convince not only the parliamentary Opposition but his own, composed of Ministers and younger backbenchers who demanded a clearer sense of economic direction.

Until then his colleagues had responded with apathy and almost wilful blindness. Despite warnings from their economic advisors that it would be hard to raise productivity per man-hour enough to recapture what had been lost and from Bridges that the planning staff was inadequate, Attlee remained convinced that exhorting the public would be enough. Ministers simply put on one side the coming convertibility crisis, though the dollars ran out faster than before. Worst of all, to ensure that the issue of manpower controls would not again be raised, the existing shortfall of 500 000 skilled workers had been written down to 250 000 – in January before the real crisis began.[2] Attlee's private notes suggest that he realised the problem ('the controls that remain are not sufficient to force the economy into the shape that is required', he wrote, early in February) but that he made an instinctive judgement about what the public would not accept.[3]

Although the government survived the censure vote easily enough, dissent rumbled on in the Cabinet. Dalton pressed for a new Minister of Planning to replace the ailing Morrison; Morrison in turn blamed the Treasury and the Bank for sterling problems. Finally, in September, Dalton and Cripps plotted to replace Attlee with Bevin and oust the now wholly incompetent Morrison. Attlee triumphed, relying on Bevin's loyalty, and packed Cripps off to the Ministry of Economic Affairs. Serious though these personal clashes were, they were perhaps less dispiriting than the revolt of younger men, like Evan Durbin, aghast at the impression of fatalism given from the top. Nineteen backbenchers protested about lack of leadership in a Cabinet drifting rather than face the remedies of manpower control, wage restraint, longer hours of work, and higher taxation for the better-off (which the 'Keep Left Group' wanted) while it waited for American aid.[4]

The convertibility crisis, seen but not admitted except as what Douglas Jay calls a 'horrid secret' in the winter, grew steadily into an overriding constraint which made planning ahead impossible, until in August it destroyed the Cabinet's hope – or exposed it as illusion – that overseas commitments, the welfare system, full employment and living standards could be maintained all together. It had long been foreseen by the Bank and Treasury officials and by Morrison who, as early as October 1946, had forecast 'another 1931'.[5] In January 1947 the Bank asked to draw more dollar credits than the Treasury would allow; at that stage Dalton still hoped that European Monetary Agreements and arrangements with sterling creditors would enable Britain to import enough without using dollars too quickly. In early March however, after encountering problems with Belgium and France, he warned the Cabinet that it might not be possible to keep supplying food to the population of the British sector in Germany.

On the 22 March, Dalton put to his bemused colleagues a harsh series of cuts in dollar imports, including food. After strong resistance, they agreed to only just over half his suggested savings of £200 million. By this stage all must have realised that the original loan could not outlast the year, and that the convertibility requirement in July would be impossible to maintain without intense austerity. The Treasury and Board of Trade gave very explicit warnings on 25 May and 24 June, yet apart from some talk of freezing the sterling balances, no new proposals were made; and Attlee could declare, on 19 July, 'it was essential that the government should meet the situation by positive action designed to preserve the standard of life of the people and maintain the position of the UK in the world'.[6]

Such measures as were discussed, before July (including a request to the TUC for wage restraint, some reductions in imports and an extension of the working day) suggest that Attlee hoped to get by with another appeal for voluntary austerity. This was not Dalton's and Cripps' intention: the Treasury saw it as essential not only to control the balance of payments deficit and protect the remaining dollar reserves,[7] but to be seen not to renege on convertibility in case the promised Marshall Aid should in some way be withdrawn. Cutting personal spending and increasing production seemed to offer the only answer.

After only four weeks of convertibility, the crisis broke on 16 August. While Bridges and Burke Trend prepared notes for the Chancellor's speech, Eady flew to Washington to warn that Britain would suspend convertibility three days later. Cripps duly put his own list of economies and higher production targets to Cabinet and in October austerity was instituted, on a basis of national needs defined by Dalton and Cripps, the economic ministers, not by Attlee.

The Treasury was able to conclude, in its version written fifteen years later, that this had been a crisis of sterling, brought about by excessive overseas and defence spending, and a lack of foreign confidence in a Labour government, justifying in effect the Bank of England's contemporary misgivings. The Cabinet ought to have faced up to Dalton's cuts in March. But at the time, Treasury and Bank argued together that, since the overseas role sought by Bevin and Attlee could only be supported on a strong pound, the burden must fall on the domestic economy. (The change is probably explicable in terms of the foreign policy needs of the Macmillan government.) But they did not go so far as City institutions, who hoped for greater facilities for the capital market and for invisible earnings; because the Treasury hedged its bets, unwilling to be seen to try to restore London as a financial and international trading centre at the expense of the public's diet.

Dalton blamed the Bank rather than his own officials or colleagues and asked Harold Wilson to conduct an inquiry into its operations. But it is doubtful if he understood what was at stake. Afterwards, the struggle to trade in a non-dollar environment, through the use of EMAs and the sterling area, could easily be seen as a vain endeavour. Britain's evasions and obvious inclination to betray its sterling creditors, and attempts to make Europeans hold sterling against their will, probably contributed to the weakness of the pound. In their defence, the Bank and the Treasury Overseas Division could say that they had of course only been carrying out the Cabinet's 1945–46 policy. The real issue lies in the Treasury's 1962 verdict: 'at least we can say that our experience . . . made such an impression that we were able to resist the temptation, in the years which followed, to offer convertibility until we were strong enough to do so with the assurance of success'.[8] That implied that the pound's strength would be built up in order to ensure both Britain's great-power role and a sound domestic economy at the price, if necessary, of cuts in aggregate demand. Crucial though the political weighting given to sterling was in economic management, this was not something that the Labour Cabinet ever discussed. Yet on that gibbet all subsequent governments were to swing, until the Basle Agreement, 1968, and the end of sterling as a reserve currency.

No political party could have asked the public to accept a ration of 1 700 calories a day, compared to 2 800 in wartime, when Britain was feeding Germans, and France was self-sufficient. Through the early autumn, while it discussed where cuts would fall, the government could only sit tight and wait for Marshall Aid. Yet even by October anything more than a trickle of dollars was uncertain. Austerity therefore took the form of longer hours, cuts in investment and reductions in purchasing power. The impact fell chiefly on wages and modernisation of public industry since the Board of Trade argued a strong case for preserving retailers' margins and business profits in order to sustain private investment.[9]

Arguments had been taking place during the summer over whether there was, in fact, a danger of wage inflation that might give a justification which could be used in public to explain such an uneven distribution of pain. According to the officials in the Treasury, BOT and MOL there was. Once again, Morrison, who thought that the TUC was ready for 'a central arbitral body, armed with compulsory powers over wage claims; and would welcome government taking a firm line, in the national interest'[10] and Dalton confronted Isaacs who with Bevin's usual backing roundly declared: 'It would involve a complete recasting of the whole system of industrial relations which has been built up in this country over half a century.'

Morrison and Isaacs were despatched to talk to the General Council who gave them no more change than they did to Attlee's public appeal in July. As the summer wore on, the Cabinet looked longingly for a voluntary pact with the TUC, while officials prepared a White Paper, embodying a wage freeze, though without statutory backing, incorporating food subsidies and price limits to stabilise the cost of living and inhibit wage claims.[11] The search for a compromise formula that was to continue for more than thirty years, failed. So in defiance of Isaacs' threat that it would discredit union leaders and give encouragement to shop stewards, Communists and Trotskyists, Dalton and Cripps brought a stern draft 'Statement on Personal Incomes, Costs and Prices' to Cabinet in November, without consulting either the TUC or the employers. Bevin's weight helped to keep the economic Ministers in a minority. Attlee propounded a compromise: they would go for the voluntary pact, holding compulsion in reserve and say nothing in public.

The TUC gave sufficient assurances of good behaviour to allow Attlee to conclude that they would, in fact, bail out the government. But by February 1948, the evidence of wage inflation provided by the Economic Intelligence Unit was such that a freeze became inevitable, Publication of a new White Paper (Cmd 7321) with the old title represented an almost complete victory for the Treasury over Foreign Office and MOL combined, and the Bevin–Isaacs' majority disintegrated. Employers had little if anything to do with the White Paper, however much its terms suited them, and the theme – that each wage claim should be based on 'national merits and not on the basis of maintaining a former relativity between different occupations and industries' – was definitely *not* discussed with the TUC, though some explanation was offered later.

Nevertheless the TUC responded more loyally than anyone in Cabinet had forecast when the freeze was first discussed, Sir George Chester spoke for the majority when he declared that the choice (as with conscription in 1916) lay between 'some authority established by ourselves – by far the better way – or an authority imposed upon us which we should of course vigorously resent'.[12] Deakin even became an enthusiast for prices and incomes policy and helped steer it through the TUC's March 1948 Special Congress. Yet he and other leaders had a hard time of it in their own unions, and their bland Congress statements belie a great deal of uneasiness. Frank Cousins especially resented Deakin's use of emotional language, such as 'the people's fight for economic survival' when condemning unofficial strikes and blaming them on Communist agitators.

Union leaders earned the tribute 'public-spirited' from a grateful Cabinet all of whom had come to share Cripps' belief that 'it can only be secured by consent. It cannot be enforced'.[13] Perhaps only Morrison believed that a wages policy could have been made more permanent, though some of the younger ministers saw it as essential to future Socialist planning. When Congress repudiated the pact in 1950, Attlee accepted it fatalistically. The essay in voluntary prices and wages restraint had never been more than a temporary expedient until Marshall Aid lifted the intolerable burden of the dollar shortage.

Even before General George Marshall's celebrated offer, the United States was becoming gravely concerned about the failure of Europe generally – East as well as West – to recover. Most countries other than Germany had, in fact, regained their prewar levels of industrial output, thanks largely to strongly nationalistic efforts of self-help. But they had not solved the problem of shortage of dollars any better than Britain and import bills had been heavily financed by American aid in the form of government loans which, like the loan to Britain, were running out. Yet those closest in trading patterns to Britain showed no inclination to share in the supposed benefits of the sterling area or the EMAs.

From the United States' point of view, it was self-evidently desirable that Britain should take part in the European Recovery Programme. But the Truman government had no illusions about Britain's productive performance and, in spite of the sympathy of very many individual Americans, the work teams set up under Marshall's plan were not to give preferential treatment but to instil efficiency while bringing aid. The USA wanted sterling retained as an international medium of exchange but still required Britain to divest herself of any lingering imperial ambitions.

In the climate of the Cold War however, when Stalin rejected the desire of some of the 'people's democracies' in Eastern Europe to accept Marshall's offer, European recovery became a purely Western phenomenon, and Britain, virtually free of Communist influence at national level, seemed the most desirable political and diplomatic coadjutor. This as much as the vigour with which Bevin and Attlee (the chief influences on foreign policy) latched on to Marshall's offer explains why Britain emerged with the largest share of aid, a result out of all proportion both to her actual need or her willingness to co-operate with the ERP work-teams, who found UK industries more resistant to their efforts to raise productivity than those in either France or Belgium.

As it became clear that Britain would not be able to establish a competitive trading zone out of the sterling area, the antipathies shown by the US Treasury and State Department in 1945–46 faded away, to be replaced by a more sympathetic, even generous appraisal of the external burdens Britain still carried in Germany, Egypt and Palestine; responsibilities in Greece and Turkey, at Bevin's insistence, were taken over under the Truman Doctrine. During 1947, as the officials prepared to bid for Britain's share, in vigorous competition with other Western European countries, they could increasingly be sure that Marshall Aid was not going to mean forcing their recalcitrant economy into surrogate American shape as seemed to be the case in Germany and Italy.

There remained three problems: would the aid carry strings detrimental to what was left of the sterling area; would it be adequate to carry the economy through the trough; and would if affect what the

1943–44 inquiries had seen as the rooted inefficiency of British manufacturing industry? There was also the matter of pride in not being seen to receive charity or moral lessons. Cripps assured the House of Commons that there would be no 'broad investigation of British industry by American specialists'. Instead, he set up the Anglo-American Productivity Council largely to prove that Britain would not simply draw the dollars and squander them on welfare payments.[14] There has to be doubt about how genuine British protestations about efficiency were quite apart from the evidence of the ERP director, Paul G. Hoffman's complaints; some of the Economic Section argued that the Treasury only developed proper planning in the process of bidding for Marshall Aid in 1947–48. Also, in bidding competitively against other European nations, as they did against Britain, the Treasury helped to negate the central idea of the ERP and increased the scepticism of its officials actually in Europe.

It would of course have been difficult to have done otherwise, since until the end of 1947 the Treasury expected to win only a small share, and sought to maximise British claims in order to assure even that. By early 1948, however, the government could be certain of a share that would make it unnecessary to cut food consumption to anything near the catastrophic levels forecast six months earlier.[15] Wild fears of malnutrition, political unrest and slump, and mistrust of American motives survived for a time, but had vanished by October 1948 when the Committee on European Economic Co-operation finally made its four year submission to ERP.

By then, Cripps had been in office as Chancellor for nearly a year. Marshall Aid opened the period he saw as the government's second chance, offering time to achieve the equilibrium in trade that the convertibility requirement had vitiated, time to raise productivity and exports not by 'American business methods' but by British dedication and co-operation. To his credit, he always emphasised that Marshall Aid should not be a panacea but an opportunity. Wage restraint and productivity formed the agenda of the most persuasive of the *Economic Surveys* in 1948.

Although this was a good year, after the fuel and sterling crises, the events of 1947–48 had several more remote consequences detrimental to the political and economic package of ideas imposed in 1944 which had, until then, guided the government's economic policy. Firstly, Marshall Aid let the government off the hook on which the convertibility crisis had impaled them. As Kenneth Morgan writes, 'it is inconceivable that their economic and social policies could have survived without the massive platform constructed by a combination of American long-term economic self-interest and British diplomatic initiative'.[16] The Cabinet slipped into the period of second chance believing it enough to rely on holding back personal spending, unnecessary imports, and wages, by agreement with unions and management. Cripps, virtually alone, had to disinter the great buried questions about productivity, investment and innovation.

Secondly, Britain's great power responsibilities and their enormous cost in foreign exchange survived, trimmed only at the edges. Combined with the move towards liberal trading which was Britain's one real response to Marshall Aid, the stresses these imposed made the pound unsustainable and devaluation inevitable (though not to the extent adopted in 1949).

Thirdly, Britain cut herself off from moves towards European economic and political integration after the Hague meeting in May 1948. This too was probably inevitable, given the line-up of Attlee, Bevin and Cripps,[17] all loyal to the sterling area and the Commonwealth (where 40 per cent of Britain's trading still took place, as against 25 per cent with Europe), suspicious of the Franco-German *rapprochement*, and also the factious part played by the Conservative Party, seeking by enthusiasm for the European movement to cut off Labour from association with European Socialist parties. A self-contained, insular view of the British economy received retrospective justification, just at the time when in Western European Union and later NATO Britain codified its European and Atlantic strategic self-image.

Long before the decision to support the United States in the Korean War at a very high price in terms of Britain's economic recovery, the Labour government had settled into a post-imperial role, distinct from what was stirring in Europe. Independence for the colonies already lay on the table. One fashionable image of the world depicted Britain at the 'centre' of three circles: the Commonwealth, Europe, and the United States. By mid-1948, Ministers might congratulate themselves that they could look forward to slow, steady growth, achieved by prudent economic management within the existing voluntary framework of mild austerity.

Whether they could succeed was bound to depend on the attitudes of industry, unions and the public. The TUC made no attempt to hide its increasing difficulties. Even in 1947, Tewson had warned Attlee that acceptance of austerity might threaten 'the incentive to produce'.[18] Unions resented giving up progress towards the 40-hour week. In the bargaining over implementation of the February 1948 White Paper 'Statement on Personal Incomes, Costs and Prices', the TUC gained at least as much from government as did the FBI and accepted that the next two or three years would be ones of consolidation. What was acceptable to the General Council, however, caused trouble on the shop floor. Pressures began to build up in the intermediate levels of major unions, where complaints about conditions of work and the freeze accompanied a certain anger that the bright hopes of 1945, vested in nationalisation and worker-participation, had turned sour. For the moment, these were suppressed by the big six.[19] The government gave what help it could, especially since the war of attrition against Communist infiltration then being directed from headquarters by Victor Feather fitted so well with its foreign policy. The decision to declare a state of emergency during the dock strike in June by a virtually united Cabinet showed how firmly the TUC stood with Ministers on questions of the national interest.

Management had a greater inducement to co-operate, firstly to ensure that the government did not try to use the 1947 crisis to turn economic management into state direction of the economy; secondly to be able to shape wages restraint while resisting as far as possible, overall price control. *The Way to Recovery* (1947) outlined the FBI's commitment to a voluntarist, mixed economy and Kipping and Baillieu took care to keep more right-wing views in abeyance, while continuing criticism of government spending and 'excess demand'.[20] The FBI's Home Economic Policy Committee complained regularly about the dead hand of state bureaucracy and the way public industries and welfare services soaked up limited investment allocations and supply of raw materials: how much of this was ritual, how much real concern, is hard to determine.

Discussion of the capital investment White Paper, in December 1947, indicates that the FBI was sensitive enough to public opinion, to press, as City institutions did, for a speedy return to the market economy. 'It is accepted that in order to maintain full employment and secure, insofar as they are obtainable, the social aims which the nation has set itself, there must be some broad, overall planning'; but it should be done by agreement, and with continuity and discipline in the labour market.[21] But where industry's share of capital was concerned, the FBI claimed that its virtuous exporting members starved, while housing – a wholly unproductive drain on the market – benefited.

Loyal collectively as they were to the 1944 ideas in consciously *political* terms, FBI members had begun to drift away wherever their firms' immediate interests were concerned – and by the end of 1948, this drift had become a current. A new language began to permeate its documents, in which 'labour' (in some undefined sense not yet 'unions' or 'the TUC') was blamed for its restrictive practices, resistance to change and outright greed.

If the two sides' willingness to make sacrifices in 1947–49 is compared on the basis of what they *said* they wished to do, the unions come out best. The TUC made a considerable effort to increase production, and responded to Cripps' first Export Conference in September 1947 by accepting that industry should benefit from Marshall Aid rather than the social services. It took a fuller part in the Anglo-American Productivity Council and the Joint Council on Productivity (which brought in outside experts and scientists) than the FBI who remained throughout rather defensive, taking the whole US Economic Co-operation Organisation (correctly enough) to be an implied criticism of management rather than unions.[22] Although it had to work hard to prevent individual unions airing their fears that 'production' was only the start of a new and dynamic form of Taylorism, the TUC maintained its support until 1952 (when the Economic Co-operation Administration ended) and union delegates continued to accompany management on the various delegations to America. There they found that the USA had more capital invested per head than in Britain, newer equipment, more professional management, better standardisation, a more productivity-conscious workforce, and a social and economic climate more favourable to enterprise, mobility and technical innovation: lessons that were only to be rediscovered after the foundation of NEDC in 1962.

Unfortunately, the Press and public remained almost totally unconcerned, and their work seems to have had little impact beyond the headquarters of TUC or FBI. Those who went to America, like the Mond group in 1927–28, were those already with open minds. The AAPC put out 58 reports: the most that one can say is that the effect was unquantifiable.

The TUC understood as cynically as Cripps that participation helped persuade the ECA to continue Britain's generous share of Marshall Aid; but it also showed a genuine concern with productivity, which the American visits confirmed, rather than the simplistic emphasis on volume production habitual in government circles. It extended downwards through unions' newly-appointed 'efficiency departments' and outwards to link up with the British Institute of Management's concern with technology and scientific management. In this sense, the FBI's fears were justified: the long-term thrust of the Marshall Aid experience highlighted management inadequacies, not those of the workforce. But this was not the view taken in the popular Press, nor was it propagated by the government whose members, caught up in the 'red scare' of 1948–49, seemed to take more note of unofficial strikes, Communists in the London docks, and Smithfield Market, and a general 'absence of real leadership' on the part of the TUC.

The Cabinet could not easily distinguish between faction, agitation, and genuine grievances in the heated, Cold War climate.[23] Blamed for matters over which it had no control, but which weakened foreign confidence, the TUC found itself constrained to accept not only wage restraint and the production drive, but also an alignment of the FBI, many civil servants and the economic Ministers which they found perverse and unfair. *Industry and the Way to Recovery* won commendation from CEPS in August 1947; the FBI's canny line-up with government in preparing the ERP bids appears to have given it a degree of licence to criticise on fiscal and industrial policy that was denied the TUC. The FBI vigorously defended company profits and salaries (while conceding dividend control) and resisted statutory control of prices in 1949; Development Councils, which they opposed on principle were damned not only as a threat to trade associations and the intrinsic rights of management, but as potential agencies of state control.[24]

So effective was their mobilising of parliamentary opinion that when Harold Wilson moved to the Board of Trade in 1949, he decided that Development Councils were too contentious a matter to institute on anything but a narrow, selective scale.[25] The FBI's 1948 campaign against cuts in the investment allocated to private industry made less impression on the Chancellor, but their continued sniping at nationalised industries concentrated with damaging accuracy on the loose system of hidden subsidies and confused social, rather than commercial accounting which the government's earlier imprecision about objectives had allowed to develop. No outright breach was involved, even in the case of steel. The FBI had far too much to lose to risk isolating itself, and left that defence to the steel companies themselves, aided and guided by the Economic League and Aims of Industry. Indeed, the FBI's natural caution might have led it to play even more cautiously, in spite of the threat involved in the state becoming monopoly supplier of a basic product, and the evidence in Labour's 1949 Manifesto that a further round would involve sugar, cement, water supply and insurance, if it had not been for accusations of being 'soft' from among its members. Kipping and his deputy, David Walker, had to argue a case redolent of corporate bias: the FBI must fight 'indirectly . . . to educate the electorate on the evils which the present policy is creating' or risk losing its privileged position. It was 'not in the national interest to withdraw co-operation from government'.[26]

But in 1949, as the government's propaganda campaign exhausted itself and complaints surged up from member firms and trade associations, the FBI slipped into a more outspoken assault on government spending and profligate public industries. This did not necessarily signify a breach of the tripartite relationship; they could still agree with the TUC on some aspects of public industry, for example on the need for a national fuel policy. But the FBI's changed attitude had a symbolic as well as a practical momentum. Membership had always been refused to public industries which were monopolies: now the FBI depicted them generally as extensions of the state, and scarcely as industries at all. Asking for bulk tariff concessions, it addressed the Coal and Electricity Boards as if they were departments of state, to complain that manufacturing industry was being crowded out of the capital market because tariffs were kept artificially low to domestic consumers in order to hold down the cost of living.

Justified as many of these criticisms were, including the FBI's charge that state sector policies encouraged 'overfull employment', they ignored the idea of interdependence which had infused the 1944 package. Where profits were concerned, the FBI leadership, like the TUC with wages, found that members' commercial interests forced even the more co-operative-minded Council members to abrogate their altruistic inclinations. At the same time, and on both sides, the wages and prices pact began to lose coherence after the first eighteen months. Then came the Korean war, with inflationary effects on the cost of raw materials and the cost of living which neither side could ignore.

City institutions meanwhile kept a low political profile and seemed content with the regularity of the government's balanced budgets and its management of the sterling debts. As far as government was concerned, markets functioned well if they allowed the state to fund its debt and if they increased the foreign exchange reserves. In Treasury eyes, the Capital Issues Committee (composed of seven bankers, stockbrokers and industrialists) served 'well and faithfully' during 1945–50,[27] and the Labour Party's old animus against the City appears not to have been reflected in the government's formal transactions. But a summary of the state of the capital market, written by the CIC in 1950, gives the impression that the City was as ready as the FBI for a breach with government on the question of industrial investment.[28]

The Bank of England, principal source of such information for Attlee himself as well as Cripps, still expected corporate investment to come mainly from retained profits, the exceptions being its own creations to help small businesses, ICFC and FFI.[29] But the 1949 devaluation weakened that assumption and led to the clearing banks' refusing to cut back on advances to established clients, regardless of the Chancellor's policy.[30] The CIC acknowledged that large companies ('all too often monopolies' – a phrase removed from the final report) would normally be able to generate their own investment funds. But they criticised government policy as being responsible for a decline in the issue of preference shares (a reference to the capital demands of the housing programme) and for weakening the whole capital market by inflation, devaluation, increased personal taxation and the high cost of labour. The CIC had turned against Dalton's cheap money doctrine, and in 1949–50 began to demand that the capital market should be regulated by interest rates, not controls; in effect asking for their own dissolution. In addition, its members had doubts about the developing practice of economic management. They raised the old spectre that British industry might become over-dependent on 'finance capital', as pre-war German industry had depended on the banks, while the over-taxed 'small investor' might desert the market altogether.

The emergence of loaded phrases such as 'wage-inflation' and 'high personal taxation' in such a document indicates that the collective interests of industry and the finance sector and of the individuals who ran them were diverging from government policy in a way which the authors of the 1944 White Paper had not imagined. The CIC's report focused on the problem of the small investor and represented him as standing for the very idea of independence and entrepreneurial risk, a talisman against planning and the ever-encroaching state. Over the next five years, this shift in financial institutions' ethos may have been more significant than concomitant changes in the FBI and the TUC.

After the consequences of the convertibility crisis had worked themselves out, early in 1948, Cripps and the other economic ministers (with the whole economic planning apparatus, CEPS, EPB and EIU concentrated under one roof) set to work to ensure that Marshall Aid would, indeed, provide a second chance. To do so, they had to develop the practice of managing the economy in peacetime. Some change in Treasury policy had already occurred with Dalton's second Budget in October 1947, when 'excess demand' had been summarily curbed by taxation. Within the next year, Treasury planners had convinced themselves that fiscal levers would be sufficient for them to control demand, production and manpower supply, despite sporadic failure of the production drive to reach targets, and persistent manpower shortages in the export industries. During 1948–49, they learned the techniques of macroeconomic management and fed on the success so deeply that confidence in the techniques became habitual, an integral part of the Treasury's wisdom, for the next twenty-five years.

This did not mean there was no debate in the rest of government on microeconomic matters and the role of private industry. On the Cabinet Economic Policy Committee, Morrison still talked of national planning and partnership, and at the Board of Trade after 1949, Harold Wilson developed a more radical scheme (see page 181). The Labour Party Research Department issued important documents on public ownership and the use of public industry as a regulator. But the government proceeded pragmatically, fearful of alienating the private sector, particularly small business and retailers.[31] The Department's document 'Socialism and Private Enterprise' received a hammering in the NEC in November 1947, after the left failed to support it against Morrison's criticism. Divisions persisted among ministers and between Cabinet and party. Compromises about the future of the mixed economy, made in the 1949 manifesto, *Labour Believes in Britain*, did no more than paper over the cracks.

Neither side could win decisively in a dispute of such fundamental significance. The left could not prevent negative action to appease business interests, such as the delays over steel nationalisation or the introduction of Development Councils; but when Morrison attempted to review the whole functioning of public industries in 1948–49 in order to win back support for them from an increasingly disillusioned business community and the TUC at one and the same time, he was stopped. The conclusions that his Committee on Socialisation had come to in 1948 ('the business of management is to manage and nowhere is this more true than in large basic industries'[32]) shows that

Morrison wished to demonstrate that public industries could be efficient, if they were soundly managed, freed as far as possible from Ministerial interference, and restricted to areas where they could better existing private services to the public.

Apart from the fact that the temptation to fix prices of energy or services in order to hold down the cost of living had already become endemic, this doctrine was quite unacceptable to the Party's officers and research department who, together with the TUC Economic Committee, saw public industries as agencies with which to plan and manage the economy. No formula could bridge this gap, though Morrison kept his campaign going, to the point of eliciting the Attorney-General's opinion that Ministers did not have legal power to override a Board's statutory obligation to pay its way.[33]

In a muddled way, and without getting to grips with the wages structures, uncontrolled costs, or the rigid pattern of subsidies, the majority of Ministers had already come to see public industries as instruments of economic management – a view which dismayed mandarins like Bridges and Plowden who remembered more clearly the decisions made in 1943–44. Morrison gave way, though he and Gaitskell fought a rearguard action and induced the Economic Policy Committee to accept a rider about state industries' commercial basis couched in terms unfortunately too vague to assist management to establish genuine independence.[34] Later, in 1949, they campaigned with more success against worker-participation, which they damned as 'syndicalist tendencies'.[35] Caught between their responsibilities to the party, unions, management and the hypothetical consumer, Ministers held on to their new licence to manipulate almost unconditionally, and failed to appoint to the Boards chairmen who might have opposed it. Public industries did not become dynamic instigators of investment, nor did the government use its purchasing power to influence suppliers' and consumers' practices; any hope of a unified transport system, or a coherent energy policy spanning coal, oil, gas and electricity, died in the lifetime of the government that set up the nationalisation programme.

Such an outcome to the public industry 'review' augured badly for Cripps' second chance, and the heat it generated in Cabinet may have encouraged Treasury planners to avoid the equally contentious issues of restrictive practices, investment and technology, all essential to any concern with productivity, and to concentrate solely on what could be done within the Chancellor's sphere of fiscal control – that is, through the Budget, and restrictions over credit and investment. Yet the government did not suffer from a lack of alternatives: within the planning staff James Meade was consistently arguing that since industry had no spare capacity and no means to create more, quickly, production must increase through efficiency and productivity – 'means which do not prejudice the great social revolution and the increased economic and social equity which the last years have brought'. Others in the Labour Party like Stephen Taylor foreshadowed Anthony Crosland in asking what would be the nature of socialism if physical controls were set aside, and redistribution were to lead to a new sort of property-owning democracy.[36]

As Chancellor, Cripps found himself in a dominant if not impregnable position, unfettered by a Prime Minister who had little talent for economic argument, and distanced from the backbenchers and the Party apparatus. Bevan and the left troubled him far less than they did Attlee who took the brunt of their rhetoric. Surrounded by his like-minded planning staff (as near as the Treasury ever came to Beveridge's economic general staff) and brilliant younger officials like Richard Clarke, Cripps could search out ways to manage the economy without creating public or party hostility, to achieve success without tears, without radical change in the patterns of work and production. The Treasury now had considerable influence in Washington, and at home Attlee always backed the Chancellor in Cabinet.

Cripps' strategy can be seen in the machinery of government review, instituted by the Treasury itself at the end of 1947 which improved the lines of communication in industry, from BOT to trade associations, and simplified the Production Authority system, but did not provide the fundamental restructuring which the House of Commons' Estimates Committee had recently asked for. It demonstrated how sceptical the mandarinate was about the practical limits of state power; and went no further than recommending extension of joint production councils in the troubled car industry. By emphasising voluntary and tripartite principles as the only alternative to a command economy (which the public would not tolerate) and depicting controls as archaic and detrimental to the natural development of the economy, it went some way towards settling the agenda of the 'second chance'.[37]

The same civil servants, under Bridges' guidance, carried on the inquiry into 1949, with a retrospective examination of how the machinery of government had worked in the five years since 1944. Since other departments objected to so much power residing in a Treasury team, the group was re-established on a broader base, in order to look at the whole field of state organisation in economic affairs, trade and industry.[38] In the near distance, they opened up the future of sponsorship and the Production Authority system, now that economic policy had been wholly gathered into the Treasury, but beyond that (and not always only by implication) they reviewed the 1944 pledge itself. Their activities complemented the productivity drive and Cripps' direct appeals to the TUC and the public. But insofar as they worked in the tripartite system (and all agreed with Cripps on the need for industrialists' full support), they had to bargain, for the FBI wanted to influence the way production (and in due course, rearmament for the Korean War) would be carried on. The Board of Trade, CEPS and Plowden, as Chief Planner, came finally to an agreement in March 1951 about the need to decentralise government planning.[39] Quite apart from the exigencies imposed by the Korean War, planning as it had been understood by most Labour MPs and many Ministers in 1945 had withered away, leaving a residue almost exactly the same as the legacy of 1944. What had occurred after 1947 was a mutation that was more or less complete when the government fell.

Enough of the groundwork had been completed by 1949 to give a reasonable chance of industrial support for Cripps' major plans. Sponsorship, the state's relations with industry, was defined neither as control, nor simply government procurement, but the method of insuring 'that government intervention in the affairs of an industry takes full account of its needs and of government policy towards it. The implication is that the department is knowledgeable about the place of its industries in the economy, watches over their requirements and interests, and gives them general advice and assistance'.[10] Whether such a minimalist doctrine would enable policy to affect what an individual firm did, when measured against a hundred other constraints in an open peacetime environment, and whether the sponsorship mechanism alone could bridge what increasingly appeared as the gap between macro and microeconomic action, remained to be proved.

Officials in the Treasury admitted that the new techniques of economic management were rough and ready, and seem to have made an effort not to encourage Ministers in the illusion that their aims could easily be achieved. But, confident in their abilities to make economic management work, and aware that Washington looked sympathetically at what they were trying to do, they gradually acquired confidence that the problems were soluble. They did not seek to formulate answers in advance of Cabinet, but their expertise and reputation was such that, with Attlee's backing, Cripps could always outpoint any opposition. The economic powerhouse served the Chancellor, not the Cabinet, and could dole out information and hence shape debates elsewhere, as it did on the EPB, without being in any way beholden to industrial institutions or unions for their views. The Treasury alone took charge of the drafting of the most influential *Economic Surveys*, those of 1947 and 1948. From 1948 one can date the emergence of the Treasury as a citadel, at times impervious to the outside world, whose denizens, without a direct sponsorship responsibility for anything but the financial sector, took an overarching interest in seeing that other sponsors did their jobs and brought their clients to heel, within the grand design. Other Ministers than Cripps, of course, amended or extended the design, usually under the spur of successive crises; but they barely touched the concept and, in the troughs and hollows between, the Treasury acted as a flywheel to regulate momentum.

Consequently Cabinet had few opportunities to question the prior importance of the sterling area, 'the only great multinational trading system in the world', as Cripps told the 1944 Association in July 1948. A mass of evidence had been built up (initially to answer Dalton's earlier criticisms that the Treasury had failed to check the outflow of dollars in 1947), to demonstrate that, faced with inexorable flows of capital in the world, Treasury or Bank could do little but react after the event, unless and until sterling had been made stable.[41] The way lay open to argue that, although it was no longer possible to use the sterling area as the bilateralists had hoped, British procurement could still be increased there, to save dollars and supplement Marshall Aid. Tension slowly grew up inside the Treasury itself between Cobbold at the Bank and OFD, headed by Sir Leslie Rowan, advocates of a strong pound, which would ultimately be restored to convertibility, and the Home Economic Department, experts in economic management, who resisted what seemed always to be calls to deflate. This tension – a derivation of the 1943 trade argument – rose in the summer of 1949 as Britain drifted towards devaluation.

The devaluation argument, as Sir Alec Cairncross points out, was not really about trade advantage, and how to maintain it afterwards without allowing wages and costs to rise and erode it (though that was how it was presented by the Board of Trade at the time) because though the eventual fall was extremely large, from $4.03 to $2.80, the effective (trade-weighted) fall was only 9 per cent.[42] As the Bank of England informed Cripps in July 1949, the lack of reserves made it progressively more difficult to sustain an unrealistic rate. Long-term factors made a reversal of the trend unlikely. Holders of sterling world-wide were finding it easy and increasingly prudent to slip out of sterling through Switzerland. The trend had accelerated recently as a result of strikes and the obvious weakness of Attlee's leadership. The US Treasury was also pressing for a devaluation with the intention of bringing the pound back to convertibility. After two years of Marshall Aid, according to the Bank, Americans looked with some horror at British rates of profitability, productivity, and at wage inflation, lack of competitiveness, and 'misuse' of what they had provided.[43]

But the Bank did not want simply to devalue, and certainly not to float the pound as had been done with great skill and success in 1931, preferring to institute a tight monetary policy without too much direct deflation at home, 'to create the conditions for a return of confidence in sterling and a new approach to the Americans'. Devaluation, it believed, would not do this by itself, without supporting measures to ensure the new rate for a term of years. That is to say, devaluation would have to come (and the Bank preferred it sooner, at a rate of roughly $3.25, rather than later), but the relief would not exempt the government from controlling home-grown inflation.[44] This may not have been a pre-emptive strike to tie the politicians down, but it certainly pinned the disagreeable choices on them. Obviously, the export industries would have to earn substantially more dollars after devaluation, but their capacity to do so remained in doubt.

Cripps opposed devaluation for some weeks not only because he feared its effect on Commonwealth countries (whose assets in the sterling area would be depreciated) but also because he saw it as a major defeat for his second chance and a clear victory for market forces over the government that would be hard to explain to the Labour Party's electorate. Gaitskell and Jay, supported by Plowden, Hall and Clarke from the Treasury, conducted the argument in favour, while at Trade Wilson took refuge in ambiguities. Dalton supported Cripps. Attlee himself seems not to have grasped the economic rationale at all; yet it was for his ear that the others competed.[45] Early on, Cripps fell ill and withdrew to a sanatorium in Switzerland. Bevin was already in decline and took no part. In the end Wilson sided with the devaluers, who also converted Dalton, Bevan, Strachey and Strauss. On 21 July, Attlee warned his colleagues that dividing the government would be worse than avoiding a decision and by 28 July a majority for devaluation existed. After further agonies of mind, Cripps gave way and the date was set – too late for Britain's best interests – for 18 August.

The new parity was decided largely by the expert advisors who picked a level of $2.80. This gave, as Roy Harrod argued in 1963, a greater depreciation than circumstances required, and much greater than had originally been envisaged. Cairncross argues that more careful management would have prevented so drastic a fall.[46] But what Treasury and Bank officials wanted was a rate that could be sustained for many years, and which would convince international opinion – and the speculators – that this and future governments intended to run the domestic economy tightly with the intention of moving gradually back towards convertibility and an increasingly liberal trading pattern. Their aim had been frustrated after the 1947 crisis; now they intended it to be enshrined in the exchange rate, possibly without most of the Cabinet understanding the implications.

Only at the last moment were the FBI and the TUC informed: nevertheless they heard before India and Pakistan – an interesting priority, only partly explained by the difference in time between London and Delhi. To the rest of Cabinet, Attlee explained that devaluation was not a disaster like 1931, and had not been done under American pressure.

Cutting public expenditure had already been debated, nervously and inconclusively; in July 1949 the Treasury had put forward a figure of 5 per cent cuts all round, with Morrison's support. They argued that increased national income during 1948 had produced 'excess demand', a flood of imports and a balance of payments crisis; that this differed from the real case for devaluation, put by the Bank and the Treasury OFD, was either not noticed or ignored. In the autumn the Cabinet settled miserably into wrangling over where the cuts should fall; each department used what leverage it had and the Attlee–Bevin–Alexander line on overseas commitments and the exigencies of the Cold War ensured that the defence departments came out on top. Housing, health services and food imports would suffer in consequence, as Dalton complained, thanks to what he called 'the conspiracy of Bridges, Plowden and the Bank'.

Ministers who thought they had instituted 'a great social revolution' found this hard to take. Yet some fought back: Tom Williams, at Agriculture, successfully disputed the cuts in agricultural subsidies. The most serious economies, as in 1947 and in all subsequent similar crises under Labour or Conservative governments, fell on investment and other capital projects rather than on current spending. (Only Bevin wisely argued that the voter should also feel pain, with an increase in the price of bread.)

Tailoring the import bill and diminishing the nation's spending power would not be enough, economic ministers argued, if wages were again to outpace productivity. The Treasury working party reported the day after devaluation that a stringent wages policy was needed if Britain were not to have to devalue again: 'wages are the largest element in the cost of manufactured goods. Since devaluation brings with it some increase in the cost of living, there is the risk that . . . a cycle of wages increases will be set off by the devaluation itself.'[47] The FBI joined in: devaluation had raised the cost of imported raw materials and if manufacturing industry were to achieve the new volume of exports demanded by a devalued pound, they must have insurances against a rise in wages.[48] Only too well aware of the contrary forces inside the trade union movement, Cabinet sent Plowden to negotiate with the TUC in September, and postponed the proposed cuts in food subsidies until after Congress had voted to continue the freeze (by a much narrower majority than in 1948). This manoeuvre virtually ensured that the TUC would not comply again. Some very wild views were aired during these weeks before Cripps delivered his Budget in November. One member of the Economic Secretariat speculated that inflation might reach 20–30 per cent in two years if wages and price control were not instituted.[49]

Without saying outright that the TUC was to blame, the Cabinet had begun to convince itself that its mandate and the entire post-war settlement depended on continuing the wages and prices freeze. Yet its members recoiled when they saw the resulting swing of public opinion among wage-earners. Government was shocked by the depths of public feeling, openly voiced in factories, where it was widely thought that exporters were to be encouraged by incentives to make high profits at wage-earners' expense. Many saw Marshall Aid as a loan which would have later to be repaid. For the first time, government felt it had failed to explain; worse, that the wartime reservoir of public altruism had run dry.[50] That both the TUC and the FBI concurred shows how strong tripartite consensus still was; but that their authority was at risk can be seen from the fact that government expected the freeze to last for six more months only, with tentative provision for a further term. In these confused terms, Cripps' second chance had until the autumn of 1950 to succeed.

Prices and profits in the export industries escaped scrutiny, giving further reason for public complaints that sacrifices were not being distributed fairly. What appears to have been a drift into wages policy (for price control did not bear so harshly on manufacturers) might have been better if it had been a deliberate strategy from the beginning, to complement a devaluation designed earlier in the year to right Britain's trade disadvantage within the dollar zone, rather than what the Treasury called a 'necessary adjustment' in August. Yet devaluation worked, in the narrow sense that the drain on the reserves stopped and the pound held at $2.80 until 1967. Taking a larger view, the attempt to tie government and public consumption down to external financial aims failed; but the onus was put instead on trade unions' wage claims.[51]

Rather perversely, the crisis benefited those who had least to do with devaluation: Attlee's leadership recovered and Cripps managed for a further year (until ill-health forced him to retire in October 1950) to carry on his domestic strategy under the continued umbrella of Marshall Aid. Exports rose, though more in the sterling than the dollar area, consumption levelled off, wages stabilised, and Cripps succeeded in trimming public expenditure without losing more public support or the allegiance of Bevan and the left. Officials who served the Cabinet Economic Policy and Production Committees, where Cripps' main work took place, still argue that the second chance could have worked, and the economy could have moved into the equilibrium which allowed renewal of collective bargaining and personal spending (which the Conservative government experienced instead after 1952) if it had not been for the Korean War.

Given Britain's close relationship with the United States, her shared view of the Soviet Union's aggressive designs, membership of the recently-formed NATO, and the line consistently followed by Attlee, Bevin and the Defence Ministers, to say nothing of the fact that Australia and Canada sent contingents, the question of whether Britain could have avoided participating in the Korean War, which broke out on 25 June 1950, is barely worth asking. Gaitskell could have advanced very powerful economic arguments against participation, but chose not to, though some Treasury officials attempted to stiffen him to do so. Attlee himself came under great pressure from the State Department on the grounds that Congress might have difficulty voting supplies unless the United States' main ally joined in.

But the war they entered turned out not to be the war they had to fight: the Cabinet could not know that when General MacArthur had apparently 'won', China (assured perhaps by Guy Burgess that Truman had promised Attlee not to use atomic weapons) would attack across the Yalu River and prolong the war by three years. Douglas Jay denies that the American government promised to help if Britain fell into a balance of payments crisis: Lord Plowden remembers that it was a tacit assumption among Treasury and Cabinet Office officials that the United States would help with the £200 million deficit on the trade balance which was predicted and which, manifestly, could not be met by Britain's exports.[52]

Britain joined, the deficit materialised, and the USA did not help. Mossadeq's take-over of BP's Iranian oil fields made things worse. Four serious consequences followed: first, that conscription exacerbated the already endemic shortages of skilled labour – yet government failed either to import enough skilled immigrants or set up training programmes (at a time when Britain's main European competitor, Germany, was drawing in highly skilled workers fleeing from East Germany, Poland and Czechoslovakia); second, direction of resources for war and distortion of civilian industrial production diminished the abilities of the machine tool industry to fulfil home orders and of industry as a whole to satisfy public demand, thus creating an inflationary surge, regardless of wages and prices control, which left home markets wide open to foreign competitors (without, however, providing a spur which might have forced British firms to face up to such competition); third, that the economies made in investment hit hardest the infrastructure of transport, industrial construction, housing and health, leaving a huge backlog of debilitated public services which alienated a public already disturbed by the events of 1947 and 1949; lastly, that Britain incurred greatly increased dollar expenditure, at a time when Marshall Aid was coming to an end.

The sheer volume of Britain's engagement in the Korean War mattered less, in domestic terms, than the fact that it occurred at a critical time for her recovery in relation to her principal competitors. The United States' economy barely suffered from the drain of manpower and some industries positively benefited from military orders; Germany suffered not at all. For fourteen months after devaluation, there had seemed a chance Cripps might succeed, if unions, management and the public co-operated. The TUC's September 1950 repudiation of wages restraint coincided with China's entry into the war, and the fatalism with which Attlee accepted it suggests that, even without the Korean denouement, the 'second chance' had failed.

Even before the reintroduction of austerity in 1947, Mass Observation and other opinion polls were starting to show Labour supporters' eagerness for renewed change. Afterwards, to instil enthusiasm for the production drives and make privation more palatable, the government began to use its whole armoury of persuasion and propaganda, ranging from Labour Party publications like *The Bridge to Socialism* (April 1948) to productions of the Economic Intelligence Unit and the COI, which in October 1948 produced its *Report to the Nation*. They had no choice: rising industrial discontent in 1948 indicated that substantial numbers of workers either had lost sympathy or positively disagreed with government policies,[53] while evidence accumulated of a revulsion among middle management, the professional middle-class and the small business sector. Unable to offer concessions to what they regarded as privileged groups, the government could only try persuasion, using new instruments, in order to rebuild the consensus of 1945. Like earlier exhortations, these all relied on the principle that if the public were told the facts, they would respond loyally.[54]

After considerable success in 1948, government propagandists put a more subtle argument into the 1949 *Economic Survey*. For the first time productivity took prior place: a much more difficult argument for government to get across than higher volume production. Future progress would depend on technical advance, new capital equipment, improved industrial organisation, not simply on a larger workforce, longer hours and 'output per man'. These strictures may have been directed at management but after devaluation the onus was to be put on their workers. Nevertheless, in his public speeches and broadcasts, Cripps, the moralist-cum-technocrat, set out a future for modern industry and a modern workforce in the international market, which would depend on a more mature political involvement than tripartism had yet produced. Drawing on the 1944 legacy, he sought continually to shape it for the 1950s.

Unfortunately the public did not buy or read the 1949 *Survey* in large numbers. They may not even have understood it. Press and BBC gave it scant space, because productivity was a difficult concept to explain, even when wrapped in talk of prosperity and social justice. 'After a long period of high unemployment and defensive and restrictive practices in many sections of industry,' the EIU wrote, 'there is not enough general understanding of the industrial politics and personal attitudes which full employment requires.'[55]

The campaign may have been too narrowly directed at trade unions, too obviously linked to a wages policy; and its tone of calm detachment suggests that Ministers may almost have given up the struggle. Cripps was seriously ill by the time it appeared, Bevin dying, Morrison discarded and Attlee hanging on while the younger generation manoeuvred for position in the devaluation debate. The level of strikes, which grew worse after the Korean War had begun, confirmed for many Ministers their worst suspicions about unions' irresponsibility, shop-floor agitation and Communists. Some of the strikes were certainly Communist-inspired.[56] Those in the docks, on London buses and at Smithfield Market in the summer of 1950 not only diverted attention from the extent to which the TUC were genuinely trying to assist, but led Attlee in particular into considering legislation so stringent that it made wartime controls seem almost trivial.[57] It was abandoned in November 1950 thanks to the efforts of the Cabinet Office and Morrison and TUC leaders; but though the latter undertook to use their own disciplinary powers, they hesitated, when the occasion came, fearing to inspire breakaway unions.

The truth was that despite the initial optimism of Deakin and Feather, the anti-Communist crusade had proved much harder than the Cabinet had expected because admiration for Soviet Russia stubbornly survived in unions like the ETU (where the CPGB dominated) and the TGWU (where it took eight out of thirty-two places on the Executive in 1948), the South Wales Mineworkers, on the London Trades Council, and at district level in the AEU, or even where the Communist Party had lost its original influence.[58] The links between Communist influence and strikes and radical dissent in unions or trade councils emphasised the cleavage between TUC leaders and their followers and probably prepared the Cabinet for the October 1950 Congress decision.

Congress' rejection of the wages freeze showed the Cabinet that the TUC simply could not act as government agent any longer, or 'control' the discontent within – which had turned out to be far more broad-based than earlier talk of subversive elements indicated. The TUC could not even be certain of retaining support for Order 1305.[59] Bridges and Norman Brook carefully damped down Ministers' Cold War tempers, played down the Communist Party's role, and pointed wisely to the generally low level of morale in the docks and other trouble-spots. Attlee conceded the point when forgoing penal legislation, possibly because he did not want the party to face the forthcoming election in conflict with the TUC, but he did so reluctantly and Gaitskell, also a protagonist of the draft Bill, later regretted it: 'the government really ought to face up to the issue of power station strikes and decide whether they can afford to treat them as ordinary industrial disputes. In my view they cannot.'[60]

Behind this, of course, lay the unacknowledged question of 1944, 1947 and 1949–50: if industry and unions would not, or could not co-operate with government, and earn their 'privileges' of high demand and profit or full employment, should the state compel them – or rather their members – to do so? It had taken six years, and a major war, within a wider Cold War that included the Berlin blockade in 1948, to bring Attlee and a minority of the Cabinet so far. Even to put the question was to doubt that Cripps' second chance existed. To relegate or evade it (as the Attlee government did and as Harold Wilson was also to do with 'In Place of Strife' in 1969) meant either that the diagnosis had been wrong – and perhaps no one in Attlee's Cabinet believed that – or that in a democratic society the state was too weak to proceed: that it must perforce rely on what co-operation unions and management would give, and on what it could do indirectly by fiscal and monetary means to limit demand; and beyond that, tailor its expectations to what had turned out to be possible.

In July 1949, during the devaluation discussion, Morgan Phillips Labour's general secretary, advised Attlee to declare a general election in order to mobilise public opinion against the malign combination of dock strikes, Conservative attacks, the dollar gap, and the expected US recession.[61] Gaitskell agreed with him: it should be done before 1950, while the wages pact still lasted. But for more than a year the party had been simmering, as headquarters and constituency activists piped in radical schemes, for broadside nationalisation and permanent planning controls over private industry. Young, left-inclined intellectuals on the backbenches confronted ageing, tired and impatient ministers on a range of issues altogether outside the 1944 package: to do with industrial democracy, banking and credit policy, control of profits, equal pay, the rights of the shop floor. The language had changed: the 1947 Conference had accepted a resolution declaring 'every individual member of the Labour Party is a shock-worker of social democracy'.

Cripps' doctrine of persuasion finally broke down in 1950. Too many members of unions, their standard of living already curtailed in 1949 and under pressure from Korean War inflation of world prices, felt betrayed by 'their' government,[62] too many ostensibly 'Labour' organisations like trades councils had started to accuse Labour leaders of 'bargaining with capitalism', for the government to try to re-exert its authority over its domain. On the other hand, too many employers were making their own propaganda out of unofficial strikes and certain shop stewards' behaviour for them to be able confidently to rely on that side of the tripartite system. (The FBI, having carefully watched what the TUC did, abandoned dividend restraint as soon as the Congress decision was known.)

In electoral terms, the government held its base: it lost none of the thirty-two by-elections before 1950, a unique record. When the election did come, before the Budget, in February 1950 it also held its numerical support.[63] Paradoxically, its only lasting loss occurred among the briefly-radical newspapers and middle-class Labour voters of 1945 who, tired of austerity, and polarised by the events of 1949–50, turned either to the Liberal Party (which polled a surprising 2.6 million votes, 9.1 per cent of the total) or to the Conservatives. But the loss of its unassailable majority and the evidence of working-class disillusion, as well as the irreparable loss of Cripps himself in October 1950, whose moral stature and capacity to set high Puritanism in a nationally acceptable imagery had given policy an authority it never recaptured, deeply affected Attlee and his colleagues.

During the 'second chance' exports rose, at least until the American recession set in during 1949. Britain benefited from devaluation without an immediate inflationary spiral of wages and prices. The Chancellor balanced his budgets, capitalised on the vestigial altruism of unions and management, and went a long way towards evolving the techniques of economic management. His policy might have survived the American recession as it had devaluation. But, even without the Korean War, the public had become saturated, incapable of further sacrifice. Clem Leslie, Director of the EIU, had wanted to put a stark choice in the 1949 *Economic Survey*: 'poverty or full employment'.[64] The Ministerial Economic Policy Committee refused. The time for such language had passed. The second chance turned out not to be an end in itself but only an overture to a drama which the intrinsically divided sections of the Labour Party each claimed to have the right to direct. If there were to be a third, it had to come *de novo*, and not from reinterpretation of what had been laid down in other circumstances, in 1944 or 1945.

6 Which Way is Jerusalem?

Compared with its vigorous start, the last two years of Attlee's administration seems a time of muddle, indecision and conflict, particularly after the 1950 election reduced Labour's majority to seventeen. It is easy to underestimate its significance. Most accounts depict a 'retreat from Jerusalem' against which the Bevanite left waged an unsuccessful campaign. In fact the government had passed through a complicated evolution, at least as far as its macroeconomic and industrial policies were concerned, which after 1949 reached a point where the pre-war and wartime guidelines that had served it turned out to be inadequate. In this hiatus a fundamental debate sprung up not about economic management as such but about what economic management was for, ostensibly between the Bevanites and the centre (comprising Cripps, Morrison, Gaitskell and Jay) but actually between the socialist and social-democratic wings of the party, which determined the way that the endemic civil war would develop during the thirteen years in opposition, but also influenced strongly the tenor of Churchill's and Macmillan's governments down to 1961.

Having been limited in 1949–50 by what it could plan because of the coming election, Labour was constrained afterwards by its narrow majority. Yet at least Attlee did not *have* to think of another election in a year, as Harold Wilson did in 1964 and 1974. In spite of rearmament's harsh requirements, there was intrinsically no reason why the Labour government should not have looked for a third chance. Not all forecasts after the election were as gloomy as those of the BEC and FBI, who looked to the rapidly falling rate of profit as costs of raw materials shot up due to the Korean War. The EPB thought that in 1951 productivity would rise beyond the 2.5 per cent increase allowed for – and it actually reached 4 per cent. Unfortunately this was soon translated into wages, profits and excess demand rather than savings, investment and exports so that

180

another serious deficit on the balance of payments began to build up.

To put it schematically, three options for the early 1950s emerged: the first associated with Harold Wilson at the Board of Trade, the second with Hugh Gaitskell, who became Chancellor of the Exchequer when Cripps was forced to retire due to ill-health in October 1950, and the third, which had nothing to do with the Labour Party and only came to light after the 1951 election, with the officials at the centre of government and at the Bank of England. They developed coterminously but must be narrated separately.

At the Board of Trade after 1947, Wilson, the youngest member of the Cabinet, picked up many of the themes his officials had been forced to relinquish in 1943–44. Having sat on the fence at first in the devaluation debate, he had been converted mainly because he saw a fall in the exchange as the required stimulus to the exporting industries; afterwards he became aware that the hoped-for benefits of devaluation were being eroded by continuing inflation and the perennial tendency of manufacturers to evade German (and increasingly Japanese) competition by relying on the home market, or orders for the Korean War, or both. He was temperamentally opposed to the sort of protection given to agriculture by Williams' 1947 Act, with its guaranteed price system, even if GATT principles had not forbidden its application to manufacturing industry other than defence equipment suppliers. His trade mission to Washington in 1949 encouraged him to think (like earlier TUC visitors) that British industry *could* be modernised to recapture export markets, and he had been optimistic enough to reassure American businessmen 'that social democracy in Britain, so far from being a halfway house to Communism, was the most live and practical alternative to it'.[1]

Back in England, he and his junior minister, Christopher Mayhew, prepared a lengthy paper, 'The State and Private Industry' which they set before a meeting of senior ministers (not Cabinet, for this was primarily a *party* document, as Wilson explained) on 17 May 1950.[2] Summing up a radical proposal more suited to the next election, circa 1953, than immediate policy, he argued that the relationship between the state and private industry – an area vitally concerned with all the great issues of full employment, exports, productivity and the standard of living – represented a 'vacuum in Socialist thought'. As controls disappeared (with his blessing, for he had long since accepted they could not be maintained) no means of influencing industry remained for the state except through the public industries, whose record had been, at least, patchy and disputable, and the levers of demand management, which the 1949 crisis had shown were not so neutral that their usage did not bear hardest on working class living standards.

The whole tenor of this paper reasserted the positions about uncompetitive private industry and inefficient management which BOT had been forced to abandon at the end of the war, buoyed up by a confidence that the supply side could be improved to meet the state's requirements and avert the recession that had already hit the United States. In such a way the vague promises of *Labour Believes in Britain* (the 1950 Manifesto) could be made credible. It was, Wilson admitted, an aggressive document, intended to turn the Conservative attack on public industries back against the private sector which Labour had so far let off its catechism of the public interest. At the same time he intended to display the party not just as defender of the working class as producers but as 'champion of the consumer' (a phrase coined by Mayhew) against the old unholy alliance of cartel-minded management and oligarchic unions, given new tripartite form by courtesy of the state itself. Steering carefully between the old left, whose primary concern remained the extension of public ownership, and the Gaitskell–Jay position, Wilson and Mayhew appealed to the substantial number of voters who in February had voted Liberal or reverted to the Conservatives because of dissatisfaction with the high prices and inefficiency of public industries, and the bleak austerity of the Cripps' years.

Daring as this exercise was, they did not for practical reasons wish to antagonise the FBI or trade associations and failed to go so far as BOT officials had done in 1944, restricting themselves to the use of the seventeen Development Councils already outlined. Some of their actual recommendations sounded unrealistic, and all required substantial legislation, which they admitted might not be easy to pass if industrialists' opposition (to permanent price controls for example) brought Liberals and Conservatives together. On the other hand, proposals for Consumer Consultative Councils in state industries, a Consumers' Charter, and improvements in the distributive system clearly had a strong electoral appeal, as did their proposed crusade against monopolies, restrictive practices, and incompetent management.

Had this come at the beginning of a five year term, say in 1946, it would have offered Cabinet a far clearer insight into how to influence the 'commanding heights' of industry – if only because Wilson demanded the information actually to identify 'key firms' and powers both to make directives effective and to implement the first stages of worker participation. Most important of all, his proposal boldly addressed the problem of vested interests in Whitehall, industry and the trade union movement, and consequently aroused deep hostility, and an all-round suspicion from which Wilson never entirely freed himself.

His colleagues reacted cautiously. Senior Ministers welcomed the section on price control (though Basil Willey and John Edwards pointed out that they would favour the least efficient firms). Douglas Jay, speaking as a Treasury Minister, disliked the powers of direction rather than persuasion, and Gaitskell, then still Minister of State for Economic Affairs under Cripps, summed up with cautious ambiguity: 'he did not believe in controls on the private sector for the sake of control. In general, his view was that we should get rid of monopoly practices and let competition work'. Attlee did not declare his hand, other than to minute that responsibility seemed to be passing to younger men, after which he referred it to Morgan Phillips for consultation with the Parliamentary Party.

Various parts were later excised: proposals for government-appointed directors on company boards and the nationalisation of ICI, and others on investment and capital allocation. It became a less statist document, more reliant on price controls and more congenial to the TUC than Wilson had intended; and his dramatic peroration, equating reform with the survival of full employment, disappeared. To say that nothing happened because Wilson resigned after the 1951 Budget, however, ignores its wider symbolism, and its legacy when he became Prime Minister in 1964. Long before he resigned, in company with Bevan and Michael Foot, over a relatively small issue and after skilful manoeuvring by Attlee and Gaitskell, Wilson's proposal focused the concerns of the new 'ideological' element in the party: that is, the Research Department, many individual trade unionists, and middle-ranking union officials like Frank Cousins and Jack Jones, as well as large numbers of constituency activists, worried about the drift of the party and its increasingly 'social democratic' outlook. However jejune some of Wilson's recommendations, it showed that the left was seeking to renew itself, to redefine its goals in contradistinction to what Gaitskell increasingly saw as the reality of a changing society – to which Gaitskell preferred the party should adapt. This was not a trivial conflict, though Wilson believed it possible to prevent and it explains why Wilson found himself increasingly in the Bevanite camp. Although Gaitskell's intellectual clarity led him to misunderstand Bevan's often muddled responses he later saw the quarrel in apocalyptic terms and wrote that it was 'a fight for the soul of the Labour Party . . . But who shall win it? No one can say as yet. I am afraid that if Bevan does, we shall be out of power for years and years'.[3]

Sheer pressure of work, and his negotiations in the USA after he took over from Cripps in October 1950, limited Gaitskell's freedom of thought to the point that his diary gives barely any indication of the fact that his transition to the point of view later associated with Anthony Crosland and the social-democratic 'revisionists' took place at the Treasury in the short period before the 1951 election.

The feud between him and the Bevanites ran on, of course, through 1955 and contributed gravely to the loss of that election. Behind the clash of personalities it was indeed a fight for the party's soul, though the Gaitskellite alternative (which owed much to Evan Durbin's *Politics of Democratic Socialism* (1940) and the thinking in Durbin's notes for an unpublished 'Economics of Democratic Socialism') did not emerge in coherent public form until Anthony Crosland published his celebrated argument in *The Future of Socialism* (1956) that capitalism had been so far transformed by what had been achieved after 1945 that equality, as well as growth and prosperity, could be achieved simply by economic management and social administration. The thesis could already be detected in Morrison's 1948–49 attempt to redefine the role of public industries in terms of commercial objectives (see page 166) and his and Gaitskell's rearguard action against worker-participation; also in the sequel which in 1949–50 set the left for the first time against what Wilson defined as the flaccid 'state corporation' model and the reactionary combinations inculcated by tripartism.[4]

In this dispute, the TUC failed to back up the Bevanites and instead sought advice from Gaitskell how to reform public industries, make them more efficient and extend their influence. Nothing dramatic ensued from two years' desultory talks, perhaps because the TUC failed to demand radical reform of the existing Coal Board and Transport Commission. Instead, the Cabinet set up an inquiry in February 1950 to adjudicate on Morrison's proposals. Having heard evidence from all wings of the party, this bogged down in the sheer incompatibility of conflicting opinions.[5] In a final plaintive minute, Morrison's office listed the unresolved questions: quality of management; relations between Ministers, Boards and Parliament; control of efficiency; consumer satisfaction; relations between workers, and management – the whole agenda, in fact, which public industries had been instituted after 1945 to solve!

Wilson's critique of industrial policy had at least had the merit that it openly took issue with existing priorities, in particular the fact that the Treasury's economic management had so far not only given priority to sterling, the balance of payments, and a balanced budget, but that it had justified this in terms of the 1944 White Paper, while calling on productive workers to carry the worst burdens. Cripps, of course, made no secret of what had been done; he told the TUC with some pride in April 1949 that Britain was the only nation which had consistently budgeted for a surplus, which would give enough capacity to tide the economy through the coming recession. The fact that the surplus, did not prevent devaluation and the 1949 cuts in investment did not shame him out of a similar defence in February 1950.[6] But by the latter date, the Ministerial Economic Committee had become restive at the appearance of a tired Chancellor in thrall to the old gods, ready to cut consumption while BOT proceeded with decontrol of industry; in these circumstances, Wilson may well have expected a better reception for his proposal than he actually received.

Critics among the Cabinet and in the TUC were not wrong to deduce from what Cripps told the Economic Planning Board and from the 1950 *Economic Survey* that the Treasury was settling into a policy based on holding inflation and wages down to safeguard the new sterling parity in a hostile world where Britain's trade was increasingly curtailed by Germany and Japan, and where import controls might soon be necessary to avert another devaluation. This inheritance and the vastly-swollen defence budget gave little scope for Gaitskell to develop a distinctive position once he became Chancellor in October in the dramatic way Wilson had attemped to do six months earlier, even though the Chancellor now had wider powers than in the late 1940s, in areas such as wages and investment.

His search was made much harder, firstly by the need for increased war expenditure which led to a particularly stringent

Budget in 1951 (at a time when the Korean War was known to be electorally extremely unpopular[7]), and secondly by the growth of a belief among the mandarins and CEPS experts that expenditure on the social services, especially health, was accelerating out of control. In a characteristically pessimistic minute, Morrison pointed out that 'there was a tendency, in education and the other social services, for expenditure to rise from year to year without full regard to the taxable capacity of the country, to a greater extent than had happened in recent years. What was desirable [a phrase that would have delighted Sir George May] must be judged in the light of what was practicable from the point of view of long-term national finance.' Cripps added, 'they were reaching the limit on expenditure which could be raised by taxation, and there was a serious danger that obligations might be entered into which the country could not meet in future years'.[8]

Gaitskell had to break away from this cast of mind if the government were to salvage anything of its claim to the voters of the 1950s to have instituted a social revolution. On the other side of what was becoming an ideological gap, Bevan was already arguing the merits of taxation as an instrument for redistribution of wealth without any limits dictated by past tradition. It was particularly damaging to Cripps that Bevan's supporters in the Party and the TUC raised the issue of poorly-paid public service workers, in May 1950 when Cripps had already considered actual *cuts* in their wages and Morrison was designating public sector pay restraint as a means 'to educate the workers, and particularly branch trade union officials, in their responsibilities, as partners, in the industry'.[9]

Had the admittedly uncoordinated left group chosen to make a public declaration in 1950 rather than resign a year later on an issue which took too much explanation, they could easily have pinned the label 'revisionist' on a Cabinet leadership much of whose outlook had come to foreshadow that of Conservative Ministers after 1951. But Bevan instead concentrated on winning a substantial victory on the Economic Policy Committee, in May 1950, by restoring the 1949 cuts in the housing programme and then hanging onto his gains despite the Cabinet's decision in July to increase defence spending to £3 400 million to meet Britain's enforced commitment to the Korean War, after the Chinese turned MacArthur and the American army back from the Yalu River. So serious for the balance of payments was the impact of Bevan's success that Attlee, Cripps and Gaitskell insisted in the Economic Policy Committee on docking the restored housing money from other budgets, and warned: 'We are entering upon a new phase in which the dangers of inflation will again become very great, and drastic steps will have to be taken'.[10]

What these were, like King Lear, they failed at first to specify, and the Bevanites did not take fright. As a direct result, the party civil war intensified: the more that payment for rearmament dominated the brokerage between the Treasury and spending departments during 1950–51, the wider grew the gap between the two factions, one defending public expenditure on welfare and services (and employment therein), the other adopting the Treasury line, if only to justify the expense of a war whose length and seriousness had been grossly underestimated. In the end, predictably, the argument came back to wages and what the Economic Policy Committee euphemistically referred to as 'social criticism' – that is, the middle class electoral revolt and the protests of those trying to live on fixed incomes. It is not surprising that, in these conditions, with a balance of payments crisis looming at the end of 1951, some of them looked longingly at Wilson's scheme for price control and talks with the USA about stabilising world commodity prices.

As Chancellor, Gaitskell had to assume that the new defence estimates, which rose to £4700 million for 1951–54 in December 1950 after Attlee's visit to Washington, could be found somehow even by charging for certain health services – at the price of the resignations of Bevan, Wilson and Foot.[11] But the impact of diverting such an enormous sum meant that the remaining advantage of devaluation was lost. Meanwhile, shortages of skilled labour accelerated, invisible earnings declined, and a new tendency developed for the public to spend savings faster than building them up. Attlee and his closest colleagues could have argued, as most of the civil servants did, that it was better for Britain to take more than its 'fair' share of the Korean War, in order to ensure that the United States did not waver in its European commitment, and that NATO should be seen to work properly in its first test. But their awareness of an international dimension which outweighed the domestic cost cut them off, historically, from the younger men of the centre and the left who wished to succeed them.

Theirs was not a position on which Gaitskell could found the sort of alternative which would last once the war had ended. Beyond the immediate budgetary and war finance problem, he and his Treasury team found themselves caught, for the first time, in the dilemma of choice between inflation and the possibility of unemployment, as

Britain's increasing uncompetitiveness and foreign penetration of her home markets became apparent. Import controls might have offered an escape from a choice between wages control which they could not endorse and reflation in which they simply dared not indulge – if GATT rules had not forbidden them. Price controls – Wilson's choice – however attractive in theory, implied arbitrary justice and excessive bureaucracy.[12] (Paradoxically, in its drive for efficiency, Wilson's industry policy seemed also likely to raise unemployment, for the same reasons as rationalisation had done in the late 1920s.)

The minutes of the Economic Policy Committee in July 1951 and the process of drafting the (never-published) 'Economic Survey' of 1952 confirmed that, for lack of an alternative, economic management would henceforth permit a strictly limited amount of inflation accompanied by ad hoc measures to control the wages of public employees.[13] Thus Labour's last year in power set the stage for the Conservative budgets of Butler after 1951, and hence the stop-go policies of the 1950s. This decision-by-default can be depicted as a Treasury victory, though it still depended, as Wilson had desired, on galvanising industry and the export trade somehow to contain the resulting balance of payments deficit. But it represented a confession that, however much ministers talked about prices, they could make very little impression on them, and virtually none on wages if they relied only on TUC co-operation.

Further cuts in public expenditure and fresh means to control wages appeared inevitable. Early drafts of the Survey resemble the pillage of a captured city. Ministers stood passively by; the enormity of what was happening may have debilitated them more than the eleven years in office.

Even if it had been published, it is unlikely that employers would have listened to the 1952 Survey's admonitions not to give into wage demands since the hot house conditions of rearmament, in the absence of controls on manpower and wages, fostered both a real growth in wages that they could not control, and the start in engineering and the motorcar industry of the 'annual round' and plant bargaining at the expense of national rates.[14] In these conditions, employers would pay simply to keep production lines going, and if they operated in the home market, pass the cost on in higher prices. Thus Beveridge's nightmare of inflation beyond responsible restraints began to take shape, though the actual *rate* was as yet very low by later standards.

If wages could not be controlled by agreement (as the TUC's September 1950 decision implied) nor by direct government controls, Gaitskell had to find another way, and his proposal for a National Wages Board, in November 1950, achieved a 'first' in the long search for a neutral arbiter with the charge of driving wages down. Thirty years of experimentation lay ahead, in which successive governments built auto-destructive monuments to the victory of optimism and the force of their own ingenuity.

There could now be no doubt that wages were rising faster than production or productivity warranted, and that unions' claims were being geared to the accelerating cost of living. Wage inflation and the development of the annual round caused as much anxiety at the Ministry of Labour as within the Treasury and led to a deep and unresolved dilemma, between MOL's wish to see wages 'stabilised' (largely by price restraint and other manoeuvres to keep the cost of living down, which of course, in turn alienated management) and their traditional support for collective bargaining. Like Trade colleagues in regard to industrial efficiency, Labour officials had to face up to the penalties for the state's interest in the labour market. Already by 1950, the Ministry's formerly benevolent image was becoming a little tarnished and in that year, with distinctly uneasy feelings among older officials, the department set up the ominously-styled Wages Division.[15]

As the TUC had warned the government, devaluation's effect on the cost of living had done more than anything to break the voluntary freeze on wages.[16] Recognition of why wages rose, however, did not mean that Isaacs and his officials at MOL would abandon their newly discovered plateau of agreement with the Treasury that there was a 'correct' level of wages, as one of them put it, 'so that there is not too much expendable money about, and that wages operate so far as they can to induce workers to go to the right jobs, and to work hard when there'.[17] As in other fields, Ministers and civil servants were beginning to discover that, once controls lapsed, economic management would have to cover a very much larger area than the authors of the 1944 package had imagined. As far as wages were concerned, this meant that the Treasury would have to devise means of taxation which were either too subtle or remote to arouse wage earners' antagonism, or sufficiently geared against middle-class and higher incomes to balance the odium; and thus a new and more complicated set of political judgments was introduced to the process of brokerage.

The Treasury tended to advise Ministers that restraint could be achieved by bearing on the public industry wage bill, combined with general exhortation and warning and reliance on the Ministry of Labour to educate both the workforce and their employers through the NJAC and EPB.[18] The gasworkers' wage claim in April 1950 exposed this assumption as unrealistic. The claim had roots in the confused state of wages among many different companies before nationalisation, and affected the electricity and other state industries. The Gas Board itself supported the union because it needed to hold skilled workers whom it believed had quite genuine grievances. The case not only put the pay policy at risk, with knock-on effects on railwaymen and miners, but brought government for the first time directly into conflict with its own (public) employees. Unfortunately, it was incompetently handled by the Minister of Fuel and Power, Philip Noel-Baker, who operated unconvincingly in a Cabinet divided between the economic need to hold wages down (and prevent a general scramble) and the political need not to offend the TUC (when there was still some hope that Congress might approve another year of the wages policy).

No machinery existed which could have kept Ministers from interfering, once this case reached Cabinet, and they soon found themselves trying to settle wages directly with a 'recalcitrant' Gas Council and enraged gas workers. Yet they shunned Robert Hall's advice to put out a public argument that there was a choice between higher wages and full employment. Perhaps they disliked his lucid appraisal: 'we want the full co-operation of the trades unions to the maximum practicable restraint (which I am afraid *they* will have to judge) without it appearing that the government has either changed its mind about the need for modernisation, or been defeated on the whole issue.'[19] Hall and the Economic Section wanted Ministers finally to decide what percentage of GNP should go to public spending and public investment as part of the conditions for full employment – but an occasion to develop what in Sweden became co-determination, and in Germany *mitbestimmung*, was allowed to lapse.

Norman Brook and others in Treasury, believing that the wages policy was already dead, wanted Cabinet simply to assert its authority over those they regarded as public servants. With a stronger Minister, such a tactic might have succeeded but the government failed to overawe the Gas Board. Since the Board then conceded claims retrospectively for all gasworkers, and the Electricity Board followed suit in September, they got the worst of all worlds. Yet they seem to have been satisfied with a bland declaration of principle, that 'government naturally assumed that the Boards would give full weight to Ministers' requests' – a charter for future *ad hoc* and ill-prepared intervention which Attlee very unwisely endorsed.[20] As Hall had had the effrontry to point out, government was in pawn to the willingness of public sector workers to bear in mind their 1944 responsibilities (which their unions had never fully acknowledged), in a peculiarly difficult case where the frustration of low-paid workers ran completely counter to what angry gas consumers (many of them on fixed incomes) expected to pay. The political choice between voters' and unions' requirements baffled the social democratic centre of the Labour Party.

Again, the young men had answers. In May 1950 Nicholas Kaldor introduced a proposal that amounted to planned permanent restraint of wages through Wages Boards. Yet, like the Wilson document, this fell short of coercion; the Party's research department took refuge in the idea of 'social responsibility', engendered by education and buttressed by price control, a chimera they were to pursue for many years to come.[21] Gaitskell then took on the whole problem, with greater logical vigour in one of his first major Treasury papers, which emphasised wage inflation and its effect on those with fixed incomes – mainly the retired, but including a large middle-class area of predominantly Conservative voters. In one of the clearest statements of his alternative viewpoint, on which later the social-democrats were to erect their philosophy, Gaitskell argued that there should be no more voluntary restraint but, instead, price stability through control of the aggregate of wages, in relation to the volume of production.[22] If this were adopted, and information supplied by MOL about the pattern of wages claims *before* they became effective, the Treasury could then adjust taxation to skim off any undesirable excess consumption. Collective bargaining might continue freely, but government would assess the result with a higher wisdom, and permit only gains which 'the nation' could afford. Gaitskell discussed three possible means of limiting wage claims; firstly utilising the TUC to bring all negotiations into line on a certain date, and thus prevent the 'comparability' argument from degenerating into 'leap-frogging'; secondly, an independent wages advisory service to publicise 'how the national interest would be affected'; and thirdly state control or a state wages agency. The latter he dismissed as too complex and politically unacceptable. He evidently preferred the second, looking like Hall towards some form of assessment made in conjunction with unions and management of what the nation could afford.

Gaitskell's proposal got no further before the 1951 election but it left an important legacy to Labour in opposition because it assumed that there was a middle ground between unrestrained wage bargaining and regular intervention by government each time the annual round occurred in public industries. It fitted well with MOL officials' distaste for any sort of coercion, and their fear that interference only undermined union leaders' authority over their own members. Moreover, it offered the basis of an *entente* with the TUC some of whose leaders had already shown themselves preoccupied with the problem of wages' drift.[23] But it would have required time to become an habitual process and for lack of time, as Max Nicholson pointed out, it remained 'hopelessly academic'. By September 1951 the TUC had got no further than a guarded, almost coded Report on Wages Prices and Profits, which referred merely to the need 'to be guided by reason and good sense' and not to take a lead from 'selfish and irresponsible people who could, wittingly or unwittingly, wreck our chances of overcoming the dangers which threaten us all'.[24]

By then, Labour was out of office. Within six months of the Churchill government all public talk of wage restraint had been set aside in the event for six years. But as a result of the discussion in Cabinet about what the full employment target actually should be (in order to submit proposals to the United Nation's Economic and Employment Commission) Gaitskell settled on a level of 3 per cent unemployment, finally conceding what the TUC had sought since 1944.[25] Gaitskell's own personal attempt to implement both the 1944 package and the principles of *Let Us Face the Future* continued in opposition where, as he complained to the Soviet leader, Georgi Malenkov in March 1956, Labour's historic perception had been altered – 'our trouble was that prosperity had made too many voters vote Tory – the situation could no longer be described in terms of a simple class struggle'.[26]

The third 'option of 1951' had quite other origins in various departmental responses to the immense economic, social and political problems of 1949–51. Senior civil servants replied to the initiatives of Gaitskell and Wilson without abandoning their underlying belief that the 1944 package needed only to be adapted to new circumstances, and without forgetting that they might have to serve a Conservative government in 1950 or 1951. But the more that the events described above concentrated power of economic management in the Treasury, the more Cabinet Office, Board of Trade and Labour mandarins, and departments within the Treasury itself, divided among themselves about ways and means and the aims which management was intended to fulfil.

No substantial redisposition of functions among existing departments and Ministers' responsibility occurred although the Treasury set up an Economic Organisation Working Group, chaired by Edwin Plowden to look at the machinery of government aspect. Most issues had, after all, been decided before 1945, and Plowden's hope to resurrect the logic of 'essential departmental functions' (which had lain unexamined since Haldane's 1918 Report) withered. (The only actual change was that the Ministry of Supply, revived briefly for the Korean War, disappeared, divided between Board of Trade and Ministry of Defence.[27]) Other departments saw no reason to challenge the statement that the Treasury was 'the dominant department in the economic field', as the Chancellor was supreme in the Ministerial Economic Policy Committee.[28] But in the course of its meetings, the Group also tried to find an organising principle on which future economic management, whose rules and standards were still in their infancy, could rest.

The problem as the Group saw it, was how government could best combine the widely-agreed aims of increasing real incomes for all, fair distribution, and the 'highest practicable' level of employment, while containing inflation and keeping the balance of payments in equilibrium. The 1944 White Paper no longer gave adequate guidance, now that they were entering the era of mass individual consumption; whereas full employment made it harder 'to have recourse to the classic use of the monetary weapon to limit inflation or to protect the external value of the currency . . . .' They concluded therefore that 'in its place, it is now necessary to exercise a far closer watch over the economy as a whole and particularly over investment policy and budgetary policy in order to secure the right balance'.[29] Considerable significance ought to be attached to the report's confirmation, for any doubters who might look to an incoming Tory government to restore the free market, that 'the maintenance of full employment will always require a degree of government intervention; and the regulation of investment and the balance of payments cannot be left to movements of the rate of interest and exchange rate, or credit policy alone, for a foreseeable period of time'.[30]

Contested though this statement was at a detailed level by Treasury OFD officials because it did not take sufficient account of Britain's position as centre of the sterling area, and by others for not specifying what should be the instruments of demand management, it became the established view of all those actually responsible for domestic policy under the Chancellor – principally the Home Economic Department of the Treasury. Against this, and evidently with a Conservative victory in mind, Norman Brook argued from the Cabinet Office that government simply could not control everything in this way; it could not even control its own public industries and their Chairmen.

Only indirectly did the Group address the consequential question (which had been buried in 1944): was it the duty of the state to aid industry, or industry the state? If the latter, then no problem of priorities between sterling and the balance of payments and the domestic economy arose; but if the state had a duty to industry, then the Treasury would indeed be divided, temperamentally if not functionally, with the OFD on one side urging external priorities, the Home Economic Division domestic interests on the other. The existence of this dilemma probably influenced the originators of the 'Robot' scheme (see page 199). But in what was becoming a habitual tendency to evade sharp conclusions, the EOWG failed to point up such a complex issue and contented itself with a final report in February 1951, 'The Relations of Government Departments and Industry' on the much narrower issue of how the Production Authority system (which tied particular industries to departments and had grown up almost haphazardly since 1942) should fit in with the better-defined sponsorship of whole sectors of industry.

It is doubtful if Ministers outside the Treasury were aware of the implications of the Group's recommendations. But the inner mandarins knew very well what was at stake: whereas EOWG wanted to retain the Production Authority system as a means for government to intervene down to the level of specific industries, Norman Brook and the OFD men wanted it abolished, lest government be sucked into a microeconomic world of competing firms where its conception of the overall national interest would be lost. 'Officials,' Brook minuted, 'are not paid to engage in the disinterested pursuit of knowledge of an industry.' Instead, it was for trade associations, properly reflecting the claims of their member firms, to address government.[31]

For twenty-four years this problem festered until civil servants again offered a Labour Cabinet a policy giving reasonable priority for manufacturing industry's needs. But in 1951, for all the EOWG's skilful argumentation, Production Authorities did not become an alternative to Development Councils, to enable government to stimulate efficiency at the microeconomic level in British industry.

Gaitskell's followers, even Wilson's, might have taken up their recommendations, for this was what government actually wished to do. But the Cabinet did not discuss the issue fully and practice continued as before.[32]

This argument revealed that there were two competing traditions among the mandarins. Brook, who had spoken from a general and pragmatic position, not as a committed advocate of the 'free market' but as a sceptic about the state's power actually to use such an instrument, accepted that a low level of intervention would continue, without radical alteration of the machinery. Unlike Bridges, whose statist temperament inclined him to think that machinery could always be made to work effectively if the willpower existed, Brook represented the liberal belief that pluralism at the centre offered a better chance of harmonious government than any logical division of functions on categories that Haldane would have recognised, because it allowed for multiple forms of friction, lateral bargaining and the free exercise of competitive self-interest. His position implied the long-term erosion of formal tripartism and would no doubt have been contested by the FBI or BEC if they had been able to interject their own arguments; although there is no evidence that their opinions were sought. On the other hand, it favoured the informal system of corporate bias; and the fact that Brook's vision rather than Bridges' underpinned the Churchill administration belies the remote, arcane appearance of the EOWG review whose outcome turned into ground rules for the mandarins that lasted until the next Treasury review in 1961.

As a direct consequence of this report, and the emphasis on macroeconomic objectives, the OFD mounted a counter-offensive later in the year. Although, chronologically, the story of Robot belongs to the Churchill years it can only be understood in the context of a sometimes passionate argument about the basic principles of how the economy was to be managed. OFD and the Bank of England had an obvious functional responsibility for the exchange rate, the sterling area, and the balance of payments, and had naturally sided with Brook against those who wanted to give greater priority to manufacturing industry and the rest of the domestic economy. Successive compromises since the 1947 convertibility crisis had left them (and in particular Leslie Rowan, head of OFD) deeply dissatisfied, because the more the practice of economic management evolved in the Treasury on Keynesian principles, the more it began to look as if the politicians were to be given subtle tools which they might misuse. They feared that, taking Keynes' name in vain, governments less wedded than Attlee's to balanced budgets might indulge in permanent deficit financing, or allow inflation to creep up, so that they might squeeze the capital market to fund government debt, which they would later repay in depreciated currency. They also doubted (as Keynes himself had) the efficacy of intervention in the industrial and labour markets designed to produce *structural* change. These were not idle fears to anyone who read the productions of either the Labour or Conservative Party research departments in the early 1950s. If governments took to living by borrowing, and allowed inflation even at a low 'controlled' level to become habitual, it seemed unlikely in the eyes of the 'guardians' of currency that they could be brought back to the path of commonsense.

To say this is not to depict a grand conspiracy, another 'bankers ramp'. The Labour government had been meticulous in keeping to the 1944 White Paper's understanding that budgets would always aim for a surplus in good years, and the authors of Robot evidently feared either the Bevanite left or an untried Conservative administration. But to bring forward a scheme intended once and for all to tie Cabinets down to sound financial principles ran an obvious risk of profound political conflict.

Even in Dalton's day, the Bank of England had begun to hint that it was time to end the era of cheap money. But Lord Catto the Governor had no means of appeal to the public beyond the Chancellor except in the velleities of speeches to like-minded City audiences. The Bank found Cripps both a more sympathetic listener and a more trustworthy figure; but after the shock of devaluation and the diagnosis that Marshall Aid was being wasted, it looks as though the Bank, in close conjunction with the OFD, began to take a gloomy view of welfare spending. It saw in the sort of state intervention proposed by Wilson, Bevan's victory on housing finance, and in the drift towards a 'permissible level' level of inflation proposed by the Economic Section, a foretaste of something well outside the acceptable limits of the 1944 package. The more the ideological divide opened up between Gaitskell and the Bevanites, and the more the Conservative Party committed itself to abolition of controls and concern for the consumer, the further what had been regarded as equilibrium appeared to recede. The confluence of this 'City view' and that of the OFD began to be reflected in the picture of British policy both gave out privately in Washington to like-minded officials in the Federal Reserve Board and the US Treasury and may in turn have influenced American officials in the European Recovery Administration.

After the defeat implied by devaluation, they retreated into a distinctly defensive view of the old tripartite division of the world, in which sterling would provide the main buffer between the dollar zone and non-dollar countries. (This view appeared clearly in paragraph 5 of the UK's OEEC submission in December 1949; which argued that because a world-wide multilateral trading system (as proposed by GATT) was out of the question unless sterling was strong, Britain had to begin a long haul, designed permanently to strengthen the reserves, with the ultimate aim of full convertibility and a new fixed parity with the dollar.) The Federal Reserve and most American businessmen of course approved. To achieve this aim, however, without American support (which the Korean War had just shown would not be forthcoming) meant that the government would have either to lower price levels, which was impossible given its public commitment not to deflate, or to reduce public spending, stabilise wages and increase productivity. So long as these remained prime aims of Cripps' and Gaitskell's policy in 1949–51, the Bank–OFD grouping restrained itself; but it waited on the first opening to assault the high cost of defence, wages, and the welfare state.

For justification, it cited evidence that devaluation had failed to stimulate British exporters to penetrate dollar markets. Insofar as manufacturers relied instead on sterling markets to cover their increased wages bill, the dollar gap actually worsened in 1949–50. But that argument did not solve the problem of the sterling balances and their threat to Britain's dollar reserves should any sterling creditor wish to withdraw large sums (as India and Egypt intended to do, for their own domestic investment). After four years of unremitting effort to create a beneficial trading pattern with sterling countries, the OFD and Bank officials had had to admit that sterling balance holders would never accept cancellation of the debts nor were they likely to spend enough on British goods to make withdrawals tolerable. To allow the pound to become convertible, with so much debt outstanding, could, in the technical sense, bankrupt Britain overnight.[33] Yet Britain could not (as the USA had hoped in 1945) simply repudiate the debts, without destroying the whole political fabric of the Commonwealth. At its simplest, India's war effort could not just be written off.

That repudiation was even discussed in the Economic Policy Committee shows how seriously the problem weighed on Ministers in the aftermath of devaluation.[34] The total sterling debt amounted in 1950 to $3 267 million, and despite a game attempt to play the 'defence against world communism' card, Ministers accepted that, here too, the USA would not be generous, even though in mid-1950 they seemed prepared to accept substantial American penetration of Commonwealth markets, as a quid pro quo for any assistance.[35]

Not surprisingly, Gaitskell and Cripps felt themselves sometimes pressed too hard by their officials. Compared with the short-term problem of financing the Korean War, and keeping some sort of balance between domestic spending and Defence departments, the sterling balances represented a more distant, though even more unpleasant form of nemesis, and it is hardly surprising that, for home political reasons, Cripps and Gaitskell resisted their officials' insistent demands to raise the bank rate and increase the reserves while diminishing public and private spending. In 1951 Dalton recorded that his colleagues were finding City opinion distinctly hostile.[36] But after attempts at a joint Anglo-American stabilisation of world commodity prices had failed in June 1951, Britain faced an import bill of horrifying proportions, without any basis for agreement on an incomes policy or dividend control to make a new austerity package acceptable; indeed without agreement even on Gaitskell's conclusion that the balance of payments problem should override all others.

At this point, and at the height of the import boom tired Labour Ministers took the decision to go to the country and lost the election. In the event, towards the end of 1951 the balance of payments position improved slightly, commodity prices fell, once the worst of the Korean War passed, and as the United States gave some support to sterling to prevent a further devaluation. But US requirements that in return the new Conservative government should institute tougher fiscal and monetary reforms emphasised how much the climate had changed. Wind and tide together made the winter of 1951–52 an almost irresistible temptation for the 'guardians', including older Treasury men like Sir Wilfred Eady, finally to put government under decent restraint.

At first Butler, the new Chancellor, resisted and allowed the bank rate to rise only from 2 per cent to 2.5 per cent in November. Peter Thorneycroft at BOT opposed all but minor cuts in imports. Both points of view fitted with the new government's narrow majority and its fear of losing new-found and volatile public support. The Cabinet found the balance of payments deficit horrifying, but hoped for relief from substantial cuts in defence (Churchill put forward economies of

£250 million in January 1952) and prepared to tell the NATO Conference, at its meeting in Lisbon a month later, that Britain could not meet its targets. But inexperienced as they were, they could not deflect the guardians' pincer movement, one arm bearing proposals for the sterling area, the other for the balance of payments.

Although its intellectual origins go back at least to 1947, Robot reached print in the memorandum 'The Sterling Area', written by Sir Richard (Otto) Clarke in preparation for the Commonwealth Finance Ministers' Conference early in 1952. So serious was the crisis, he argued, that the sterling area system was threatened, and Britain's capacity to export and compete against the USA might therefore be eroded. Since Britain could neither live up to her responsibility as centre of the sterling area, nor opt out, she was likely to continue to borrow short-term from balance holders and remain perpetually vulnerable to devaluation any time there was a downturn in the world economy.[37]

This mordant diagnosis set off a vigorous argument inside the Treasury. 'Traditionalists' like Bridges joined by Gilbert and Ince (MOL) wanted to try the 1948 solution again: tripartite talks, leading to an agreed package of wages and prices restraint and cuts in imports, whether in dollars or sterling. The 'new radicals' of OFD and the Bank, led by Rowan, Sir George Bolton and Otto Clarke (hence the acronym Robot) with support from Sir Frank Lee at Trade, hesitated to put such an austere and politically intolerable proposal to a new Cabinet. Butler who of course took part in the discussions, went so far as to consult Gaitskell as an 'old friend', only to discover that, though the ex-Chancellor agreed with the diagnosis, he would give no cross-party support.[38]

Panaceas gave no relief: the November manoeuvres did not stem the drain on the reserves; Churchill got no help from Washington in December, and the Commonwealth Finance Ministers, having extracted assurances from Butler that the sterling area would continue, then denied him his main requirement of a joint agreement to combat inflation collectively and restrict imports all round. By the middle of January 1952, circumstances had brought the Cabinet sharply up against a choice for which they had been almost unprepared, and which at once divided it on ideological as well as practical grounds. It is not surprising that they gave Parliament a seven-week Christmas recess.

In seeking to sever, with one cut, the Gordian knot of sterling balances, the balance of payments, home-grown wage inflation and, excessive public spending, the authors of Robot conceived of letting the pound float, making it convertible to non-sterling balance holders but blocking the balances themselves; and renouncing both the European Payments Union *and* the commitment to full employment as the cardinal principle of economic management. The scheme only slowly took on such daring dimensions but, from the start, they doubted if Ministers would have the nerve to see it through.[39] Whether they hoped to finesse them, in ignorance, is unclear. As yet few others even in the Treasury knew what was being discussed, but Robert Hall and Plowden, while admitting the extent of the crisis, demurred early in January at such drastic action. Cameron Cobbold, who had succeeded Catto as Governor of the Bank in 1949, supported the idea of a package designed to sort out the sterling area, strengthen the reserves, and curb inflation – all with eventual convertibility in mind – though he did not necessarily follow his own advisor, George Bolton, all the Robot way.[40]

Meanwhile, before Butler introduced the scheme, a dispute broke out in Cabinet on 14 January over the extent to which import cuts and reductions in food rations would be necessary to stem the drain on the reserves. Butler's demands seemed unnecessarily high and politically almost intolerable, reducing as they did the standard of basic nutrition, and consequently endangering industrial production. Ten days later, he made some concessions but held to his demand for 'disciplinary action', that is, cuts in consumption to 'bring home the crisis to the public'. If not, 'foreign confidence in the pound' would collapse.[41] Butler's later reputation for Florentine diplomacy suggests that his language was designed to soften up his colleagues for Robot, as well as to introduce further cuts in defence – which of course the Chiefs of Staff would contest. As if to foreclose debate, he brought the Budget date forward to 4 March.

On 7 February, backed by the Bank and the majority of Treasury officials, he put Robot to the Cabinet, but only in veiled form. However he had by then accepted Cobbold's argument that the sterling area no longer served Britain's interests, as against Thorneycroft's contention that it still held considerable trade advantages. Bridges was right to suspect that the Chancellor's hint spelled the end of cheap money and the start of tougher credit control – and hence rising unemployment.[42] Cabinet policy in other areas confirms this more aggressive note. By now the Robot group had a slogan – to take the strain off the reserves and put it on the exchange rate – whose attraction disguised the fact that they proposed to lock Britain's creditors in a much narrower prison than had been envisaged in 1944, and to accord them 'foreigner' treatment if they tried to break out.

Robot can, of course, be seen as an assertion of Britain's reasonable self-interest after playing fair for too long, a self-interest no more objectionable than the American position in 1945–46, and certainly not something which can be judged summarily as 'right' or 'wrong'. Its authors, by their own admission, overstated the case to convince the waverers. Butler seems to have accepted their argument in its entirety, and to have imagined that, if the pound fell after being floated, the Cabinet would have to concede his austerity measures.[43] Rowan, the most obviously political of the three Robotics, may have seen the scheme as a means to strengthen the Chancellor against his softer colleagues' too-cosy acceptance of the Labour Government's social welfare legacy.

But other departments winced at the likely repercussions on the Commonwealth, Britain's foreign policy, and her defence contribution to NATO. The Treasury attempted to meet their objections by asserting in dramatic terms that 'the economy is not working in a manner which enables us to pay our way or to maintain our external objectives. Without major changes, these objectives, *which are fundamental to our existence as a Great Power* [my italics], will be swept away in major crisis . . . The size of the problem is so great, and the consequences for the future so devastating to the national life, that the whole of the national resources must be thrown into it.'[44] At times, this language so bordered on fantasy ('we have to drive the Americans and the Germans out of the world markets'), that it is hard to know how far it was meant to be taken at its face value. Whether Robot would, in fact, strengthen the reserves, remained a matter of faith to which, by the end of February, and under Rowan's evangelistic guidance the whole Treasury had largely committed itself.

Confronted by such a Manichean view of the world, the chief sceptic, Robert Hall, Director of the Economic Section, moved rapidly into opposition on the grounds that Robot would disrupt trade, destroy the sterling area and the future of demand management, and cause widespread public unrest. Heightening the tension, he argued that it would commit the government to political suicide by forcing it back to the equivalent of automatic deflation. When Churchill met a selected group of senior Ministers on 20 February before Robot had even reached Cabinet, the lines of battle had been set out and the post-war settlement put at risk. Relying on Butler's conversion, the Robot team played for the Prime Minister's support. In returning to the Gold Standard in 1925, Churchill had confessed his inability as Chancellor to judge and had turned to others for advice. Now, faced with an even more difficult choice, he let Butler argue the case to an audience that included Oliver Lyttleton, champion for the City, Lord Swinton, Henry Crookshank and Lord Woolton, all of whom approved, and Lord Cherwell who did not. The latter played for time by asking for another meeting after the weekend, with detailed papers.[45] Reliant as ever on 'the Prof's' advice, and politically more sensitive than he was economically astute, Churchill accepted the delay.

Opposition now coalesced around Hall, at official level, and Cherwell among the politicians.[46] Arthur Salter, Treasury Minister of Economic Affairs, declared himself against, because of the effect on Dominions and NATO, and because the possibility of 'semi-starvation' at home would be exploited by militant unions on one hand and the Soviet Union on the other. Appalled at these developments, Bridges tried to contain the damage, while siding with the Robotics. The next meeting of Ministers, on 22 February, brought together the same group as before, together with the Chief Whip, James Stuart, and the Home Secretary, Maxwell Fyfe, a veteran party manager. Once again, Cherwell stood alone, though Woolton conceded that they would have to ask the advice of Eden, the Foreign Secretary. To allow for that, the Budget was postponed for a week, until 11 March.

But Eden was already in Lisbon for the NATO meeting. Officially to apprise him that the senior Ministers were going ahead went Eric Berthoud; unofficially, to explain the dissidents' views, went Plowden carrying the views of Hall and Salter that Robot would put half a million men out of work. 'The situation would be so unpleasant that Ministers would face seriously now what they have so far failed completely to face. I doubt if they themselves understand this point as yet'.[47] According to one account, Eden felt overborne by the weight of numbers, and took refuge in the suggestion of another election.[48] Plowden thought this absurd, and persuaded Eden to ask for the whole thing to be deferred till his return.

Eden's doubt, and Cherwell's conviction, swung the political balance: soon Ted Leathers and Lord Swinton joined the opposition while instead of being overborne by Treasury officials, Hall and Plowden appealed direct to Butler, on whom they made sufficient impression for him to ask them for an alternative proposal. What that would be probably did not greatly matter: Butler's request undercut the Robotics' assertion that there *was* no alternative.

The Cabinet met, in great secrecy, on 28/29 February,[49] and Butler, rather diffidently now, put the Robot case, followed (after Cherwell's rejoinder), by the Hall–Plowden alternative which amounted to a harsh domestic package raising Bank rate to 4 per cent but intended not to prejudice full employment. Malcolm MacDonald, Colonial Secretary, argued the disastrous impact of Robot on Commonwealth opinion. By the end too many doubts had been voiced: Maxwell Fyfe even hazarded a figure of ten million unemployed! Butler defended Robot ably enough, but without total conviction, waiting perhaps for the *force majeure* of a collapse of the reserves later on to force his colleagues into sense. Churchill summed up: if they were not united, it was better not to try Robot at all.

Almost by default, the Cabinet fell back on the alternative. Bank rate would rise to 4 per cent, accompanied by heavy cuts in defence, capital investment, and imports (£200 million) and new restrictions on trade. Ministers now argued their departmental briefs, and Butler was able to deal with them seriatim. Defence suffered least – losing a mere £40 million, rather than Churchill's original £250 million; food subsidies were cut by 40 per cent and cheap money died after a lifetime of exactly twenty years. Any hope that Butler had of making the economies hurt all round vanished as Tory landmarks, defence, industry and trade resisted the tide and consumption, chiefly working class basic expenditure, suffered most.

Robot remained, in theory, open for discussion and that battle took some months to die away. OFD and the Bank gained their victory over the level of Bank rate, but knew that they had lost the real campaign to put a permanent constraint on the spendthrift politicians. They had not even wrested back from them power to fix Bank rate in future, which became a source of dissension for years to come. Wiser than Rowan, Cobbold did not complain. He had done what he saw as his duty, as Govenor and remained sensitive to the 1944 emphasis on full employment. But Rowan, convinced of his own rectitude and the need to enlist market forces to curb 'this complacent interregnum', continued to batter the Chancellor with memoranda, only to be countered by Cherwell with the one argument bound to catch Churchill's ear, 'it is no good harking back to Victorian times . . . the people will not accept mass unemployment'.[50] After Robot's failure the guardians of the temple would have to adopt a different strategy, at least for another twenty-odd years. But though Britain's balance of payments position improved, and the reserves soon built up, they had inflicted a lasting wound on the post-war settlement.

If the Labour government had been able to agree on a permanent sequel to Cripps' second stage, it might have been possible to hold the three sectors of the City, industry and trade unions together in the skein of reciprocal responsibility woven in 1944. Instead, under the stresses of the Korean War and their own members' dissent, they sprang apart, each no longer sure of the rewards for service but increasingly aware that the future need not be bound by austerity and self-restraint. In short, they had had enough.

Of the three, the trade union movement showed both the most obvious dissent and the greatest loyalty. Months before repudiating wages restraint in September 1950, the TUC had left government in no doubt about the objections of many thousands of union members, and their inability to go on trying to hold the line.[51] Productivity rose by 5 per cent in 1950 (despite productivity campaign evidence suggesting that the public had become satiated with exhortation) which made it harder for the 'big six' to advocate restraint with any real conviction. Though the TUC's Economic Committee readily admitted that they 'had a higher responsibility than that of merely reflecting public opinion', they could not completely ignore the radical demands of the shop floor, nor those identified with the Communist Party, such as the ETU's call for the control of profits.[52] They had criticised the budgets of 1949 and 1950 and grew disturbed at the quarrels between Gaitskell and the Bevanites; and seem to have been puzzled by Wilson's policies, since the abolition of controls appeared to destroy the government's capacity to plan fair shares and consumption in the future.

Tewson and his deputy, George Woodcock, did what they could to help and planned the TUC's special Conference in February 1950 so as to put the best face on the 1949 devaluation; as Woodcock wrote, 'the TUC's policy about wages is firmly based upon the need to re-establish confidence in sterling and to achieve monetary stability at home and abroad during the remainder of the period required by Britain to establish its industries and trade on a firm and self-supporting basis'.[53] Tewson went so far as to tell the EPB that it was better for the economy to cut food imports rather than raw materials, and earned for the TUC the tribute 'very responsible' in the 1950 *Economic Survey*. In return, the government's replacement of Order 1305 by Order 1376 (which provided for legally binding arbitration, but removed the restraint on official strikes), offered a sweetener for unions' grievances.

Very few in the central organisations of industry or the City at this stage wanted to trade wage restraint for full employment; but as the consequences of devaluation and the Korean War eroded employers' profits, their representatives on the EPB began to let off increasingly sharp warnings about the future of one without the other. According to the FBI's spokesman, Sir George Cunningham, public not private industry should take the strain. By mid-1950 the government's long honeymoon with management had ended. Although the TUC's rejection of wage restraint provided a public signal to withdraw from the tripartite front, the FBI had already been trying for six months to push up prices in order to sustain profits and investment, with Board of Trade support.

The FBI got on less well with Gaitskell than with Cripps and under his Chancellorship declared openly that the Production Authority system had become irksome. As Sir Hartley Shawcross, President of the Board of Trade after Wilson's resignation, developed plans for a Monopolies Commission, and a new location of industry policy to replace physical controls, the FBI embarked on a sustained defence of restrictive practices, resale price maintenance, managerial autonomy, and industrial priority for investment which differed only in presentation from the self-regulatory philosophy of Allan Smith and Lord Weir in the late 1930s.[54] Equating the national interest with the interests of industry conflicted with the Wilson–Mayhew attempt to make Labour a 'consumers' party' and with BOT–Treasury hopes to make industry efficient enough to fulfil the state's need for exports and provide a firm base for full employment.

On the three issues of restrictive practices, industrial location, and investment incentives, the FBI's defence probably affected collaboration with government much more than their opposition to Wilson's schemes for regulating the private sector, or their support for the steel companies' and Tate and Lyle's resistance to nationalisation because it cut at the ten-year-old tripartite accord, not just at Labour's 1945 programme. (The steel takeover had, after all, been delayed by Attlee in 1947, partly to win FBI support.) The will to co-operate had weakened; more and more, industrialists looked to the Conservative opposition.[55] The FBI's document *A Policy for Solvency* (1951) reflected the results of their direct contacts, and of the new economic liberalism surging up among individual firms and in the service industries.

The BEC had also swung into opposition, concluding after a number of wage adjudications such as the AEU's large claim in 1949, that government had betrayed its side of the 1944 contract. Subsequent gloomy protests to Gaitskell about inflation and labour shortages, and the impact of rearmament on exports, were intended quite clearly to substantiate an argument that they, not the government, should act to control wages. The BEC also argued that Britain's contribution to the Korean War was beyond the nation's capacity or real interests. Although that did not signify outright hostility to the Labour government, the language of criticism of wage inflation, state expenditure, and the profligacy of public industries which boiled up from among Council members made the relationship antagonistic.

The Capital Issues Committee's 1950 Report (discussed on page 165), indicated that the City and its markets had also broken with the 1944 contract, insofar as continuation of controls and restraint of market mechanisms was concerned. At the centre of government, in mid-1951, civil servants were considering putting to Ministers a modification of the planning and Production Authority system intended also to emasculate the surviving Development Councils, in order to meet City and FBI/BEC complaints; they differed among themselves chiefly over the extent of decontrol, with Norman Brook as ever inclined much more than Bridges to favour swingeing amendments.

The intensity of tripartite collaboration diminished sharply after 1949 and reached its nadir in 1951–52, just at the time that the 'guardians' Robot strategy emerged. After ten years in which Britain came very close to instituting the corporate state, this conjuncture cannot be seen as accidental. Rather, it represented a revolt by the memberships of each of the parties to the 1944 political contract, against the accumulation and perpetuation in peacetime of restraints and controls. The transition might not have gone so far, given the natural tendencies of the FBI, the BEC and the TUC, if it had not been for the Korean War; but it is unlikely that government could have suppressed it much longer in the changing economic circumstances of the early 1950s.

Rearmament for the Korean War and the reimposition of austerity meant that TUC members would suffer individually more than the shareholders or managers, so that the more loyal the TUC tried to be to the Labour government, the more unions and workers ran out of control,[56] and the more stimulus was given to shop steward leaderships in industries such as car production, dock-work, shipbuilding and aircraft; with consequences only realised in the later 1950s and '60s. If individuals had to work harder, they wished also to spend their earnings and not to save – indeed, they wanted to use up existing savings.[57] Yet only in the expanding industries, notably consumer goods, were profits high enough to meet such wage expectations. These were to be the growth industries of the 1950s, able to pass on high wages, in more or less permanent competition for scarce skilled workers. They gave birth to, and some deliberately propagated plant bargaining (already stimulated by the wages freeze in 1948–50, together with increased overtime and other distortions of the labour market) and the 'annual round', and went in at the same time for labour hoarding to safeguard themselves in times of future peak demand – a complex process which served to emphasise the money wage as the key index of trade union success.

In less fortunate industries, unions had to claim maintenance of existing differentials if their members' places in the old pecking order were to be held. Endemic tendencies to concentrate on wages, in relation to the cost of living and the earnings of other comparable groups, combined with these new phenomena to produce what employers and politicians of all three parties came to see as a dynamic process capable of quite different economic effects from the mild wage-inflation of the late 1940s. (Unit wage costs rose from 100 in 1948 to 103 in 1950, 114 in 1951.) But because of archaic accounting practices based on historic costs, the real effects on profits and companies' cash flow remained largely hidden for a crucial period down to the late 1950s.[58] Equally, because restrictive practices, poor management practices, and low utilisation of technology continued almost unchecked, the elasticity and competitiveness sought by the Board of Trade, which could have met high wages and still delivered high profits (as in Germany in the 1950s and '60s) remained obstinately out of sight. If the 'consumer society' existed in embryo, even before the Conservatives came to power in 1951, so did the vicious spiral of relative decline continue, as it had before.

So vast a development cannot simply be blamed on the Labour Government. But these were not inevitable consequences of the post-war settlement and it is fair to point out that Labour's choices after 1947, such as entry into the Korean War, or its selection of 3 per cent as the maximum level of tolerable unemployment, or its decisions to take serious account of the rise of middle-class hostility after the 1950 election,[59] gravely limited their own or their successors' capacity to manage the economy so as to achieve the sort of equilibrium demanded by the 1944 package. For lack of that equilibrium, the self-interest of the institutions and their members superceded their original perception of the national interest and led them to evolve new ones more in conflict with each other.

Once this process had begun, propaganda or political education alone could not hold them back any more than the government could restrain the striking gas and electricity workers or dock workers resisting the 1950 dock labour scheme.[60] The 1949 Productivity Campaign had over-extended the apparatus of propaganda, without increasing its returns. Government itself at times ceased to treat tripartism as a means of keeping political equilibrium in industry. During the 1950–51 rash of strikes (which some Cabinet Ministers took to be Communist-inspired and subversive, to the point where Attlee seriously considered penal legislation (see page 177)) the senior Ministers refused to discuss aspects of their emergency preparations to counter subversion with the TUC but they did consult chairmen of public industries, who presumably passed on the gist to their colleagues in the FBI and the BEC.[61] The fact that some TUC leaders agreed with what was proposed does not minimise the conflict between Labour leaders' professions about bolstering union leaders' authority and their reluctance to bargain for the TUC's support. The Party took a similar line: the Research Department's 1951 plans for economic recovery did not depend in the old way on tripartite collaboration. Meanwhile, in the Conservative Party, a more thorough-going revulsion found expression in almost nineteenth-century language about the supremacy of Parliament particularly among more traditionalist members of the incoming administration, like Sir David Maxwell Fyfe, the new Home Secretary.

Labour lost in 1951, yet its popular vote increased. The Conservatives won because the Liberal vote, swollen in 1950 by many middle-class electors who had voted Labour in 1945, collapsed, making them the principal and predictable beneficiaries. Labour had failed to provide a coherent, publicly appealing sequel to its 1945 programme and did not remedy this until after two years in opposition, with the drafting of a programme which was in turn overtaken by events before the 1955 election. Neither Gaitskell nor the Bevanites were wrong (in 1950–51) to play for a hypothetical election to be held in 1953–54 and there is no intrinsic reason why Attlee's Cabinet should not have survived the winter of 1951–52, as well as, or better than Churchill's did, subsequently to benefit from improvements in Britain's international trading position. If Attlee had waited till the middle of 1952, Labour would (on Gallup poll figures taken then) have won.

It would be unwise to look to the centrifugal tendencies of any of the three governing institutions studied here to explain Attlee's decision to dissolve, or the result. Only one of them carried any mass electoral weight and it was the TUC which did most to keep alive the spirit of tripartite collaboration partly for reasons of loyalty to 'its' government, partly because it had a much more strongly-held and deeper long-term interest in it than either of the central employers' associations. In any case, it was not until the tenor of press comment about wage inflation and unofficial strikes began the process which was to make trade unions actively unpopular, that the FBI, the BEC and the City shrewdly joined it to their existing complaints about controls, austerity, and the holding down of the public's desire for immediate consumption gratification; they did not create public demand, but only tried to manipulate it.

The younger ministers were probably right in their strategy: Gaitskell's conclusion (in 1956) 'their prosperity had made too many workers vote Tory' can be read earlier in his and Wilson's various attempts to harness the electorate's desire for prosperity without abandoning the party's *raison d'être*. After 1949–50, the Attlee–Cripps–Morrison triumvirate's vision of how the 1944 package could be given a distinctly Labour tinge while remaining faithful to the doctrine of overall equilibrium and balanced budgets looked out of place. The problem (which was inevitable given the federal nature of the party) came when their successors, not all of whom shared the 1944 assumptions, asked for what ends, beyond full employment, should they manage the economy? If the answer differed radically from post-war practice, it had to be found in the party's ideology, because the sort of management designed to meet the minimum requirements of unions, industrialists and bankers could not lead to redistribution of wealth to any one group but only a larger share of a larger cake.

To point out that corporate bias leads to profoundly conservative arrangements only demonstrates that party radicalism – of the right as well as the left – tends to be detrimental to tripartite arrangements and vice versa. What is notable about the initiatives of both Wilson and

Gaitskell, and the whole period 1949–55, is that mainstream Labour Party thinking continued to entrench the ideas of interdependence and collaboration.[62] The possibility that competition might erupt throughout the political system after twenty years abeyance since the formation of the National Government in 1931, threatening at times primary, class-based conflict, was restrained for another fifteen years first by Conservative governments and then by Labour until the mid-1960s.

The Attlee government only partially fulfilled the 1944 White Paper's aims. The sterling area as the 1944 authors conceived it and the pound's level of $4.03 could not have been held beyond 1949 by a Britain which was a full member of GATT and NATO. The fundamental restructuring of manufacturing industry which they envisaged was aborted by a combination of management and labour (and financial institutions which shrugged off their shareholders' responsibility for enforcing it) aided and abetted by a government seeking reconstruction without political disharmony. In this sense, Henry Morgenthau, Vinson and the other Washington critics who faced Keynes in 1945–46 were only too prescient. But they demanded something the British electorate would not permit, which the Attlee government believed democratic rule could not have enforced. By any standard, Labour in power gave social reforms worthy of popular sacrifices, and repaired the lost chance of 1918 with fairness and social justice, as the 1944 White Paper required. It abandoned planning (which was never part of the package), gave inadequate terms of reference to the public industries (which were) and staffed them mostly with underpaid and often incompetent administrators. It balanced its budgets and kept public borrowing low, as required; it failed to legislate adequately for monopolies and restrictive practices but it went as far as it could towards liberalising trade. It set a target for full employment far higher than any but Beveridge and the TUC had dreamed was possible; it suppressed consequent public demand with the result that incoming Conservatives were able to claim credit for the prosperity that actually arose from the great gains in productivity between 1947 and 1950.

Labour ministers absorbed the ideas of 1944 and established them as part of the Labour Party's values (which a Conservative government might not have done). But it went beyond, as a government must: in sustaining Britain's role as a great power, it attempted to maintain economic growth and living standards at home while governing a third of Germany, sharing with the United States an interest in Europe, the

Middle East and South-East Asia, and in the foundation of NATO, and in undertaking a level of rearmament in 1951 with which neither the machine tools industry nor the exporting industries' earnings could cope. As it had inherited them,[63] so it left a legacy of world-wide commitments which the nation, on any rational commercial calculation, could not afford and from which its immediate competitors did not suffer – and which indeed its successors at once tried to shuffle off.[64] The limits of the 1944 accord were, quite simply, that it was grounded in a rationality whose landmarks had, by 1951, ceased to exist.

7 Parties and Institutions 1951–56

Coming after a decade of privation, and before another decade of unease about whether prosperity could last, the five dulcet years of what one historian calls 'Churchill's Indian Summer' permitted an extraordinary set of real gains in economic and social life by almost every individual and group in Britain. Part of this can be credited to the government's managerial skills, at home and abroad; yet these might hardly have existed had it not been for the metamorphosis which occurred in Opposition. The electorate had not trusted the Tory Party in 1945 – nor in 1950. That it did so in 1951 was partly fortuitous, partly a result of a slow-growing transformation begun at the centre, quite deliberately, by younger men than Churchill, who feared that otherwise their party would be relegated, perhaps permanently, like the old right in France, Belgium and Scandinavia.

During the 1945 election, Conservative Party organisation had failed on almost all counts: its main economic committee had not even produced the election document in time. The bland tone of Central Office statements had been at odds with Churchill's combative style, which was in turn the natural consequence of over-reliance on his aggressive advisers, Lord Beaverbrook, Brendan Bracken and Lord Cherwell. A year was required simply to recover before Churchill gave Lord Woolton, the new party Chairman, and R. A. Butler, Chairman of the Research Department, a mandate for reform. Shortly after, in a speech to the National Union, Butler set out some of the principles of what he would do, but it was some time before he could complete the preliminary changes in organisation which gave him a team capable of the job.[1] Even after Harry Hopkinson and Ralph Assheton had started to reform the parliamentary party structure, and Butler had control of the Advisory Committee on Policy and Political Education as well as the Research Department, Central Office lagged behind, more content to represent opinion in the party as a whole rather than to mould it to cope with post-war demands.

While Woolton concentrated on fund-raising, Butler turned to basic policy formulation. Both assumed that they would be several years in opposition and that general philosophy would for some time matter more than detailed policy. Meanwhile, preoccupied with global strategy and defence, Churchill showed little interest and only reluctantly agreed that Butler should start on the questions of labour, industry and taxation.[2] From the Industrial Policy Committee that Butler then set up, stocked with young men of Keynesian persuasion who had been in, or were touched by, 'middle opinion' in the 1930s like Harold Macmillan, Oliver Stanley and Derick Heathcoat Amory, as well as those experienced in finance and industry like Maxwell Fyfe and Oliver Lyttleton, came the *Industrial Charter* which Butler intended to be a new 'Tamworth Manifesto' marking a definitive breach with the party of Neville Chamberlain.

The authors concerned themselves with the politics of industry, labour and finance, rather than industrial policy as that had been understood by the post-war Board of Trade, but they did go to some pains to take evidence from businessmen working in the regions as well as from the FBI or small business spokesmen; and they drafted their document with care for the sensibilities of an unenlightened 1922 Committee, so that the *Industrial Charter* successfully bridged the gap between advocates of a free market and still-influential Tory corporatists like Leo Amery. In its insistence on full employment as the basis for future policy, it reflected the contractual element in the 1944 White Paper, but it put rather less emphasis on the state's role – at least where intervention might threaten potentially favourable interest groups. It tiptoed, for example, around the issue of restraining monopolies and reforming restrictive practices.[3]

The Charter accepted that public ownership of transport and energy would remain, albeit with some decentralising, and that 'planning' in the tripartite sense would continue. In Butler's retrospect, it gave the public 'the assurance that modern Conservatism would maintain strong guidance over the operation of the economy in the interests of efficiency, full employment, and security; to provide a philosophical alternative to socialism, in stressing the importance of the individual in the mixed economy; and thirdly a charter to the worker offering him employment assurances, incentives, and individual status'.[4] This third element was contained in an annexe called *The Workers Charter* which promised the trade union movement that Conservatives would proceed in industrial relations, not by legislation but by consultation (using tripartite instruments such as NJAC), and which even gave a hint of measures to be taken against bad management.

All this would have been acceptable to the 120 industrialists in 1942 and it probably restored credibility to the party in TUC eyes, not least because it showed that there would be no attempt (as was happening in France and Italy) to set up Conservative unions, or even a Conservative TUC.[5] In launching it on the Party, Butler had Eden the shadow Foreign Secretary and Churchill's heir-apparent on his side. But in spite of their attempts to win over Churchill himself, before publication in May 1947, he sat on the fence, and it remained 'unofficial' until the annual Conference, when a major struggle took place between the new wave and the old right. In the event (as Topping, the principal Agent had foretold) 'Waldron Smithers and Co.' went down in defeat, while Churchill and the hesitant majority of the centre-right wisely swung with the wind from the constituencies.

Butler's group consolidated their success with other documents, less dramatic and more attuned to particular interests such as the farmers' lobby (the *Agricultural Charter*), and women (*A True Balance*). Their cumulative effect served to display the party as a broad-based potential government, inspired by fresh thinking appropriate to the post-war world, grounded in the settlement of 1944–45. There would be no revanchism. Meanwhile, reforms of the apparatus continued, insofar as Churchill allowed them. A Shadow Cabinet grew up, under the title of 'Committee of Chairmen' but the leader remained absent, unwilling to prejudice his power by engaging in disputation. Other committees developed institutional links with the FBI and the BEC and worked hard to fight nationalisation of iron and steel and road transport. The Secretariat and the Research Department merged in 1948, allowing rein to the young turks such as Reginald Maudling, Enoch Powell and Iain Macleod whose coruscating ideas stood out in sharp contrast to those of Woolton and the party managers who believed in building up cash and membership, and cared less about policy and electoral appeal.

But *The Industrial Charter* did not represent total victory, and the reforms of organisation recommended by Maxwell Fyfe's much more sober-minded committee, in 1948, while breaking the power of the Constituency Associations, brought the newly enlarged Research Department under the control of Woolton, thus ensuring that 'policy' would have to be validated in turn by the National Union, the parliamentary party, and Churchill himself. On the other hand, Maxwell Fyfe's reforms also curtailed Central Office's influence on constituencies' choices of candidates and prepared the way for the 1950–51 inrush of gifted younger men, mainly of middle-class origins, who had served in the war and who found the Charters an appropriate antidote which they could apply to soften bitter memories of the 1930s among their working-class constituents.

Central Office's managerial mentality was blamed severely for its failure to take advantage of the Attlee government's problems during two crucial by-elections in 1949. Faced by demands from agents and party workers for clear, comprehensible policies, Churchill had to abandon some of his natural reluctance to be tied down to detailed pledges. This turned out to be the signal for much infighting as Woolton and Butler each sought to give characteristics of their own to the general document *The Right Road for Britain* (1949). Oliver Poole and David Beales campaigned for a free enterprise theme against Harold Macmillan's and Quintin Hogg's advocacy of the mixed economy. The final version veered towards the latter and, unusually for a manifesto, embodied some of Hogg's effervescent wit. But the 1950 manifesto, *This is the Road*, included few actual pledges from *The Right Road*, the rest being excised by Churchill.

During the 1950 election campaign, the party concentrated more on the government's economic trouble than on its own alternatives, let alone those contained in the Charter, and oscillated rather uneasily between attacking the Liberal Party and wooing Liberal voters. Conservative candidates demanded detailed policies to wield against their Labour opponents, who were disoriented by the economic crisis, and divisions among their leaders. But the party's capacity to satisfy them was limited. Michael Fraser's restatement of the Workers Charter, 'The Worker in Industry', for example, ran into opposition from the Labour Committee and differences over the extent of denationalisation and the future of welfare policy continued to hamper the party up to the 1951 election despite its evident need to attract dissident Labour and floating voters. Such was the climate of uncertainty that Central Office feared to publish

costings of Conservative health policy, and the crucial decision to
aim for 300 000 houses a year was only taken after a surge of
enthusiasm during the Conference in 1950.[6]

Nevertheless this strategy paid dividends a year later, when the
Liberals, disheartened and short of funds, put forward fewer
candidates and lost, overall, almost two million votes, more than
half of which went to the Conservatives. Without that swing they
could not have won because Labour actually increased its total
poll.[7] Before the 1951 election Churchill kept ultimate control of the
Research Department's lively ideas, rewrote much of the manifesto
himself, and then as Prime Minister downgraded the Department to
public relations work and the servicing of backbench committees.
Like all politicians in government he did not want to be beholden to
claimants outside Cabinet to be the party's conscience, whether they
were Butler's officials, or the One Nation group, founded in 1950 by
Cuthbert Alport, Robert Carr, Iain Macleod, Angus Maude and
Enoch Powell. Though they lost influence over policy creation, they
had ensured that since 1946 the party had accepted the post-war
settlement (which they understood to mean the welfare state, full
employment, and the mixed economy); and they had set down
markers for the future of sufficient significance to the party at large
to prevent the leadership interpreting this commitment in a way that
ignored the importance of sustaining its appeal to organised labour.

Because Churchill did not find it necessary to implement this new
ethos when appointing his Cabinet and junior ministers but instead
chose to balance the various currents and traditions among his more
senior colleagues, the centre-left/centre-right division stayed open
throughout the early 1950s. Hoping to contain disruption by
avoiding policy discussions, by appointing very senior Ministers as
'overlords' to control spending departments, circumscribing his
Chancellor R. A. Butler's freedom of action by setting watchdogs
round him, and by refusing to name Eden as his heir or set a date
for his own retirement, he actually stultified some of the energy and
inventiveness of a gifted Cabinet.

The divisions showed: especially in the questions of how
government should work and what should be its industrial, labour
and financial policies. From the start, between the 1950 and 1951
elections, the Research Department had been primed with
information about how the machinery of government had been
adapted by Labour ministers in Cripps' 'second stage', because
some civil servants thought it vital that Conservatives should have

decided before the election whether or not to continue it.[8] The staff generally approved that the Treasury had become the central department of state but, while they accepted that it should have responsibility for monetary policy, they resented the fact that an 'overview' appeared to rest in the hands of civil servants. More generally, Churchill and his colleagues disliked what they saw as the plethora of interdepartmental committees, whose number had steadily increased since 1945, taking them as a sign that Attlee had been run by his mandarins. They intended both to reverse the process and to subordinate departments more clearly to individual Ministers' initiative.

But they did not plan to dismantle the sponsorship system, nor the tripartite arrangements which flowed from it. In this, as with their campaign against controls and planning, they followed the line taken by the FBI: production departments and the Production Authority system should be downgraded but not abolished, so as to allow industries to resume self-government, free from dependence on the state, without losing the advantages of access to advice and protection from the state. About Development Councils and Shawcross's proposed anti-monopolies legislation they were more positive, in agreement again with the FBI, and defended the rights of management against state intervention, even where that was intended to stimulate greater efficiency. With its intimate knowledge of the discussions going on in Whitehall in 1950–51, however, the Research Department could run ahead of the Committee of Chairmen and it began to circulate plans for investment incentives, new forms of organisation to change public into semi-public industries (such as Robert Shone's experiment with the Iron and Steel Board) and means to correlate government fiscal policy with industry's needs. In a further extension of the concept of industrial self-government, they also discussed ways in which banks and City institutions could finance industry, without the need for direct state participation.

Into this shaping of a Conservative industrial policy, which had already gone well beyond the simple statements of the *Industrial Charter*, the FBI and BEC successfully injected many of their own views.[9] The embryo small business lobby, operating at that time mainly through the National Union of Manufacturers (NUM) and the Chambers of Commerce, had less influence. On labour policy no direct overtures were made by – or to the TUC, but the Research Department argued consistently against committing the party to a wages policy by legislation. Its fear to alienate the unions found a response in Churchill's insistence that full employment, good industrial relations and rising working class living standards constituted the new face of Tory democracy.[10]

Since the future Conservative state was to abjure industrial controls and labour legislation and since all the leaders now realised what a political disaster it would be if they were seen as the party that wished to restore a reserve of unemployment as a spur to productivity and discipline, the planners had to work out how to make industry's claims to self-regulation balance the three institutions' 1944 responsibilities to the state. The immediate onus would lie with the Board of Trade, where Churchill placed the young Peter Thorneycroft, and the Ministry of Labour where he chose the experienced lawyer, Walter Monckton. Churchill gave Thorneycroft no especial brief but his clear instructions to Monckton (see page 257) and the more equivocal phrases of the 1951 manifesto suggest that he was well aware of the danger of letting loose once in office, a wide-ranging discussion between the ideologues on the party's Labour Committee who wanted to curb union restrictive practices, and those who either feared, or like Eden and the One Nation group did not wish to take on the TUC in a struggle, and who certainly had no desire to legislate on contracting out of the political levy, or the secret ballot.[11]

Part of Monckton's brief appears to have been drafted not by the Labour Committee but by the sub-committee on 'union problems' which recommended that a Conservative government must recognise the trade union movement 'as a full partner in the state, to be consulted equally at government level and at the shop floor. The trade union movement has now firmly established itself as one of the three interests that support our industrial fabric . . . an essential safeguard of freedom in an industrial society.'[12]

The furthest that future Ministers would go was to use the NJAC and the NPACI as 'educative forces' to exhort unions and industry – a course prudent perhaps in the context of their narrow 1951 majority, but one which soon appeared unreasonably timid. On the external financial side, they accepted the City's requirements almost without question. In 1949 they had sought to defend the pound against devaluation; several seem to have concurred with that trend of opinion in the United States which believed that Britain had wasted Marshall Aid.[13] It followed naturally that a Conservative government should build up the gold and dollar reserves, aim again for convertibility, and seek to make devaluation work by restraining industrial costs (principally wages). It is hardly surprising that the majority of Ministers at first welcomed Robot: they had much earlier absorbed the view that some sort of internal self-discipline was necessary in government, as well as in the trade unions. They also realised that the sterling area could no longer serve Britain's interests (as they imagined was possible in 1945) nor London's 'rightful position as the financial centre of the world'. But not until 1953 or 1954 did Ministers or party headquarters fully understand that the United States had a greater interest in Britain's joining a European trading association than in her standing as a 'third circle' between the dollar and the rest of the world.

Because policy had not been made in opposition but only compromises between the claims of centre-left and centre-right, between the Committee of chairmen and headquarters staff, and between party and outside business interests, Churchill's government seemed less prepared for the sorts of financial and industrial problems that the Korean War left them, than for those of foreign and defence policy. Under a pragmatic leadership remote from ideological impulses,[14] a question such as Robot would be decided on its merits and immediate political repercussions rather than with a long-term strategy in mind. Churchill's intentions were, at best, vague as Monckton and Butler both discovered. 'In this crisis of our island life, when the cottage homes could so easily be plunged into penury and want, we must not allow class or party feeling to be needlessly inflamed' might be a good vade-mecum but inadequate as a ministerial brief.[15] Churchill's conduct of business in the House of Commons nostalgically reflected the bipartisan days of Coalition; but his insistence on furthering the housing programme and the end of rationing and controls at all costs were straightforward reactions to the government's narrow victory in 1951, and the evidence of opinion polls that Labour retained its popularity for at least another two years.

In circumstances where they could not hope to win another election until the rewards of cautious pragmatism showed, say by 1954–55, Churchill chose to avoid more policy-making than was strictly necessary. The Research Department even ran into trouble by trying to define the essential difference between the new Conservatism and Socialism in order to respond to Labour's 1953 programme, *A Challenge to Britain*, and the Cabinet accepted Churchill's recommendations not to publish a response at all, despite the programme's obvious public attractions. Discussion of fundamentals was deprecated as it had been in the Coalition after October 1943.

Only in the low key of discussing their 'electoral value' was the Research Department able to look at sensitive issues without the surveillance of ACPPE and the 1922 Committee and even then it was assumed that voters would be more interested in tangible rewards, houses and consumer spending, than 'political matters'.[16]

Very substantial matters were therefore decided as they arose, either in conformity with principles agreed before 1951, or on lines acceptable to the competing interests whose appeasement government desired. It became impossible for the more active minds in the party organisation to pin Ministers down to issues like industrial productivity; the subject was relegated to the level of Board of Trade–FBI discourse. The Wilson–Gaitskell argument about how to stimulate industrial efficiency survived, in Tory shape, in the supposed antithesis between state intervention and individual managerial responsibility, but the argument was not advanced much before 1955 in spite of increasing evidence that neither theoretical position led to a contemporary policy adequate to keep British industry competitive. Yet for a younger minister like Thorneycroft as for many Conservative backbenchers, and the Powell–Macleod–Maudling group, the agenda had already changed leaving the *Industrial Charter* far behind. Something more was required to improve the quality of management, labour relations and mobility, the level of investment and usage of technology, product design, marketing and service, if Britain were ever favourably to compete with the United States and a renascent Germany.

The 1951 pledges had been too general, and too carefully balanced, between the demands of traditional Tory voters for an increase in individual freedom and the provision of incentives and blandishments to trade union members, to serve as a guide for five years. Yet Churchill as late as 1954 vetoed a proposal by Thorneycroft to legislate for some of the Charter's proposals about Development Councils. The government's signal successes came in other fields where the centre-left centre-right tension gave way to electoral calculation, where a minister like Macmillan had a wide-ranging brief to build 300 000 houses at no matter what cost to other capital investment,[17] or like

Monckton to harmonise industrial relations. Thorneycroft did have a clearer *ministerial* policy than most, which led in 1953 to the Monopolies Commission. But he proved unable to draw his Cabinet colleagues into a general policy for industry, even on their election commitments: in spite of its great symbolic importance, denationalisation of steel and road haulage proceeded rather slowly, dogged by difficulties in the capital issue market.

From the point of view of those like Monckton and Churchill, who wanted to re-establish the party in the public mind as standing for harmony and prosperity after the lean Chamberlain years, the absence of rigorous analysis of where their pragmatism was leading may have been an advantage. Butler was not permitted, for example, to reduce Macmillan's housing targets on the grounds that other capital investment was preferable; nor was Osbert Peake, Minister of National Insurance, allowed to argue either the future cost burden of old-age pensions and the health service if current trends were prolonged, or to pursue reintroduction of Beveridge's principle of insurance (which Attlee's government had abandoned when introducing means-tested National Assistance). Lord Cherwell found it hard to bring up even the less obviously contentious issue of the future of higher education. (Not until 1956 did his and Woolton's support for the idea of technological universities, superseding the old technical colleges (as the 1944 Percy Report had recommended) reach the stage of a White Paper; even then when it became clear how backward Britain had become in research fields such as nuclear technology they emerged only as Colleges of Advanced Technology, in conformity with the traditional views of industry and universities.)

Whatever else can be said for Churchill during his 'Indian Summer', he actively discouraged both innovation and critical thinking; and he delayed Eden's succession beyond all reason, thus helping to prevent a lasting settlement of the outstanding arguments between centre-left and centre-right. When the research and policy-making process resumed, two years too late, in 1954 it was tied down to the drafting of an election manifesto, and was subsequently again curtailed, during Eden's first uneasy year and the Suez débâcle. The best time thus slipped away, so that by 1957, as the Brazen Head said to Friar Bungay, 'Time *has been.*' Failure, for example to confront the problems of wages, productivity, investment and exports, failure to provide an authoritative case for participation (as the FBI already wished to do) in the early stages of the EEC, to counter the dominance

of Eden, the Foreign Office and the Atlanticists, could not
subsequently be remedied.

The Labour Party's restless activity in Opposition contrasts with
Conservative complacency – or pusillanimity – in economic and
industrial matters. Cut off abruptly from responsibility after eleven
years in office, distanced most of all from day to day concern with
foreign affairs by the growth of passionate internal debate over the
principles of nuclear armaments, the Cold War, and Germany's entry
to NATO, with the Bevanite–Gaitskell quarrel unsolved, yet
conscious that the election had been only narrowly lost, the party
simmered with an intellectual liveliness that might have brought it
back to government had Churchill's serious stroke in June 1953 led to
an election.[18]

But at the top, Attlee who was by then in his late sixties, looked tired
and disillusioned, as did his senior colleagues; he seemed content to let
disputes resolve themselves while still exercising enough discipline to
forestall the Bevanite left, who at the time the party civil war broke out
in the open, at the Morecombe Conference in 1952, held six out of
seven constituency seats on the NEC,[19] and roughly one quarter of the
parliamentary party, but had few bases in the trade union movement.
Meanwhile in Parliament Labour made no concerted attempt to harass
the new administration.

Lacking a parliamentary vehicle, the debates of 1951–54 took place
inside party headquarters, chiefly on the Home Policy Committee, set
up by Attlee soon after the defeat, whose membership spanned the
various interests and factions. They quickly concluded that, with the
balance of payments deeply in deficit, Britain was stuck in a hazardous
position which allowed neither full liberalisation nor convertibility of
sterling; controls and import restrictions must therefore be retained.
They suspected that the Conservatives would do no better than Labour
had done in 1950–51 and that, after winning the next election, Labour
would have to institute a salvage operation rather than legislate a
workers' charter. The direction of economic policy thus maintained
continuity with the era of Cripps.

Fears of losing full employment and the post-war gains, and of being
forced into deflation because of another American recession,
accompanied by grave balance of payments problems and a flight of
capital, were not unrealistic in 1951–52; they formed part of the Robot
case to Butler. But if the HPC's diagnosis of weaknesses in the

economy ran close enough to that of the Treasury, without its emphasis on wage-inflation, their remedy of cutting consumption in order to release funds for state-directed investment wholly misjudged the underlying trends of consumer expenditure and voters' aspirations and were not alleviated by talk of the 'social wage' and profuse public expenditure on services and welfare.

The HPC's gloomy prognosis led the Labour Party to project a new apparatus of planning including import controls and state direction of investment, which emphasised Development Councils in a way reminiscent of Wilson's 1950 proposals. Apart from the TUC's habitual resistance to what it called 'leftist proposals' aimed at union restrictive practices, most of this was approved by the unions at NEC weekend conferences in the early part of 1953, leaving only the unresolved disagreement between bilateral traders, as Balogh was at this time, and multilateralists such as Gaitskell. The tone of discussion documents remained resolutely that of a party which saw itself as if it were in government, ready again to manage the economy while treating the Conservative years as an unavoidable hiatus.

The result, *Challenge to Britain* (1953) originated with a distinguished team of economists: Kaldor, Balogh, Richard Kahn, Lewis, Joan Robinson and Robin Marris. But in attempting to bridge the gap between Gaitskell and Wilson with the somewhat bland assumption that both were primarily concerned to transform capitalism in Britain and make business internationally competitive,[20] *Challenge* represented a triumph of the intellectuals over the realities of party conflicts rather than the high point of convergence imagined by Samuel Beer when he wrote *Modern British Politics* in 1965. Attlee and his old guard still confronted the Bevanite left on the NEC while the fundamental division between social-democrats and socialists ramified in multiple fissures among the constituency party activists and union leaderships. With its proposals to nationalise whole new sectors (chemicals (ICI), electrical manufacturing, machine tools and parts of the aircraft industry, as well as steel) to abolish the public schools and extend comprehensive education at the expense of grammar schools, and to tax wealth more severely, *Challenge* went far further than *Let Us Face the Future* and left the social-democrats in disarray.

As Austen Albu pointed out: 'to put a programme of this sort before the electorate will require political courage, expository skill, and a united party'. The latter quality proved unattainable as a large section of the unions' membership, skilled workers suffering from narrowing differentials, and lower paid public service workers hit by the cost of living, joined party activists who had been challenging Attlee's leadership and the dominance of the 'big six' on the TUC since at least 1952. To meet a rush of demand for fresh thinking, the HPC brought out an election manifesto in March 1955 appealing to marginal voters on the old platform of fair shares in the distribution of wealth, and greater equality;[21] it offered a gesture of sympathy to the 'casualties of the consumer society' which grossly over-estimated the altruism of the rest of the electorate who preferred to share in the benefits mass consumerism offered.

Lacking access to government sources of information about economic trends, and rejecting Joan Robinson's warning that four years of Conservative fiscal policy had created overfull employment and very high consumer demand, the party's leaders miscalculated the extent of recovery that had already taken place in 1953–54, so that the depression which they planned to divert arrived *after* the 1955 election, making their updating of *Challenge to Britain* anachronistic and electorally unpalatable.

An impressive list of proposed reforms of central planning and the role of the Treasury and plans to solve the balance of payments problem and give priority to industry, to control capital movements, banks and City institutions and to regulate the sterling area and investment, which in theory brought the Gaitskell–Wilson controversy to a conclusion favouring the latter, was thus lost, leaving the party's intellectual core at odds with itself for another seven or eight years. The programme would have given priority to industry under the guidance and through the agency of Development Councils, at the expense of the exchange rate, the sterling area and the balance of payments. In that sense it cut hard at the banking and financial systems, falling just short of nationalising credit but providing for permanent restraint of the capital market. Whether it could have been implemented in a country as vulnerable to international financial pressures as Britain must be extremely doubtful. But its legacy conditioned Labour government thinking once Harold Wilson became leader, and influenced industrial as well as financial policy from the inception of the DEA in 1964 to the 1975 Industrial Strategy.

Outside, in the electoral marketplace, Labour lost 1.5 million votes in 1955, with shattering effects on its leaders' morale and the status of its intellectuals among constituencies and with the trade unions. In the short term, the disaster led Attlee and Gaitskell to conclude that, after four years of armed truce, the party could no longer afford its quarrel with the left, or the elaborate ratiocination needed to produce compromises, when the electorate willed otherwise. Attlee resigned shortly afterwards, handing the struggle over to Gaitskell who, after being made Party Treasurer (as a result of a manoeuvre in which he willingly accepted the patronage of Deakin and other members of the 'big six') had effectively held a reversionary lien on the leadership. Bevan soon began his journey back into the fold, by preparing to abandon unilateral disarmament; leaving the New Left to seed itself lower down in the party hierarchy.

The 1955 defeat has been attributed to two main factors: to the success of a blatantly electioneering budget, put together against Butler's better judgment; and to the inappropriateness of Labour's programme. It should be added that neither industry nor the majority of the TUC General Council and union memberships approved of *Challenge to Britain*'s reversion to state intervention and control. Beside that catalogue of errors, to have foreseen that the economic crisis would arrive, later in 1955, counted for nothing. In the prolonged post-mortem, the HPC concluded sadly that *Challenge* had 'suffered too much from its reliance on the inevitability of economic difficulties as a vehicle for bringing Labour to power'. Over the next year, the NEC commissioned much research into how British society had changed, and why working class voters had reneged on the party that (they claimed) had given them full employment. The results were ambiguous, fostering on one hand conclusions that led Crosland and Gaitskell to proclaim social-democracy as the future for Labour, and on the other arguments favouring the socialists' pursuit of planning and equality.

In January 1956, Gaitskell and Wilson could still sit uneasily together at a meeting of the Socialist International to discuss economic planning, industry and the state. Yet the social democrats thought they knew what their real constituents wanted: standing in a white sheet at the end of the year, Gaitskell told members of the 1944 Association, 'there was a danger that, in regard to certain fundamental matters, the Party was getting out of touch with the electorate'.[22] The assembled businessmen who for ten years had shown the Labour Party nothing but sympathy left him in no doubt that, in their view, unions and management were together committed to the mixed economy, consumer satisfaction, and industrial self regulation, not to further planning and state control.

In the years from 1951 to 1956, the Conservative Party had no reason radically to try to change the relationships between government, industry, unions, and the financial institutions, which consequently developed (much as they had done in 1940–44) along lines determined by practice and the result of mutual competition to gain their particular ends. But the experience turned out to be unsatisfactory enough to stimulate the revival of an older tradition, which looked to the sort of views about disengagement expressed by Baldwin in the mid-1920s (though it did not yet cast back to the liberal anti-statism of Bonar Law). The 1956 White Paper 'The Economic Implications of Full Employment' (Cmd 9725) marks an important turning point not only in the balance between centre-left and centre-right areas of Conservatism but in the party's changing overall conception of the state's role. Government sought to divest itself of some of the responsibility for managing the economy at full employment which Labour governments had superimposed on the 1944 White Paper, in order to place it firmly on management and unions – returning, in fact, to the 1944 spirit of reciprocal obligations which both sides of industry seemed by then to have forgotten.

But in 1951, Labour's rules were still acceptable and accepted almost unquestioned. The TUC, being at risk of association with what was now the Opposition, put out a statement immediately after the 1951 election: 'we expect of this government that they will maintain to the full the practice of consultation. On our part, we shall continue to examine every question in the light of the economic and industrial implications.' What was, for them, merely a restatement of 'longstanding practice to seek to work amicably with whatever government is in power',[23] amounted to renewal of a licence for self-regulation under a just state.

TUC leaders tried afterwards to equate this neutrality with their loyalty to Labour's ageing leaders, by holding back the left's demands, and toning down the list of new firms for nationalisation in the 1953 programme, *Challenge*;[24] they incurred instead accusations of being backward and conservative from those who planned it and who looked to Woodcock for support in future, rather than to the old-fashioned, complacent Tewson. Some of the charges were accurate. Until about 1954, the TUC avoided asking itself questions about the implications of full employment and the consequences of high demand on wages, prices, and industrial efficiency – even when employers and government officials came up with answers they did not like. Instead, as if rooted in the late 1940s, they argued the case for maintaining high demand as insurance against a recession which never came, at a time when unemployment ranged around the totally unprecedented level of 1.8 per cent; they grew suspicious even of the schemes for taxation and welfare payments gradually to redistribute wealth being discussed by the Labour Party Research Department and the NEC.

These years confirmed the established post-war pattern of corporate bias. The TUC had always since 1940 seen the state as the main instrument of change and became more statist as time passed. While they claimed to represent their members' interests in the evolution of policies and hoped to participate in government in implementing them, they expected that government, rather than the tripartite accord of employers and trades unions, would actually guarantee the 1944 package. Consequently, so long as a Conservative administration carried on the job satisfactorily, the TUC would seek to deny the existence of class struggle or of any primary conflict which might prevent them, in political logic, from continuing. (Thus they chose to define the actions of the FBI and BEC in 1950–51 as being tactical, not a fundamental breach with the post-war settlement.) This attitude led the General Council instinctively to deprecate Labour party radicalism, especially in the research documents prepared by economists.

When problems grew, in the mid-1950s, the TUC expected to assist in solving them. But because the problems were those of the modern labour market, already altered (or distorted) from the familiar post-war model, they set up tensions within the trade union movement. By 1955–56, the TUC found itself caught between its role as a governing institution with responsibility for wage moderation, and its members' response not only to the measurable cost of living but to the new world of shop floor competition fostered by fifteen years of full employment. Something that the TUC had assumed could not occur did, in fact, occur as government and civil service, as well as employers, began to blame wages for price instability and export failure. Worse, TUC leaders could see, as could all contemporary commentators, that the sense of restraint required by the 1944 package had ceased to apply at plant level, where it had been replaced by a very different conception of members' interests that already took full employment for granted.

The investment boom that might have matched rising wages with productivity in the long term (rather than in the short-lived spurt of 1949–51) failed to occur under Labour's Conservative successors. At the same time, removal of dividend restraint, and the return of a certain level of conspicuous consumption after wartime and post-war absence, indicated to the TUC that their idea of 'fair shares' was being abandoned. For some years after 1951, however, Conservative labour policy gave the TUC more or less what they required, and counter-balanced fiscal concessions to middle class and business opinion. So long as this continued (and Churchill and Monckton judged it very shrewdly) the TUC could not easily complain.

Yet this was exactly the time when plant bargaining, leap-frogging wage claims, unofficial strikes, and 'indiscipline' first began to affect the unions' once-favourable presentation in the press. Put on the defensive, but unable to control what was going on, the TUC could not 'solve' the contradiction between its responsibilities to its members and its responsibilities to government, and with increasing dismay had to watch government begin to concern itself more directly with the problems of industrial relations, manpower, and the labour market.

Some of the blame falls on Tewson himself. He lacked the vision to see that the old methods of building up unions' size and authority had led into forms of arteriosclerosis accompanied by leaders' dogmatic assertion which ordinary union members and their branch officials, as well as headquarters staff, resented. When it came to discussion of general principles, fragmentation occurred: even on the NPACI and NJAC, union leaders by the 1950s were beginning to speak for their own unions rather than as members of the General Council. Yet the TUC's committees, basking in the assurance that the Conservatives backed full employment, continued to be preoccupied with detailed analysis of the government's fiscal policy rather than with the changes taking place in the labour market and the movement as a whole.

Such generalisations are borne out by the histories of a number of issues. Productivity had always been an important target for the TUC, as its participation in the Anglo-American Productivity Council (later the British Productivity Council) and the work of its own Production Committee shows.[25] In the wake of Wilson's Board of Trade plans, the TUC also developed an interest in industrial organisation, and the analysis of monopoly practices. As part of the full employment bargain, they were still, in 1950–51, actively discussing how to make the workforce more efficient and how to train branch officials in management techniques. They concluded (after a number of delegations had visited the United States) that American methods of scientific management were not necessarily detrimental – indeed, that 'progressive management is bound to introduce new production methods'. Unions should not contest these, but negotiate 'on level terms . . . where possible, techniques leading to improved industrial efficiency should be encouraged'.[26]

The TUC had come this far once before, in the bilateral talks with employers in 1929–30, when displacement occurring as a result of rationalising industry had been at issue. Now, assured in an era of full employment that those made redundant would be employed elsewhere, they affirmed that 'full employment does not mean that workpeople can expect to remain indefinitely in any particular job'. Butler welcomed such arguments, in December 1951, as a sort of alternative to wage restraint. The TUC's concern with good management and what the Production Committee called a 'constructive association, in which the TUC can actively participate in securing industrial progress, and in which such association encourages those human relations which are at the basis of a dynamic industrial democracy' was still very much alive at the end of 1954. According to the TUC's Production Committee, 'Trade unions are as interested in industrial progress as is management. The maintenance and development of their pay packets and standards of work and living are dependent on industrial progress.'[27]

Those who dealt with Monckton and the benign Ministry of Labour accepted that many reforms such as shift-working ought to be accepted in the higher cause of full employment (although even among Production Committee members some doubts crept·in about how to cope with the deterioration in industrial relations in 1955[28]). But their vision of an industrial concordat, assuring the principle of union self-regulation against legislative interference, began to look rather archaic once unions' public image began to worsen, and once Iain Macleod the new Minister of Labour introduced the idea of a code of conduct, intended conventionally if not legally to bind the two sides.

Meanwhile, in contrast to the demure attitude of the Production Committee, the TUC's more powerful Economic Committee grew suspicious: even though their fears that Butler might return to deflation evaporated after 1952.[29] Committee members thought the Treasury's monetary levers too blunt and abstract to discriminate between what was 'merely profitable' and what was 'desirable in the public interest'. From then, divisions increased inside the TUC between those who were willing to try to do what Butler urged and those who resisted being sucked in to another voluntary wages policy like 1948.

The Economic Committee's unwillingness to compromise (for which Woodcock was chiefly responsible) confined itself to wages and barely influenced the TUC's rather indeterminate publication *The Control of Industry* (1953). Nor did the Labour Party's programme, for the TUC seems to have been more concerned with the balance of payments and industry's competitiveness, than with using Development Councils to galvanise incompetent management.[30] Sceptical of the party's intellectuals, especially where further nationalisation was concerned, the TUC tried to respond to the changing climate as the world economic upturn demonstrated Britain's long-term competitive weaknesses, by putting difficult questions about the country's declining share of world trade – a greater threat to full employment, in the eyes of some unions like the TGWU, than even the possibility of deliberate deflation. This led them away from the Labour Party line on planning and controls. Early in 1954 a long Economic Committee analysis of German and Japanese competition, the state of the sterling area, and the strength of OEEC, shows that the TUC had woken up to the existence of a new and potentially hostile world.[31] Soon after, reports from Courts of Inquiry into engineering and shipbuilding disputes demonstrated the new significance attached by Government and public to wages and industrial indiscipline.

It is of great significance that in the spring of 1954 the Economic Committee discussed whether to argue out what it called the 'economic problems surrounding wage claims' and the abuses exposed by these reports, and decided against. Until then they had been able to rely if not always on the sympathy of MOL officials at least on that of the Prime Minister who, for example, after a TUC complaint that Monckton had rejected a number of wages councils' awards in 1952 overrode his Minister of Labour to the dismay of the Treasury and the BEC. But over the next two years, the character both of MOL and Cabinet outlooks had changed, putting trade union leaders on the spot. One side of the Committee argued that, if these reports were not accepted as valid, it would produce dissent; the other that if they were, it would lead government back to a wages policy. Both sides saw that the problems were indeed as serious as government and the Courts of Inquiry claimed, but instead of working with a still-friendly but increasingly demanding Conservative government, they decided instead to take the easier course and throw the onus back onto employers, by complaining how little profit went back into investment, and how high dividends made it hard for unions to seek wage restraint.[32]

Experience of how the wage freeze of 1948–50 had worked and an inability to conceive of a solution in which unions would not be the minority partner to an increasingly aggressive management probably explains why the TUC's centre came so far but baulked at the consequences. The TUC might well have responded more in tune with government's requirements during 1955, especially after the Conservatives won the election. But they could not then do so (and might well not have been able to in 1954) because union members simply would not have allowed it at a time of mild price inflation when collective bargaining had the advantages of a seller's market, shortages of skilled labour, and employers' propensity to pay. After the harsh autumn 1955 Budget, and the government's attempt to get convertibility at the price of consumer spending, (see page 270) the TUC suddenly found itself free of the dilemma: it could now attack government, first for the 'election hand-out' earlier in the year, then for the apparent assault on working class living standards, which continued during Macmillan's period as Chancellor well into 1956.

While different committees of the TUC (often comprising the same people, working on different agendas usually determined by government departments) tried in various ways to react to a new range of problems vastly different from those of 1944, the 'big six', newer but less assured than in Attlee's day, hung together on the General Council in support of what Monckton tried to do, for fear of something worse. What Deakin wrote in 1952 (about NUM opposition to Saturday shift-work) was typical: 'independent action for political purposes within a parliamentary democracy would be suicidal, bringing repercussions in its train which would completely undermine the influence and authority of the movement'.[33] There was no lack of thinking about wages and inflation among individual union General Secretaries, only of agreement on how to break out of the dilemma created by full employment that Beveridge and his colleagues had foreseen. Deakin's own TGWU Executive Council minutes reveal him no longer thumping the table, but treading cautiously between his more demanding members and increasingly resistant employers.

Thus it was not Frank Cousins'[34] rise that *caused* trouble: as a symptom of deep-rooted discontent, he merely articulated a view fundamentally opposed to the style and content of the TUC as it had been under Citrine and Tewson. Two significant changes had already occurred before he took over the TGWU from Deakin in 1956. First in time, stemming from the car industry in the West Midlands and the Coventry Toolroom agreement of 1942, came the rise of a new form of shop stewards' organisation (quite different from that of 1916–21) which up-and-coming officials like Jack Jones were determined to use to introduce informal decentralisation and rank and file participation and to break the monolithic power of Deakin himself and other union bosses. Before 1955, this and the plant bargaining which characterised it had not spread much beyond the car industry and it was not directly responsible for Cousins' promotion.[35] But the presence of increasingly radical lay members on the TGWU Executive and the vociferousness of its Congress greatly influenced Cousins' early years in office, pushing him and his deputy Harry Nicholas towards the decentralised, federal structure which Jones was later to institute.

The second great change in trade union patterns occurred over a longer time-scale as white-collar, clerical and supervisory unions (who had formerly been classified by employers as 'lower management' in an attempt to deter them from forming links with, or being sucked into mass unions) found their status, privileges and differentials threatened by the growing power and influence of large manual unions. Some saw the attractions of forming special divisions of existing unions, such as TASS actually inside the AEU, despite employers' rearguard actions; others formed new groups like ASSET (later ASTMS). These cut across old alignments. Yet change came haphazardly: some unions like the AEU under Carron resisted the rank and file movement for many years; or like the GMWU under Cooper, found it unnecessary to alter the habits of the 1940s. Others, such as the Communist-led ETU fostered it, or like the steel unions, took advantage and continued to negotiate wages in relation to productivity with the new Iron and Steel Board. The phenomena of 'wild cat strikes' and general indiscipline which began after the mid-1950s to obsess commentators on industrial relations was, in 1955, characteristic of only a minority of Britain's factories, mainly confined to engineering, and it is possible that a different decision by the Economic Committee in April 1954 to seek a basis for wage bargaining in productivity and profitability could have won majority support from those who still valued full employment as a living gain.

These were not, unfortunately, years in which employers themselves spent much time evaluating the real basis, as opposed to the historic basis, of profitability. Despite the jeremiads of the EEF and BEC, car barons and newspaper proprietors were the first habitually to give in to plant bargaining and accelerating wage demands to keep production lines going and perhaps also to bankrupt their competitors. Those who stood out, like Sir William Rootes, found their competitors keener to steal their business than to show employers' solidarity. There was therefore no outside stimulus for the

TUC to put its own house in order. Change was passing them by (for the TGWU or GMWU now usually settled their own inter-union disputes according to the Bridlington Agreement rather than involve the TUC's good offices). Its own press, the *Daily Herald* and *Labour*, an unattractive monthly, had ceased to ask important questions, and worst of all the rank and file was starting to set wage standards in certain key sectors far ahead of the cost of living. Significantly, the arrival of Cousins coincided with the Economic Committee's failure to consider the key report 'Trade Unions and Full Employment in a Changing World'.

Clouds then gathered quickly. Although Iain Macleod made a brave defence of British unionism, at the 1956 Conservative Conference, the White Paper on the implications of full employment had already hinted that full employment might in future be dependent on wage restraint. After a decade in which unions had stood high in public estimation, a series of strikes in the docks, railways and the newspaper industry, during and after the 1955 election, accompanied by detailed reports of bad behaviour in what were now seen as trouble centres such as the car plants at Dagenham, led to a general and increasing perception of unions as an impediment to, if not yet a malign influence on economic progress. Only too well aware that many wage claims in public industries like the railways were beyond the industry's capacity to pay, and that the only defence against press unpopularity was reforms which the TUC were quite incapable of imposing on member unions, Tewson delayed action too long, while Woodcock waited, unwilling openly to challenge the ageing General Secretary. Meanwhile the aggressive attitudes which Cousins's language embodied, and the employers' collective response, divided the General Council too deeply for it to produce a coherent response, even to the continued survival of its old enemy, the Communist Party.[36]

A damaging and well-documented case had thus built up in government, among employers' associations and in the press against the trade union movement, collectively, for permitting a state of affairs in which established procedures such as the National Docks Labour scheme continually broke down, or where public sector unions like the Railwaymen put forward claims which their industry manifestly could not pay except out of government subventions, and for doing nothing to discipline shop stewards responsible for the state of anarchy revealed by Courts of Inquiry, for example, into the Briggs Motor Bodies Works at Dagenham. These observations all emphasised wage-push inflation and the damaging effect on the economy of annual increases. Poaching between unions, by no means always the TGWU, flagrant abuses in the Communist-dominated ETU, and the struggles of ASLEF to retain train-drivers' already archaic practices, provided the sort of evidence that led to a growing majority of Gallup poll respondents to state that government was too weak in its attitude to union reform.

In private, TUC committees accepted that some of these charges were valid: that strikes which had doubled in number between 1945 and 1955 damaged the economy, and that competitive plant bargaining and aggressive union expansion threatened the future of the industrial relations system.[37] But they could not endorse those in the Conservative Party who demanded legislation to curb abuses. Self-regulation, they insisted, remained the only way to control behaviour in conditions which were 'exactly the opposite of those in which trade unionism had developed'.

Having baulked at examining wage inflation in 1954, the TUC looked for that sense of responsibility required by the post-war settlement – and found it wanting. Tewson inclined to blame the younger generation which had never known mass unemployment; others saw more clearly that, since 1947, the TUC itself had lapsed into a branch of 'economism' which had encouraged emphasis on the money wage to become again, as it had in the early 1920s, the measure of a union leader's success. Their wartime contribution, which government, civil servants, and employers had found so admirable, had somehow slipped out of public awareness. But they had no recourse except to strengthen the rule book and offer the promise of self-regulation which looked impracticable if not improbable in the light of the recent past. As a means to fend off legislation, and after a conversation with the new Prime Minister, Anthony Eden in June 1955, Tewson prepared to strengthen the TUC's disciplinary powers, using Rule No. 11, which was less stringent than numbers 12 and 13, but represented the maximum coercion that member unions would permit.[38]

At this stage, when employers were continually relaying their fears to government, the Ministry of Labour's traditional preference for voluntary bargains, and Eden's inexperience in home affairs and rather vague benevolence towards 'labour', combined to give the TUC a little time. Since March 1954, when Monckton had approached the TUC for a strengthening of existing negotiating machinery ('an extension of self-government in the determination of wages and conditions') MOL and the TUC had been sparring over how far government should go beyond conciliation and the endless search for better procedures, in the drafting of more formal – though not necessarily any more binding – codes of conduct. In 1955–56, in much the same way as it conceded that a wage problem existed, the TUC came close to accepting that radical change in industrial relations would be necessary; but delayed as long as it could, at least until after the 1956 Congress had given it a chance to prepare delegates for what was to come. In the event, and to Cousins' undisguised relief, a badly-managed Congress waxed angry about the government's fiscal and foreign policy, and set out absurdly high terms for co-operation.[39] Then came the disastrous Suez adventure, Eden's collapse and resignation, and the credit squeeze followed by further austerity early in 1957. By the time that had passed, Britain appeared to have a new, rosy future in the European Free Trade Association (EFTA). For reasons not dissimilar to those of the BEC and the FBI, the TUC preferred to close the lid on self-examination, in the hope that better times would make it unnecessary.

———————

However much introspection TUC senior staff or General Council members allowed themselves, they assumed that they were still on the same side as employers and government in retaining a tripartite view of industrial politics, based on the assumption that full employment remained central to government policy. By 1957, as industry and the financial sector began openly to compete with them with alternative statements about the national interest this had ceased to be accurate. While the BEC followed the FBI rather passively on most questions to do with trade and competitiveness, and let the idea of a merger lie when the FBI brought it up again in 1953, they became increasingly concerned to the point of obsession with wage inflation and shortages of skilled labour caused, they believed, by over full employment in the state industries.

For the first year or two of Churchill's government, the BEC relied on the NJAC, the Chancellor, and the evidence put in to EPB by its own 'statistical department', to educate unions in the effect of wages on costs. Local employers' associations had already drifted out of touch with headquarters during the late 1940s and become baffled by the complexities of dealing with government departments,[40] (a development which may explain part of the NJAC's slow decline) although as a central co-ordinating body, the BEC Council still saw itself as responsible to the national economic interest, for national wage settlements; but not, however, for the terms offered by individual companies. The BEC was intrinsically as hostile as the TUC to plant bargaining. Conservative in procedure, its Council disliked equally Monckton's and MOL's attempts to extend arbitration, and Conservative backbenchers' talk of changing the law; this was so even where the sensitive question of the closed shop was concerned, since most BEC federations found it a convenient arrangement.[41] They also cried down attempts by Monckton or Thorneycroft to legislate aspects of the Conservative *Workers' Charter*. Matters like Communist infiltration and strike ballots, they preferred to leave to individual unions; on most issues in the mid-1950s the BEC appeared committed to the old tripartite formula as the proper way to introduce change.

But on wages the BEC's member federations soon developed an intransigence reminiscent of the wage-cutting early 1920s. After Butler's appeal through the NJAC for voluntary restraint in 1952, they became disinclined to translate higher productivity into wage increases. They saw the 'annual round' as a stimulus to union negotiators that would lead expectation to run ahead of industry's capacity to pay. Council at once interpreted Butler's 1954 target of a permanent annual balance of payments surplus as a signal for permanent restraints. Each time that Monckton or MOL conciliators gave way on the big set-piece strikes in public industries, they complained of damage, primarily to exports, because the culprit could simply pass the cost on to the home consumer, and betray the national interest.[42]

Since it was government's Danegeld in the public sector that was blamed, the BEC increasingly saw itself as representing employers' interests against both government and 'labour', a polarisation quite absent from the FBI's outlook. With the fervour of a marginal group, BEC propagandists constructed a public campaign based on the argument that wage inflation and shop floor indiscipline were the primary causes of relative decline. Their phraseology reveals an attitude which had been in abeyance for many years;[43] as does the feeling that the FBI had again gone soft, by taking up ideas of profit-sharing and co-partnership, which the times could not afford.

By 1955 the BEC had come habitually to talk of 'capitulation to the threat of strikes'. Yet this language was not ostensibly directed against the TUC, nor even primarily against unions, but against shop stewards 'seeking maximum trouble out of the smallest grievance', also against fellow employers who sold out the employers' real interest and in the process undermined 'moderate' union leaders, out of weakness or for short-term advantage. Like the TUC, they had a vested interest in bringing the tripartite machinery to bear on their own members as well as the opposition. But their avoidance of direct conflict with the unions (as when they conspired to delay an MOL plan to put the subject of 'wages' on the NJAC agenda) waited only for the 1955 election to confirm the Conservatives in office. Thereafter the BEC campaigned for a government declaration to point up Britain's high costs as the explanation of uncompetitiveness. Having been rewarded in 1956, by *The Economic Implications of Full Employment* they played on the change in public opinion, whenever possible, and encouraged member federations to form a sort of employers' front, the most obvious case being EEF resistance to the AEU's 1956 wage claim.

Although in that case, the Chancellor, Macmillan replied to the EEF's invitation to government to 'make it clear to the unions, the government and the country, that the union demands are wholly irresponsible and must be rejected', by referring them to the responsibilities laid down on both sides rather than only on government by the 1956 White Paper,[44] the EEF and BEC continued to believe that the Conservative government shared their feelings until they were finally let down (as they believed) by the Macmillan government in 1957 (see page 312). But where public industries were concerned, blame fell entirely on government for its supine record, as the BEC pamphlet *Britain's Industrial Future* (1956) made clear. The BEC thus cut itself off not only from attempts to renew the state sector of industry but also from the dominant strand of Conservative thinking represented by Eden, Macmillan and Macleod. However much it welcomed any statement that could be interpreted as 'moderate' or 'realistic' emanating from the TUC, the drift leftwards shown at the TUC's 1956 Congress, the rise and early activities of Cousins and the TUC's patent inability or unwillingness to check the spread of plant bargaining, presaged a more complete rupture. This change might have been less significant if it had not been for the shift in public and press perceptions of what was wrong: arising concurrently, the new anti-union animus added emotional momentum to detailed corroboration.

The FBI Council had been cautious neither to diverge too quickly from the Labour government nor to welcome too openly its Conservative successor. Its membership was much too diverse to risk overtly political action, and it retained an old fear from before the war, of being seen 'in restraint of trade', which Thorneycroft's introduction of the Monopolies Commission in 1953 did nothing to diminish. The 1950 'Next Five Years' conference had also given it a benign public face. Yet by 1957 it, too, had slipped into a stand-off attitude towards government, largely out of disgust at the way economic management was practised to the detriment of industry's interests. Even in November 1951 its document *A New Policy for Solvency* contained criticism of the small rise in bank rate Butler had been forced to make, and of the introduction of controls over hire purchase, which bore heavily on the consumer goods and car industries in the domestic market, making it more difficult for them to plan research and development programmes and to contend with competition in export markets from Germany, Japan and the United States.

Uneasily aware that this argument could be turned back by the Board of Trade and Treasury against a sluggish uncompetitive British industrial base,[45] and that the sterling area and other once-assured markets like the Middle East were becoming fragile, the FBI presented another export-orientated face to its members, giving them support and information through the Dollar Exports Board, trade delegations and fairs, and through Foreign Office auspices in Chinese and Far Eastern markets. But they did not make clear whether they wanted incentives – export credits and 'concealed subsidies' – from government as occurred in France through the Office of the Plan, or merely the removal of what employers regarded as 'disincentives' such as high public expenditure, high personal tax rates, and state industries' privileged access to finance for investment.

The government's 1953 *Economic Survey* attempted to refute the charge that private industry had been starved of capital by claiming that its share of total investment had risen from 26.5 per cent in 1948 to 32 per cent in 1953. But concern about the malign effects of frequent changes in fiscal policy on industrial performance (necessary, according to the Treasury, to regulate demand) led the FBI to denounce the 1955 autumn Budget and, by implication, its election-oriented precedessor. The fact that welfare and social services were also pruned did not offset employers' antipathy to what was already being defined as 'stop-go'. When an FBI delegation complained to the new Chancellor, in February 1956, that the demands of *A Policy for Solvency* had not been met, Macmillan merely referred them as he had the BEC to the White Paper which broke with 1944 precedent not only in putting the onus of self-restraint on industry and unions, but also in redefining the sovereign rights of Cabinets to make policy.

Even in the field of export credits, the FBI made no headway against Treasury arguments when the squeeze came, in 1955–57. Butler and then Macmillan, together with their officials, tended to assume that the major part of capital investment would continue to come from retained profits (at the expense of shareholders' short-term interests) rather than from the capital market. But as the FBI could now see, profit margins were beginning to shrink. Some large firms operating partly overseas now speculated about the true cost of operating deficits, and about the nature of their accountancy practices, in a world where slow inflation was becoming endemic. But the majority of FBI members, and the FBI itself, continued to argue about stability and full capacity and low unit costs, without in practice realising how hard this was for the Treasury to achieve by fiscal levers alone.[46] It was, in any case, a poor recipe for innovation and entrepreneurial risk-taking.

Inadequate performance which a mere ten years before had seemed remediable, now became endemic. At the Board of Trade, Thorneycroft transformed the Anglo-American Productivity Council into the British Productivity Council in 1952, in an attempt to cure some of the shortcomings exposed by the Korean War but, in so far as its work had any effect at all, it served to promote backward or average firms to the – still inadequate – level of better ones. Some eighty regional Production Committees existed by 1957 but despite full backing from the FBI, they encountered perennial problems in the secretiveness and suspicion of firms competing with each other, in the weaknesses of trade associations, and in the continued survival of a mass of small firms, reliant on sheltered domestic markets, which were unable or unwilling to reform their practices or their low productivity.

The FBI had offered to assist in 1951 when BOT first proposed a Monopolies Commission (Cmd 8274) for fear of more direct government intervention, for example against retail price maintenance, if it did not. But it continued to argue that the commission should argue each case, singly and on 'expert terms' rather than apply broad 'ideological' guidelines. The national interest would then emerge empirically as the sum total of remedies for individual abuses; almost inevitably the picture would be so confused as to do little damage to FBI members. Moreover, they argued, the national interest should be equated with government's picture of the overall economy, not the rights of the consumer, as Wilson had argued and as Thorneycroft was initially tempted to do.[47]

Thorneycroft and Sir Frank Lee, BOT Permanent Secretary, wanted much more than this: a Monopolies Commission powerful enough to break through just the inertia and vested interests which the FBI sought, if not to preserve, at least to expose as little as possible to a general political assault. They intended also to meet GATT and the United States' protests about unfair and illiberal trade policies. The Attorney General, Sir Lionel Heald went so far as to talk of formulating a general direction to the Monopolies Commission – exactly what industrialists most feared – in December 1955.

The FBI responded as it had done in 1950–51 by arguing a contrary case in stupefying detail, and briefing heavyweight ex-Ministers and backbenchers such as Oliver Lyttleton and Sir Arnold Gridley to speak out on the party's Trade and Industry Committee.[48] They won: talk of a ministerial tribunal lapsed, principally because Conservative backbenchers feared that a future Labour government would use it to enforce control. Instead the Monopolies Commission remained unable to develop a synoptic view of competition policy: when the government set up the Restrictive Practices Court (which at least had powers to prosecute in cases of individual abuse) they gave it similar narrow terms of reference. Following in the tradition of commercial law, the Court built up precedents only slowly and eschewed general arguments, as the FBI had hoped.

More was at issue here than simply recrudescence of the restrictive mentality of the 1930s. By the mid-1950s, the FBI had reason to worry about Britain's share of world trade, even about the security of its domestic market if British firms were to be exposed to free competition without the protection of restrictive practices and resale price maintenance. The problems raised by BOT in 1943 had manifestly either not been solved, or solved less effectively than in Germany and Japan, whilst American competitors, during the Republican administration of Eisenhower, retained their shelters more or less intact. Unable to say this publicly, the FBI had recourse to more specious defences, such as maintenance of quality control and after-sales service, arguments which of course surfaced again in 1963 when Edward Heath finally abolished resale price maintenance. They failed totally, however, to suggest alternative means of making manufacturing industry and the distributive system competitive, other than through mergers and rationalisation of company structures – a development reminiscent of the late 1920s which stock market operations were beginning to favour and which grew rapidly during the next decade. Growth of the giant firm and multinational corporations, thus obscured from all but BOT officials the endemic problem of incompetent medium-sized firms which survived the fat years, only to become casualities in the harsher late 1960s.

The FBI reacted much more positively to opportunities opened up by the early stages of European integration. Britain had declined to join in the Schumann Plan in 1950, largely because of fears that it would involve supra-national commitments. This view, continually deployed by the Foreign Office, dogged Britain's attitude also to development of the European Coal and Steel Community, though a delegation did go as observers to the Messina Conference. Among FBI members, the Iron and Steel Federation argued that to dismantle the British tariff would leave home producers prostrate in front of European competitors, and that any link with the ECSC would harm Commonwealth preference schemes. On the other hand, some of the larger firms individually represented on the FBI Council liked Jean Monnet's plans and welcomed him to England in September 1954. The FBI staff believed it possible to act as brokers in the evolution of ECSC between the ISF, the Iron and Steel Board (successor to the nationalised industry) and Britain's steel users, but were not prepared to argue anything detrimental to national interests. Consequently the FBI as a whole listened to Eden and the Foreign Office and backed Britain's entry to EFTA, as a second-best option, in the hope that a combination covering most OEEC countries, and including the Six, would eventually become possible.[49]

Nevertheless, once serious talks began about the creation of a European Community, in 1955, the FBI began to be afraid that Britain would be left out. Diffidently, because of official hostility, they put forward the idea of British 'association' (a proposal not dissimilar to de Valera's for Irish inclusion in the Commonwealth in 1921) searching, in fact, for a position where Britain could retain both its privileged EFTA and Commonwealth access, while achieving tariff reductions with the EEC.[50] Such a position was not tenable for long, but it represented an advance on the government's position at the time, obsessed as Ministers were with the Suez operation and its diplomatic aftermath (see page 253).

During what, in retrospect, were prosperous years, the FBI's authority extended itself, even into BEC territory. But within its own organisation, as well as through the NUM and Chambers of Commerce, the small business lobby began to protest against their subordination to the interests of medium and large firms. As yet, small business had little weight on the FBI Grand Council but through the 1950s their complaints about the price paid for corporate bias and the government's continued restraints on entrepreneurial activity slowly acquired first a hearing and then some status outside, in the financial press and among certain economic commentators.[51]

Having been still close to the TUC on issues such as national energy policy (where a joint initiative led to the setting up of the Ridley Committee in 1951), the FBI had turned away from tripartism as a method of influencing government policy five years later. Even before the 1956 White Paper put responsibility on management and unions and appeared to detach government from its post-war interventionism, the FBI, like the BEC, had made a series of pre-emptive strikes, accusing government of failing to control public utility prices, energy costs, and wages generally. The restrictive autumn 1955 Budget, coming after Butler's first over-optimistic one, appears to have been a signal which put both of the industrial institutions on the defensive, accentuating the ideological aspect of their thinking, and exposing what their real mentality had become. In April 1956, they replied to Macmillan by disclaiming the responsibility laid by the White Paper. At the same time, they accused the TUC of not fulfilling its obligations and claimed that the balance of power had swung too far, and perhaps irretrievably, in favour of trade unions.[52]

In public, both combined to urge wage restraint on their member firms and associations in order to bail out the government (an unwelcome duty from which they were excused once the TUC's 1956 Congress had rejected wage restraint). But in private, both had delivered notice that they expected government to help them hold back the tide of union power. This occurred a full two years before the Inns of Court Conservative lawyers drafted their well-known pamphlet. *A Giant's Strength*. In deeply defensive mood, the FBI Council began to advise its members to postpone capital spending, in order to forestall a credit squeeze (which came about, in any case, in 1957), with disastrous implications for the future. Here was a turning-point as significant as the 1956 White Paper. Given its natural political affinity, the FBI had wished to stand by a Tory government through the bad years after 1955, but because of internal incoherence and the competing claims of its different sectors, it mounted instead a defence against government, and against the way economic management had developed. In sharp contrast to its public ethos the FBI turned to vilify public spending, public industries, and the practice of deficit financing; yet in spite of the 1956 White Paper it expected government still to deliver stable demand.

After the abandonment of Robot, which was finally laid aside in May 1952, the Bank of England pursued its second line of policy with a rather greater freedom of thought than had been possible under a Labour Chancellor. Cobbold, the Governor, followed Norman's tradition and held back from discussing with Treasury officials, or even Robert Hall, the Chief Economic Adviser, the principles on which money supply was controlled, or Bank rate regulated. (This did not preclude discussion with the Treasury in the light of the prevailing political and economic situation.) Until 1956, Cobbold preferred not to accompany the Chancellor on his visits to Washington; when he did so in the aftermath of Suez it signified that the Bank's still-considerable autonomy had been curtailed. The era of summitry which followed involved the Prime Minister and Foreign Secretary as well as the Chancellor in speaking for the Governor: opportunities for him to speak in his own right diminished.

A similar change occurred in most Western countries, even where a federal Constitution gave the Governor greater formal rights, as in Germany or the United States. After the mid-1950s the private co-operation of central bankers, which had run almost without interruption since the First World War, declined in political if not financial significance, though of course central bank officials continued to meet regularly at Basle, and could rescue sterling, as late as 1961, on their own initiative. The way the Bank represented government policy to the banking system and other City markets was inevitably affected by this loss of autonomy though its diminished status did not affect the way these markets responded to its advice, for example with the extension to finance houses and hire purchase firms of informal credit control in 1960.

Apart from predictable disapproval of the April 1955 Budget for its electioneering tendency, the Bank's only real disagreement with Butler occurred over convertability (see page 277), later that year. Unlike Rowan and the OFD, who had continued the Robot campaign, Cobbold accepted the primacy of the Chancellor's political position while continuing to argue for an anti-inflationary policy designed to stabilise sterling and produce balance of payments equilibrium. Butler's restrictive budget in 1953 exactly fitted these requirements.

Until 1955, Bank and Treasury remained in agreement, though few Treasury officials shared Cobbold's concern, influenced by his German and French central bank colleagues, about the dangers of even a 2–3 per cent inflation rate. Despite this somewhat unfashionable worry, the Bank accepted that full employment and a constant high level of demand would continue to be primary aims of government economic management.

Being the government's agent for funding its debt by the sale of gilts, the Bank could only influence the pattern of borrowing by recalling government to the 1944 pledge not to run unbalanced budgets except in bad years. There was no way to prevent slipping into a pattern of deficit financing except to stand firm on the exchange rate; to deny even the possibility of another devaluation, in the hope that a fixed exchange rate and eventual convertability would, in the long run, help to restrain government borrowing, and state industries' wages and costs, and also keep the reserves high enough to prevent such a crisis as 1951–52 recurring. This standpoint brought the Bank much sympathy from Thorneycroft and his BOT officials, insofar as it helped to prevent the government sheltering industry from competition, or isolating the economy by 'artificial' means. So long as the division between OFD and the Home Economic Section bedevilled the Treasury, and so long as the Permanent Secretary Edward Bridges (who did not retire until 1956) sympathised with the Bank's views on political and diplomatic grounds. Cobbold was listened to. But his real influence could not be compared with Norman's great authority and it suffered severely in 1955 from the extravagant stop-go swing of two misjudged Budgets. In particular the old-fashioned deflation of the second one weakened what remained of the 1944 political contract between the governing institutions, in which the Bank and (rather more remotely) City institutions still had a considerable interest.

Somewhat paradoxically, the Bank emerged as the last defender of the 1944 package, an advocate of a constant prudent restraint which it believed was the last hope of preventing both pendulum swings of policy between governments, and the bogy inflation, without impairing demand or full employment. Misunderstood at the time and later,[53] this was not an ignoble dream. So long as Churchill listened, and influential elder statesmen with City backgrounds like Oliver Lyttleton, the Bank could plead effectively the interests of the sterling area and its advantages as a market together with the conclusion that, in default of further American aid, it was necessary to aim for an eventual return to convertability. But it was vulnerable at all points to international and centrifugal domestic forces and to the temptations to cut corners for political ends to which all Cabinets and Chancellors are exposed.[54] A policy of constant restraint was simply not one that Churchill's harassed successors could risk, in the election year 1955 or afterwards. The Bank's definition of the national interest had therefore to compete, without special weighting like any other in the political marketplace, and sometimes came home among the also-rans.

This was still a time when the Bank, confident in its own research capacity and analysis, barely consulted even the Committee of Clearing Banks about its submissions to the Chancellor on economic policy; and when clearing and merchant banks, and the Stock Exchange went their own way without much doubt that the capital market served industry adequately (and in particular that ICFC and FFI served smaller firms). The new generation of bank chairmen, like Anthony Tuke at Barclays, and Sir Oliver Franks at Lloyds, remained content to follow the lead of small banks like Glyn Mills in developing export finance and the medium-term market, in order to tap the vast funds accumulated by insurance companies. Apart from sharing the same convictions about inflation, wage rates, and strikes, City institutions and their directors probably gave little time to worrying about trends inside British industry or the trade union movement. An awakening occurred during the 1955–57 watershed, as a result of successive governments' attempts to squeeze the supply of credit – which in themselves represented a breakdown of the Bank's informal mechanisms and weakened its sponsorship role.[55]

Meanwhile, the instruments of an earlier government's belief in tripartite consultation, the NPACI, NPAC and EPB continued to focus management and union interest until the White Paper of 1956 shrugged off part of the state's responsibility. But even their own records suggest a gradual decline in the level of genuine participation. The right things were said, the correct gestures made: these remained important centres where competition for advantage among institutions and influence over Ministerial policy occurred. But it was becoming clear to all the participants that transactions were not binding and could not again be the basis for a general economic or political contract. To achieve consensus in the mid-1950s would have involved too much sacrifice of self-interest, too much conflict with member firms or unions. The years after what must be seen as a 1945–55 extension of wartime mentality, witnessed the establishment, in each institution, of a distinct post-war ethos. This evolution (or in some aspects reversion to an earlier ethos on which the war had made only a limited impression) set limits to the prospects for the post-war settlement and economic management even before relative economic decline set in.

8 Men and Issues

During the first five years of Conservative government, the parties and institutions drifted out of sympathy with the political ethos of the immediate post-war consensus in response to changing external conditions and their members' increasing discontents. Those who staffed industry's and unions' central organisations, however, and even more the Civil Service mandarins, still took for granted the existence of a common interest in the 1944 White Paper's blend of mutual advantage and reciprocal obligation – if the leaders of the institutions could only be made to accept them. But the mandarins had first to contend with a novel impediment: the Churchill government's suspicious attempts to rearrange or downgrade their functions.

Incoming Conservative ministers suspected that the higher Civil Service had become too closely identified with their Labour predecessors through Attlee's system of interdepartmental committees. At the personal level, they soon realised that they had been wrong, for the Permanent Secretaries had no need to draw on their 'chameleon' talents to realign themselves; Sir Godfrey Ince with Monckton, Sir Frank Lee with Thorneycroft, Sir Norman Brook with Churchill.[1] But collectively the belief that Attlee and other Labour Ministers had been influenced or even subordinated to Civil Service practice remained. The fact that Brook had challenged Bridges in writing a different machinery of government agenda for them, much less reliant on the use of interdepartmental committees than the system Bridges defended, began a rift between the Treasury (where Bridges, though he gave signs of being worn out after his indefatigable years of wartime service, remained Permanent Secretary until 1956) and the Cabinet Office to which Churchill appointed Brook to serve him almost personally as Cabinet Secretary. Churchill's attempt both to run the Cabinet with 'overlords' and hold his Chancellor, Butler, under supervision reinforced the tension at Ministerial level. Butler slowly established a sort of parity but even by 1955, when Eden became Prime

247

Minister, the centre looked more as it had under Baldwin than under Attlee, with the Chancellor taking main responsibility for economic affairs, the Prime Minister for defence and foreign policy. A system which had worked just about adequately under Churchill, left Eden at a serious disadvantage, not least because of the antipathy in which he and Butler held each other.

Until 1951, the question of how demand should be managed had been worked out under Treasury auspices, with the aid of the Central Economic Planning staff whose evolution Bridges and Hall, the Chief Economic Adviser, had overseen. But Brook's scepticism about the efficacy of economic management added to the disagreement between the two top mandarins. He positively welcomed the new government's assertion of a more market-oriented approach, and Butler's defence of Robot in 1951–52. Bridges attempted to hand on the old priorities, in a list of economic problems worked out by Lee (BOT) and Emmerson (MOL).[2] But Churchill wanted simply to diminish the role played by bureaucrats, especially that of the Treasury in planning, not to take on a Whitehall agenda.

Churchill intended to keep the main lines of policy in his own hands, as he had done during the war, and his system of 'overlords' was intended to facilitate this in peacetime, rather than to revolutionise the way that Cabinet worked. He chose as his four co-ordinating Ministers, Cherwell, Leathers, Anderson and Woolton, men with whom he felt at ease. In the event, Anderson refused, and the domains of the others turned out to be too diffuse and probably too large. Virtually all senior civil servants criticised the idea as inefficient and beyond proper parliamentary control – deficiencies that Woolton actually admitted.[3] Churchill finally abolished them in September 1953.

A drive to diminish what he saw as Civil Service manipulation would probably have occurred in any case, once the period of scarcity and rationing ended. The interdepartmental committees Churchill deplored had mostly vanished by 1953, to be replaced, if at all, by informal meetings of Permanent Secretaries; senior civil servants generally resumed their distinctive attitudes in a departmental geography closer to the 1930s. The innate tendency of Treasury, Board of Trade or Ministry of Labour to develop conflicting policies, as a result of their functions and sponsorship links with financial, industrial and labour institutions had until then been restrained by a conscious effort to emphasise interdependence;

but from the early 1950s they began again to look like separate fiefs. This had the effect of imperilling the Treasury's primacy in economic management. The Treasury countered first by setting up committees of inquiry into various major topics, under the aegis of Sir Thomas Padmore, and secondly by emphasising that balance of payments equilibrium and the stability of sterling counted more than either full employment or industrial prosperity.

Bridges and Brook united in trying to prevent the outbreak of conflict over fundamental policy, as their actions at the time of Robot show. That there was a danger to the post-war settlement if departmental frontiers became established as firmly as they had been before the war was a view widely shared: 'If those of us who have lived all our working lives in Whitehall and have studied the Whitehall organisation,' Lee wrote, 'give up as hopeless all attempts to reform it from inside then what hope is there of reform in our time?'[4] But Churchill resisted any wide-ranging machinery of government debate, and Woolton dismissed the Padmore Committees' reports in scathing terms, in 1954. So long as he was there, Bridges saw himself as holding together the elaborate and subtle apparatus of the 1940s,[5] and the informal meetings of Permanent Secretaries evidently still fulfilled what may be called adjustment functions or brokerage between departments. But in the five years after 1951, a transition to a more departmental structure did occur, leaving the Civil Service centre more exposed to the balance of opinion in Cabinet, less able to argue a coherent interdepartmental case for the particular sort of economic management prevalent since 1947, or for a general equivalence between the claims of the various interests outside.

Since Churchill held the reins, yet took little detailed interest in the domestic economy, the spending departments reverted to their traditional adversarial relationship with the Treasury. The Board of Trade and Ministry of Labour had in such circumstances to find their own levels. Under the relatively junior Thorneycroft, the former discovered itself in an anomalous position frequently outflanked by the FBI's direct links with the Conservative Party – a disadvantage from which MOL, given Monckton's mandate from the Prime Minister, did not suffer. Given that the Ministry of Agriculture[6] and the Ministry of Transport and Civil Aviation[7] retained their full sponsorship practices, the resulting pattern of government-industry relations became a curious hybrid, part state influence, part reliance on a supposed free market.

The Conservative Party's Conference commitment to providing 300 000 houses a year, and the powers allocated by Churchill allowed Harold Macmillan to remodel the Ministry of Housing on the lines of the old Ministry of Production, able to override other departments' claims to skilled labour, plant and capital, or Treasury attempts to regulate their supply. That the houses were built suggests not only that political priorities ranked above concern with industrial capital formation, but that such energies, otherwise deployed, might have revolutionised the already hidebound and unprofitable public industries the Conservatives had inherited. Construction on such a scale may have been good for full employment. But more than any other time in the post-war era, the early 1950s were already years of over-full employment on one hand, of inadequate investment in manufacturing industry on the other. Britain could barely afford such hothouse developments, especially when Butler reduced investment incentives by £200 million, in his restrictionist budget in 1953.

It is easy to argue that if Peter Thorneycroft had been more senior in the Cabinet pecking order, BOT could have argued a more rational order of priorities than tying up so much available capital in this way. But he had been chosen not as a Minister for Industry but as a good Commons performer and a token that the Tory Reformers had not been excluded. Able, determined, interested in the development of British industry as a matter of political philosophy, Thorneycroft fitted well into a ministerial tradition that began with Cunliffe–Lister in the 1920s and continued, after a bad patch in the late 1950s, with Edward Heath. At one with the gifted Permanent Secretary, Sir Frank Lee, he steered BOT away from Wilson's legacy of Development Councils and the whole policy of effecting change by state leverage, in favour of liberal trade, reduction of monopolies, lower taxes on industry, and an eventual place for Britain within an as yet unspecified European bloc. As had been intended in 1942–44, government would set the context of free competition, forcing industry to become efficient so that it could take advantage of a wider market.

Whether or not Thorneycroft's should be seen as early 'supply-side' policy, his ideas fitted well enough with the ethos of the party's Trade and Industry Committee, under its Chairman Oliver Lyttleton, and forward-looking industrialists like Sir Richard Costain and Sir Henry Pilkington, whom Thorneycroft chose as his private advisors. But the FBI disliked them, partly because BOT failed to establish priority or even parity for industry as against balance of payments considerations, and partly because they did nothing to alleviate dividend restraint, nor hasten the process of denationalising steel and road transport. Kipping, the FBI's Director General went so far as to write, 'Disenchantment was mutual. Genuine consultation, and any question of mutual involvement of shared policy-making waned.'[8]

So long as Thorneycroft and Lee concentrated on the trade context, the FBI's feeling that BOT was failing to assert itself against the Treasury rankled – although it diminished sharply after Butler's income tax concessions in 1953. But given the events in Europe it mattered much more to the FBI to settle whether Britain's trading future lay in a European combination or the sterling area. Ministers and departments differed strongly: the Conservative old right, now represented by Leo Amery and Lord Salisbury, fought for imperial preferences, while the Bank, most City institutions and the Treasury OFD backed the sterling area and the advantages of building up a Commonwealth financial community. The Foreign Office threw its whole weight against British participation in the early stages of European economic integration (see page 253). What amounted to a restatement of the case for bilateralism rested not on Britain's imperial legacy but on genuine doubts whether GATT liberalism could be a realistic aim, given Britain's imbalance of trade with the United States and the rest of the world.

Thorneycroft, supported by the Chief Economic Advisor, Robert Hall, argued that this analysis was already out of date, citing the way that the Robot episode had revealed unexpected divisions among the Dominions. Britain's trade with the Commonwealth and even the sterling area was shrinking and the vaunted preferences now meant little; Canada had long since moved into the US orbit, Australia was already entering it, while India and Pakistan had become major trading partners with the USA, according to a BOT Survey, May 1952, conducted by Sir Edgar Cohen.[9] In terms of capital, the Commonwealth was a drain which even the Bank of England admitted Britain could barely afford. In arguing so, Thorneycroft and Lee of course followed what the Dollar Export Board and the Anglo-American Productivity Committee had been saying for seven years. Churchill seems to have accepted BOT's point of view, for he closed down the Cabinet Committee on Commercial Policy in July 1952; overborne afterwards by Salisbury and the anti-BOT lobby, however, he gave assent to an extension of imperial preferences, which he ordered Lyttleton to defend at the Party Conference.[10]

In due course, the Treasury discovered that BOT's analysis of the pattern was correct, and when the Dominions showed themselves lukewarm, preferences were slowly discarded. It took time to wean the party from its ancestral responses (Salisbury and Amery never gave in) but, with Churchill's backing, Thorneycroft finally vindicated his policy of trade liberalisation at the 1954 Conservative Conference. The concessions that he had by then gained for the Commonwealth in GATT negotiations probably did more than preferences could have achieved, at this late stage.

But BOT could never play a straightforward hand as a Ministry of Trade because it was also a Ministry of Industry – without the powers or nationalistic ethos which enabled the Japanese Ministry of International Trade and Industry later to contribute so greatly to the development of both. Ironically Japan's entry into GATT tested BOT's faith in freer trade and its susceptibility to party electoral calculation. Given the uncompetitiveness of much of British industry, Thorneycroft had to ask whether the government should welcome this spur to efficiency, even if it meant bankruptcies or unemployment, or seek to protect the home market under cover of buying time to adjust. In schizophrenic mood, and very much as the FBI desired, BOT now reverted to its 1930s habits, and started talks about anti-dumping and 'restoring equilibrium', which meant in practice, through the medium of the Anglo-Japanese Trade and Payments Agreement, 1954 and the 1957 Customs Duty Act, restriction of imports, particularly Japanese textiles, which upset both the free-traders in Cabinet and the Eisenhower administration.

Even in its restrictive guise, BOT could not please everyone. Thorneycroft refused to control the entry of cheap Commonwealth textiles, which enraged Lancashire manufacturers as well as the Americans, and worried Party officials, fearful for marginal seats in the North-West in an election year like 1955. Eden, as Prime Minister, tried to shift Thorneycroft before the election; and Churchill had to intervene to pacify the Lancashire Cotton Board.[11] Conversely, where exports were concerned, BOT could count on the support of both Eden and Churchill for increasing trade with Eastern Europe and the Far East, although Butler quibbled about the degree to which tax incentives and export credits might conflict with GATT or offend the Inland Revenue.

The extension of the Export Credit Guarantees Department to include banking in April 1954 coincided with an improvement in the visible trade deficit, just at the time when BOT found itself in complete sympathy with the FBI on removing import quotas on European trade. But what might have been an occasion for BOT to examine the advantages of European economic integration slipped away. Little if any discussion in Cabinet occurred in 1954–55. Churchill and Eden took charge and excluded not only Thorneycroft but others like Macmillan and Maxwell Fyfe who might have supported some degree of integration from a question they believed to be for the Foreign Office alone. In a Cabinet paper written in June 1955, Thorneycroft favoured an EFTA association with the EEC but he was overridden by a combination of Foreign Office, Treasury and Cabinet Office, aided by the Ministry of Agriculture which reflected, quite simply, the hostility of British farmers.

Thorneycroft was constrained after this to approve withdrawal from the Messina Conference. He had in any case been under the impression – sedulously fostered by Eden – that the Coal and Steel Community was an unwieldy creation put together by 'unstable countries'. Like the Foreign Office, Trade officials led by Herbert Andrew still saw Europe through suspicious eyes and preferred involvement on British terms or not at all. Not until about 1956 did the myth of the 'three circles' – dollar, sterling and the rest – finally die away. Even then the Bank of England and OFD only grudgingly admitted that BOT's analysis of how the sterling area had lost its value had been right; and the Salisbury group never forgave Thorneycroft. As the Suez invasion showed, Eden failed to recognise the fundamental change in Britain's international position; disaster at Suez of course curtailed some of Britain's most sheltered markets and ended her economic hegemony in the Middle East, while India's political threat to withdraw its sterling balances further debilitated the sterling area.

There was no chance after Messina that the British government would try to follow in the path of the Spaak Report, with its supranational overtones.[12] From January 1956 Eden took the lead in resisting pressure from Eisenhower and Dulles to line up with Spaak and the European movement before it was too late to join the incipient Community. Despite FBI pressure and Thorneycroft's doubts, the Cabinet sought to retain what sterling area benefits still existed, together with the special relationship with the United States *and* to increase trade in Europe – although the government's public statement on the future of EFTA, in December 1955 wrapped this up in a more palatable form. Neither Thorneycroft nor his officials had been prepared to go as far as Monnet, Spaak and Schumann. Another four years' experience was required before the inadequacy of EFTA as a holding position became clear enough for Britain's belated application to the EEC to proceed.

In two other fields, monopolies and restrictive practices, and also regional policy, Thorneycroft briefly exhumed some of the questions buried by his predecessors. He and Frank Lee were at one in disliking the restrictionist mentality of the FBI and the TUC, and their departmental inquiry led on to the 1953 Monopolies Commission Act and the Restrictive Practices Act 1956. But on the crucial issue whether the Commission and the Restrictive Practices Court should work on general principles of investigation, as opposed to taking each case on its merits and relying on Ministers to refer to them specific abuses for reform, Thorneycroft and the Cabinet took the FBI's side; equally, under Monckton's influence, they refused altogether to touch trade union restrictive practices. Paradoxically, Thorneycroft supported general, rather than selective incentives to investment, though some evidence of selectivity can be discerned in BOT use of the 1954 Capital Grants Act.

BOT emerged as more of a friend of industry (as the FBI defined friendship) than the Thorneycroft–Lee combination might have led its civil servants to expect; certainly far from the intrinsically hostile role of which Wilson had dreamed six years before. The practice of tripartism and sponsorship survived, in the NPACI, but mattered less than the BOT's much closer, informal linkages with the FBI and the fact that BOT emphasis now lay less on galvanising industry by enforced competition than on facilitating exports, stimulating investment, and leaving industry to take its chances, or not, as the case might be. Again, as in 1944, an opportunity was missed, because a more interventionist policy might at least have influenced those key sectors of industry like machine tools production which were already developing symptoms of arteriosclerosis.

The mid-1950s witnessed unparalleled regional prosperity even in Northern Ireland, so that the incentive to do otherwise was absent. Nevertheless, the obstacles to growth the NEDC was to diagnose in 1962 in the 'Orange Book' had come into existence at least a decade before; some of them dated from much earlier stages of Britain's industrial revolution. BOT's own investigation in 1942 had pointed to industry's habit of passing on costs to domestic consumers, leaving those competing in export markets to become 'Cinderellas'. Government stimuli had gone some way to make exporting profitable and to increase productivity in the late 1940s, without significantly improving what a later generation would call non-price factors – product design, quality, after-sales service, among others. All that had been said in 1943–44 about the inability of the FBI or trade associations to induce change applied ten years later, at a time when it could be contrasted with the German example, where trade associations were both compulsory and more powerful.

It is of course hard to generalise or make simple distinctions between large and small firms. In industries prone to underinvestment, overmanning or resistance to change, there were always firms which ran counter to prevailing trends. But those who worked, for example, in the EEF recall the rigid attitudes of Engineering Council members at this time and of its Director General. In 1952 when Ramsay retired, the Council chose a 'safe' successor, on no better grounds than that on controversial policies he might entice back the car manufacturers who had relinquished membership some years before. EEF politics seemed to follow parallel to the decline in engineering productivity that had become visible during the Korean War. Meanwhile, the leading car manufacturers themselves, eager not to lose sales by letting the production line stop, met wage demands at plant level throughout the 1950s as if the golden years would never end. Thinking more of their cash reserves in a possible recession than about future markets, they neglected to invest in new plant and technology, so that 'new models' emerged as variations only in chrome trim. A similar fear of new product design afflicted textiles, while shipbuilders and heavy engineering companies continued to build for existing markets with little thought of how rapidly demand might change. The machine tool industry stagnated and buyers, even from Commonwealth countries like India, began to turn elsewhere.

These were to be the dinosaurs of the 1960s and '70s, as the old staple industries, coal, steel and textiles had been in the 1920s. Even where they had an export trade, it tended to be concentrated in semi-imperial or politically sheltered markets. British firms produced no car for the European market in the 1950s, to rival the Volkswagen or Citroën's DS19, but contented themselves either with offering upgraded 1930s products like the Standard Vanguard or appealing to a luxury market with ponderous production-line imitations of custom-built cars. Insular self-satisfaction predominated, and distortions of the manufacturing markets were enhanced by a taxation policy which offset low managerial salaries with a range of private perquisites. The British Tabulating Company broke off its links with IBM on the bland assumption that it could satisfy the home market – and was overtaken by 1960. Public industries (with the notable exception of the Gas Board, and the Coal Board under the chairmanship of Alfred Robens) exemplified many of the worst features. In such a busy, profitable era, with constant high consumer demand liberated after a decade of austerity, there was little time to reflect on whether companies would always be able to sell all they produced. Trade unions assumed too easily that unemployment had been abolished, manufacturers that competition no longer mattered. Those like Courtaulds or ICI who watched the trends because they had much foreign business, however, understood the rise to commercial supremacy of Germany, followed by Japan, and did act, so that well before 1960 a division existed between the survivors and the incipient disasters like Alfred Herbert, once the finest machine tool manufacturer in the world.

A feeling that unions were gaining a serious advantage on the shop floor ruffled this mood of collective complacency about the time of the first serious 'stop' in government economic policy in 1955–56. Many industrialists had hoped that the EEF would speak for all employers in standing up to the AEU, and were deeply distressed when the Macmillan government reneged, as they thought, on its promise of support to the engineering employers (see page 312). Here was a marker in the establishment of an alibi for managerial failings. Yet the hallmark of the period was an act of almost gratuitous thoughtlessness. Leonard Lord, head of the British Motor Corporation issued dismissal notices for 6000 car workers in the summer of 1956, just before the men went on holiday, without prior notice even to their unions or MOL. More than any other single event, this embittered industrial relations in the car industry as the uneasy years began.

To the outlook of trade associations and employers, the later fifties brought an accumulation of worries. But until then, BOT exhortations and warnings had made virtually no impression. Sponsorship in industry had come to mean nothing more than a measure of dependence on the FBI or BEC for representation accompanied by a genial expectancy of government benevolence. The Thorneycroft–Lee innovations and attempts to improve competitiveness hardly touched the feeling that, despite the hiccups caused by balance of payments problems and sterling's perennial weakness, the 1944 package was still working and no general appraisal was needed. For lack of access to Cabinet archives, it is not possible to say what was government's overall perception, but Ministers certainly did not try to rouse the rather lethargic Conservative Trade and Industry Committee to look at foreign competition. In the most significant case of the period, the Churchill government gave the steel barons pretty much what they wanted when steel was denationalised, perhaps without realising that by adapting the pre-war state corporation model when setting up the new Iron and Steel Board, they were replicating the cartel conditions of the 1930s.[13]

Churchill chose Walter Monckton for the Ministry of Labour because he was a man without a political past, a lawyer with a long experience of labour issues and a gifted conciliator. He gave him a simple brief: to reassure the trade union movement that a Conservative government would not introduce penal sanctions in any industrial relations legislation, and to make sure that government was not disrupted: 'Winston's riding orders to me were that the Labour Party had foretold grave industrial troubles if the Conservatives were elected, and he looked to me to do my best to preserve industrial peace. I said that I should seek to do that by trying to do justice . . . without caring about party politics.'[14] Churchill gave him consistent support (though he did at times go over his head and correspond with Tewson directly) as did Malcolm McCorquodale, Chairman of the Conservative Labour Committee.

Since MOL's main function had thus been reduced to one of conciliation, Monckton found himself at home among his officials, like Godfrey Ince, who had accepted that manpower controls should not be restored, even for the Korean War. Conrad Heron, who became his closest advisor, saw Monckton as a fellow bureaucrat who would listen to advice and argue the Labour department's case in Cabinet with a lawyer's fluency. All three agreed that any attempt to guide the labour market should be done in association with the TUC and the BEC, through the NJAC. In drafting his proposals for codes of conduct on the basis of the *Industrial Charter* rather than legislation, Monckton followed in the tradition of prewar Conservative Ministers like Arthur Steel-Maitland; and he rapidly established a rapport with TUC leaders who saw it as natural that he should lunch with Tewson, Deakin, and other sympathisers on the General Council like Tom Williamson, Will Lawther, Lincoln Evans of the ISTC, Tom O'Brien and Alan Birch.[15]

In the Commons he got on equally well with the Labour spokesman, Alfred Robens, later Chairman of the Coal Board.

Within his own Party, Monckton had a harder time, for even the subject of conciliation soon roused strong passions. Central Office staff and the Research Department still stood by the Charter's principle: change by slow, incremental stages should be formalised in procedures and conventions rather than legislation. Backbenchers' demands for legislation against the closed shop, or for making union election ballots mandatory, gave Monckton a difficult time during the 1953 Conference but had no significant resonance outside the constituency organisations. Wages however were a far more contentious subject. Although Ince might tell his colleagues in MOL 'we have the best wages policy in the world', Treasury officials by 1956 regarded the claim as economic nonsense, an attempt to shroud reality with nostalgia and mystery which unfortunately appealed only too strongly to Churchill's romantic vein.

Wages would have been a difficult problem under any regime and without employers' insistence that wage-inflation had become a major problem. The Korean War's distorting effect on the cost of living lasted until 1953, and lead sectors of industry early on established a process of leap-frogging claims which not only widened differentials between, for example, metal workers and textile workers, but on a much more serious scale distanced a buoyant private market from public industries. As Churchill probably realised, Monckton would be judged by Cabinet on how he preserved peace in such conditions. 'The old oil can' (as David Margesson, once Chief Whip, called him), was so stretched after 1954 that he collapsed from illness briefly, and for two months early in 1955 had to give way to his junior minister, Harold Watkinson. If nothing else, this overriding obligation to the party prevented him from implementing his real policy which was not to be a wages arbiter or broker but an innovator of ways to formalise procedures of industrial relations, very similar to the line that was later taken by the Donovan Commission.

As a wages broker, he sought always to introduce the 'neutral mechanism', the arbiter or court of inquiry which could bring a sense of a wider national interest to bear, much as his predecessor George Askwith had done forty years earlier: 'to examine and explore the field of conflict and reduce it patiently to its narrowest limits and there to indicate a way in which . . . the parties might find a way of getting together.'[16] So long as this was the intention, and Courts of Inquiry the method of clarifying general principles, the TUC gave him goodwill and did not attempt to challenge the results. But it objected to his interference in 1952 with Wages Boards, and to the use of emergency powers against oil tanker drivers a year later; individual unions and middle-ranking officials, who suspected that his methods would work to the detriment of poorly organised and low-paid workers, took dissent much further.

The radicals in the union movement saw behind Monckton's codes of practice not an extension of the informal system of industrial relations which had grown up in the previous fifty years but an alternative thesis that behaviour in the labour market should be regulated by contract law. This was certainly a view becoming popular on the right of the Conservative Party but it was not Monckton's. Nevertheless, wage disputes created more antagonism than might have been expected, and made it harder to implement his real policy. What created problems with his colleagues was the duty Churchill had laid on him of keeping the government out of trouble with the nationalised industries – none of which were under his control. Like the Attlee government's dispute with the gas workers in 1947, claims and settlements in electricity supply, shipbuilding and almost annually on the railways affected overall public policy and threatened the Treasury strategy of wages and prices equilibrium. After the 1953 railway strike, the Chief Whip, Harry Crookshank, asked Monckton pointedly whether a settlement made over the head of Sir Brian Robertson, Chairman of the British Transport Commission, would not set a dangerous pattern of concession. 1954 brought strikes in mining, engineering, electricity and on the railways again, as state employees attempted to catch up with the elusive leaders in private industry. Cabinet Ministers began seriously to worry that union claimants were now no longer content to abide even by settlements reached the previous year; yet they still tried to hold back wages in public industry for fear of stimulating worse inflation outside.

Monckton could not be a free agent, an individual court of conciliation, nor could he bargain with the TUC when individual unions simply refused to be tied down by his subtle procedural nets. Meanwhile the BEC stepped up its gloomy warnings, and after Forbes Watson had been replaced by the more dynamic Sir George Pollock, moved to create an employers' front with the FBI, directed as much against public industry itself, as the wages bargaining system.[17] Worst of all, in the long run, was the fact that the independent Courts of Inquiry which Monckton had, perforce, to appoint enunciated principles which were neither to ministers' nor employers' tastes, nor (in the case of Lord Justice Morris's inquiry into shipbuilding and engineering) the unions'. In spite of the principle enunciated in the crucial Cameron Report, in January 1955, which, to government's horror, favoured 'a fair and adequate wage' and laid down that if the nation had willed this as an end, it must find the means even if the railways could not afford it out of their own budget, the train drivers' union ASLEF remained on strike in order to maintain its old differentials *vis-à-vis* the railwaymen.

The railway strike of 1954 which gave rise to the Cameron Report provided the crux. A powerful animus gathered against Monckton during December, when the Cabinet seemed unanimous in refusing to let BTC go into debt to pay its wages bill. Monckton too gave the impression of wanting to stand firm; but Churchill and Woolton ordered him to give way, because they were afraid of what transport paralysis during the winter would do to the Budget and the party's election prospects.[18] Electoral calculations remained secret: 'Monckton's way' collected the odium. There is no evidence that Churchill's government faced up, even to the extent that Attlee's had done in 1947–48, to the problem of public industry wages, where increasingly powerful unions backed relatively low-paid workers' claims to equivalence with the most profitable parts of private industry, regardless of the full employment for which, only ten years earlier, it had been assumed they would be extremely grateful. The lack of a clear political statement about responsibility (such as Attlee frequently gave) lies at the door of government, not Monckton alone.

Fearful of opinion in the constituencies, and of a critical press, Churchill and his ministers passively accepted that they had to redress a wages' imbalance, without asking if it was already balanced in other ways. Instead of taking what was probably the last opportunity to ask what public industries signified in the economy as a whole and the labour market in particular, the Cabinet decided to fight each claim *seriatim*, with the result that the inquiries and settlements built up, remorselessly, a pattern of comparability which had not been envisaged by the architects of nationalisation but which constrained all future governments down to 1978–79. As Anthony Seldon points out, the very choice of 'neutral', almost judicial instruments to settle disputes between the state and its own employees in fact devalued the state's authority. 'In order not to prejudice the government's posture of impartiality, the Ministers and other government spokesmen refrained from comment on the substance of the dispute, even if it was widely held that the union's claim was unrealistic'.[19] When reports were published, ministers found themselves having to recommend them to both sides, thus demoralising the Boards of public industry and leaving a legacy of ambiguity which the 1956 White Paper failed to resolve.

Where private industry was concerned, Monckton tried to stiffen Sir George Pollock and the BEC to resist the engineering workers' claim in 1955, and advised the EEF in the same sense.[20] They reacted mistrustfully, uncertain about the Eden government's collective resolve. Neither Monckton nor Churchill should be singled out for blame when, at varying times and for different reasons, Macmillan, Butler and Woolton all justified the settlements that were made in order to legitimise the new Conservatism among the mass of eleven million trades unionists. Nor is it reasonable to blame union leaders, already deeply worried about the way power was draining down to the shop floor and concerned quite legitimately for public employees whose low wages condemned them to a marginal position in the consumer society that was developing quickly by 1953–55. The TUC itself could not bear to be seen as sluggish or in restraint of shop floor pressure or, perhaps worse, to act in defence of a Conservative government less than two years from a general election which Labour confidently expected to win. Instead they went as far as seemed prudent not to alienate a favourable Minister of Labour: in standing by Order 1376 and by not supporting ASLEF's long strike after the Cameron Report, nor opposing the declaration of a state of emergency in May 1955.[21]

Monckton and Watkinson saw that there was a way out of all this, if only 'industry' could respond and achieve the higher profitability which would have made a wage-inflation debate otiose. This miracle of course occurred in Germany in the 1950s, under the Adenauer–Erhard administration. For lack of it in Britain, profit margins began to narrow, and senior Conservative ministers, aligned more closely to City opinion than to the industrial interest, do not appear to have realised how rapidly the chance of stopping deterioration was slipping away.

The Ministry of Labour's long policy of reordering the skilled labour market by better training and measures to increase mobility, so that redundancy would not necessarily be the price of modernising production, rested at this time on reducing competition for skilled labour through the flexible use of Order 1376, and the operation of labour exchanges. Monckton's own method of solving disputes by building incrementally a consciousness of common interest in wages and profits had some successes but in the end only reinforced the conclusion of what was becoming a small group of cynics in his Ministry that the state was weaker than in wartime. Government could not now do more than create a climate of educated opinion 'as a partner in this enterprise with employers and organised labour'.[22] Unfortunately, the Treasury had concluded that an equally long-term wages policy was required – hence Butler's 1952 appeal in the NJAC to both sides to link wages and productivity was followed a year later by another, based on the threat of inflation to Britain's vital export trade. Much as the BEC appreciated his efforts, the Cabinet were not prepared to proceed without TUC agreement, which was not forthcoming. Nothing more occurred until 1955 – after the election – when the combination in previous months of the Cameron Report and a wave of apparently uncontrollable strikes in the docks, newspaper production, and yet again, on the railways finally led them back to the idea.

It is possible that a deal with the TUC might have been tried then, during Eden's brief premiership, when Macleod had taken Monckton's place at MOL and Macmillan was at the Exchequer. Macleod turned out to be only slightly less emollient than his predecessor: he only toyed with the idea of a restrictive practices Commission to investigate trade unions and was soon deterred by the prospect of stirring up hostility. But Eden and Macmillan, like Lloyd George in 1919, were baffled by the contrast between the General Council level of the TUC, which still seemed aware of the 1944 responsibilities, and the local level of the trade union movement which, in their eyes, had become utterly irresponsible.

Monckton's last advice to Eden, in September 1955, had been to try by his personal authority to bring the two sides together to discuss an equitable, voluntary form of restraint in the interests of the nation as a whole.[23] A continuous line can thus be traced from 1944, which runs on to 1962–63 and the Labour government's negotiations with the TUC in 1965. But even if it had not been for the Suez disaster, it is doubtful if Eden was the man for such a negotiation. Worried as he was about inflation, he found it hard to accept that the actual system of industrial relations had degenerated: lacking experience of industry or labour after his years at the Foreign Office, he could not see how rapidly the trade union movement had altered, making Churchill's easy generalisations of 1951 completely out of date. Eden was lucky, who only kept in touch with congenial leaders like Deakin and Carron at one remove through his PPS Toby Low. Macleod had to cope with the much more perplexing phenomenon represented by Frank Cousins, and the rise of challengers to the old big six, such as Hugh Scanlon in the AEU.

Eden planned for talks with both sides at Chequers in the summer of 1956. It is doubtful, given his misjudgment about the power of the TUC leaders he knew, if they could had led far, even if they had taken place. Tewson's conversations with Eden (see page 234) and his talk of tightening up the TUC's Rule 11 to cope with the refusal of ASLEF to accept the Cameron Report, depended on Tewson's very limited capacity to mobilise a deeply divided, irresolute General Council. In any case, as Monckton and Maxwell Fyfe both pointed out, many Conservative backbenchers would resist interference by the TUC with the liberty of individual members of unions to bargain as they wished: they would in fact prevent the TUC from becoming an effective corporative instrument.[24]

Meanwhile, other vociferous backbenchers who had cried 'Danegeld' ever since Monckton's appointment, lined up with the BEC and FBI to predict an irreversible shift in the balance of power, unless legislation were brought in to prevent it. Conservative lawyers of the Inns of Court duly drafted what became the seminal pamphlet *A Giant's Strength*. However much Macleod defended the TUC to a hostile 1956 Conference, attitudes in the party were veering against the practice of co-operation, to the point of denying that common ground existed. One of the many elements in the 1956 White Paper was that Eden and his colleagues tried to prevent this happening by playing off the BEC against the FBI, by referring responsibility back to unions and management, and by hoping that gradual deflation and the 'price plateau' in public industries (from which they expected significant results) would take some of the heat out of wage expectations.[25]

One pointer to the changing attitude about wages can be seen in Beveridge's contemporary worries about the whole system of collective bargaining. In a number of influential articles in 1954–56, he argued that inflation was destroying the fiscal basis of social insurance, and would make the cost of the welfare state ultimately intolerable; in answer, he advocated a permanent wages policy laid down, not by the government but by arbitration tribunals.[26]

Of greater importance, inside MOL, at a more junior level than Ince and Emmerson, grew up a belief 'that national priorities, in the labour and industrial relations field since the war had been fundamentally wrong'.[27] Because of their mutual connivance, government, employers and unions together were living in a fool's paradise of full employment – as Treasury officials had warned them, ten years earlier.

For the first time since the war, concern about wages led to common ground between MOL and BOT, in the feeling that efficiency mattered more than political harmony, and that the two might no longer be compatible. This coincided with a failure of the demand management 'fine-tuning' on which the Treasury had so far prided itself; and with the appointment of Peter Thorneycroft as Chancellor of the Exchequer.

Speaking in very general terms, the mid-1950s marks the end of a stage begun in the mid-1930s, during which the relationship of Britain's foreign trade and her manufacturing was favourable. Afterwards it deteriorated slowly, to about 1963, when a more rapid downturn began. 1950–54 was also a period of historically high growth – though obviously less dramatic than the immediate post-war years – and of an extremely high level of employment. Yet profits fell drastically as a result of lack of competitiveness and wage inflation after wages restraint collapsed in 1950. Labour's share in total national income rose steadily (thanks to increases in the employers' national insurance contribution made by the Attlee government, against which the BEC and FBI repeatedly protested). Supply constraints, in particular shortages of skilled labour, explain the low growth in productivity after 1952; the most serious failing was not so much the low volume of investment (though that amounted to barely more than 50 per cent of most OEEC competitors) as its direction into fundamentally defensive strategies, whenever managers and owners patched up existing plant rather than applying money to re-equipment.

Such a wide-ranging phenomenon invited many explanations after the mid-1950s when its serious dimensions first came into clear focus. Some were straightforward, even simplistic: wage-inflation or 'union power', reverberated in the press and increasingly among employers. Conversely, the thesis that management was incompetent or defensive was more difficult to argue on a factual basis at the time, and more difficult for the readers of most newspapers to understand. A few commentators recalled the Macmillan 'gap' and accused the financial sector of caring more about overseas earnings than about the home industrial base. Others, among them the FBI and the TUC, turned on the Treasury and blamed it for the uncertainties and cutbacks of 'stop-go', and for the lowly place given to industry in the priorities of economic management. They tended to argue that the 1944 aim of equilibrium had been pursued not by hard bargaining and mutual assistance between government and the two sides of industry, as had originally been intended, but by the use of fiscal levers, such as bank rate and credit control in ways detrimental to the real economy. Treasury hegemony (as Samuel Brittan was later to argue in *The Treasury under the Tories* (1964)), also forced unions to become obsessive about money wages and prevented any government from consistently pursuing growth, as Erhard had done in Germany. Required to choose after 1945 between the unpalatable alternatives of a socialist command economy and unfettered free enterprise, it appeared that the mandarins had picked instead a middle way which failed on most counts other than the creation of political harmony.

The Treasury's defence – or rather the defence put up later by Treasury officials – was that they had first to discover how to do the job that Cripps and his successors had willed them to do; that their fine-tuning worked well between 1950 and 1955, and again from 1957 to 1960; and that their efforts were undone by the politically-orientated budgets of 1955 and 1959 drafted with forthcoming elections in mind.

For lack of access to Treasury documents, only an interim judgment can be made. Nevertheless, it is clear that in the years 1952–56, when world factors were more generally favourable to Britain's economy than in any subsequent period, the apparent success of economic management had a profound effect on its future practice. The more the 1951–52 crisis receded in memory, the more Butler's period as Chancellor came to be seen as the model for what the Treasury should do, and how it should regulate its relationships with other departments and they with the institutions.

Churchill's promotion of Butler to the Exchequer which, only five years after the *Industrial Charter*, hinted at a leftward turn may be explained by the absence of a preferred alternative: Oliver Stanley had died the previous year, Oliver Lyttleton was too committed to the City, and Woolton did not seek the job. Initially, Churchill set watchdogs around him, and behaved somewhat ambiguously during the Robot episode. Butler had therefore to contend with his rivals on the Economic Policy Committee, and in Cherwell's Statistical Branch; he had also to argue a politically unpopular case against Macmillan's housing expenditure. Not until after Cherwell retired in November 1953 did he enjoy a period of very considerable authority – though that was saddened and confused by his wife's illness and early death. It is not surprising that he adopted a low-key style of presentation. Moreover, he inherited a financial predicament about which the party's planning in opposition had given him virtually no guidance. In September 1951 when Churchill chose his Cabinet, the dollar deficit was already $1200 million, the balance of payments approximately £500 million, worse if taken across the sterling area. Treasury officials warned Butler at once that the crisis might be more serious than that of 1931, and then prepared him for the rise in bank rate, and the manoeuvres which ended with Robot.

Butler found the Treasury divided and not only in its opinion of Robot. The serious rift of principle between OFD and the Home Economic Department ensured that the Chancellor would often receive conflicting advice. Much as he enjoyed tackling hard intellectual problems, Butler liked the support of officials and missed the near-unanimity on which previous Chancellors had relied. He had few friends in Cabinet, and to Eden and Macmillan it appeared that he was run by his officials. This was not so, indeed the reverse was true, for Butler had to be an intellectual broker, but the Treasury kept its divisions so quiet (Robot itself remained a matter of most intense secrecy for more than twenty years) that it seemed so.

Robot's failure had both a cathartic and a divisive effect on the Treasury. Older officials, sceptical of Keynesian techniques, like Sir Bernard Gilbert lost influence as did Leslie Rowan himself. Butler continued to rely on both, however, as an antidote to the new orthodoxy about which he was much more uncertain than his public utterances allowed to appear (as his initial welcome for Robot and the fact that the traditionalist, Sir Herbert Brittain, headed the Home Finance Section after Eady, suggest). Bridges and Padmore took rather less part than these three in policy evaluation through the Budget Committee.[28]

Butler acquired an excellent team of technocrats, led by Robert Hall (who was finally detached from the Cabinet Office with the rest of the Economic Section in November 1953). These favoured a strategy of fiscal equilibrium based on analysis of national income and expenditure, implemented through the Budget and its fiscal levers, and accompanied by a fairly rough-and-ready monetary policy. Policy aims were clear: to keep industrial costs low, particularly wages, but also the cost of living, on the assumption that exports would then rise and produce payments equilibrium. From the advisors' point of view it also had the merit of being almost free of influence either from the FBI, the TUC or from the Conservative Finance Committee – a right-wing body led by F. Assheton, Lyttleton and Harry Crookshank from whose free market dictates they tried to shelter their Chancellor.

In terms of organisation, the volume and importance of planning declined sharply; Plowden resigned from EPB in 1953, and rather against Butler's inclination (which favoured tripartism) the whole apparatus sank rapidly into insignificance, leaving so little direct legacy in the changed climate after 1955, that it was necessary to go to the French model in 1961–62 to find a basis for NEDC.

None of the Treasury officials, with the exception of Rowan, wished to revive the Robot drama; but it soon became impossible to hold down the conflicts of principle among officials and between Butler and his more demanding colleagues who expected him to produce electorally palatable budgets whatever the circumstances. As soon as inflation began to fall in 1952–53, unemployment rose – marginally, in retrospect, but enough to frighten the Cabinet, as Woolton's correspondence with Churchill in April 1953 shows.[29] The politicians feared both unemployment *and* inflation, as Scylla and Charybdis, and imagined that the technique of economic management would give them an instant remedy from either. Officials preferred a light touch and a longer view. The legacy of Robot, however, ensured that they would not respond as a united body and that Butler would therefore lack what is normally one of a Chancellor's main weapons.

Against the Keynesian majority, who accepted a small degree of inflation as an inevitable consequence of what they were trying to do, the remaining Robotics and their acolytes, Otto Clarke, Leslie Rowan, Edward Playfair and Denis Rickett, made cause with the Bank of England and the Conservative Finance Committee in emphasising inflation as a greater danger than unemployment. Both sides (for in intellectual terms they really were adversaries) competed directly for the Chancellor's ear, rather than going through the Permanent Secretary; and Bridges, rather supinely, did not stop them. Crying 'foul' at what the restrictionists were doing, some of the members of the Economic Section spoke out so openly that they alienated Ministers, making them suspicious that the argument was ramifying across Whitehall, and that both sides were adopting ideological positions. Butler had therefore not only to tune his decisions so as not to lose the confidence of his colleagues or cut across what Thorneycroft and Monckton were trying to do, but also to decide between rival experts how swiftly and strongly to respond.

Tensions within the Treasury continued to bedevil the process of policy formulation after Butler left the Treasury in December 1955 and during his short period as Chancellor this so irritated Macmillan that he brought in a diplomat, Sir Roger Makins, after Bridges retired, in order to discipline what he regarded as intellectually arrogant officials. Makins succeeded in reasserting the office of Permanent Secretary as a buffer between rival officials and the Chancellor, but he could not compel them to agree and this dissension certainly inhibited the evolution of a general ministerial strategy for either industry or the labour market, until the arrival of Sir Frank Lee from the Board of Trade in 1960. Whether the basic problem, the choice of an expansionist or restrictionist economic strategy, could have been solved in intellectual terms, given the limited experience of economic management then available, is open to question. The next Chancellor, Peter Thorneycroft, and his juniors Enoch Powell and Nigel Birch did not propose an alternative when they resigned in 1957, but merely adopted the arguments of the Treasury minority. Through these years, whoever was Chancellor had to make his own decisions, without benefit of an official 'overview'; which may have been constitutionally correct but was not what the architects of 1944 had in mind.

The fact that the argument took place at one remove from Cabinet, leaving the Chancellor less insulated from his officials' doubts than his recent predecessors had another consequence. By 1956 a few of the Keynesian officials, including Robert Hall, were coming round to part of their former opponents' conclusions: that wage inflation had become an inevitable consequence of full employment, at the level of unemployment by then habitual. But they saw that the corollary, that higher unemployment would provide natural restraint, was not something which they could say in public, nor to Ministers other than the Chancellor. Because a proper discussion among Ministers was not mounted in Cabinet, the devious way in which this new scepticism was phrased came as a surprise to Macmillan and probably contributed to his disillusion, since he had expected to find only expansionists in the Treasury. Inhibited from conducting an investigation into what the optimum level of full employment ought to be, in the conditions of the mid-1950s, by Churchill's and then Eden's awareness of the serious electoral repercussions if it became public knowledge, Treasury officials had to rely on the work of Professors Paish or Phillips outside in academic life.[30]

For three years Butler steered successfully, establishing a reputation as a remarkable Chancellor. The package of economies adopted in his budget, after Robot had been abandoned in Spring 1952, looked fair in political terms, though industrialists complained about the end of cheap money, and union leaders of the effect that cutting food subsidies would have on wage demands. Careful presentation disguised the fact that there was not much trade-off between the new Excess Profits Tax and the reduction of income tax which transferred £300 million to those on fixed and middle-class incomes – first signs of the Conservative Party's sensitivity to groups whose demands would rise steeply later on in the 1950s.

As Philip Williams argues, this budget shows that Butler did not follow directly the same premises as Gaitskell, however appropriate the term 'Butskellism' appeared to be in practice afterwards.[31] After an attempt to curb government spending in 1953, the 1954 budget increased investment allowances and suggests that Butler worked quite closely with Thorneycroft at BOT. The removal of hire purchase restrictions in August 1954 pleased industry, as did the fact that bank rate fell to 3 per cent. 'Invest in success' Butler told the party Conference that year, promising that it would be possible to double the standard of living in twenty-five years.

The most important development of these years however occurred in Britain's strategic outlook, because Butler's cuts in expenditure and taxation were taken with the novel argument in mind, that the hydrogen bomb had made conventional defence forces almost obsolete. The decision actually to go nuclear was not taken until a long and contentious Cabinet debate in July 1954 and remained so sensitive that it did not become public until the 1955 Defence White Paper. But it followed directly from Churchill's proposed pruning of the defence budget in 1951–52 and the increasing acceptance by the United States of a doctrine of 'massive retaliation';[32] and from other attempts to break out of the constraints imposed by Britain's post-imperial commitments, such as the defence of Hong Kong (abandoned, despite Chiefs of Staff protests, in April 1954) and the presence of troops in Egypt and Cyprus. Taken together with the exogenous economic conditions that helped, after seven years of austerity, to keep unemployment under 2 per cent and inflation under 3 per cent, this trend makes Butler's achievement less remarkable than it seemed at the time.

But when it came to the Budget for Spring 1955, with an election imminent, Churchill, Eden and Macmillan all put Butler under considerable pressure to expand the economy faster than he or his more cautious officials thought wise.[33] Distraught at his wife's death, Butler succumbed, lowered income tax and conceded £135 million to consumption. Whether this one budget can be blamed for the financial markets' reaction in the autumn and the subsequent unstable conditions of 1956–57, which did much to harm Eden's brief period as Prime Minister, is still a matter of dispute; but the consensus among economic historians is that it came on top of a swell in consumer demand and expectations, triggered off as early as 1953, which had been facilitated by the substantial wage increases of 1953–55.

What is undeniable is that politics took priority. Samuel Brittan later charged Butler with starting the cycle of election budgets, a judgment which is unfair in view of the pressures put on him to change his own earlier intention.[34] Even Bridges and Gilbert, fearful of a Labour victory and the implementation of the radical 1953 programme, wanted to stimulate demand and ensure Tory success, though Hall and the young William Armstrong counselled otherwise. The expansionists must have known, as they planned the 1955 Budget through the preceding winter, that if things went wrong monetary and fiscal means could not bring the economy under control quickly enough without a measure of overkill. Butler had admitted this at the Commonwealth Prime Ministers' meeting the previous January.[35] Butler did, of course, also stand convicted by his 1954 budget endorsement of that year's *Economic Survey*'s prediction that if Britain priced itself out of export markets through high costs and wages 'we should be taking a short cut to national bankruptcy'. The 'stop-go' pendulum, swinging faster with each year, began a derogation from the standards of fiscal prudence and political morality set by the 1944 White Paper which had been faithfully endorsed by Cripps and Gaitskell and previously maintained by Butler himself. It is no defence to say that subsequent Labour governments did the same.

In the summer, after the Conservative election victory,[36] the balance of payments crisis duly arrived. Whether it was primarily a crisis of confidence in the pound, as Hall and the Party's Research Department argued, or a direct result of an imprudent Budget (the point of view of the Bank of England) made no difference to the outcome. Butler had to bring in severe restraint in July, which failed to check the tide of demand sufficiently, so that he had to introduce a further credit squeeze and an emergency budget in the autumn.

It is worth asking where four years of Butler's demand management policies had led. It was certainly not true, as *The Economist* claimed in a valedictory tribute, that he had presided over the transition to a free market economy and guaranteed the value of sterling.[37] A cynic might say that Butler's success had been indistinguishable from exogenous factors favourable to the economy and that, at the first major difficult choice, his sound judgement had been distorted. At a more general level, it is clear that the Treasury had not yet mastered the techniques of fine-tuning, nor established a statistical basis (beyond the figures of unemployment and the index of production) which would allow them an advance warning of balance of payments trouble. In political terms, the Treasury had failed (as was perhaps inevitable given its internal divisions and the reluctance of ministers ever to envisage restraint) to establish a position as a neutral policy machine conducting a purely technical exercise. Careful reading of the March 1956 White Paper (Cmd 9725), *The Economic Implications of Full Employment*, suggests that its officials would have liked to state more bluntly that full employment enhanced union power, and weakened employers' capacity to resist; and that a wages agreement was essential. Here Hall, Bridges and other Keynesians found common ground with the restrictionists whose caution Macmillan (who became Chancellor in December 1955) already deplored; but when the Chancellor refused to listen, it is hardly surprising that the general tenor of the White Paper laid down that it would be enough if employers and unions reverted to the responsibilities accepted in 1944.

The struggle within the Treasury continued through the 1955–56 crisis and during its aftermath, ensuring that, at a critical time for her development in relation to major competitors such as Germany and Japan, Britain decided neither for growth nor wages and price equilibrium but an unstable mixture of both. In spite of Macmillan's long-held desire to expand, defend full employment and liberalise trade, he was constrained to announce a further round of restraint and cuts in investment in February 1956. Those who wanted to stiffen his White Paper's stand on wages and prices saw in its language a retreat from government, and the state's role in industrial and labour markets, which his April Budget (the so-called 'savings budget') did nothing to reassert. If the Treasury had spoken with one voice, it would have been easier for Macmillan to present a more statist document – as he probably wished to do – but for that to be possible the underlying problem would first have had to be solved. The extent of confusion among officials may, not unfairly, be gauged from the fact that in September 1956 Macmillan assured Eden and the inner Cabinet that the Suez adventure would not be halted for reasons to do with the external financial situation, only to reverse his stance as soon as the repercussions on sterling and the hostile reactions of sterling holders like India (which threatened to withdraw its balance in an attempt to bring the military operation to a halt) became clear.

This was a period which Macmillan glossed over in his memoirs though it deeply affected his attitude as Prime Minister, for he never really trusted his own chancellors (other than perhaps Heathcoat Amory) not to succumb to their officials' pessimism. He felt himself imprisoned and frustrated, impotent to do more than argue with his officials and the Bank about a series of measures, like increasing the price of gold or floating sterling, which were designed to break out of the cycle of restraint. Hopes that a wages and prices arrangement might be got between industry and unions, on the back of the White Paper, did gain support from the employers, in particular the EEF, because the President, Macmillan's old friend and colleague at Housing, Sir Percy Mills, put the Federation's considerable prestige behind the government's policy of a 'price plateau' for public industries, and urged his members to resist the AEU's very substantial 1956 wage claims. Macleod and Macmillan gave the EEF assurances of support (despite the fact that Carron, General Secretary of the AEU, was known strongly to resent the political implications). When the EEF's director general asked what the two Ministers would do if the government backed down during the predicted strike, Macmillan replied that he would not wish to be a party to such a government.[38] But as Prime Minister, he had to preside over a government that did back down only six months later.

The failure of Suez demonstrated for the first time how vulnerable the UK economy really was. Afterwards came the nadir, drawings of £201 million on the IMF, and £264 million of standby credits, simply to get through the winter while relations with the United States were repaired. Suez by itself neither disproved the hopes vested in expansion, nor validated the new regime adopted when Thorneycroft became Chancellor, in February 1957. But it did mark the end of a coherent period, lying between the Robot crisis and the adoption of a consciously different economic strategy and it gave an extra edge to Treasury arguments about the need to prune defence spending and adopt a cautious policy towards European organisation in the aftermath, while the Treasury, Cabinet Office and Board of Trade (Makins, Brook and Lee) coped with the financial repercussions.

How deep the arguments about economic policy ran, and how they crossed the normal lines of affiliation in the Conservative Party, as well as among government departments, can be seen in two related fields: public industries' management and convertability of the pound. In a government which had proclaimed when in opposition the need for denationalisation, it was natural that the free marketeers should regard as corporatist relics of the 1930s those of their colleagues who wanted to retain a state-owned infrastructure, providing assured cheap energy, transport and health, education and welfare services, and tripartite links with industry and unions. But whatever the centre-right had hoped for, Churchill ensured that privatisation would proceed no further than steel and road haulage, and in either case no faster than the investing public would take up the shares.

On the other hand, because of suspicions among this group that it would lead to increased intervention, Churchill's idea of an 'overlord' for state industries also disappeared.[39] The civil servants also advised against something which had been rejected twice already, in 1944 and 1950. Padmore's Treasury Committee instead confirmed that each Board would stay in the orbit of its sponsor, whether Fuel and Power or Transport. Thus an opportunity to ask what, in Conservative terms, public industries were for, and whether an integrated transport or power system had virtue in its own right and not just as 'socialism', passed almost before ministers or the party realised that it existed. Instead, Macmillan, Butler and Duncan Sandys (who set up the Iron and Steel Board on the model of the state corporation and left it to Robert Shone, its first Chairman, to develop) worked within the narrower focus of aims set by industry's demands – that is, the provision of cheap steel, or cheap road haulage.[40]

The result only partly met the City's demands for a public demonstration against state ownership, and failed to vindicate the doctrine of free competition, yet it fell short of providing the infrastructure service to industry which the old Tory corporatists had envisaged. Not till 1961 did government seriously address the problems of accountability, cost effectiveness and commercial management. Public industries' costs (and hence in theory their wages bill, but in practice their debt ratios) were instead put to the service of other objectives such as holding down the cost of living. The cutback in investment in Butler's 1953 budget hit all public industries severely, and in British railways, under a supine management, investment almost ceased. Only the Coal Board, under Alfred Robens, proceeded with demanning and modernisation gently and, on the whole, with NUM consent.

Public industries were made more accountable to Parliament, through the Select Committee on Nationalised Industries in this period but this was done more to satisfy backbenchers' hostility, and the FBI's long campaign against their privileged access to government loans, than to make them efficient – though the Committee did succeed in arguing out some of the principles which were to be written into the 1961 White Paper (see Volume 2). Government-commissioned reports on individual state industries conflicted with each other: the Flack Report recommended reorganisation to create a stronger Coal Board; but attempted reorganisation in 1953 actually weakened the BTC. Ministers steadily refused to refer public industries to the Monopolies Commission for fear of losing the powers to control prices,[41] and thus placate consumer or electoral interests which they had built up in defiance of Morrison's original terms of reference. Competition flourished between electricity and gas, but coal production was protected against imported oil by the use of hydrocarbon duties, and coal supplies were imposed on the Central Electricity Generating Board's power stations in order to lower its price to domestic users. Doctrine required the servicing of debts, yet when these became overwhelming they were written off, rather than inflict true costs on the public, which would then be reflected directly in the cost of living. The burden instead fell on increased indirect taxation or government borrowing.

Here, in multiple evasions of the principles laid down in the post-war settlement, government itself, in Conservative pragmatic hands, and with the FBI as cheerleader welcoming each move, whittled down the strength of the state's reciprocal obligations to industry and the financial sector, which had seemed self-evident in 1944. It failed to replace them with a coherent alternative. As Anthony Seldon puts it 'the Conservatives were ambivalent . . . having a political distaste for their success, but fearful of the industrial and financial consequences of their failure'.[42] Recurrent interference with management policy and the levels of wages made life hard for Boards which were, in most cases, composed of mediocre appointments, the best who could be got, given the low level of public salaries. The one Minister who had a theory of what might be done, Thorneycroft, was too junior to facilitate the emergence of a statist-commercial rationality which might have established itself (as Shone and Robens sought to do) in the interstices between Labour's 1953 programme and Conservative 1950's practice.

Whereas government avoided stirring up the problem of public industries' management, it became deeply involved in the question of convertibility of sterling; this reflected the greater political leverage of the financial sector. The 1944 White Paper laid down that consumption and industrial investment should rise only when the balance of payments permitted. Whether a surplus could be achieved without investment and sustained home demand was not a question asked in the public document. Under the Labour governments, the tautology of this reasoning had been avoided by restraint of personal consumption and the Production Campaigns' exhortation to produce and export. Once controls had been abolished and consumer expectations raised, after 1952, the balance of payments deficit became a perpetual constraint, nagging at best, at worst signifying crisis. Early on in Churchill's government, the Treasury attempted to pre-empt the political process of decision (which it feared, correctly, would usually go in favour of the consumer, rather than industry or the balance of payments) by laying down a rule which amounted to restating part of the Robot case: 'The UK will only be in a sound economic position when it has both achieved a substantial surplus in its external accounts, and a high level of productive investment. If a high level of social investment is also to be maintained, then the country must be prepared to limit its consumption accordingly.'[43]

It was easy enough to suggest subordination of the political flexibility inherent in economic management in a crisis as severe as 1951–52, when both the TUC and the FBI could accept the principle. The Treasury ruling thereafter caused much more trouble. But in all the subsequent arguments, the spending departments and sponsors failed to break out of the prison imposed by this Treasury-defined agenda so that arguments in the Budget Committee and Cabinet about where cuts should fall were almost always settled in favour of the strongest sponsoring department, or the one which actually handled procurement like the Ministry of Defence. It became very hard, for example, for the Board of Trade, with its relatively weak backing from industry, to argue the claims of export sectors against those, say, of defence-related industries such as aviation. In general, fiscal burdens and consequent distortions of markets tended to fall on industries reliant on domestic consumer demand first, and on investment programmes generally, since these always offered the greatest savings at what looked like least short-term cost.[44]

Robot had been intended ultimately to put government in a position where it could not, logically, in order to appease domestic interests, try to break out of the balance of payments constraint by means which the Bank and Treasury regarded as suspect. Having lost it, other means had to be found, in order to try to ameliorate the problem that economic management was not a neutral process to be ordered by a rule-book. The Treasury had its eyes on preserving fundamental national interests while permitting the stable growth in manufacturing industry which the Churchill government assumed, almost without question, would in the long run assure the elusive permanent surplus; looking thus to legitimate lower taxation and the high spending of a consumer society. For this reason, Plowden told the EPB as early as December 1951 that the problems of the next decade would not be those of the domestic market but of international finance and stability of the currency.

Taking up the road to convertibility after the 1947 disaster seemed at the time a separate and arcane subject, but was in fact very closely related. All Chancellors after 1951 looked longingly at the option of floating the pound, and all were immediately advised to forget it and concentrate on creating conditions in which sterling could again be made convertible, rather than risk what amounted to another devaluation, with unpredictable effects on the cost of living and inflation. An argument which seemed novel in 1952 had gained by 1961 in sophistication what it had lost in freshness, rather like the old 'Treasury case' against spending on public works in the 1930s.

The technical means by which OFD and the Bank tried to proceed matter less here than their political implication, which was that anything other than sound measures would not remedy the economy's real deficiencies.[45] As heresies are worse for true believers than mere atheism, so unsound means were worse than no means at all. An ingenious scheme by Robert Hall, for example, was damned as 'fearful', whereas Robot had merely been 'frightening'. Late in 1952 came an OFD attempt to get convertibility on the back of a hypothetical $1 billion loan from the United States, an unrealistic project which might have resolved all the sterling area problems, but which the Eisenhower administration not unreasonably refused to entertain.[46] Because of Butler's success in building up a modest surplus in 1953, pressure on Britain's reserves diminished for a time; yet to maintain such a surplus required a steady increase in exports which, as the FBI advised, was impossible. Nevertheless, in February 1955, with Butler's agreement, the Bank began gently to dismantle exchange control.[47] Encouraged by initial success, the Bank and Treasury moved on, with a scheme for a new European monetary agreement to modify the existing European Payments Union in which the pound would range between $2.78 and $2.88, that is, float within a 5 per cent margin.

Butler became uneasy because this amounted to using government's scarce dollars to help certain favoured holders to get out of sterling. But he agreed, since it obviously made the sterling area more acceptable to international companies as a trading base. Unfortunately, a speculative wave developed in the summer as a direct result of the Spring Budget and the rise in domestic inflation. As Eden and Butler already knew from their discussions with Eisenhower and Foster Dulles the United States would provide no assistance.[48] In July they realised that another devaluation might be imminent. At the Bank, Cobbold stepped back and jettisoned the EMA scheme rather than endanger parity. The domestic credit squeeze followed at once (which Butler rather slyly blamed on the Bank). At a meeting of finance ministers at Istanbul in September, Butler categorically denied that convertibility was still under consideration and at the same time hinted at his forthcoming autumn Budget.

Measures taken to control inflation, consequent on the Spring Budget, became inextricably confused with external operations of the currency. Speculation, on the assumption that a convertible pound would fall far further than 5 per cent, together with the government's justified fears for the reserves, undid the attempt to establish convertibility, and led to arguments between Bank and the Chancellor over how stringent the autumn Budget should be. Those most concerned (the narrow circle of Prime Minister and the economic ministers) realised that any further search for convertibility would have to take the pound's fixed parity for granted. Favourable conditions did not occur until December 1958.

This rather confused chain of events confirmed that, from 1953 onwards, the balance of payments would receive firm priority: not firm enough to prevent an electioneering budget in April 1955, but strong enough to make the October measures inevitable. Since in the five years that followed wages were not brought down, nor was efficiency improved to compensate for the consequences of 'stop-go', manufacturing industry's competitiveness suffered and its profitability steadily declined. This is not what any of the competing institutions wanted, but it exemplifies the fundamental dilemma of all governments after 1951: measures taken to preserve equilibrium in the short-term made it more difficult to sustain over a long period. The good was enemy of the best.

Deflation hit capital spending on the industrial base, public industries and the social infrastructure, more than consumption, not because the mechanisms chosen were inherently inadequate to control the latter, but because their impact on the cost of living was very soon reflected in wage claims, actual wages, and consequently in spending regardless of fiscal constraints – a disturbing phenomenon which Eden's government, at the height of the Suez business, understandably preferred not to face. But the government was not blamed – at least for that – in the Suez aftermath. Unions carried the can, as Central Office had foreseen, and perhaps intended;[49] and this expression of press and radio hegemony increased the defensiveness already shown inside the TUC, and perhaps also unions' more general hostility to technical change as well as their obsession with money wages, which had always been stock responses to renewed fears of unemployment.

The 1956 White Paper blamed both sides of industry, more or less impartially, for Britain's problems, and represented at least an attempt to be fair, while withdrawing the state a little from the position established during the previous sixteen years. But what was actually done, in conditions of economic difficulty between two very different crises in October 1955 and October 1956, reveals a new chiaroscuro in Conservative ideology. Externally the value of sterling had been demonstrated to be a reflection of Britain's international stature, not its economic performance – in contrast to contemporary France, where the Plan allowed for progressive alteration of the value of the franc. In the domestic economy, inflation now presented a defined enemy, an intruder which could, it was believed, be squeezed out, rather than accommodated in order to facilitate growth, as the Keynesians wanted, and as the followers of Erhard had actually done.

These conclusions and the weight their exponents now had in the party influenced many aspects of policy during the next five years, in particular pay policy as it evolved after 1957. Under Churchill's benign administration, Conservatives had mostly accepted the post-war settlement bequeathed by Labour. They had solved few of the fundamental problems, preferring a policy of accommodation to the countervailing demands put forward by the various interest groups and strands in the electorate. But they had managed the economy well, by their own standards, and by the measure of public expectation. The nub was wages. Eden's government, and then Macmillan's, discovered that whereas Attlee's had limited the consumption of the whole nation, they had to bear on the desires primarily of the working class majority, or permit unemployment to rise – a dilemma from which they shrank, instinctively as well as rationally.

That wages should outstrip profits and dividends, and create inflation to the detriment of Conservative supporters living on fixed incomes, and thus redistribute wealth to a largely Labour-voting mass was, of course, a nightmare for the middle and lower middle class voters who had remained loyal to the Conservative Party even in 1945. Herein lay the second dilemma. Loyalist voters might as yet have no other possible allegiance but they weighted heavily in the constituencies and with party activists, and their complaints, though easy enough to placate at Conferences before 1955, penetrated more deeply in the years of vulnerable administration during and after 1956. Suez sowed dragon's teeth at home as well as overseas. As Iain Macleod discovered when addressing the Conference in 1956, it would become progressively harder to defend tripartism, concessions to trades unions or working class opinion; harder to fend off the BEC lobby or Aims of Industry and the Institute of Directors, whatever the 'One Nation' ministers now in power personally desired.[50]

By the mid-1950s and probably soon after the end of Marshall Aid in 1952, it was becoming harder for government to manage demand in the way that original Keynesians had imagined. Once consumption, freed from controls, began to rise rapidly, there was a need for saving, in default of which high taxation or enforced saving (caused by a simple lack of goods to satisfy demand) had to be maintained. But the range of consumer goods proliferated; meanwhile to meet the demands of their loyalist voters, taxation and government expenditure had to be lowered. Almost inevitably, Conservative governments abandoned the 1944 White Paper's prescription, and the Attlee government's bleak integrity, and slipped into more or less permanent deficit financing.[51] Treasury and Bank officials gauged accurately, as well as cynically, that it would be so. Even if initially Butler and Macmillan acted in Keynes' 'ideal' form – that is, by borrowing to cover excess expenditure – they did it in years when it was not necessary because full employment already existed at a level beyond the imagination of the authors of the 1944 White Paper.

It was possible, in Butler's budgets in 1953 and April 1955, to reduce taxation largely to the benefit of the middle class and fixed income groups, small savers, and all those who naturally felt dispossessed by unions' collective bargaining successes. But the concomitant emphasis on indirect taxation, hire purchase or credit restrictions, hit both manufacturing industry and working-class spending expectations. The government derived no benefit from its conscious decision not to provoke trouble by reforming restrictive practices, because working-class voters *as consumers* were already becoming conscious of an interest in lower prices which restrictive practices impeded.

No obvious way out of the tunnel leading to the trap of wages policy existed in Eden's day. As his election speeches and the whole record of his personal convictions showed, Eden had no wish to be remembered as the saviour of a petty bourgeoisie by reducing working-class living standards. He loathed and tried to mitigate the deflation of 1955. But electoral calculations ruled, earlier in the year: hence the equivocation in Cabinet over Thorneycroft's policy on textiles, for fear of losing seats in Lancashire, and the need for an election budget which took 2.4 million people out of the income tax net altogether. During the election, Eden consciously tuned his programme to what the party hoped was the new Tory electorate, the upper, skilled working class.[52]

Similar forces operated during the drafting of the 1956 budget. Eden fought for two days against Macmillan, whose resolve had been stiffened by his officials, to retain subsidies on bread and milk. Although that budget did benefit manufacturing industry, it led on to yet another distortion via the 'price plateau' imposed on public industry in order to retain the sympathies of the public as consumers.[53] As Butler put it, subtly highlighting the Prime Minister's inexperience while deflecting the blame, 'he paid me the compliment of expecting me, more than the Chairman of the Party, to be responsible for Conservative success in the country . . . .'[54]

After the Tonbridge by-election with its astonishing swing against the government in a predominantly middle-class area, in April 1956, ominous evidence developed of a middle-class revanche, beyond the control of the party's propaganda apparatus. Later in the year came even more damaging results at Torquay and Taunton, both part of the Conservative heartland. Nevertheless, the Research Department stuck to its conclusion that if the reactionary feelings these reverses implied were appeased (by altering the tax system from direct to indirect means, and by restraining wages), far greater losses would be incurred elsewhere, in electoral terms and to the economy as a whole.[55] The liberal-minded centre-left of the party preferred by persuasion and education to revive the memory of reciprocal responsibility in the trade union movement, rather than to bring in legislation designed to alter the balance of power.

Unfortunately, the 1956 White Paper, which embodied a viewpoint common to party headquarters, Eden, Macmillan and Macleod received very little tangible response. This may explain why, by mid-1956, the Research Department was turning to the alternative of a wages policy, which brought it into conflict with Macleod and Eden and, in the end, the Cabinet majority. The strength of an idea whose time had come, however, led to its adoption a mere nine months later.

The rupture in Anglo-American relations, and with the Commonwealth over Suez, healed surprisingly quickly in 1957 and left, even more surprisingly, little permanent impression on British politics. It was still possible afterwards for government to envisage Commonwealth trade and outward investment as a dominant British interest, in which insurance, banking and commodity services remained 'so closely linked to the existence of Empire as to appear at times as extensions of British foreign policy'.[56] Third world countries continued to occupy Ministers' attention, as surrogates for the sort of growth that Britain itself found so elusive, a condition for which the governors of their Central Banks had been assiduously trained in the previous decade. Labour, in turn, true to Attlee's legacy, took up this white man's burden after 1964.

This forms part of the standard explanation why the British government failed to participate in the early stages of European integration, and rejected the recommendation of the Spaak Report in May 1956. The British plan for EFTA only reached the stage of public formulation in October – not the most opportune moment. But Suez revealed the real limits of Britain's autonomy in the world: Macmillan, Selwyn Lloyd and Butler all accepted in retrospect that it became *economically* impossible to continue the venture.[57] At the height of the crisis in October 1956 an alternative existed: to devalue, freeze American assets, and restore the exchange controls so recently lifted. According to the advice of the Treasury and the Bank, this would have wrecked sterling and domestic credit policy. The decision epitomises the tendency towards crisis avoidance in British government. Rather than choose either alternative, the inner group of Ministers abandoned their ailing, distraught leader, and opened up communication with the United States through the one door that had not, by the end of November, been bolted. It was inglorious, but it showed where the balance of interest lay.

For good reasons of foreign difficulty, the winter of 1956–57 constituted a hiatus in domestic industrial and labour policies; yet it brought the end of an age of innocence in which it had been possible to assume widely and freely that economic management, conducted by the limited fiscal means available once a year through the budget, would suffice to keep Britain in balance and deliver what each party to the 1944 political contract required: full employment, rising living standards, and stable prices.

The adjustments made between 1951 and 1956–57 in response to changing economic conditions and political demands of course affected both two main parties and all the institutions. They had not been enough to prevent centripetal tendencies in each threatening to modify (though not yet to abrogate) the post-war settlement. As external conditions grew less favourable, the doubts they caused weighed down a Conservative administration initially less certain of its road than Labour's had been, which in due course divided on lines only too similar to the division previously confined to the Treasury officials. Unlike Churchill, Macmillan, as Prime Minister after Eden's resignation in January 1957, could rely only on faith not certainty; faith (to quote Macleod's statement to the NJAC) that 'there is no reason why we should not have an economy which expands steadily, uninterrupted by crises and price rises, in which all classes of the community find themselves better off as years go by. Given peace, it would not be unreasonably optimistic to set ourselves the aim of doubling the standard of living by 1974.'[58]

9 Threats to Equilibrium 1957–61

Like an overfall in the tide, caused by an upsurge striking a rough configuration in the ocean bed, the years 1955–57 created powerful eddies of disruption, but did not alter the underlying currents in government. The history of the next four years could be written in terms of Conservative success in survival, particularly in the unprecedented feat of winning the third election in a row in 1959. But the field of industrial, labour and financial politics began to be dominated by the dissatisfaction of institutions, themselves concerned about worries, and even anger among their members. Meanwhile, inside government and its departments, the antitheses between growth and the balance of payments, between employment and price equilibrium were not synthesised, and instead an attempt occurred, in 1961, to break out of the cycle in what looked like novel ways.[1]

Behind this phenomenon lay a much broader social change, one aspect of which manifested itself in the late 1950s by-election 'revolt of the middle class', another as the increased mobility and higher expectations of those in the higher-earning end of the working class – which some contemporary sociologists called 'embourgeoisement'. Both disturbed the pattern of Conservative policy making and exposed some of the fissures in the party's ideology.

In much the same way as Churchill before them, Eden and then Macmillan tailored their governments' appeals to the public in 1955 and 1959 to the demands of the skilled worker, typically in the rapidly expanding engineering and consumer goods industries, sensing that the Labour Party's hold on this area of electorate had been weakened in the austere late 1940s. To put it crudely (as Lord Birkenhead did of the party's extension of the franchise to younger women in 1928) they imagined that they could secure it for a progressive Conservatism which refrained from taking a position hostile to trade unions, which gave their members a rising standard of living, and ensured that the economy provided for their

283

requirements, whether houses, holidays with pay, or cars and other material symbols of the new acquisitive society.

The Labour Party derived a different answer from the same, often conflicting evidence, but failed to set it in a winning programme until 1964. Embourgeoisement turned out to be a dubious concept, as the work of J. Goldthorpe and D. Lockwood showed, in *The Affluent Worker* (1969). They observed a marked change in the picture of a stratified working class given by Seebohm Rowntree and Caradog Jones before the war: a substantial number of non-manual workers was now behaving in ways formerly supposed to be middle-class. They were more mobile, had higher, individualistic aspirations and ambitions for their children; and, unlike the 69 per cent whom Goldthorpe and Lockwood characterised as traditional working class, refused to accept that society was immutable and that their future would resemble their past.

The 'embourgeoisement' thesis was an illusion, product of middle-class imaginations; the change fitted into a longer trend in which white collar workers would eventually outnumber manual or blue-collar ones. Only a minority of skilled and white collar workers behaved as the thesis would have required: what signified most was their capacity to make their aspirations as consumers effective, and that many more of their children subsequently rose in the social scale.

But in political terms the argument probably stimulated well-documented middle and lower middle class fears of decline in a scale which began in the 1950s to be habitually measured by access to and possession of expensive objects and expensive pleasures – on which electoral commentators soon fastened. Much of the history of the Conservative Party during its nine remaining years in office after the 1955 election thus became a counterpoint between concern for loyalists' anxieties and the consistent attempt to cut off the affluent worker from voting for their opponents.[2]

At the very start of the Macmillan administration, the Research Department submitted an analysis of the 'middle-class revolt' which highlighted taxation policy and the favours supposedly shown to unions and the working-class voter. Apropos of the disastrous results at the Tonbridge and North Lewisham by-elections, a CRD official wrote: 'it is essentially an uneducated mentality and it springs from emotional and social rather than economic strains. It has many characteristics: a basic insecurity feeling in the psychological sense that comes out in the demand for protection and a certain jingoism . . . and a resistance to change.'[3] He went on to document the existence of much suppressed resentment among professional people and black-coated workers, who feared loss of status as much as diminished spending power in the face of an encroaching, prosperous, better-educated working class, and also among small businessmen and shopkeepers who were actually doing quite well but were dissatisfied because their higher incomes, in an inflationary climate, could not buy the desirable objects they now aspired to own.

CRD had no answers that did not involve alienating far larger numbers of Tory working-class voters in marginal constituencies. It advised caution 'not to upset the small shopkeeper class'; yet within two years it had begun a study of abolition of resale price maintenance, an issue likely more than any other to do precisely that.[4] For the party officials, as for Macmillan, these feelings had to be appeased when elections loomed, but were not to be allowed to dictate party policy.

But what was party policy as distinct from the vague benevolence expounded by Eden? Butler – once the leading radical mind – seemed content in these years to become a great reforming Home Secretary, since he was excluded by Macmillan from any chance of using CRD to stir up the party's thinking, even when he became Chairman. To set out policy, Macmillan appointed a Steering Committee, where he took the chair, flanked by Edward Heath, the Chief Whip, Butler, Hailsham, Macleod and Michael Fraser. Here an overall list of priorities was first established in December 1957, once the Suez episode had been forgotten. Macmillan later used the Steering Committee (to which Lord Home and Oliver Poole were later added) to run both the parliamentary party and the Central Office machine.[5]

'Forgetting Suez' involved the creation of an official propaganda effort in the capable hands of Charles Hill, later BBC Director General; in other spheres it meant evolution of a modern colonial policy in which independence became not a remote destiny but an immediate virtue, borne on the 'wind of change' – that famous phrase, originally applied by Baldwin to India, which Macmillan used with great effect in Southern and Western Africa. With remarkable prescience, Enoch Powell took the point in February 1957, only four months after the Suez disaster: 'The Tory Party must be cured of the British Empire, of the pitiful yearning to cling to the relics of the bygone system (and fight for them if necessary at the barricades and in other division lobbies) while at the same time proclaiming the wonders of a new system whose foster parents were

Attlee and Nehru. Economically and politically we need what the younger Pitt of 1784 stands for: what (and why) the Empire was and what (if anything) the Commonwealth is, must be made clear to ourselves till it hurts no longer. The courage to act rationally will flow from the courage to see things as they are. The Tory Party has to find its patriotism again, and to find it, as of old, in "this England".'[6] But Macmillan, Macleod and Heath drew a different conclusion, for they did not favour little-England idealism, in their policy towards either Europe or the United States.

The deep conflict which followed, ending with Powell's resignation less than a year later, originated in a clash over concepts of Britain's future role in the world, but it spilled out into domestic policy and was resolved over the 1957 budget (described on page 292). The 'one-nation' group, Macmillan, Macleod and to a lesser extent Maudling and Heath, faced their former associates, Thorneycroft and Powell, and reacted against their ideas for solving the dilemma about which interests among the public economic management should serve, rather than – initially at least – developing their own. They seem in 1957 to have been stuck, unable because of their *Industrial Charter* heritage (and more remotely that of the 'Next Five Years' and 'The Middle Way') to develop the means to do what Thorneycroft and Powell did, by espousing categorically one of the competing Treasury strategies. But if the leadership consistently refused to retrench, at the price of curtailing consumption, the Research Department was making its own controversial contribution by developing a critique of wage inflation at which the Cabinet could not baulk[7] any more than it could at the issue of 'trade union' power with which wage inflation was inevitably coupled in the constituencies. In 1956–57, Eden and Butler had consistently evaded calls for legislation to limit or abolish the closed shop, or to deal with unofficial strikes; but an indication of how Ministers were later swayed by the evidence of what was actually going on can be found when, with the Prime Minister's support, in September 1958, Macleod floated the idea of a Royal Commission on trade union restrictive practices.[8] Nothing came of it, despite Conference talk, mainly because the majority of employers preferred to live peaceably with unions and the closed shop, rather than provoke trouble gratuitously for the sake of 'individual liberty'. As if appalled at his own temerity, Macleod took care to reassure the TUC with an MOL pamphlet on 'Positive Employment Policies' (1958) which advocated full government co-operation with unions. But on wages and unions' bargaining strength, the leadership could not finesse protests from industrialists and those in the party who, rather than deplore the BMC sackings in July 1956, had seen them as the first blow in the war against over-manning.[9] Party officials felt bound to take notice. 'Is the present legal theory, that trade unions are the same sort of body as a local tennis club, adequate?' one of them asked. 'Trade union law is fifty years behind Company law.'[10] In the Inns of Court, Conservative lawyers had already drafted *A Giant's Strength*. The age of innocence had passed and by 1960 Heath could only cope with demands from the People's League for Freedom for an even wider-ranging Royal Commission by pointing, rather lamely, to the Conservative commitment to 'sharing prosperity' and to George Woodcock's attempt to reform the TUC from within.

Whatever Ministers said in public, a habit developed in the party of blaming trade unions, which the Steering Committee and Heath, the Chief Whip, struggled to prevent turning into mere anti-socialism. By 1959 (according to Toby Low, his Junior Minister) even Macleod's opposition to legislation to deal with trade union abuses had been somewhat eroded. But Ministers responsible for the Treasury and Board of Trade, whose officials and the Cohen Council (CPPI) measured the immediate inflationary consequences of plant bargaining and of wages inquiries, notably the Guillebaud Report (see page 303), were considerably more sensitive than the Minister of Labour to protests from within the party. (Macleod's resistance to the trend may even have caused Sir Norman Brook, now head of the Civil Service, to send Sir Laurence Helsby, a stern Treasury man, to succeed Emmerson as Permanent Secretary at MOL in 1959). Yet to the despair of those backbenchers of the growing 'new right'[11] who had applauded Thorneycroft's and Powell's stand and seen in Heathcoat Amory an intelligent and upright sceptic of the way economic management was developing, Macmillan continually brushed aside fiscal restraint in the pursuit of expansion. The majority of the Cabinet concurred, and the internal opposition – for so it was – had to be content with the hope (similar to that of Cobbold, Governor of the Bank) that in the long run overseas investors would see what was being done, and by running down the reserves would force the government to put on the brakes.

Such a threat could be credible only so long as the balance of payments retained its priority; and thus the divisions between external and domestic Treasury departments transmitted themselves into party life. But there was no recourse against a Prime Minister who knew his own mind (in contrast to Eden), who placed expansionists in the key departments, and interfered with (or in the case of Selwyn Lloyd sacked) his Chancellors if they succumbed to the alternative. Just as it had been impossible to question the doctrine of full employment so it became near-impossible to argue against the proposition – which had, after all, already worked in Germany – that productivity, growth and new exports would pay for higher living standards. Given that they had the choice, Macmillan's Cabinet majority preferred to keep industry and wage-earners content, rather than the fixed-income middle class; and in making the choice they assented to that moderate rate of inflation which Hall and other Keynesian economic advisers had indicated as early as 1951–52 was an inevitable corollary of expansion.

Being confined to a minority, without ministerial exponents after Thorneycroft's resignation in 1957, dissent had little impact on overall policy, but its existence may explain the government's apparent inability to take on other major economic questions, for example how the machinery of government could be extended so as to pass on to industry the results of scientific advance (though Lord Hailsham did become Minister for Science in 1959) or how public industries might be made at once competitive and publicly accountable. It is significant that an inquiry into their future, by Butler in October 1956, had been delayed precisely because its members at once divided between right-wingers who wanted only to privatise, or at least sell off the profitable parts of each state holding, and the centre-left who wanted to see an efficient state infrastructure serve the rest of private industry. The initial thinking which culminated in the 1961 White Paper on nationalised industries took place elsewhere, either in the Civil Service or in CRD (where the importance of the new phenomenon of rationalisation, mergers and industrial concentration led to a preoccupation with resale price maintenance and other restrictive practices, and with the improvement of management).[12]

Whether it was better to regulate demand by credit control or taxation and what should be the future of sterling raised similar differences of opinion, although both sides accepted the prevailing view that the pound's value measured both the government's determination and the strength of the British economy.

Through all this can be seen the manoeuvring of two wings of the party, which led outside commentators to see in the Prime Minister himself a split personality – 'the duke's son versus the crofter's grandson'. Macmillan, like Lloyd George, steered a divided party alternately by blandishments and force through four years of gradual relative economic decline which it would have been hard, by any means then in favour, to reverse. To the public who returned the party to office in 1959 for the third time in succession, he was depicted as Supermac, the prestidigitator who kept the show on the road. A large measure of cynical appeal to interest groups indeed infused the 1959 manifesto and the election campaign to the dismay, amongst others, of Heathcoat Amory. Macmillan's own phrase 'the problem is how to present what is, in fact, "safety first", into a policy which looks as if it is moving forward' seemed only too accurate.[13]

By 1959–60, the right wing was drifting apart from the centre-left majority and dissent had acquired substantial support from industry generally, the FBI and the BEC in particular. But the 1959 election postmortem did not address the major question of whether the Conservatives could permanently remain a party of working-class appeal in worsening economic conditions (which was already a problem for Gaullists in France and Christian Democrats in Germany and Italy); but instead concentrated on how to exploit Labour's catastrophic decline, bearing in mind Michael Fraser's dictum that elections were won in the time between elections.[14] Absence of a coherent parliamentary opposition had a curious but lasting effect on the nature of the government's strategic planning (begun by Butler, Fraser and Heath 'the party's main impresario' in November 1959). Instead of making a radical break with the past such as would have been needed if Labour had presented a real challenge, it aimed merely to harmonise policy differences, far enough in advance of the next election in 1964.

Unfortunately, by 1961, the party had to defend itself against an economic crisis, and the lowering problems of the Central African Federation. So far-reaching and serious were the personality clashes and the scandals of 1962–63, that long-term policy-making almost ceased, debilitating from the start the 'new era' which the application to join the European community, the founding of NEDC and the change to a more consistent policy for economic growth in 1961 (described in the next volume) were meant to introduce. One CRD official described as 'too much footwork' the elaborate and slightly desperate policymongering of the time. Meanwhile, what were in reality ideological divisions festered, as the still impotent dissenters threw up ideas about public industry, industrial relations, taxation reform, and the future of small business which the leaders did not wish to hear but which they could not entirely ignore.

This passage would have been very much easier if economic management had been able to produce a reasonable equilibrium instead of the recurring fits of 'stop-go' which antagonised industrialists in the key areas of consumer goods and car production, or if Macmillan's appointment of Sir Roger Makins as Permanent Secretary had healed the intellectual cleavage in the Treasury. Makins instilled enough discipline to make sure that the Chancellor would, henceforth, be presented with a coherent view rather than competing ones, but he could not produce a reasoned alternative rule to obviate the pendulum swing from stop to go and back each time that the indicators warned of rising inflation or rising unemployment.

It might also have been easier if the government had floated the pound, or gone consistently for industrial growth and let the pound fall in a succession of small devaluations, as occurred in France and as some US Treasury and Federal Reserve officials expected it to do as a preliminary to British entry into the EEC. But the British Treasury was more or less united against the idea, after their failure to get convertibility in 1955, because to judge from the level of black market operations on the edge of the sterling area the pound's fall would have been about 20 per cent – enough to give a severe twist to the cost of living and consequently to wages.

For lack of access to government archives it is impossible to say for certain that Treasury officials were excessively cautious because they were only too aware of the dangers of getting into the minefield of political repercussions in this Cabinet; but it does seem that, apart from responding to House of Commons' criticism about expenditure control by setting up the Plowden Committee, they followed the rules of demand management evolved in the previous ten years with an uncritical fidelity. But even if they had tried to modify the rules in the period after Suez, the decline of Britain's share of world trade would have made it hard to achieve equilibrium for any length of time. The reserves may have appeared more stable than in 1951 or 1955–56; but since Britain was slipping into semi-permanent deficit financing (especially for the pre-election Budget of 1959), cautious debt management became crucial as a means of offsetting speculation against a weak currency. A stronger reason for prudence was the size of the storm caused by Thorneycroft's attempt to cut through existing practice.

Thorneycroft became Chancellor in January 1957. A liberal trader, in favour of European economic linkages but not monetary integration, he held strong views about the need to restrain wages and consumption until industry should be efficient enough to compete internationally. He also concurred with the Bank and the FBI about returning to sterling convertibility at a fixed parity: a view which naturally brought him into close alliance with all those officials who feared that, since April 1955, the Conservative government had been drifting towards spendthrift policies and excessive borrowing.[15]

Thorneycroft's outlook was not uncongenial to Macmillan during the difficult months of re-establishing relations with the United States and restoring unity to a party divided three ways over Suez. For a time, orthodoxy ranked higher than expansion. But the Chancellor soon found that he missed Sir Frank Lee, did not get on well with Makins, and preferred the authoritarian views of Leslie Rowan to those of the Treasury expansionists.

His first budget in 1957 passed the test of making concessions to industry and maintaining popularity by avoiding deflation at home at a time when unemployment came near to half a million. It was well received by commentators of most persuasions, who were not to know that the Cabinet, unwilling to risk losing trades unions' sympathy so soon after the 1956 troubles, had jibbed at the Chancellor's proposal to make a statement about incomes policy.[16] The most that Thorneycroft could do was to set up the Council on Prices, Productivity and Incomes (CPPI) (otherwise known as Cohen Council) in August 1957, with the intention of educating public opinion in the wisdom of the 1956 White Paper, that unions and employers rather than government were primarily responsible for restraint. The CPPI, he hoped would suggest, on the basis of statistical inquiry, what the nation could afford, and might succeed where the NJAC and EPB had failed, in teaching the two sides of industry (primarily of course the TUC) the malign effects of unrestrained wages.

This represented another attempt to revive the 1944 accord, not by personal moral authority in the manner of Attlee and Cripps but by appealing to a neutral, expert authoritative body. If the public responded favourably, it would then save government from having to use its fiscal levers to create the hated 'stop-go'. Unfortunately, the next financial crisis, set off by a 20 per cent devaluation of the French franc, hit Britain before the CPPI began work. Speculation based on the imbalance of the pound among European currencies caused the reserves to lose £166 million in the second week of August. Devaluation seemed once again inevitable, accompanied by revaluation of the German mark. The problem could be blamed on the same endemic weaknesses that Suez had revealed, although it was accentuated because of leakages through the so-called 'Kuwait gap', the measure of convertibility for non-sterling balance-holders allowed since 1955 which the Bank had now to abrogate.[17]

Thorneycroft had to follow the example of Butler's second budget in 1955, but with greater severity, for each correction now significantly exaggerated the pendulum swing. Bank rate thus rose in September to 7 per cent, its highest peacetime level since 1918. The credit cuts reduced bank advances by £2 000 million and capital expenditure in the state sector by £1 500 million, the harshest blow to industry in post-war history: and this occurred at a time when the balance of payments was actually in surplus and the economy was not overheating. To safeguard the sterling parity, Britain was forced into a period of stagnation if not actual recession. Treasury officials defended what was done, without much conviction, in EPB and it may well have been that some of them would have preferred to float the pound immediately.

Macmillan, Makins and the expansionists resisted the deflationary package but they were ultimately overborne because the parity of sterling had become inextricably entwined with Britain's national status and the balance of her whole economic policy.[18] The result was perhaps the least satisfactory compromise possible, for it avoided a direct assault on consumption at the price of debilitating industry and undermining managerial confidence in government, as well as reducing the state's capacity properly to run public industries, all for an exchange standard in whose increasingly artificial level probably only a minority in the Treasury now believed. The struggle also identified Thorneycroft and his junior ministers with the OFD/Bank axis, and what remained of the Robot tradition; personal attributes of the subsequent crisis should not obscure its deep political, even ideological significance.

So pervasive was the expansionists' disillusion, even rancour, afterwards (for Macmillan resisted the rise in bank rate and the credit squeeze longer than the Treasury or the Bank had expected) that Makins instituted a Treasury inquiry into the practice of economic management which included the obvious question: could the new CPPI's reports not be used to establish an internal wage/price equilibrium which would inhibit inflation and give sufficient stability to the pound, in foreign eyes, to eliminate speculative raids on the reserves? That led straight into a wages policy, even though the CPPI's findings did not substantiate the wage-push explanation of inflated industrial costs with anything like the decisive logic employed by Treasury Ministers. On a separate front, but in phase with the normal cycle of Treasury argument with spending departments, Thorneycroft determined to put an end to the process by which government expenditure now rose at a rate which automatically pushed it into unnecessary and harmful deficit financing, in clear contravention of the principles of sound budgeting laid down by the 1944 White Paper.

Whether inflation and money supply were also linked in Treasury Ministers' minds is not certain; the chief protagonist was guided not by doctrine but empirical judgement.[19] That wages in public industries and local authorities were out of control seemed a more obvious deduction than any about money supply – a subject which at that time rarely came up at Cabinet level. Thorneycroft proposed, simply, that no rise should take place in nominal government expenditure, during the coming year: this signalled a cut in real terms which was bound to be reflected in the wages of state employees. The autumn negotiations with spending departments turned into an internecine war which ran on throughout the winter, finally exposing to Cabinet what had occurred during the years of the Treasury's prolonged internal dispute.

A myth about the 'early monetarists' has since developed. Their stand at the time looks rather incoherent and barely amounts to more than a statement of principle; in one sense, it was no more than the Treasury's traditional hostility to the spenders. While the influence of Rowan and the 'Robotics' should not be ignored, there were other Treasury officials who also saw 1958 as the year in which profligate state borrowing could at last be checked. Not only the 'Robotics' believed that spending on welfare, education and health had slipped out of proper control. Recently vindicated in public by the Bank rate Tribunal, and secure in the knowledge that with bank rate at 7 per cent they could assure the IMF that the pound was now stable, the Bank and most Treasury officials could form up together on grounds which they had first put to Gaitskell in 1950–51.

But Thorneycroft had no backing in Cabinet because the Chancellor must always rely on the Prime Minister during the 'annual round', and in this case Macmillan unbendingly opposed what he regarded as a bid to overthrow the whole conception of state-guaranteed industrial growth and full employment. Instead of supporting his Chancellor, he took the side of the spenders, in private ways. Faced with their tenacious tactics, Thorneycroft realised by the end of 1957 that he would fail. He could have conformed, as Amory did later; he could have worked the fiscal and monetary levers to curtail consumption, even if he failed to control government spending. But that was a different issue. From personal conviction, and under the considerable influence of Powell and Rowan, he decided to stand fast, hoping at least to strengthen the Treasury by going out on a point of principle.

Although in public Macmillan later dismissed the whole affair as 'a little local difficulty', great efforts were made to prevent resignations. Makins mobilised the expansionists in the Treasury and elsewhere and tried personally to wear down Thorneycroft's resistance, only to find him stiffened, by Powell, whose greater intellectual rigour enabled him to locate the argument on high political ground. After three days' wrangling in Cabinet, the gap narrowed to £30 million, a figure which those who wanted to avoid a crisis put 'within the margin of budgetary error'.[20] But elision of the logic of sound finance was not what the Treasury team wanted. Instead they sent an ultimatum to the Prime Minister. Macmillan instructed Makins and Brook to make a personal appeal. The two mandarins met Thorneycroft, Powell and Birch at No. 11, just before Macmillan went abroad, but made no impression. Resignation by all three followed; Leslie Rowan retired early in 1958.

Macmillan, who had already decided to choose Heathcoat Amory as the next Chancellor, won with ease, for Thorneycroft and his friends found it no easier to explain their stance to the Commons than Eden had in 1937, bound as they were by the secrecy convention not to reveal what had really been at stake. In retrospect, the episode can be seen as a sort of catharsis, which left the Treasury exhausted. Makins took care not to let it get involved again in such 'high politics', and in a sense 1958–59 formed a sort of interregnum, which ended with the arrival of Sir Frank Lee from the Board of Trade, vested with a rather different authority. But the Thorneycroft argument did not die, for it had been beaten by force, not reason. Like certain rivers in the desert, it went underground, its only open exponents being Lord Cobbold, who urged it from time to time on a well-armoured Prime Minister, and Hall and a handful of Under Secretaries, none of whom now could hope for top promotion, late converts to the view that full employment had been set at far too high a figure.

Amory, a liberal trader like Thorneycroft, but more popular in the party and much more compliant to the Prime Minister's wishes, was a good administrator, a much-liked healer in the Treasury, who understood the whole business of national income forecasting, a technician who eschewed the sort of general reflections at which Butler had excelled. By implication, he accepted an impossible charge: to meet the pressure on sterling without resort to deflation, yet nevertheless to stabilise prices and wages. Lacking the sort of insight into industrial weaknesses given by Thorneycroft's Board of Trade experience, he chose the only way permitted by the weakness of sterling and Britain's international position: that is to abandon the crusade against public expenditure (but not the economies that had already been won) and to continue the credit squeeze. He was fortunate because the previous two years' policy during a world recession now brought rewards: a decline in the rate of wage increases, a balance of payments surplus, and a rise of less than one per cent in prices – ideal conditions in which to face the election of 1959.

Amory proceeded cautiously at first. 'We are not yet strong enough to give the economy more than a minor stimulus,' he told the Commons in the 1958 Budget speech. More significantly, he redefined the government's guarantee of full employment not in terms of a percentage level of unemployment, as Gaitskell had done in 1951, but as 'the provision of regular productive employment for all who are able and willing to work . . . We want to see production and employment just as high as we can, consistent with the value of money'.[21] Indirectly, almost by the back door, and without gratuitously attacking the level of government expenditure, Amory reiterated the 1944 White Paper commitment without explaining that many of his officials were coming to rely on a small but constant margin of unused capacity and unemployment in order to achieve slower and, they hoped, steadier growth.

Amory added a panegyric on the value of the sterling area, completely at variance with BOT opinion and the evidence of the Treasury's own working party on British trade, which was clearly intended to build on the success of recent Commonwealth Conferences and to prepare the way for the full convertibility which he finally introduced – at a fixed parity of course – in December 1958. Thereafter, if equilibrium were to be maintained, a balance of payments surplus would be essential. Deliberately placed in that prison, but in far less advantageous conditions, future Chancellors were to find their margin of manoeuvre gravely curtailed, and their route into Europe almost impassable.[22]

Two years of 'fine-tuning' followed. Unemployment rose over 500 000 without causing the sky to fall, but the credit squeeze restricted growth sufficiently for Macmillan to urge a resumption of public industry investment and government spending. Alarmed at the electoral implications of an unemployment figure of 620 000 in the 1958–59 winter, but made more optimistic by the signs of surplus and high reserves, preconditions for growth for which they had waited over three years, and forgetting the example of April 1955, Cabinet put Amory under considerable pressure to produce an expansionist budget. According to his own account, Amory feared that it was the wrong part of the cycle for a stimulus, and referred back not only to Cobbold but to the Committee of Clearing Bankers.[23] In the event, the Prime Minister added his own twist to the spiral by increasing the cut in income tax at the standard rate from 6d to 9d, pushing an extra £60 million into consumption. This decision was taken quite deliberately as an alternative to lowering the Bank rate, against the Bank of England's advice, and after consultation with the Prime Minister's own friends among the bankers.[24]

Macmillan's concern with re-election at a time when the Labour Party seemed to have lurched far to the left was not only understandable but shared by the leaders of industry and the various financial markets. The Bank and the Chief Economic Adviser found themselves almost alone in pleading financial rectitude which may explain the tentative way Amory put forward his Budget as if appeasing Nemesis. As Samuel Brittan pointed out, five years afterwards, the 1959 budget stimulus did come too late in the cycle, at a time when production was rising steeply, accompanied by shortages of skilled labour and excessive demand, the classic symptoms of overheating. Yet it was not simply an election budget. The election did not come till October, and the increased majority, a feat without precedent in modern history, can be explained also by other factors. The expansionists aimed at something higher than expunging the memory of Suez and retaining the Conservatives' upper working class votes; they hoped, like Cripps in 1948, to break through the economic constraints into a pattern of sustained growth, like a regiment of tanks piercing the deep lines of trenches in a First World War battlefield.

For one more year the pattern of trade and wages and the experience of convertibility seemed benign. But industry soon began to issue warnings about domestic overheating. Amory used this as evidence in support of his planned restrictionist budget in 1960; but Macmillan, supported by Norman Brook, refused. Instead, Amory issued a veiled warning, raised Bank rate from 4 per cent to 5 per cent and introduced a new, much more sophisticated form of credit control

which, through Bank of England requirement of special deposits from
clearing banks, bore directly on the banking system, but left it to the
banks to discriminate between private and industrial borrowers. Much
less arbitrary in its effect on volatile consumer industries than hire
purchase controls and purchase tax, this system might have appealed
more to industry if the Treasury had not continued to use the old
controls as well.

Tired of resorting to such devious tactics, Amory resigned in July
1960, leaving a warning of trouble to come unless the government
introduced an incomes policy. His mild squeeze on credit had had
barely any effect on employment, now regarded as 'overfull' by almost
all Treasury officials, some of whom had begun to doubt the principles
of demand management as they had understood since 1951.
Despite favourable world conditions, exports remained sluggish, while
basic wages rose by 6.5 per cent in 1959–60, reinforcing existing beliefs
in the Board of Trade about industrial inefficiency and throughout the
whole government machine about wage-inflation as the prime reason
for the failure to achieve equilibrium. Cobbold warned that unless
wages were curbed, devaluation would follow. Hall now believed that
full employment had created sheltered areas more or less outside the
scope of government demand management.

Having nearly been a scapegoat once, at the time of Suez, Selwyn
Lloyd, Amory's successor, knew better how to ride two horses at once;
no less of an innovator, he argued his officials' drafts with more
effect than Amory who had tended to expect logic and reason alone to
guide debate. The new Treasury Permanent Secretary, Sir Frank Lee,
unlike Makins, distrusted Macmillan's gospel of fiscal stimulus to
industry, arguing with a wealth of BOT experience that concessions
would allow employers to pay high wages for industrial peace and
forget to count the cost. In January 1961, the Cabinet finally
confronted the possibility that the previous nine years' experience
might no longer be an accurate or even approximate guide. The
complaints from industry, commerce and unions which fill the EPB's
minutes probably had some effect in bringing them this far: but the
spur was once again a forecast of balance of payments problems. Novel
remedies offered ways out: the first, to regulate employment itself,
hence the introduction of a payroll tax and other regulators, the
second, to widen Britain's market by entry to the EEC and to institute
indicative planning on the French style.

Nemesis in 1961 ended a twenty-year period, perhaps the springtime of economic management. Doubt could no longer exist that wages (which were now rising steadily faster than productivity) contributed to inflation; some government economists suspected that inflation had only been held at relatively low levels by continued weaknesses in the price of traded goods, particularly raw materials, through the 1950s. In default of a deflationary programme like Thorneycroft's, the combination of statistical argument and pressure from employers in 1960–61 made a wages policy inevitable. But until a new crisis arrived to give government the political excuse to go beyond the reasoned advice of the CPPI, they did not know at which point to begin.

The crisis occurred some time after the crucial debate in Cabinet in January had set out in embryo the alternatives of further regulation and EEC application. Treasury officials had long been searching for new levers which could be used at any time between budgets, and which would avoid the gross interruption of investment patterns and planning whose effects had been worst in the consumer goods and car industries. Since the Inland Revenue refused to entertain Robbins' 1943 idea of variable taxation or insurance contributions (as the Customs and Excise did for a sales tax) and since a straight payroll tax appeared unacceptable to the TUC, attention turned to the 'regulator' – a power at any time to vary certain existing taxes within a 10 per cent margin, which Lloyd brought in, with other rather more cumbersome measures, in his April 1961 Budget.

By then the dimensions of the balance of payments crisis, which had already frightened the Cabinet in January, were only too clear. But Ministers were riven by disagreement whether to go for a full wages policy (to replace the 'guiding light' set by the CPPI) or to rely, as before, on wage earners' voluntary response to political education. Until the summer neither side prevailed.

The fact that the Cabinet was blocked did not prevent the Bank of England from preparing counter measures. Knowing in advance that the German mark was to be revalued, concerned for the stability for the dollar after the 1960 Presidential election returned the untried John F. Kennedy, and aware that an extremely ill-judged move to make government stock tax-free to foreign holders had sucked in £500 million of 'hot' money, but debarred by the Cabinet's indecision from either raising Bank rate or preparing exchange controls, Cobbold and his officials used their links with European central bankers with great effect to concert defence measures in February. When the mark was revalued on 5 March, followed immediately by a run on sterling, the

£300 million stockpile made available by this 'Basle arrangement', allowed Britain four months in which to react. But a sort of paralysis among Ministers prevented action; until in July when the deficit had reached £445 million, Lloyd acted out of sheer desperation.

According to officials serving at the time, devaluation was discussed in the Treasury early in 1961. It would have been surprising if it had not been, since President Kennedy's newly appointed Treasury advisers certainly expected devaluation, and took their precautions.[25] Some of them indeed saw it as essential for Britain's future, although other experts including Professor Milton Friedman would have preferred a floating exchange rate. Apart from the prestige vested in the rate, the main British objection was almost a moral one: that devaluation could provide only a temporary breathing space before the increased cost of living forced wages up again, and once more priced exports out of the market. This view, of course, rested on a profound pessimism about British entrepreneurial activity and worker behaviour for which there existed only too much empirical evidence; but it is also possible that the Bank and Treasury officials misread the advice to sustain the rate from New York and Washington, given by officials who had served under the previous administration before Kennedy's liberal-minded nominees fully established themselves. During the four months respite, given by the Basle agreement, Treasury officials, advised by Cobbold (who retired shortly afterwards) and Hall, backed up at one remove by the FBI and the BEC acting in concert, took advantage of Cabinet indecision to put their principal desiderata firmly on the agenda. Publication in May of the OECD report 'The Problem of Rising Prices' made a wages freeze more palatable. The exercise of tying ministers down to a virtuous pattern which Lloyd undertook was obstructed continually, not only by Macmillan, but by Maudling, Macleod and Heath, each of whom was determined not to break faith with the *Industrial Charter* by imposing a statutory freeze on the Tory working man. The triumvirate demanded in the name of social justice (in return for Lloyd's necessary but ill-timed surtax relief to higher taxpayers granted in April) commitments to increase corporation tax and to tax short-term capital gains.

In the long run, the fact that Selwyn Lloyd had to take crisis measures in July ensured Macmillan's whole-hearted support for the 'dash for growth' which began in 1962. Lloyd's measures were almost certainly more severe than would have been necessary in April, and much worse than if they had come in January when the Cabinet wrangle began.[26] Yet it is hard to imagine that the government could have taken such a harsh set of decisions in January, *tout court*, for they grievously undermined the new Conservative philosophy and the position with which Macmillan had first identified himself in the early 1930s. The evidence suggests that six months skirmishing took place, inhibiting any decisive result or even discussion of carefully-planned devaluation as part of the Basle Agreement.[27] It was not until the climactic weekend at Chequers, 20–22 July, which Lord Cobbold also attended, that Lloyd finally used the regulator to its full extent, cut back credit and public expenditure, raised bank rate again to 7 per cent and laid down, without prior consultation with employers or the TUC, a 'wages pause'.

Macmillan and the Tory radicals failed to maintain the balance of equality or sacrifice because Lloyd insisted on resisting increases in Income Tax and the employers' National Insurance Surcharge in order not to upset industry and commercial interests. The reason that no formal discussions took place with anyone outside the centre of government, in contravention of established EPB practice and the 1948 precedent[28], may have been due to a change of opinion in the Ministry of Labour, associated with the arrival as Permanent Secretary of Sir Laurence Helsby in 1959, and in 1960 a Minister, John Hare, who became the first, post-war, to line up with the Chancellor on wages policy. Yet Lloyd himself, according to one Treasury source, disliked the whole business and hoped, perhaps as late as April, that it could be avoided. Without the documents it is impossible to be sure, but it looks as if the experts and officials guided Ministers to the water of necessity and this time, unlike Robot, made sure that they drank.

The crisis broke on an almost unprepared public. Even 'informed opinion' had been deceived by the apparently high reserves, swollen by 'hot money' and the Basle cover into underestimating what became the worst deficit since 1951. The government itself underestimated the repercussions: the shock to investment outraged industry almost as much as the pay pause did the TUC. For the first time since the war, and under cover of an extraneous threat, the state had brought wages under direct control. Both sides blamed Lloyd, the Prime Minister and the Cabinet, in that order.

Sir Frank Lee was ill and in Paris when the measures were announced, but the Treasury, collectively, took great care to explain for the guidance of future generations of officials why they had been necessary.[29] This may have been intended to offset criticism from other departments such as the Board of Trade for not having reflected more and earlier about the deteriorating patterns in labour and industrial affairs; in other words, for not having prepared for the unthinkable by analysing the true cost of full employment. Given Prime-Ministerial direction and the government's electoral mandate, such an inquiry could only have been conducted in the Radcliffe Committee. The real failure of these years may have been not to have given Radcliffe the extensive terms of reference of the 1929–31 Macmillan Committee, and asked him to examine the phenomenon of relative decline, as well as the malfunctioning of the capital market. Yet in its evidence to Radcliffe, the Treasury contented itself with rebutting the Labour Party programme, and denying that comparisons could be made with the French system of pre-empting a percentage of savings for industrial investment. Thus the onus of examining the relationship between wages, profits and productivity fell on a non-governmental body without any formal powers at all, the far-sighted but grossly-overworked CPPI.

A widespread feeling among civil servants that time had been wasted may explain the decisive aspect given to the new policy in 1961–62 (which is discussed in the next volume), just as the odium which fell on Ministers probably accounts for the personal lead subsequently given by Macmillan; and for the way contemporary economists portrayed him either as an irresponsible Pied Piper, leading the neo-Keynesians to destruction, or as an apostle of growth whose single-minded authority alone could ensure the participation of industry, unions and the public.

Those institutions which might on general political grounds have been expected to be most supportive of the majority tendency in Cabinet experienced similar doubts about the practice of economic management. For different reasons the banking system and larger manufacturing and service industry companies resisted the 'stop' end of the swing; but their complaints tended to diminish in direct proportion to the effectiveness of the government's wages policy. The 'voice of industry' lost some of its directness while the lead taken by the Bank of England held City opposition to the operation of the special deposits scheme more or less in check.

Nevertheless the Bank lost a further tranche of its autonomy, and became more of a conduit for messages to which the Chancellor and Treasury wanted the City to listen;[30] it was by-passed, probably for the first time, by Macmillan's communications with Monckton and the Midland Bank in August 1957. In the City itself, the rise of a new, more aggressive form of merchant banking associated with Kenneth Keith and Siegmund Warburg began to erode old, customary certainties. Lord Cromer, who became Governor in June 1961, lacked Cobbold's power of persuasion to make effective the warnings Governors habitually gave about government borrowing and deficit Budgets.[31] Sterling convertibility by implication prevented the Bank from arguing that excessive borrowing curtailed or 'crowded out' the private sector; the new generation of Treasury officials, headed by Lee, probably thought that it did.[32]

On the other hand, the Basle Agreement demonstrated what the Bank *could* still do to give a government time, by capitalising on the goodwill that then existed among European bankers and the enthusiasm in Germany and the United States for British entry to the EEC. This, and credits from the IMF, saw Britain through to 1962, despite continued fears of speculation (revealed to members of the EPB) after the July measures. Lord Cobbold attributed continuing weakness to the fact that foreign holders of sterling saw 'something that was wrong in the internal economy';[33] yet it would be quite wrong to think that the Bank wanted to break with full employment. Like the Treasury in 1951, it wished only to expose the true cost to the national interest (as that was defined by the financial sector) and to revise upwards, perhaps to the original 1945 range of 3–5 per cent, the working estimate of what full employment actually should be.[34]

Meanwhile, the Bank revived some of its once-flourishing links with industry and began to take an interest in improving the quality of management for the first time since the 1930s. It gave some encouragement to the insurance companies, notably the Prudential, in particular cases where directors' incompetence had endangered institutional shareholders' interests.[35] The clearing banks, by developing the post of Chief General Manager, by training their personnel in export finance, and by following the lead of merchant banks more closely, did more at the time to orientate themselves towards exporting and satisfying the needs of domestic industry, a slow change (or form of corporate Darwinism) which in turn facilitated the merger boom of the 1960s, and Britain's increased financial links in Europe. Lloyd's, for example, made a decision in the late 1950s to ease out of India, minimise their operations in post-colonial Africa, and to concentrate on Europe.

But these stirrings did not develop momentum for another decade and received their greatest stimulus in 1974–76 in very different and more apocalyptic conditions. Nor, despite the advice given by prominent City men on appointments to their Boards, was much done about state industries' management record, chiefly because to do so would have required an impetus from government which at that stage was absent. It was recurring cutbacks of investment plans, as much as inadequate direction, which caused British railways to convert to diesel only with excruciating delays (and backward glances at the virtues of steam); steel developments were badly retarded by the denationalisation drama, water and sewage struggled simply to maintain their Victorian heritage, while the Central Electricity Board toyed with the idea of nuclear power as something for a distant future.

Public industries' chairmen, however, did form something like a common front in order to contest the claims of their public service workers to parity of wages with private industry. The tendency accelerated after the 1959 Guillebaud Report on pay on the railways enunciated the new principle of comparability – regardless of whether the industry could pay. Guillebaud probably also provided the stimulus for government to reflect on the future of state industries, which led to the White Paper of 1961. As far as entrepreneurial activity was concerned, tight control by sponsor departments overlaid by Treasury control of investment and the governments' persistent interference with pricing structures suffocated initiative even at the level of middle mangement. Confronted with public apathy or outright hostility and the stand-off attitude of the FBI, the Boards tended to concentrate simply on keeping their undertakings running, rather than take risks in research and development, even though such risks were less (because not tied to commercial calculation) than in private industry. Gas and to a lesser extent electricity excepted, public industries provided a dismal history, with the railways as the worst example.[36] Sponsor ministers may have acted as advocates for their claims when negotiating with the Treasury over expenditure, but their performance records were so poor that it was hard in crises like 1955 or 1961 to argue that their investment programmes should be exempted. Even in the drafting of the 1961 White Paper, the Treasury seems to have been more interested in them as agencies of demand management with which to control prices and hold down wages.

The way in which public policy on industrial and labour problems had been addressed since the war began to change in the late 1950s. Industry and unions, increasingly disturbed by evidence of Britain's relative decline and bad industrial relations, anguished over causes and remedies yet. Unlike financial institutions, they failed to reach answers, principally because they remained representative of their members whose innate competition for the benefits of affluence prevented lasting accommodation of their separate interests. Government policy appeared to their central institutions as a product which could be moulded to their demands: something much more malleable than in the sterner days of Stafford Cripps. Consequently competition between them took place more at the level of self-interest than had been customary before the mid-1950s. The documents of the FBI, BEC and TUC mention the national interest less often, and contain a higher level of recrimination and criticism of each other.

For the first time since the war, this pattern put both the Board of Trade and Ministry of Labour in an anomalous position, being neither spenders nor departments with a functional right to membership of the governing centre. (The centre itself under Eden and Macmillan comprised the Prime Minister, the Foreign and Defence Secretaries and the Chancellor of the Exchequer, a constellation made explicit in the composition of the inner cabinet at the time of Suez). In a more vituperative climate of bargaining, political weighting of the sponsorship given to the TUC, FBI or BEC diminished; for John Hare at Labour or Reginald Maudling at Trade, these institutions ranked as supplementary bodies, not intrinsic parts of the state; as no more than recipients of advice and information, suppliants for favours or compliant providers of assistance in solving problems. It was for Ministers and their departments to define, analyse solutions. Tripartism declined in favour and it is not far-fetched to suggest that, some two or three years in advance of Britain's application to join the EEC, government began to take on some of the directive attributes normally ascribed to the French system.

The difficulty each of these bodies had in controlling their own members (whose inadequacies or bad behaviour, in MOL and BOT eyes, constituted a major part of the problems) helped to devalue their status with government and obviate the possibility of common action, after 1956–57. Since the Board of Trade and Ministry of Labour were developing a slightly different, more authoritarian outlook on what was the national interest in each sector, and since Hare and Maudling injected this into the pluralistic bargaining process inside government rather than responding to TUC or FBI opinion, some of the explanations for Britain's poor industrial performance stuck. Wage inflation and managerial incompetence became standard terms of recrimination, embedded in what ought to be called the hegemony of the Conservative era. Not surprisingly, the NJAC and NPACI deteriorated, becoming occasions for ritual confrontation and the handing down of government information – or disinformation – rather than the sort of discussions which had previously assisted or changed behaviour. In their place (and somewhat to the detriment of the spirit of the 1944 package) departmental ministers laid down policy, or if they could not, left it to the Chancellor to regulate their markets instead. Surviving industrialists and trade union leaders who served on tripartite bodies at this time, and who asked why it was that Britain attempted to carry the burdens of the sterling area, Commonwealth investment, and a wide-ranging overseas defence commitment, to the detriment of domestic expenditure, recall the strong impression that civil servants thought these matters too complex for them to be allowed to discuss.

In the years after 1956 and Britain's withdrawal from the Messina Conference, the Board of Trade concerned itself mainly with the development of EFTA in contradistinction to an EEC which it saw as a vast cartel actually opposed to liberal trade. As a result, it drew closer to the Foreign Office and Cabinet Office than it had been under Thorneycroft. The Permanent Secretary, Sir Frank Lee was a master of detail, politically acute, who co-ordinated civil service opinion and did much to facilitate consensus in Cabinet. Contact with the FBI on other issues declined, because the FBI's main contention, opposition to 'stop-go' policies, was directed at the Treasury. From 1959–61, Maudling seems to have combined with Amory at the Treasury in seeking to manipulate existing BOT regional organisation to help maintain full employment in an inexpensive and unobtrusive manner. The practice continued under Edward Heath in 1964, during the time when Maudling was Chancellor. Aware of this, the FBI gave extra emphasis to its own regional network, as much to improve its access to government as to serve its members' needs.

As far as domestic industry was concerned, BOT watched the burgeoning process of concentration with enthusiasm. Mergers and takeovers which proliferated as the 1960s began, encouraged by profitable stock market conditions, appeared to offer an alternative means to recover Britain's lost competitive position in world trade. The problem was to ensure that the greater size of leading companies would increase efficiency and lead to economies of scale, not to more effective price-rigging and market-sharing practices. The traditions followed by Thorneycroft and Lee in founding the Restrictive Practices Court and developing the Monopolies Commission, continued with Maudling. BOT policy favoured and facilitated mergers, yet at the same time worked to eliminate restrictive practices, a trend that culminated in Edward Heath's abolition of resale price maintenance in 1963. This dual strategy depended, of course, on the pertinacity of the Court and the Commission.

Opinion inside the Board of Trade towards EFTA and the EEC showed a similar dualism. General scepticism about the latter and downright hostility to certain of its aspects such as the Common Agricultural Policy conflicted with the evident weakness of EFTA and the plain fact that the sterling area and Commonwealth trade continued to decline as the Dominions developed major trading links with the USA or, in the case of South Africa under the Nationalist government, as it attempted to diversify to forestall political constraints. A minority in BOT had always been in favour of the EEC and by 1961 the department was poised, ready to abandon Commonwealth preferences and espouse a pro-European policy, though not necessarily by application to join the Common Market.

Preoccupied with such international matters, BOT officials relegated their former concern with particular 'industries' although individuals, like the former IDAC official Leslie Robinson, kept up specialised connections. This was not a period of close interest in the quality of management, or the level of research and development,[37] but rather of a growing disillusion with the effects of government planning, and the capacity of the FBI or trade associations to achieve change. BOT did not even keep the FBI closely informed of the government's EEC negotiations in 1961–62. Part of the Thorneycroft legacy, in fact, led to disengagement, leaving industry to solve its own problems within the liberal trading and free capital market context. From the mid 1950s onwards, the Board collectively tended to preach the virtues of open competition, and tried to abolish conditions in which manufacturers could make easy profits in sheltered markets.[38] In such conditions, its 1942–43 vision of a 'Ministry of Industry' receded beyond the horizon.

This in turn enhanced the Treasury's contention that wages should be restrained for, in a freer market, and in the end without resale price maintenance, employers would not be able to pass on higher wages in the form of higher prices. BOT–Treasury discourse concentrated entirely on macroeconomic direction of the economy by what were now traditional means. Nothing comparable to the contemporary growth of the MITI system in Japan or the French Plan can be detected in Britain, and ministers saw no need even to inform themselves about what was going on elsewhere.[39] The tension between equilibrium and growth dominated all their discussions.

The fact that the Minister of Labour in the years after 1959, John Hare, came to agree with Selwyn Lloyd that the pay pause was necessary and that he supported it into the period of the National Incomes Commission symbolised a profound change inside his department, which can only partly be explained by the appointment of a former Treasury official, Sir Laurence Helsby, as Permanent Secretary. A different attitude to unions in which they no longer appeared as a beneficial force in society began to pervade it in the 1960s. Though the old guard of Emmerson's day regarded this as a derogation from what the department once stood for, younger men like the future Permanent Secretary, Denis Barnes took the abundant evidence of union bickering, sectional greed and outright malpractice in industries like car production and the docks and railways to mean that the trade union movement as a whole, unrestrained by an incompetent TUC, had gone back on its supposed pledge to behave responsibly and could no longer be trusted to fulfil the duties that the achievement of full employment had once envisaged.

Some of this can be traced back to the TUC's dismissal of the CPPI's reports, some to Macleod's wish to embody aspects of the Workers' Charter in legislation, giving legal rights to individuals rather than to unions as collective bodies. In the mid-1950s, MOL officials had been wary of any mention of legislation, particularly if it had not been agreed with the TUC. Emmerson believed that reliance on the law would weaken the 'conditions of work' element in collective bargaining and induce unions to concentrate even more on the money wage;[40] and Macleod responded for a time by working through the NJAC instead to win agreement to codes of practice.

Macleod believed, as most of his 'One-Nation' colleagues did, that strikes represented a breakdown in the normal pattern of industrial relations, caused by specific and remediable events.[41] The younger officials however, who remembered how unions had conformed to national needs in wartime, but had no memory of the 1930s, were less inclined to accept Emmerson's view or Macleod's philosophy, given the actual strike-prone conditions of the late 1950s. They preferred to make a different sort of bargain with the TUC by legislating (citing Bevin's Catering Wages Act 1944, or the 1948 Agricultural Wages Act as precedents) on contracts of employment, compensation for redundancy, and recourse for unfair dismissal. This is not simply to be seen as an adoption of the old high Tory view of Sir Henry Maine that the way forward consisted of progress from status to contract; they were proposing to lay down conditions in which there would be less excuse for unions and shop stewards to justify bad behaviour by recourse to talk of exploitation and class struggle.

As Macleod's first tranches of legislation, the Terms and Conditions of Employment and The Wages Councils Acts showed, this view became the departmental ethic. Heath, who stayed at the Ministry only for nine months and had no real chance to do more than see Macleod's Acts into practice, liked the formulation and passed it on to John Hare, who continued it with the major Contracts of Employment Act 1961, and the planning of the Redundancy Notices and Payments Act 1965.

In the Ministry of Labour's acceptance of a wages policy and a legislative framework for industrial relations, the outlines of a new, Conservative contract with the union movement can be discerned. Although it was still couched in the phraseology of tripartism (and occasionally utilised historic memory of the war), in its emphasis on contractual agreements, embodied in legislation giving individual workers access to the courts, and in its encouragement to use them for redress not only against employers but also their own unions, it resembled contemporary Swedish and German procedures.

But while this contract took account of the abundant evidence of bad industrial relations[42] and changes in the balance of power highlighted in *A Giant's Strength*, it envisaged that the law would work to alter behaviour only indirectly and on terms favourable to unions rather than their employers. Ministers and their officials still thought it necessary to protect workers' interests against unreasonable action by their employers: the memory of the 1956 BMC sackings had not yet been transmuted generally into a beneficial attack on overmanning. Few imagined that the law should be used to bring penalties to bear on unions or remedy over-mighty union power in collective bargaining, other than the Inns of Court lawyers and the right wing of the Conservative party. Nor did the legislation which was passed represent a break in the government's commitment to full employment, because 'overfull' employment was still believed to be a fault of management, one which more open competition would remedy in due course, while growth would lead those put out of work, safeguarded by the new laws, to find congenial employment elsewhere.

At the same time, the Ministry hoped by tripartite discussion to wean unions away from their traditional concentration on money wages, to encourage them to consider conditions, training, terms of service, or pensions, and to use due restraint without an overt wages policy. Officials believed that the new TUC General Secretary, George Woodcock, concurred with these and other aims such as setting up Industrial Training Boards. But tripartism had grown very rusty. By 1960 the NJAC's main occasion was its annual Christmas party. After the political events of 1955–57 it seemed easier to use the legislative programme to focus discussion. Unfortunately, such was the evidence of wage inflation after the Guillebaud Report in 1959, that MOL came under great pressure to abandon its traditional stance as a conciliator, and to take up a committed position. While they placed some reliance on TUC co-operation, chiefly from survivors of the old big six like Carron and Williamson, officials ceased to argue the case against a formal wages policy or legislation to cope with manifest abuses.

Although MOL still contested the Treasury case for a wages policy as late as 1957, the Engineering Employers Federation withdrawal from its attempt to outface the engineering unions that same year led it to conclude that employers collectively no longer had stomach to fight. MOL consented to take part in discussing the Treasury's next attempt in 1960, which took shape as the CPPI's 'guiding light', and made no serious attempt to prevent the 'pay pause' a year later nor the establishment of the National Income Commission; nor did it object when the National Economic Development Council (NEDC) was superimposed on the NJAC in 1962. Like the Board of Trade, it had distanced itself from the institution it once wholeheartedly sponsored. It ignored the complaints of both the BEC and TUC against its new emphasis on a legal framework (which brought Sir George Pollock and Frank Cousins into a bizarre alliance) and it finally came round to compulsory restraint of wages. The impetus for the latter came from the Treasury but it would have been hard to impose without MOL acquiescence.

At headquarters level, the BEC and the TUC surveyed the decay of tripartism in this period with distaste, amounting at times to a sort of cosmic despair. But the FBI, caught up in its enthusiasm for Europe, showed a surprising vigour, which culminated in the 'Next Five Years' Conference at Brighton in 1960, and led on directly to its support for the formation of NEDC and association with the EEC application. Dissatisfaction with 'stop-go' led the FBI not into the gloomy, Cassandra-like warnings of the BEC, but a determination publicly to project 'industry' as a dynamic entity, and a preoccupation with reform of economic management and government machinery. Leaving behind memories of its often reactive behaviour in the mid-1950s, when the research staff had struggled, with PEP and NIESR help, merely to keep pace with Treasury papers, the FBI moved into a position where, for the first time since 1949, leading firms made use of its research in their own plans to penetrate EFTA and then the EEC.

The first stage of the great wave of concentration (which by the late 1960s halved the number of major firms in many sectors) before foreign-based multinational corporations established themselves, was based on the premise that, as competition externally became more difficult, economies of scale and increased monopolistic power would safeguard domestic market share. Regardless of the Monopolies Commission's mild strictures (which were, in any case, restrained by the belief that aggregation and sheer size did actually promote efficiency), and facilitated by the speculative energies of the stock market and the developments in merchant banking, takeovers and mergers proliferated even before 1961.[43]

Selwyn Lloyd's July 1961 squeeze failed to deter concentration even though, on the FBI's estimate, it cut back industrial growth by a full two years. Ever since 1955, reiterated use of the fiscal levers and regulators had made corporate investment, planning, and research and development increasingly problematic. Concentration may, indeed, have occurred partly in response to fiscal oscillation. Complaints about 'stop-go' were not confined to the car and consumer goods industries, but were common to the majority of large firms and trade associations and also public industries, so that on the main issues of the day, the FBI found itself more united than at any time since the war. Where investment was concerned, they acquired allies, for Cobbold (unlike Norman in the inter-war years) accepted that bank rate at any level over 6 per cent acted as a substantial disincentive.[44]

In their disillusion with the results of demand management, the FBI drew on the May 1960 OECD Report and successive documents from EPB which demonstrated that Britain's relative decline was accelerating. What gains occurred in the reserves and the strength of sterling seemed inadequate to offset the shock that Selwyn Lloyd administered in July 1961. The government's view of EFTA as an alternative to the EEC also provided reason for complaint, since the FBI had always assumed EFTA membership would lead either to a form of association with the EEC, or to an even wider grouping within OECD.[45] With so many members keen to penetrate European markets from a secure basis of high demand at home, the FBI also deplored what looked in 1961 like the start of a permanent wages policy.

This is not to say that they disliked restraint, for which they had asked in 1955. Only later did they object to its corollary, a prices freeze to match the public industries' 'price plateau'. But they were offended by the way the 1956 White Paper distributed blame for inflation on employers as well as unions. They had supported the EEF in 1957 and had been downcast by the government's failure, after Suez, to support resistance to a major strike. But at the same time, in July 1957, the FBI had opposed dividend restraint, so that their policy came to look adventitious when it was not simply self-interested.[46]

In their combined evidence to Radcliffe, the FBI and the BEC pointed out the sharp decline in profits since 1956, prayed for a counter-inflationary policy, and for the first time, in denigrating 'overfull employment', cast doubt on the economic wisdom of full employment itself. They hazarded a level of 3–4 per cent unemployment as suitable, when accusing the government of neglecting necessary structural reform out of fear of 'transitional unemployment'. Equally outspokenly, and in tune with City opinion, the FBI argued that the money supply had been allowed to rise too quickly. Existing controls, they argued, were inadequate and Bank rate had not been used with sufficient vigour. Rather perversely, the FBI went on to complain of the malign effect of the 1957 credit squeeze and government's 'arbitrary and capricious' interventions in the capital market and the pattern of bank lending.

Such a set of views, as Peter Mathias points out in his history of the FBI, represented the limited consensus of large member firms, not the sum of opinion in all trade associations and small businesses, whose credit needs and investment patterns differed widely. On their behalf – and probably accurately – the FBI stated that the resources available to small businesses provided by ICFC and FFI, over and above the normal capital market, sufficed. (The Radcliffe Report bore this out, but it seemed to make so small an impression that the FBI subsequently set up its own public relations apparatus to ensure that government was left in no doubt about what were industry's future needs. Their Industrial Trends Survey, which appeared for the first time in February 1958, at last gave accurate information, in advance of government's own statistics, with which to contest Treasury or BOT expertise, from a position of authority.)

Assumption of industrial leadership inevitably brought the FBI into the BEC's preserve of 'labour' questions. The BEC had staved this off for a time by consenting to give joint evidence with the FBI to the CPPI; but they could not avoid coming to terms with the FBI over the question of whether or not industry ought to submit to price restraint as *quid pro quo* for wages policy. The BEC believed it should but its membership was divided; the FBI said no because (as Sir Hugh Beaver put it) prices unlike wages were governed by general competitive economic conditions.[47] Two years at least before Selwyn Lloyd invited them both to join NEDC, the idea of a merger again became popular, the better to face up to a wayward government and a divided, sometimes hostile TUC.

In the mid-1950s the BEC manifested symptoms of extreme defensiveness and what amounted almost to paranoia about the decline of Britain's economy. This morbid state of opinion cannot be attributed to a single cause: it arose partly out of member federations' awareness that profits were declining at such a rate that only a firm stand against increased wages could provide short-term relief; partly from the belief that government had abandoned the struggle and that Macmillan in particular had sabotaged the EEF's attempt to curb the engineering unions in 1957.[48] To try to quell discontent Macmillan and Macleod both found it expedient to address the BEC's 1958 Annual Conference.

The BEC had been substantially reduced in stature because the largest firms like ICI, BICC or Courtaulds now habitually conducted their own bargaining with trade unions. Except in engineering and public industry, its component Federations themselves lost ground, *pari passu* with the declining importance of national wage rates. Meanwhile the process of concentration and the spread of automation in factories exposed both the overmanning and the restrictive practices which employers had allowed to become endemic in the fat years after 1951. Although the car companies at last returned to the EEF in 1957 (probably in dismay at the government's attitude during the AEU dispute), their savage competition and willingness to indulge shop stewards' plant bargaining made them a source of weakness rather than collective strength. No one in the engineering industry was likely to forget that when Sir William Rootes had tried to stand firm in an earlier dispute with the AEU, his competitors had stolen his business, ignoring the EEF's patient request to combine.

BEC jeremiads lost some of their force because their language differed only in its intensity from what had been said five or even ten years earlier. The argument that excessive money wage settlements benefited no one, because the money was soon eroded by inflation, had always found a response from the TUC; but it was obvious that the TUC could not now control what its own committees privately diagnosed as a disease. In 1957 the BEC decided to develop a more public presence and shed its old conspiratorial shell;[49] but its new orientation also involved attacking government more openly, which offended senior members' view of how such things should be done. It also meant acknowledging more publicly their member federations latent hostility to trades' unions, which Sir George Pollock had managed to mitigate in his actual dealings with the TUC. BEC discussions in the late 1950s tended to start from an assumption that union moderates had been eclipsed, and that Congress had become a playground for truculent agitators and politically-minded extremists.

For some time yet, the BEC Council took care not to set wage inflation in the balance against full employment nor to ask government to impose a standstill. But they made contact with Makins in 1957, hoping that the Treasury under Thorneycroft would make wage restraint a reality without unpleasant 'political' repercussions. Later, in November 1957, they put the whole gloomy litany against the 'annual round', wage-earners' inflated expectations of immediate gratification, and excessive government spending and high personal taxation, in their evidence to the CPPI. Thorneycroft's resignation ended any hope that the government would restore sound sense by putting its own house in order and in 1958 the BEC at last spelled out that inflation followed directly from full employment.[50] Nevertheless, rather than offend the Macmillan administration's deepest principles, and being unwilling to repudiate a fifty years' link with the state, they chose to accept the reassurances offered by Macleod and Macmillan. On the one hand they welcomed the work of the CPPI as heralding a return to the responsible days of Stafford Cripps, and on the other they acknowledged the impetus for trade union reform generated by George Woodcock.[51]

In 1959–60, however, the figures of strikes grew so bad[52] that the government itself reached a point where they had to find another means to recreate good industrial relations, more effective than the CPPI's carefully-reasoned, powerless reports. Facing up to major strikes remained politically unacceptable; yet they were equally unwilling either to use the BEC's argument that wage inflation must be offset by allowing unemployment to rise, or to study in any depth, using the Ministry of Labour's conciliation agencies, what actually had gone wrong inside the system of collective bargaining. That left nothing to do but control wages directly.

As Lloyd moved towards the pay pause in July 1961, the BEC ran to his support. Any pretence that voluntary restraint might work had vanished. Whether from fear, or as a result of a real change of outlook, in their panic-stricken reaction to the Guillebaud Report's 1959 endorsement of comparability regardless of the Transport Commission's capacity to pay, the BEC admitted that certain matters had become too grave to be left to unions or employers to settle, within the old canon of self-regulation. For the first time they proposed a tripartism by invitation to government not, as previously, the other way round.[53]

But the BEC had already sown dragon's teeth, when it wholeheartedly approved MOL's choice of reform. Council members supported the Macleod–Heath–Hare chain of Acts,[54] only to ask that they be extended to curtail the closed shop. Whether urging worker participation, on one hand, or legislation to restore discipline by restricting the application of 'immunity' (under the 1906 Trades Disputes Act) only to disputes involving 'registered unions' not in breach of contract, on the other, the BEC made itself politically salient. They welcomed Hare's support of a merger with the FBI, agreeing with him on the need for united industry to face up to the TUC; yet they kept contact with union leaders and used the (unreliable) information given them by Carron and Williamson to suggest that the TUC recognised the effect created by full employment in encouraging 'strikes and agitation'.

Since they believed that neither procedures nor the industrial relations system were to blame, but full employment itself, the BEC's strategy in relation to the government looks distinctly devious. Yet at the same time they accepted that 'full employment was a settled policy from which no government could defect, and unless we priced ourselves out of world markets, there was no question whatever of returning to the conditions between the wars'.[55] Whether Council members really believed that they had interpreted the TUC correctly is not clear, but in July 1961, just before the pay freeze, they decided to press for a new, national tripartite bargaining system, whose decisions were to be enforced by legally-binding agreements. Only in this way, they believed, could plant bargaining be brought under control.[56] This was intended as a message to the Chancellor, encouraging him to proceed with his proposal for what later became NEDC. They appear to have known nothing in advance about the pay pause which they were reduced to welcoming rather huffily, as a temporary measure to buy time until their own larger proposal could be put into effect.

But the BEC had very little idea how to bring this about without undermining the voluntary industrial bargaining system by which its members lived. They imagined that it would be possible to restore the responsibilities encapsulated in the 1944 White Paper by giving legal sanction to the results of free collective bargaining, without asking what working conditions would have to be created in each factory *before* either side would voluntarily submit to such a procedure. They could not, therefore, satisfactorily answer the CPPI's request for information about 'how a free country can maintain full employment, economic growth, and rising standards of living, and at the same time avoid inflation', for they did not choose to repeat what they had said in 1958, that that was impossible without a rather higher margin of unemployment.[57]

Such were the diffuse reactions of the Conservative government's assumed friends. Supportive as their pronouncements were in form, in content they menaced not only the current practice of economic management but the nature of the post-war settlement. It would be incorrect to speak yet of the settlement having enemies. But the tone of FBI and BEC discussion implied more than grumbling about the failure of government and the TUC to keep to their various obligations. The ideas behind the settlement had become outdated, inappropriate to the exigences of European integration, technological change, and the cult of the giant firm. Whether in the emphasis given to American methods of management education or to the age of automation (to use the title of Sir Leon Bagrit's 1964 Reith lectures), discontent with the way industrial politics worked provided the only common ground between the central institutions of industry and the TUC, both of which by 1961 had come to see each other as the 'other side'.

10 The New Opposition and the Old

In spite of its 1951 pledge to work with the Conservatives so long as they played fair with the labour movement, and in spite of its fears of being identified as part of the 'opposition', especially at a time when the governing party was led by the principal author of *The Middle Way*, the TUC distanced itself after 1959 from both the government and the Civil Service in a way that would have astonished the architects of the 1944 White Paper. Although its members still shared many of the FBI's aims, such as an enlarged international monetary system and Britain's eventual integration in the European Community[1] (even if for different reasons), it became less inclined to work with them and positively antipathetic to the BEC. The main source of conflict with government and employers was wages and the question whether, at the alarming rate which developed after 1956, they caused inflation; but the internal condition of the labour movement itself virtually precluded real co-operation. Profound changes took place in the late 1950s which affected the direction and leadership of most large unions, at exactly the moment of greatest involvement in the Labour Party's fratricidal struggles. Any call for sacrifice or wage restraint like that put out by the TUC in 1948 would have led to member unions' rebellion or even disaffiliation; a conclusion which crippled politically those members of the TUC's main committees which had to review the dismal evidence that seemed to justify their critics.

In the context of union history, TUC caution towards Monckton and Macleod and its distrust of the intellectual chain leading from codes of conduct to legal definition of individual unionists' rights, is not hard to understand, even before the growth of public hostility to abuses in unions' behaviour found a sounding board in a predominantly Conservative press. Members of the General Council had never entirely trusted Conservative ministers nor the Treasury not to allow unemployment to rise as a means of disciplining

316

workers; nor did they believe, after a decade of experience, in the ability of either to maintain a balance between wages and the cost of living in the interests of the majority of the population. But the credit squeeze and cuts of October 1955, coming after what the Labour Party had denigrated as an election budget, particularly angered the TUC because it seemed to be the first clear breach of the 1944 political contract. For a body without the clear leadership Citrine had once provided, these grievances became a reason not to look too closely at restrictive practices or structural rigidities; especially when reform was held out by Conservative ministers as a requirement for continued full employment, which most union members had by then come to take for granted.

Wide, and in union eyes uncritical, acceptance of the wage inflation thesis unsupported by a complementary analysis of employers' shortcomings, increased the sense of dissociation, at the same time as its consequences (in what government policy required) threatened union leaderships' extremely limited authority over their own members. Tewson and his colleagues' admission that a problem existed won some sympathy from Eden, but the General Council were simply not able to enforce more stringent rules over member unions, even if they had got Congress to accept their amendments. Meanwhile, profound personal and ideological divisions ravaged the Council and created a climate of morbid defensiveness towards the outside world, the very reverse of what a perceptive strategy for re-establishing trade union popularity would have dictated. At the same time, the TUC had to face, in a rather bemused way, the unexpected change inside the Ministry of Labour, after more than fifty years of conciliatory benevolence, accompanied by what they saw as a threat to industrial relations' legal foundations that had been secure since 1906.

In these conditions, the TUC reacted negatively to the strictures of government or employers (such as the FBI pamphlet, *Britain's Industrial Future* (1955)), even when many of its leaders were aware that criticisms were valid. Individual unions indeed tried to reform themselves: the AEU's 'Plan for Engineering' in 1956 led to an inquiry into the state of the industry whose report confirmed many of the points made by the FBI [2] They also contributed, as part of the TUC's submission to the Radcliffe Committee, ideas about reforming the investment market which germinated later in the form of a proposal for a City Economic Development Committee and a National Investment Board. But the overall response was always defensive.

On the Economic Committee, and among headquarters staff, criticisms of union shortcomings and ideas about reform circulated, but the General Council's membership was becoming so diverse, and Tewson's leadership so pedestrian that they could not be drawn together. By the time that George Woodcock, who had a clear if limited vision about where the movement ought to be going, came out of the shadows where he had withdrawn in despair at what was being allowed to occur, it was too late to try for more than administrative changes. The TUC could not be other than what member General Secretaries willed even though its Economic Committee had, for example, considered the 'problem of full employment' and the disorderly behaviour of shop stewards as early as 1955.[3]

On the evidence of its central organisations' minutes the TUC was only too aware, from Gallup polls and the press as well as from official inquiries, of how strikes in the car industry (at seven times the national average) appeared to the public at home and to international opinion.[4] A number of significant and highly-publicised closed shop and victimisation cases gave substance to press criticism in these years: *Spring* v. *TGWU* (1955), *Bonsor* v. *Musicians Union* (1956), and *Hartley* v. *Thornton et al.* (1957) while the ETU ballot-rigging court battle provided all the evidence that organisations like Aims of Industry required to substantiate the Communist bogy. Empirical evidence fortified an ancient prejudice in the Conservative party which had only been partly anaesthetised by *The Industrial Charter*.

Judging from what was said at the time many individual union leaders realised that consumer demand had reached a pitch where it could not be satisfied out of domestic production. Exports had to rise to match the imports that then flooded in if the exchange rate was to hold (as they accepted was proper) or if real wages were not to fall. It was understood that trade could not penetrate the dollar area much more nor, so long as the Cold War lasted, Eastern Europe, and that, for lack of sterling area demand, the future lay in trade with EEC and EFTA countries. But they saw no reason to accept, on the government's or employers' terms, an argument which put all the onus on recapturing Britain's international competitive ranking on wage-earners' productivity and restraint.

In trying to define the national interest in a common return to post-war obligations, the TUC acted sensibly but put itself in pawn. Being quite unable to 'control' individual unions, it could not meet the expectations that its claims to government and public as a governing institution aroused; nor could it easily defend the limited returns on its bargaining with government either to militant car workers or low-paid public service employees who watched old differentials widen with every annual pay-round. From a position of political disadvantage, exacerbated by internal dissensions, the TUC simply could not do what it wanted, as its confused reaction to successive credit squeezes in 1956–57 showed. At the same time, fears about the *general* level of living standards and employment grew. Arthur Deakin, for example, had for some time been unsure of the Conservative commitment to full employment, and the TUC declared in February 1956 that the government 'had given rise to fears in the minds of many workpeople that their living standards are in danger'.[5]

Yet the TUC could not easily disengage from its habitual dance. To Ministers, they might bluntly declare, 'people put out of work in one part of the country could not be expected to move to another part to find work', but the Economic Committee realistically accepted that redeployment was an essential element in the labour market.[6] Some of Woodcock's discussion papers might, if adopted as TUC public policy, have formed the basis for a rejoinder to the 1956 White Paper, on which bargaining with the Chancellor could have begun,[7] but the General Council could not reach unanimity and instead refused to endorse the White Paper because it did not renew the 1944 guarantee of full employment.

A minority on the Economic Committee (where most of the discussions about the future of the labour market took place) believed that 'full employment required a change in the outlook and policies of trade unions, as traditional policies could themselves undermine it'. But the majority thought that to put out such a statement would weaken individual unions in their negotiations with employers and would never, therefore, pass Congress.[8] In the autumn of 1956 the debate about change was postponed to await Congress' opinion. Then came Suez and indefinite postponement. Nothing in Peter Thorneycroft's policy during 1957 encouraged the TUC to think again, because Treasury cuts in public expenditure were seen, not as a reinterpretation of the state's fiscal role, but as a fundamental alteration of the 1944 accord, weakening government's own capacity to ensure full employment.

The wage inflation thesis now seemed to be an imposition to be learned by rote, excluding discussion of the future of the economy.

Meanwhile, the TUC began to realise that, in presenting its policy, the government had begun to distinguish between the interests of public and consumers, on one hand, and that of trade unions on the other. (Attention focused on the plain fact that between April 1956 and April 1957 basic wages rose by 8 per cent at a time when productivity was stagnant, and when public industries had adopted the 'price plateau'.)

The more government requested it to put its house in order, the more Frank Cousins, leader of the TGWU since 1956 and increasingly the focus of internal opposition to the big six tradition, demanded that the TUC cease its equivocation. In June 1957, after a climactic debate about whether or not to continue its self-examination, the TUC decided not to give evidence to the CPPI on the grounds that it differed from the 1944 accord and could be no substitute for negotiating with government. They wanted to call Thorneycroft's bluff (in that he had hoped that the CPPI could decide 'the public interest') but, realising that a forthright refusal would give government a major hostage, they haggled instead, trying to extract a promise that the CPPI's reports would not be used to interfere with any particular wage dispute nor with wage bargaining in general.

Cousins's fear of a trap, after the TUC conceded, was proved correct (though not in the sense he imagined) when in December he and his colleagues had to face up to the seven difficult questions put to it by the Council about the future of collective bargaining. Hard to simplify for members' consumption, and barbed despite their neutral language, these questions exposed all the TUC's internal divisions as well as its shaky economic theory.[9] (The same would have been true of the employers' organisations of whom such questions were *not* asked.) It is clear from their initial response that most union leaders believed wages were not inflationary, but accepted that there were far too many strikes for trivial reasons, and that they did not have time to wait for a Labour government before confronting the subject of reform. Equally, none was prepared to sign a statement to that effect: 'Trade union officials had a pressing responsibility to, and were under pressure from, their members who were concerned that their real standards should not be depressed.'[10] In the end they gave evidence to the CPPI, but condemned its report when it was published.

The public was not to know how many of them had admitted the critics' case and discussed remedies. Instead, denigration increased.

Union leaders closed ranks rather than face the contradiction between their representative functions and their role *vis-à-vis* government. The nineteenth-century tradition took precedence over one established only in 1916. Had Thorneycroft remained in office and kept up the pressure, they might nevertheless have been forced to do so: this awful possibility was actually discussed in November 1957, as part of a wages bargaining strategy that relied on the Swedish model and German 'concerted action'.[11] But what seemed a defence suitable also against a future Labour government was tightly conditioned by a prerequisite of 1 per cent unemployment in conditions of price stability; and it was almost entirely erased from the TUC's subsequent 'statement on the economic situation'.

During the next two ragged years, while the TUC and the Labour Party were riven by disputes, the most powerful unions and shop steward combines continued to force up wages in competition with each other to the inevitable detriment of industry, the elderly and the lower paid. That wages led directly to inflation became a thesis etched irrevocably into the ethos of government departments, which also fed the Press and constituency activists, so that the same story trickled back to Ministers from what looked like all points of the political compass.

In 1958–59, inconclusive discussions took place with the new Chancellor Heathcoat Amory about the margin of spare capacity and unemployment, and the likely results of a shorter working week of forty hours. The TUC's commitment went little further than a desire to keep its access to government and recover its former public status. It welcomed the Radcliffe Report, but rationed 'co-operation' only to proposals from which all hint of wages policy had been strained, and which were unlikely to damage the Labour Party's chances in the 1959 election. Indeed, in one pre-Budget meeting in February 1960, union leaders revealed that they saw *any* gains in productivity as a licence for concomitant wage increases, a view which probably encouraged the Treasury to embark on its wages policy.[12] One immediate result was that Selwyn Lloyd did not consult the TUC about the pay freeze in July 1961.

Yet in an anguished post-mortem on the Briggs Motor Bodies Factory Report, in 1959, Towson confessed to the General Council that 'full employment has brought new problems. The material gains which have been achieved . . . have, in the minds of many people, removed the need for solidarity and dependance upon union machinery. Gradually, conditions have developed where it is possible for some people, by the selfish prosecution of their own interests, to do better for themselves as a small group than by working through their union.'[13] Like Donovan ten years later, Tewson put the blame on shop stewards and would have liked to incorporate them into union local branches, but his paper gave no inkling that he understood the economic and social changes which had created the shop steward phenomenon, nor how union leaders might respond.

Selwyn Lloyd's hints about a new tripartite forum to replace the NJAC revived the mood of co-operation early in 1961. The Economic Committee indicated that 'if effective planning [the new catchword] was to be possible, the trade unions might be obliged to modify some traditional attitudes and accept industrial change which would accentuate the unfavourable position of some declining industries' – in other words, create redundancies. Guarded as this language was, it was allowed to lapse as soon as the Basle arrangements for sterling took effect. Yet when the freeze came in July, although the TUC castigated the measures' deflationary consequences and inequity, it did not oppose their introduction. Such an ambivalent reaction suggests that its members realised how weak their position was, in political terms.

In defining what was eventually to become the National Economic Development Committee, Lloyd spoke of 'a joint examination of the economic prospects of the country, stretching five years or more into the future . . . [which] would try to establish what are the essential conditions for realising potential growth'. Unlike the more politically aware Economic Committee, the TUC Production Committee as a long-term ally of the British Production Council, could welcome the proposal unequivocally. Then and later, cleavages ran inside the TUC, as well as between General Secretaries; but overall, the TUC distanced itself from parties, being, 'interested in balancing a developing economy with the minimum oscillation. The political party [Labour] out of office, on the other hand, is interested in exploiting differences . . . and in causing embarrassment to the party in office'.[14]

Outside, among union members, the pay pause brought a more direct form of trouble, especially in public industries. Once full employment had become habitual, the TUC could not persuade public sector unions that their lower rates of pay should be seen as offset by job security. Nor had they faced up to the question of whether these industries were to be 'run as a social service or on a commercial basis'.[15] Instead they had welcomed Guillebaud's comparability principle as a way out. Now the pay pause hit groups like nurses who ranked high in public esteem as well as others the public judged less meritorious, like London bus drivers and Post Office engineers. More than anything, a sense of betrayal among employees of the state held the TUC back from joining NEDC to which it was finally invited in September 1961. Nevertheless, the TUC's reactions to the July measures represent the end of one story, those to NEDC the start of another.

Tewson handed over to George Woodcock in Autumn 1960, just at the moment when the General Council took up its long-postponed discussion about shop stewards and what to do with them. This transition owed nothing to the great, formative changes which took place in these years in the trade union movement which can only be mentioned here in order to suggest why the General Council found itself at odds so often. Discord has often been presented as caused by the impact of a new wave of General Secretaries, taking over unions which had once been run by the old 'big six'; but that is to trivialise its dimensions. Frank Cousins was, certainly, an unruly member, and Jack Jones his successor and Hugh Scanlon (who took over as President of the AEU in 1968) soon justified their nicknames of the 'terrible twins'. But at issue was not only the role which shop stewards and local representatives were to play, in unions as different as the TGWU, ETU, GMWU, or AEU, but the nature of the democratic process inside many more unions then these four giants.

The widest change came about roughly a decade after the eruption of consumerism and less than a generation after what may be seen as the economic emancipation of the manual and semi-skilled working class. It occurred, predictably, in the most profitable sectors of manufacturing industry, where employers were prone to pay out rather than face strikes, and where plant bargaining was making greatest gains. Public service industries (apart from key personnel such as power station engineers) and most smaller firms in private industry followed at one or several removes. But shop stewards in these sectors tended to see national wage rates and the often ossified hierarchy of unions such as the General and Municipal Workers as anachronisms which prevented their members gaining comparability. This awareness created not only new bargaining techniques and demands, but in due course produced new types of General Secretaries, ranging from the leaders of aggressive white collar unions like Clive Jenkins of ASSET (later ASTMS) to Frank Chapple of the newly-liberated ETU.

Cousins, whose radicalism lay in his political attitudes on national issues (such as his campaigns against nuclear weapons and the EEC) rather than any great innovation in his union's direction, remained uneasy about this trend, as his traditional mode of building-up of the union by another one million members showed. But Jack Jones positively welcomed the emergence of a vigorous, spontaneous shop-floor leadership, for he believed that by bringing lay (non-official) members on to all union committees, and by decentralising the mammoth structure of the TGWU in order to create eleven distinct federal units, he could develop a more representative institution capable of surviving in the new climate. Others of more old-fashioned persuasion like Sir William Carron (AEU) and John Cooper (GMWU) fought the trend as long as they could, in the latter case into the 1970s, refusing to accept that shop stewards could in any sense be the shock troops of a new form of democracy. Hugh Scanlon's conversion to the appointment of lay members to AEU committees ranks as a crucial turning point, among other skilled unions; (and also for employers, because the EEF had for long defended the engineering industry against both 'shop steward power' and the subtler, more intrusive threat of white collar unionism in new bodies such as DATA and CAWU (later APEX)).

Ministry of Labour officials and Conservative ministers, who ought to have known enough not to rely on stereotypes about shop stewards and unofficial strikes, seem to have been too *bouleversés* by the disparity of the evidence or too much addicted to the idea that it arose from agitation to ask *why* this had occurred within ten years of the voluntary wages policy of 1948. What Jones and the radicals saw as an overdue solvent of authoritarianism, and a reasoned response to physical changes in various industries, they defined (in the same way as did more orthodox TUC members and the Labour Party's centre) as a derogation of responsibility on union leaders' part, amounting in some cases to a licence for anarchy. It was in this state of mind that the government resisted the seven-week-long London bus drivers' strike in May 1958 seeing in it, not Cousins' set-piece fight with overtones of class conflict, but a deliberate provocation of authority, threatening the stability of wages throughout the public sector.

The growth of white-collar unionism, product of industrial change, technological innovation and a transformation in the use of energy, caused less political controversy but affected the composition and internal affiliations of the General Council to a much greater extent, far into the 1960s and 1970s. The power workers' union, EPEA (later EMA), for example (which had been formed in the 1940s as a result of an initiative by Citrine, Deakin and Lincoln Evans, intended to prevent the Communist Party being in a position to shut down power stations) subsequently made cosy arrangements with the TGWU and froze the electricians (ETU) out of supervisory grades in the electricity industry. Others like APEX, already a mass union characterised by an anti-strike tradition and a belief in tripartism, or the Civil Service and local government unions (CPSA, NALGO) or the bank employees' union, NUBE, rapidly increased membership as the service sector grew, and vied with ASTMS for a place on the General Council. TASS and ASTMS in contrast, under pressure from manual workers' encroachment, developed notably leftist traits, not so much because this was their members' natural political alignment, but because it took much longer for their strikes to become effective so that higher strike pay – and hence higher political consciousness – was required.

A vast variety of layers of opinion conditioned unions' behaviour in the decade 1955–65 and produced a range of responses whose bewildering complexity can be read in the 1968 Donovan Report. It was unfortunate for the future of industrial relations that governments drifted towards voluntary and then involuntary wages policies since the effect of both the changes sketched in above was to exacerbate competitiveness between unions, and concentrate attention on the money wage as the best index of success. Conflict on a national scale then became inevitable.

There was, of course, no single panacea; it would be possible to argue, for example, that shop stewards and the workers they represented were too insulated from contact with senior management, and knew too little of the state of companies' finances to realise how their annual claims might be destroying firms' profitability and the future base of their industry; this would be a reasonably accurate description of affairs in the British Motor Corporation or for the Clyde shipyards, but it would not apply to ICI or Courtaulds, firms with a broader transnational base. On the other hand, looking across whole categories of occupations, no matter what firms were concerned, it can be seen that the gap between manual and skilled workers narrowed in this decade, as a result of a series of annual flat-rate settlements won by the big battalions of the TGWU and GMWU; but at the same time a skilled union like the engineers had the power to force employers (the EEF) to maintain existing differentials, even if they could barely afford the consequences.

As the Macmillan government saw only too clearly, the effect of the 1959 Guillebaud Report (which endorsed the principle of comparability originally advanced by Cameron in 1953) allowed public sector unions to break out of the strait-jacket in which the Attlee government had more or less managed to confine them. Conservative ministers, in particular at the Treasury, did not admit that this battle had been categorically lost – hence the pay pause in 1961, when Selwyn Lloyd attempted to re-establish order in the government's own bailiwick, even at the price of outraging opinion among railwaymen whose settlement had already been arranged with Dr Beeching, or the nurses who had had their legitimate expectations frozen.

The transition from national to plant bargaining as the means to improve on basic wage rates was in itself a neutral, apolitical process. Plant bargaining might seem as anarchic to Ministry of Labour officials brought up in the pre-war tradition as it did to Sir William Carron and his colleagues; but to industrialists, particularly in the various plants of large companies, and to many economists, it appeared an appropriate recognition of market forces. But the breakdowns it caused, the accumulation of short, restricted strikes were probably more costly than Cousins' set-piece battles. Nor did shop stewards' activity represent a revival of the quasi-revolutionary movement of 1917–21. But, of course, the impact of 'wild-cat' strikes, and patent abuses in sectors of the car and print industries, were hostages to the press and became the material for sharply-pointed attacks such as the film *I'm All Right, Jack*. In so far as their behaviour tended to set the local membership against an apparently unresponsive hierarchy, and revealed a disparity between particular or regional interests and union General Secretaries' awareness of the TUC's and the national interest, shop stewards of the late 1950s and early 1960s did, however, appear more politically radical than their actual claims warranted. Language and presentation, taken out of context, came to matter more than sober analysis. Also, although the early combine committees in no way resembled the 1920–21 Councils of Action, Communist Party and Trotskyite groups undoubtedly latched on to shop-floor grievances to make political capital.[16]

What government and MOL officials believed was happening in 1960–62 mattered as little at this level of the union movement as the lucubrations of a slow-moving General Council. For reasons both of circumstance and temperament, George Woodcock's reforms and proposed amalgamations were directed at union structures and the relations of unions with the state. Although his impatience can be explained by his feeling that the movement's incoherencies were increasing, their administrative tinge seems oddly at variance with trends in factories, as if he were still trying to remedy the problems of the 1940s. Inter-union rivalry for members had led the AEU and GMWU to see the TGWU as an aggressor, barely bound by the rules of Bridlington; smaller unions tended to make alliances with larger ones, in particular with the TGWU, so that they got unwarranted representation on the General Council; such habits ensured that faction faced faction on all the main committees.

Yet for the chance to revive general agreement with government that all the institutions had pledged themselves to in 1944, Woodcock had waited through the troughs and hollows of the late 1950s. He saw as few others did that full employment could no longer be taken for granted; that the TUC could only postpone, not prevent, consideration of vast changes in the labour market and in the shape of British trade unionism. Eager to take up the proposals laid aside in 1955, he saw reform in terms of amalgamations (as many contemporary businessmen saw the future in mergers and rationalisation) and in making bargains with government. His outlook was more truly corporatist than Bevin's and his rather mechanistic approach lacked the drama required to carry a mass membership. He envisaged the TUC not as an integral part of the movement, like a parliament, but as a separate managerial layer providing services and policy instruction to member unions; and his intellectual gifts and personal remoteness accentuated the natural tendency of General Secretaries to speak *de haut en bas*. Strong unions, strong companies, and receptive government constituted his ideal tripartism.

But the General Council took its tone very much from below in the late 1950s, and even the Economic Committee rarely discussed questions which might have led to a dialogue with government, such as what a union alternative to 'stop-go' might be. Given the TUC's inability to adapt quickly or reform itself to government's requirements, the impact on government of what it did therefore diminished, by the standards of the previous fifteen years. Moving towards dictating the pay pause, government needed its co-operation less, although paradoxically some union leaders may have absorbed more of the Conservative case for reform than Ministers realised.

Meanwhile, suspicious of 'theory', General Secretaries starved the headquarters organisation, regarded the staff as bureaucrats (to Woodcock's chagrin) and tended to think that money spent on research was wasted unless it served their own union's direct interests. Apparently the only escape from a sterile argument about the merits of as yet untried legal regulation and discredited self-regulation lay in what government offered in return for its wages policy in 1961: a combination of guaranteed growth, a new tripartite body, and entry into the wider EEC market.

These developments cannot be isolated from the Labour Party's own deep dissensions. Cousins himself took an active part in the crusade against nuclear weapons, an intrusion into the party's central dilemma which finally left him dangerously exposed because like any other individual General Secretary, he retained power only because, in the last resort, his members allowed him to – and members did not welcome the TGWU being thrust into minority status in the party's eyes. Cousins was not any more sympathetic to the Labour left than he was to his own shop stewards but if it came to a choice between them, he preferred the latter. When he found that he had to join Harold Wilson after Gaitskell's death or be relegated to political nullity, faction in the Labour movement as a whole diminished rapidly.

After the Labour Party's defeat in 1959, Anthony Crosland published a very influential essay, 'Can Labour Win?' His conclusion that the extent of class cleavage in Britain had declined, drew its evidence from the increase in white collar employees and the numerical decline of Labour's 'natural' manual worker constituency, around which he wove a persuasive argument about the dissolution of old working class urban communities, the unpopularity of unions and the consequences of vastly increased social and geographical mobility. Some of the party's traditional policies such as state ownership seemed to have been left, high and dry, or positively rejected. In this landmark of the social democratic trend inside the party, even state spending on welfare and the social services appeared to have created an alienation effect; Crosland argued, like Goldthorpe and Lockwood, that the more affluent, upper working class now aspired to middle class standards of life and house ownership – and that Macmillan's chance phrase 'You've never had it so good' was, literally, true. If Labour could not count much longer on habitual working class votes, its appeal must turn towards the fluid centre. Old socialism needed to be refashioned.

Hugh Gaitskell had ventured onto the same territory when in office in 1950–51, and in his private intellectual peregrination had probably predated Crosland by five years. But this remained a minority view even after the loss of the crucial 1955 election. To judge from its discussion documents, Labour Party headquarters spent the time between 1956 and 1959 concentrating on the future of EFTA, changes in the sterling area, and, at home, on problems of demand and wages. The Home Policy Committee in particular moved towards a concept of indicative, rather than command planning, which took account of the TUC's marked scepticism about further nationalisation.[17] During 1958 it examined the unpleasant paradox that, in a mixed economy, stable prices and a strong currency could not easily be reconciled with full employment and full capacity. In the end it concluded that the party should adopt a policy of planned, selective investment, which treated each case 'on the merits, and in accordance with clearly set out priorities'.[18]

The intellectual capital jointly invested by the party and the TUC in the concept of a state interest in industry, rather than wider state control, gave Labour a stake in indicative planning, and can be seen as leading directly to Harold Wilson's establishment of the Department of Economic Affairs in 1964 and to George Brown's initiation of the National Plan. But in the rough world outside, the labour movement experienced its deepest divisions since the late 1920s.

TUC leaders had encouraged Gaitskell's successful bid against Bevan to become Party Treasurer in 1954 and facilitated his rise to the leadership a year later. In terms of political patronage, he was thus as much the TUC's nominee as Attlee had been in 1934. For another two years the TUC stridently proclaimed the need for unity in order to undermine the Bevanite left, who were ensconced, with constituency support, on the NEC. But the union front broke down from within at roughly the same time as the radicals in the party pushed onto the agenda of Conference, constituencies and parliamentary party the doctrinal argument about how socialism was to be achieved. Radicalism of course covered a wide range of opinion, for the followers of Bevan did not necessarily agree, *tout court*, with Richard Crossman, whose *Planning for Freedom* came out in 1956, nor with the trade union left and Cousins who for a time seemed to be their spokesman. But after 1955, as the labour movement faced the problem that welfare capitalism had already provided the majority of the electorate with security, leaving a bleak future for 'real socialism', the various strands could at least concur in criticising Attlee's leadership, and the bureaucratic and inefficient inheritance they now claimed his government had left behind.

Meanwhile the Gaitskellites (to use the simplest term) developed in *New Fabian Essays* the lineaments of a more beneficent state, concerned less with ownership than management, as the means to transfer wealth, induce equality and improve industrial relations and organisation. Into this strand fits Crosland's *The Future of Socialism* (1956) and Strachey's *Contemporary Capitalism* (1956), both of which influenced the 1957 party programme *Industry and Society*. With a certain amount of legerdemain the latter incorporated the views of the Bevanites[19] (apart from Cousins, who remained a sceptic, and some of the old right on the General Council who preferred to stand by a traditional Morrisonian approach to state industry).

Divisions centring on industrial policy broke out again after the 1959 election as part of the post-mortem which ranged widely and often viciously through the Party's whole doctrine and strategy and at once undid the two year old temporary settlement. Although it has sometimes been presented as a personal struggle for power, in the wake of a third electoral defeat, conflict touched the deepest principles and the very nature of the party. Beginning at a meeting in October, ostensibly to say farewell to Hugh Dalton,[20] the argument focused on structural reform and the reassessment of Clause 4 of the 1918 Constitution – the commitment to public ownership of the means of production and distribution. In the end, every issue from the party's policy, ethos, and attitudes to nuclear weapons to the appropriateness of its working class image, were subsumed with long-term structural tensions between intellectuals and trade unionists into one question put at Gaitskell's instigation: who should control and elect the national organs of the party?

But at the November 1957 Conference, Gaitskell chose to wrap up the fundamental definition of where authority lay in talk of modernisation. Thus sidetracked, competition developed over the next two years between rival claimants to design a new appeal for Labour's hypothetical 'natural constituency'. At first, Labour Party-affiliated unions stood uneasily by, afraid to expose their own disunity to an already hostile public. Most trade unions still claimed that the TUC had founded the Labour Party and retained a prescriptive right to prevent its factions risking the future of the whole labour movement: it was better, they argued, not to prejudice the outcome by becoming too involved too soon. Thus Cousins was allowed to operate virtually without restraint when asserting the right of the NEC and of the party Conference over the leadership (as the Independent Labour Party had attempted to do in 1928–29), even though the General Council majority and most of the staff, from Woodcock downwards, clearly supported Gaitskell in his move to modernise the party's outlook by downgrading the significance of Clause 4. They deprecated Cousins' emphasis on state control of industry, but at the same time they suspected the parliamentary right as well as the left of wishing to diminish union leaders' share in determining strategy; they disliked Gaitskell's forcing tactics and found themselves ill-at-ease, personally, with the intellectuals who took his side.[21]

Such was the bitterness and confusion that many trade union leaders were prepared to support a compromise (even one proposed by Crossman, who had little love for the TUC) which concentrated on the arguments of J. K. Galbraith's *The Affluent Society* in order to exploit the unpleasant side of modern capitalism, its commercialism and social injustice. Gaiskell had already, by limiting his aim to the amendment of Clause 4, signified that he did not wish to provoke a struggle *à l'outrance* by questioning the balance of power between parliamentary party, NEC and the TUC. But by the end of 1959 Gaitskell could no longer control the volatile forces that threatened civil war. At the NEC, in March 1960, he forced his amendments through, after several votes, in spite of the pleas of middle-of-the-road trade union representatives like John Boyd (AEU) and Harry Nicholas (TGWU) to defer, for peace's sake.[22] Public attacks on Gaitskell rose in a crescendo of disloyalty even in the once-loyal PLP and among trade union-sponsored MPs.

Morgan Phillips, the Party Secretary, also tried to separate the debate about policy from the dispute about who should control the party, before too much damage had been done. Skilfully, he used the electoral research of Mark Abrams to challenge Crosland's thesis about the party's mistaken public image and the decline of its 'natural constituency', in a challenging paper on 'The State of the Party' presented to the NEC in July 1960.[23] Meanwhile, trade unions favourable to Gaitskell had approved the NEC's amendments to Clause 4. But in September, in an attempt to forestall a complete split in the party, the TUC refused to ratify them. Briefly but decisively, the TUC took the lead, and at the party Conference at Scarborough the amendments fell by a 2 to 1 majority. Gaitskell was beaten, not by the left, who alone could not have mustered such a vote, nor by Cousins and the TGWU, but by the massed ranks of General Secretaries who valued stability above theory, unity above radical inquiry.

Had they been presented with an overt and logical social democratic programme to replace the 42-year-old compromise, the outcome might have been less clear cut. If Gaitskell had not risked so much, the TUC would have been very unlikely to have gone so far, and been identified in public with Cousins and the unilateralists, who also won their Conference vote on abandoning nuclear weapons. As it was, Gaitskell read the sign and withdrew on the major issue of Clause 4 (which had always been a surrogate for altering the balance of power in the party) to concentrate on the lesser issue of nuclear disarmament. On that, he 'fought and fought again' for a year and salvaged his leadership at the next Conference at Blackpool in October 1961 by a majority of 3 million votes, thus reaffirming the principle established by Macdonald in 1928–29 and confirmed in Attlee's time that, whatever Clause 5 of the 1918 Constitution declared, the Conference could not, in fact, dictate policy to a future Labour administration.

Although the NEC still asserted its claim to be 'custodian' of Conference decisions rather than a mere advocate for them to the parliamentary party,[24] unity was gradually restored, even before October 1961. Challenging Gaitskell for the leadership, Harold Wilson had chosen to appeal for unity, revealing that he as representative of the Left had no interest in Labour as a faction-ridden, perpetual opposition. When he lost, by 81 votes to 166, the various strands of the left, their minority status exposed, split apart. Michael Foot and his friends rebelled, only to have the party whip withdrawn. The fortuitous alliance of intellectuals and trade unionists dissolved as soon as trade union-sponsored MPs again felt free to vote; in the event they turned against Crossman in the election of party Chairman. Within the parliamentary party, Charles Pannell shrewdly stage-managed Gaitskell's rehabilitation, while, outside, the Campaign for Democratic Socialism took over some of the struggle during 1961 to reverse the nuclear disarmament decision.

Gaitskell's recovery owed something also to fears about the trend of by-election results in 1960–61, which showed a marked swing from Labour to Liberals. But the effect of the rather haphazard *rassemblement* of trade unions during the summer of 1961 was much more significant. USDAW retreated from the unilateralist camp in May and the NUR followed in July, leaving Cousins and the TGWU in isolation. After October, Gaitskell exploited his victory in order to debilitate Cousins politically and re-establish the party's authority *vis-à-vis* the TUC. Cousins survived, largely because only the leader of the TGWU could, in that generation, destroy himself. But faction-fighting ceased; and the real issue about who should control the party fell into abeyance for another fifteen years.

As a historian of the Labour Party Conference, Lewis Minkin blames Gaitskell for trying to alter the balance of power and establish parliamentary party sovereignty at the expense both of the constituency parties and the TUC, arguing that it would have been better not to have disturbed an arrangement laid down long before the war which still worked adequately. But if Crosland were right, the fundamental argument between socialists and social democrats would have broken out anyway, as it did in the mid-1970s. By withdrawing from his strategic position, Gaitskell ensured the return of a sort of peace, grounded however much less stably than before. But the Gaitskellites and later Social Democrats were to argue that it would have been better to have pushed it to a conclusion, even to divide the party, in 1959–61, in conditions where it could subsequently have come to terms with a society that had changed out of all recognition since 1918, rather than postpone adjustment to a time when 'consensus politics', national prosperity, full employment and the post war settlement could no longer be taken for granted.

In the end, as had happened in 1934 when Bevin destroyed George Lansbury's leadership, TUC leaders disposed. The old right, the centre and the various proponents of revision came together, a confluence which confirmed for Harold Wilson the inalienable merits of unity. For a time it seemed possible to plan for government and the future, and disregard improvements to the diffuse party mechanism which almost everyone had recently been criticising. But these multiple compromises inhibited the party's capacity to plan either for socialism or social democracy. It could no longer, if it ever could, dissociate itself from the trade unions. Its ideology would henceforth have to be made compatible, in terms of practical politics, with that of the TUC, an outcome which could not but satisfy the latter, the purveyor of financial support.

After 1961, the ideas contained in *Industry and Society* returned to the agenda. Because economic growth was what Gaitskell had assumed the electorate wanted,[25] Labour now set itself to appeal to the non-class, or trans-class voter, with a pragmatic emphasis on planning as something natural, suggested rather than imposed by the state, in order to remedy the injustices and remove the inefficiencies of modern capitalism. With the added magic of technological innovation and investment in scientific education, this provided a theme for a new style of manifesto, *Signposts for the Sixties*. But the need not to relinquish the party's roots led it to attack not only the old demons such as extravagant wealth and oligarchic power, but a new one, the grossness of the consumer society which set it at odds with what very many working class, Labour voters most desired.

Although the Labour Party's subsequent debates on planning and on the rival merits of EEC and EFTA came to different conclusions from those of Macmillan's government, they were grounded in a remarkably similar premise about the interdependence of sustained growth and indicative planning. The advantages of a European trading association,[26] the pursuit of economic growth, and the idea of translating tripartite discussion into improved industrial relations and better working practices through a new forum where industry, unions and government could meet, ran as vigorously in Labour Party headquarters as they did in Conservative Central Office. Yet so isolated had the party become in the bad years before 1961 that the measures taken by the Macmillan government, Selwyn Lloyd's announcement of the National Economic Development Council in 1961, Britain's decision to apply for EEC membership, the White Paper on nationalised industries, and the decision to give greater priority to industry, took it by surprise. Only among the economists was there more than a vague acquaintance with the French experience and the concept of planning had advanced very little since Wilson's time at the Board of Trade. Gratified to find itself at peace, the Labour Party was deeply disconcerted at the possibility that the planned, prosperous Britain they dreamed of instituting was about to become a Conservative reality.

11 Conclusion: 1961

Identifying turning points in history is a risky business on which few historians agree for long. But within a clearly defined area of study, patterns do at times change together, in a way that affects the subsequent development of each: a conjunction. Compared with the Suez affair's impact on Britain's world standing, or with the results of the 1964 election, the year 1961 may not seem significant. But this volume ends there for sound reasons. From various causes, and according to different time-scales, each main participant in the history of industrial politics had by then become sufficiently disillusioned with the way that the post-war settlement operated, and in particular with governments' economic management during the 1950s, to require radical reform.

Whether that meant restoring the settlement or trying to relegate it, as being something intrinsic to the immediate post-war, transitional years, no longer an appropriate guide to the 1960s, depended on the balance of opinion inside each institution, as well as on the lead given by government. Whereas majority opinions imagined that the intentions of the 1944 White Paper were still valid (even if they no longer phrased it that way), quite vocal minorities now looked back to earlier models associated with freer markets or to concepts of socialism, neither of which had fitted into the accepted limits of practical political and economic thinking in the previous twenty years.

These internal disputes grew up inside the existing competitive relationships between industrial, labour and financial organisations, the political parties, government and government departments, introducing a note of what might be called ideological dissent, though in fact ideological claims were usually denigrated by the majorities or outside observers as self-interested – the implication being that their practical expression contravened the prevailing view of the national interest. Groups as different as shop stewards forming the early

335

combines in the car industry, merchant bankers seeking to develop new financial markets, or managers using public hostility to wild-cat strikers in order to reverse a shift in the balance of factory power, found themselves targets for recrimination from other sides, phrased in terms of loyalty to an earlier set of political understandings about how rewards and obligations should be balanced to produce restraint and equilibrium.

Few if any groups in the 1950s saw themselves in outright opposition to the post-war settlement. They complained only that stop–go policies, wage restraint, exchange control or industrial indiscipline frustrated their natural energies and the contributions they could otherwise make. Probably very few individuals, and only at the political extremes, believed that the faults were already irremediable. What was known statistically of Britain's external circumstances indicated that, provided reforms were made, the extremely comfortable life enjoyed by virtually all citizens was not threatened. Unlike the cosmic despair of the mid-1970s, pessimism concentrated on specific abuses and in fact added weight to the reformers' case. Britain's capacity to sort out such problems was not seriously doubted: and the memory of wartime organisation, though no longer a guide, still taught that self interests could be harmonised, rationally, if only competing groups could agree on a mutually attractive set of incentives.

If greed could be appeased by the promise of steady, planned growth, fears of losing the gains already made completed an optimistic equation. The defence of full employment, the welfare state, educational standards, and the standard of living had an obvious public appeal.[1] In terms of parties' simple electoralism, or institutions' response to their own particular constituencies, willingness to make some concessions and to join in a political *rassemblement*, rather than seek a radical break with the recent past, was natural enough.

But this *rassemblement* around the idea that the post-war settlement's aims could be recast in a mould better suited to the 1960s differed in important respects from what had happened in 1944. True, the two main political parties moved after 1960 towards similar positions on industrial and some labour market issues; so did the FBI, and to a lesser extent the BEC and the TUC. True also, the new reforms were conceived of as complementary, even if they did not form a complete package, and they were hedged about with similar conditions concerning wage restraint, higher productivity and removal of restrictive practices. Their genesis also owed at least as much to government departments' work as to ministers' lead (though the Prime Minister, Harold Macmillan, conscious of how much latent opposition there was behind him in the party, put his personal authority behind the general strategy).

But the 1961 package of reforms (which comprised EEC entry and access to a vastly larger market; creation of an effective tripartite forum for discussion of all the questions buried before, to do with Britain's declining economic position; radical changes in state-owned industries; new methods of planning and control of public expenditure; and priority for planned, sustained growth over considerations such as the balance of payments) differed from what was done in 1944 in three important respects. Demand for reform came more from outside government and was couched in the form of severe complaints; the reformers' own degree of commitment was less; and the package was put together at the end of its authors' time in office, not at the beginning.

The complaints originated among institutions and the public and were precisely and vigorously focused by a Press and television no longer under any sort of government control. Quite unlike wartime, when the planners worked in an unusual climate of isolation, assessing institutional and public opinion rather than reacting to it and working to a schedule which presupposed two or more years of coalition government after fighting stopped, their late-1950s successors had to contend with a factious crescendo, in a political context where Labour and Conservative Parties had already begun to contend the same ground. What occurred looked – and was – closer to sectional appeasement than the Olympian neutrality of judgement in 1944.

Mandarins at the Treasury, Board of Trade or Ministry of Labour did indeed develop their reforms in the light of what they thought had gone wrong during the 1950s; but few of them were convinced that sustained growth could be achieved in the way that their predecessors had believed full employment could be achieved. Although the 1961 White Paper on nationalised industries appeared to offer a full solution to one endemic problem, other reforms such as the creation of NEDC and the PESC system of public expenditure control were put forward tentatively; EEC entry itself remained in doubt and the likely terms uncertain. The new package therefore had to make just as many unproved assumptions; yet circumstances required of it a high rate of success in matters which earlier experience showed to be inherently improbable. In spite of the emphasis laid on planning (a key word but an ill-defined one) the 1961 package had fewer, thinner foundations.

The third factor amounted in itself to a sort of conjunction. The centre of gravity of the Cabinet changed when Macmillan dismissed Selwyn Lloyd as Chancellor in July 1962. Other sackings and promotions, in the so-called 'night of the long knives' went far beyond the scope of a normal reshuffle – although they did little to diminish faction – and gave prominence to the generally like-minded group of Reginald Maudling, Iain MacLeod, John Hare, Enoch Powell and Edward Heath, each of whom in his own departmental strategy owed something to the work of the long-term planning group set up by R. A. Butler at the Research Department at the end of 1959. Far-reaching changes also occurred in the Labour Party, associated with the arrival of Harold Wilson as leader. But the most significant break in continuity took place in the civil service and institutions where an unprecedented number of senior officials reached retirement age around 1961.

At the Bank of England, Lord Cobbold handed over to Lord Cromer after twelve years; Vincent Tewson had left the TUC in 1960 after holding the post of General Secretary since 1946 and Sir Roger Makins had already been succeeded by Sir Frank Lee at the Treasury in 1959. Lee in turn was followed by Sir Laurence Helsby in 1962. The Chief Economic Advisor for eight years, Robert Hall, was followed by Alec Cairncross. After Sir Norman Brook's retirement from the Cabinet Office and as Head of the Civil Service in 1962, the job was divided, the Cabinet Office going to Sir Burke Trend, the Headship to Helsby. At the Board of Trade, Sir Richard Powell established a fresh line of thinking in the early 1960s, and at the Ministry of Labour, Sir James Dunnett consolidated the change of ethos began under Helsby in 1959–61.

This departure of a whole cohort of mandarins and officials, followed in 1965 by the retirement of Sir Norman Kipping after twenty years' service at the FBI and of Sir George Pollock from the BEC, coincided with widespread uncertainties about Britain's external position, the future of her industry and the methods used by the government to manage the economy. New men helped to fix different attitudes in the bodies they now ran, often to the extent that change can be called a change of mentality. Once those who had actually operated the wartime mechanisms had retired, their successors who had only studied them from subordinate posts were more easily able to adapt their by now idealised memory to the situations they observed among Britain's main competitors, France and Germany. Men in their fifties or early sixties were unlikely to abandon the experience of fifteen intellectually formative years, but were more likely than the previous cohort to be open to European currents of opinion and proven experience.

For perhaps the first time since 1914, when a devastating shutter fell, cutting off outside influences, many of Britain's leaders repeated the policy peregrinations common to admirers of the Bismarckian state in the 1890s. (Their models of state intervention came more from France than Germany, however, and they ignored for another decade the work in Japan of MITI, the Ministry of International Trade and Industry.) This occurred five years before publication of Andrew Shonfield's *Modern Capitalism* (1965), which is usually seen as the landmark of influence filtering down from academic to professional levels. Just as Shonfield was to do, they extolled the virtues of France's industrial policy and its elite administrative tradition furthered by the state education system. The impact may have been confined to attitudes rather than policy, because nothing so schematic as, for example, the FBI's conclusions drawn from comparisons of France with Germany, the Benelux countries or Scandinavia was actually put into effect; but a change of attitude in which admiration for European state systems burst out after a lapse of fifty years cannot be written off as merely symbolic.

Two personal cases exemplify change: in 1959–60 an internal Treasury reorganisation merged the Overseas Finance Division with the Home Economic Division in a single, large Finance Group. The intention was to remove any chance of the old discord recurring, but it led to something rather closer than before to the Economic Ministry that Lord Haldane had advocated in 1918, and also to the appointment to head it of perhaps the most gifted and dynamic Treasury official of the new generation, William Armstrong, an expansionist who believed in state intervention and tripartite collaboration, and a convinced European. Secondly, Sir Frank Lee, Treasury Permanent Secretary since 1959 but long an opponent of any sort of wages policy, returned after the July 1961 wages freeze announcement (which he had missed, having suffered a heart attack in Paris) *plus royaliste que le roi*, to urge his colleagues on to make it permanent through the new mechanism offered by NEDC.

If one adds together the reforms recommended in the Plowden Report,[2] the 1961 White Paper on the future management and financing of state industries, the formation of NEDC on lines derived from the French Office of the Plan, and a new Whitehall emphasis on administrative expertise and business schools, something novel and more generally directive appears to have been at work. The word 'planning', though ill-defined, slipped into policy-makers' daily language. Support from European governments and banks for Britain's entry to the EEC seemed more assured after the Basle arrangements earlier in 1961, and with the installation of J. F. Kennedy's administration in Washington. Emulation of European arrangements carried with it possibilities of changing at least some aspects of the British state itself.

William, now Lord, Beveridge, who had been there at the beginning, spotted the end of a twenty-year cycle. Having spent a decade ruminating on the Frankenstein monster of full employment and the consequent peril of inflation he had helped to create, in 1961 he too began to advocate a planning mechanism on the French model of the Commissariat du Plan.[3] A vast shift of opinion was taking place among the politicians, administrators and moulders of opinion.[4] All took courage from what they believed public opinion to desire, so that the next three years vibrated with confidence about industrial growth. It seemed that only the details needed to be worked out

Without pre-empting discussion of the changing nature of state organisation which I hope to develop in Volume 3, or suggesting that only one set of interpretations arises from the variety of patterns described here, some conclusions can be drawn about structural evolution and cyclical patterns in institutions' mentalities after World War Two.

The war emergency made close co-operation with government by the central organisations representing industry, trade unions and the financial sector vital to national survival. Naturally, it also stimulated the element of corporate bias in their organisations. During the emergency, they became to an unparalleled extent interdependent, constituent parts of the rapidly extended state. Recognising that what was happening might provide a supplementary and probably sounder basis for extending wartime political harmony and economic efficiency into an unpredictable, hazardous peacetime world than immediate reversion to two-party politics, Coalition Ministers and their officials planned a comprehensive reconstruction package which took careful account of failure in and after World War One. Prolonged discussions began in the nadir of the war, which combined a thorough analysis of Britain's inter-war problems with as good an estimate as conditions allowed of what post-war realities would be.

By 1944, the date beyond which growing differences between the Coalition partners made long-term policy-making virtually impossible, the officials had ready for Ministers' approval the concept of a unified post-war settlement, constructed so as to offer each constituent partner to a proposed political contract what it most desired. A high and stable level of employment, which all wanted, though for different reasons, became the central principle which government, as the prime mover, guaranteed as its part of the deal, and which focused in turn the obligations which government required from each.

Other elements, such as the 1944 Education Act, formed part of the package, but it was the 1944 White Paper on employment policy that laid down the framework within which political equilibrium, economic activity and social improvement could be balanced. In practice if not by deliberate design, acceptance of its principles conditioned much of what Labour governments did after 1945, and in a modified form what Conservative ones did after 1951. But the working rules for maintaining balance developed afterwards, in two stages; in the transition period of crisis and austerity to 1949, and in the following decade when external circumstances turned out to be unprecedently favourable. Successively, as the Labour Party came to terms with the gap between its pre-war party strategy and Britain's post-war dilemmas, and as the Conservatives adapted to the existence of the post-war settlement, political parties and their perceptions of electoral demand put their own stamp on the settlement and altered public perceptions of what balance was. Nevertheless, so substantial were the advantages of association with the state in this period that corporate bias flourished and, at the end, administrators, governing institutions and politicians alike committed themselves to reforming rather than abrogating the system they had created.

The post-war settlement marked a distinct break with the past, as was the intention of its authors. Their assessment of what ought to be done, of course, grew out of their own understandings of what had been wrong in the inter-war years; but their ideal solutions rejected older models of state activity based on market forces and the lower levels of corporatist activity prevalent before 1940. Precisely because they looked back for lessons, however, and created the new order out of the old, incorporating the main political forces on which wartime state organisation had been built, their efforts were more broadly acceptable and had greater chance of binding the future than had the alternative plans of outsiders or party research departments. They also capitalised on the public's new perception that the state had become the fount of reform, in order to stamp their ideas with a state seal; that Beveridge and Labour Party publicists competed for the public's attention, raised the stakes without vitiating the guarantee.

Locked in already in their own self-interest by voluntary commitment and personal participation, industrialists, trade unionists and bankers accepted the proposed contract not by putting signatures to any document but by seizing the advantages and fulfilling their obligations – albeit, as time passed, only after being prodded to do so. During the transition, down to 1949–50, reciprocity turned out to be almost as altruistic as the authors of the 1944 White Paper had expected, although some institutions proved less responsive than Attlee and Cripps imagined Labour's own additions of universal welfare provision and social security merited. That the main objectives of 1944, an export-led programme of economic recovery, sound budgetary practice, self-generated industrial investment, technological improvement and a stable currency were, with the exception of the last, maintained, can be ascribed as much to the work of the initiators and to the success of Attlee's administration in balancing public and private expectations in the context of Britain's precarious international position as to Labour's own plans for reform.

The political stability created by this unprecedented harmony between Ministers, sponsoring departments, institutions and the public sustained British governments through the successive crises of 1947, 1949, 1951, 1956 and 1961, in sharp contrast to the reconstruction plans of World War One which succumbed during the first financial review in 1919. The settlement was not only a break with the past; it became an organic part of the state. Simple institutional momentum cannot explain why the great majority of policy-makers continued to defend it against accumulating criticism from left and right far beyond 1961, and why they upheld its ideals as central to the normal expectations of political life. Hegemony of an idea as much as the steady rise in living standards which accompanied it (and which was, of course, buoyed up by the long post-war boom after the Korean War), at the same time greatly altered the public's work and leisure patterns of life and aspirations.

Criticisms made in the late 1950s were, therefore, not directed against the settlement itself, nor primarily at extensions made under the Attlee government such as nationalisation of basic industries, but at weaknesses which derived from Conservative economic management after 1951. Partly because the language of moral obligation had been overused during the late-1940s' production drives, at a time when the government held back consumer demand well beyond the limits of political expediency, the sense of reciprocal obligation decayed rapidly – as unions' and industries' determination to break free from price and wage restraint in 1950 showed. Afterwards, as defence budgets were reduced and most remaining controls abolished, it became possible to maintain stability by indirect means. The Conservative governments of Churchill and Eden avoided discussing fundamental problems of industry and the labour market (which deeply divided the Labour Party, in opposition) by relying increasingly on fiscal intervention to run the economy at the hypothetical point of equilibrium between inflation and unemployment, excess consumption and consumer affluence.

The new techniques and mechanisms worked well enough at the time, but as all economic historians of the period point out, they led to accelerating swings of policy and distortions, even imbalances, which prevented British industry from establishing a fully competitive international position. At the same time, they eroded many of the safeguards built into the 1944 White Paper, which Attlee's governments had rigorously observed: a mild degree of inflation, government deficits in good years as well as bad ones, and a failure to keep consumer spending in line with productivity, constituted political as well as economic backslidings. In 1961, these derogations still seemed remediable; but if one counts them as modifications to a system, they undoubtedly impaired its capacity to produce political equilibrium; and as the next volume will show, after 1966 made its future and even its survival problematic.

Within the Treasury, the only department with the necessary skills and status to work out the rules of economic management that allowed governments to retain control behind an appearance of fiscal neutrality, full employment came eventually to be seen as detrimental to other national aims. Yet, for political reasons, it could not be challenged, even at the low level of unemployment prevalent in the 1950s. The unpleasant paradox that the longer the fat years lasted, the wider grew the gap between contemporary gratification and future competitiveness, was one that only officials fully appreciated: hence their reservations about the nature of reforms in 1961 and their insistence that they be accompanied by a more effective agreement with trade unions restricting wage increases. Five years before a Labour government drove into this one-way street, a trend had been established in which a Treasury-defined view of wage inflation came to dominate Whitehall to the detriment of future governments' policies for industrial growth and competitiveness.

In such an important area of the polity, growth to maturity of the concept that unrestrained wages prejudiced economic management made it all the more surprising that the leaders of institutions, particularly of the TUC, eventually subscribed to the new package. A system which appeared to allow governments to deal with the public fairly painlessly, in electoral terms, had imposed on them a cumulative burden, making it harder for them to fulfil their obligations both to the state and to their members. The rewards from co-operation steadily declined during the 1950s, and restiveness surged up from the shop floor or local managers at the restrictions which their own central organisations or outside bodies like the Council on Pay, Productivity and Incomes tried to impose. The fact that institutions' leaders joined the 1961 *rassemblement* (albeit with considerable reservations) argues that, on their national assessment, advantage and altruism still coincided. They judged the settlement worth reviving; but in a less onerous form, shorn of a number of accretions from both the transition period and the 1950s.

In the years after 1940 a peak of interdependence was created and perpetuated between government and the central institutions representing manufacturing industry and trade unions. Even though the financial sector deliberately stood aside from formal arrangements, it too was closely linked; and although most of the wartime machinery was later allowed to fall into disuse, informal co-operation accompanied by an uniquely high level of corporate bias lasted so long and was so widely accepted that an historian is able to speak of it as a system – not separate from, but complementary to the party political and parliamentary system. It included as partners the main producer organisations in Britain, and allowed them fruitful access to government. In turn, governments which were unable to achieve their aims in other ways worked sufficiently closely with the institutions for them to be able to justify to their own often more independent-minded members the bargains which they tried to make.

This system survived in spite of Britain's slow relative economic decline, her reduction to second-power status and the erosion of the sterling area, factors which might have been expected to call in question some of its aspects on the grounds that it encouraged cartel-mindedness, introspectiveness and aversion to risks, low productivity and over-reliance on secure or domestic markets. Criticisms certainly developed in the late 1950s, but of a different order, amounting only to partial, not total opposition. Institutions complained that they were either not getting the share due to them, as partners, or that others were reneging on their obligations. But because the system allowed for competition between them, while reinforcing each member's status against outsiders, and because it helped to limit conflict to bounds acceptable to themselves as well as to government and the public, the partners to the original 1944 political compact chose to employ – in public – a language of political harmony which encouraged some academic analysts to forecast a decline of conflict and the virtual disappearance of political ideology.

In comparing 1961 with 1940, the most notable common feature may well be the survival of this sense of interdependence, accompanied by a belief that outright conflict was an aberration, to be remedied by a return to first principles. Otherwise, it is clear that the formal tripartite mechanisms had run down. When NEDC was formed, it was envisaged as a looser, more flexible body than the NJAC or NPACI, less tied to specific departments. (Even so, City institutions refused to consider membership, guarding their autonomy.) Governments' policing powers had also decreased, first with the erosion of Production Authorities, and the reduction of sponsorship to an administrative process, secondly with the retreat to fiscal means of economic manipulation. Only in the areas of agriculture, aerospace, and defence procurement (where it had already existed in the 1930s) did sponsorship imply close, even corporatist arrangements. The system was, therefore, more informal, much less obviously statist than those operating at the time in France, Austria or Sweden.

The partners were by 1961 drawing less from it as rewards and were consequently more likely to evade or deny what had originally been accepted as responsibilities. Individual firms' or banks' determination to benefit from access to European markets probably eroded the idea of reciprocal obligations as much as did the spread of plant bargaining or governments' propensity for deficit financing. Whereas there had been a clear advantage to each in association in 1944, later disadvantages weighed rather more heavily; the partner which stood to gain most by the early 1960s was the government, as it tried increasingly desperately to achieve equilibrium between the apparently incompatible aims of rising living standards, stable prices and full employment. The reforms were bound, therefore, to depend more than the earlier programme on achieving short-term success: with the partners so uneasy, there could be no initial period of transition.

Since acquiescence in its rules now had to vie with growing self-interest inside each institution, the system also became vulnerable, like any cartel, to its members attempting to undercut it – in political terms – by appealing upwards to government or outwards to public opinion, in order to disable other competitors. Politicians such as Cripps and Morrison knew very well how important it was to bring the public's legitimate expectations, either as consumers or taxpayers, to bear as a discipline on irresponsible institutions. A similar strategy lay behind creation of the Cohen Council (CPPI) whose reports were intended to educate public opinion about the follies of wage inflation, or later, the appointment of the Donovan Commission to study how industrial relations might be given a more rational, publicly-acceptable framework. But as both these cases suggest, later governments were tending to work up opinion against one side, without much pretence of even-handedness.

Trade unions reacted defensively (as management was to do when the position reversed itself in the mid-1970s). The TUC's publicity efforts could scarcely compare with those of the FBI or BEC which operated, in any case, in a climate markedly more anti-union than that of the 1940s. Yet public opinion could no longer be mobilised, as in wartime, nor harnessed as it had been in the production campaigns. In making their bids, governments had to develop new populist techniques, just as Prime Ministers displayed heightened and idiosyncratic styles for the new medium of television. Such appeals disrupted what had once been accepted as the conventions. They also introduced an element of uncertainty, since consumers' interests, once aroused, might run counter to those of trade unions and manufacturers alike.

By this time, the nominal balance of power between institutions had lost its wartime stability. (One cannot talk of *equivalence* of power, except for a very short period from 1940–44.) What had been imagined as an evolutionarily stable system (to borrow John Maynard Smith's phrase) that could both restrain competition and inhibit the emergence of any alternative, evolved into something more complex and unstable, where balance proved increasingly difficult to achieve. If the BEC and FBI had merged, if the trade union movement had been more highly co-ordinated, it might have been easier for governments and civil servants to use their corporatist tendencies – and it should be noted that this merger, and reform of union organisation, were specific aims pursued by governments in the mid-1960s. But, as of 1961, each institution's documents suggest that, while its links with government still appeared necessary, it feared others were using theirs to gain permanent advantage; furthermore that each blamed government for failures to hold the disciplinary ring and to satisfy all their incompatible requirements.

At the centre of the post-war system of government, civil service mandarins had acted as mediators, brokers and initiators. Under ministerial authority, they had put together the 1944 package, guided it through the transition period, and then worked out the ground rules of peacetime sponsorship and economic management. These functions grew harder as they adapted to a more strictly departmental organisation under the Conservatives after 1951. What the state desired could still be transmitted downwards, but bargains were more difficult to make and often impossible to hold. Late 1950s' experience suggested that co-operation was something which governments could no longer command and perhaps scarcely even bargain for. A pervasive sense that the British state was unduly weak may explain both the attraction for reformers of more directive European models and the Macmillan government's attempt to reinvigorate co-operation by its gamble on sustained growth after 1961.

As Britain emerged from the transition period of post-war austerity, each institution had, quite naturally, sought to take advantage of more open conditions to stabilise its power before the new became the normal. Each continued to try to write the agenda on which government policy would be based and to shape the outcome, in order to fulfil what it thought its members' requirements were. That in itself might not have debilitated the system. But it did prejudice the fulfilment of what governments since 1944 had grown used to see as partners' obligations; and when governments reacted, say, by setting down a wages policy, the shock to established practice in turn strengthened the critics inside each who argued that co-operation with the state was both onerous and unwise. When a government went further, and addressed one of the complex issues buried in the mid-1940s, such as restrictive practices or labour mobility, disharmony tended to grow. The worst threats to the system in 1961 lay in a loss of common ground where deep interests were threatened (such as trade unions' response to Ministry of Labour legislation, or manufacturers' to the abolition of resale price maintenance) which resulted in a quite widespread feeling that it might eventually be impossible to resolve anything without cutting down the power of one or more institutions.

Only a handful on the right and left of politics argued that the system itself was at fault and that its success had been due only to the temporary elimination of self-interest by an external wartime threat. Nevertheless, the disparagement of trade unions and of the TUC for its inability to control their behaviour, which became habitual in sections of the Conservative Party, can be seen as a symptom of more general discontent with the sort of system in which such abuses could occur, and of a line of thought, updating Friedrich von Hayek's critique of the state, which emphasised the rights and duties of the individual rather than those of the collective or the interest group.

Very many more critics observed that the search for political equilibrium resulted in agreements at such a low level of compliance as to be useless except in unusually favourable economic circumstances. They also argued that it led to the rapid growth of a low-level, apparently permanent set of government commitments such as incentives to industry to invest or modernise, restrictions on location and building, and regional policy. These were not only divisive and inequitable in distributing rewards to some firms or groups of workers, not others, but their contents caused deep, even ideological contention inside the Conservative government and the Labour Party in opposition.

An awareness of failure certainly gave a pointer to the reformers (and emerged very clearly in NEDC's first main publication in 1962, *Conditions Favourable to Faster Growth*) for it was clear that, whatever its other uses, the system had not been apt to seek out and solve problems. Corporate bias induced reaction to events rather than innovation. Practice had also benefited larger, well-established institutions, densely stratified and slow to change, to the detriment of growing unions, small businesses, or the new style of merchant bankers. The activities of shop stewards in the late 1950s, for example, were universally portrayed as disruptive, scarcely ever as a response to new needs in a rapidly changing industrial relations system; in contrast, company mergers (which over the next decade were to create one of the highest degrees of concentration of any industrial nation) were, again almost universally, seen as beneficial.

The fact that even institutions' support for the 1944 contract had become strictly conditional had three direct effects. It put the reformers in the position of having to produce success quickly – probably too quickly. Secondly, it implied that if reform failed, future governments would have to take directive powers whether or not these were to their liking. In 1950, Attlee and his colleagues had admitted quite simply that a wages and prices freeze could not be enforced. Their successors, more self-confident perhaps about the art of political management and certainly under much greater pressure from public expectation, ignored both the precedent and the modesty. Finally it put at risk – in theory and in due course in practice – full employment, core of the 1944 package. In 1955 it had needed an iconoclast like Peter Thorneycroft to suggest that the economy would be easier to run in balance if unemployment were allowed to rise to between 2 per cent and 3 per cent. Five years later, at levels of unemployment still far below Gaitskell's 3 per cent pledge, full employment was being blamed (as it already had been in the United States by economists who emphasised the fears of Beveridge and Michael Kalecki about unions' monopoly power and the decline of industry's profitability) for a range of evils such as wage inflation, low mobility, restrictive practices, poor productivity and overmanning. Denied open debate in the expansionist years, this latter issue simmered and spilled out into other channels. A substratum of hostility came into existence at a time when politicians' willpower weakened, and the public learned to fear inflation more, which significantly conditioned economic policy after 1966.

The sort of pluralism described here was not a competition between outside institutions to influence a supposedly neutral state, nor what is sometimes called bargained corporatism, between the state and interest groups that can deliver what they promise. It was one in which the main interests in the nation prolonged their natural competition into the very centre of government abetted by those departments of state with which they had a sponsorship affinity. Precisely because their co-operation was believed to be vital if governments were to achieve economic growth and political stability, they remained governing institutions, part of the extended state. Even if they were not equivalent in power to each other, governments believed that their strivings could be held in a sort of equilibrium; albeit with increasing difficulty.

Had the civil service and successive governments of the 1950s and

1960s remained as closely linked in their interpretation of the post-war settlement as in Attlee's day, the problem of maintaining balance between interests might have been mitigated. But the very inception of the settlement had brought about a change in the way civil servants looked at their role that in the long run tended to distinguish politicians' and mandarins' conceptions of how the national interest should be defined. Mandarins had always been policy-mongers but wartime incorporation of governing institutions in the extended state gave them a more obvious tutelary function than had existed in the often muddled, suspicious relationships with outside interests during the inter-war years. For a long period, effectively from 1938–39 to 1949–51, civil servants acted as brokers between the state and its new associates, filtering out messages which they knew the government could not accept, on the way up, and adding advice and state requirements on the way down.

Close association, and often a general sympathy with a sponsored industry or institution, accentuated the process of competition between departments of state, in the Cabinet and elsewhere at the centre of government (Sir H. Llewellyn Smith had warned in the 1900s that this would occur if a Ministry of Labour began to represent the interests of trade unions in the way that the Board of Trade represented those of employers). Superimposed on the traditional tensions of Cabinet government, between Treasury and spending departments or between the inner group of ministers concerned with finance, foreign policy and defence, and the periphery, new sets of tensions set, for example, one part of the Treasury with the Bank against another part which identified with an expansionist Prime Minister and the needs of manufacturing industry. By 1961 a whole range of incompatibilities – an Atlanticist external strategy versus a would-be European trade policy, competition policy versus restrictive practices, defence procurement at odds with a rational location of industry, or flexible labour market versus full employment – were straining to its limits the civil service's harmonising capacity.

Sponsored institutions were no more equal in their political weight at the centre of government than they were outside it. Once the era of manpower budgeting had ended, the Ministry of Labour could never again rival the Treasury, nor could the Board of Trade before 1971 establish its 1943 claim to be a Ministry of Industry. Prolonged deadlock was, therefore, unlikely, unless the Prime Minister set himself to support a weaker competitor against a stronger – though this did occur, fairly explicitly, and against the Treasury, at the end of 1957 and in the first half of 1961. Nor were relationships so fixed that they enforced rigidity. Over time, a department's attitude to 'its' area could change; Labour, once devoted exponent of 1940s trade unionism, had recoiled and become almost hostile by the mid-1960s. Trade alternated between protective caring and harsh prescription for the British manufacturing industry. Only the Treasury showed any consistent respect for its institutions, the City and financial markets, and for their views on the national interest.

Nevertheless, the volume of high-level brokerage required departments to maintain their tutelage, a need that was extended the more institutions evaded or ignored their obligations under the post-war settlement. The practice of economic management also required political as well as economic guidelines, and could never be entirely neutral. Where ministers were disinclined, or unready to provide them, even mandarins as robust as Bridges, Brook or Lee would have felt exposed if they had not understood that the efficient working of the post-war settlement was itself both an end and a justification for their activities. Long after 1961 they continued to view the 1944 arrangements as a political contract to which all partners, even governments, could be held. In that sense, the civil service acquired a wider but legitimate, historic mission. Without in any way discounting responsibility to Ministers and parliament, and without asserting countervailing power, mandarins could continue in peacetime the essence of their wartime work. They became, in effect, guardians of the settlement's stability, as the Bank of England remained guardian of the currency.

This elite was fortunate in that it could still credibly depict itself as manager of the system, 'making democracy work', while serving Ministers properly in their departmental contexts. Between ministers and mandarins, the fundamental affinity which had characterised the war period survived the 1950s. But by the 1960s, it was being threatened inside the government by structural stresses which led the Ministry of Labour, for example, to evolve means to impose good behaviour on trade unions. Externally, it was also threatened, firstly because the Labour Party's long exile from power had made its leaders unfamiliar with Whitehall, yet had not prevented them from assuming, in making their electoral appeals, that they would have a free hand when returned to office in 1964; and secondly by a wave of scepticism, inspired, variously, by the Press and television mockery, and by a broad public revulsion from the doctrine that 'the man from Whitehall knows best'.

The 1961 reforms were intended to prevent any one partner backsliding and to make it possible for the British economy both to become more efficient and to grow faster. In so far as they purported to define the state's objectives – though far short of what was being done in contemporary Germany or France, let alone Japan – civil servants as well as their Conservative ministers hoped that the work could be done not only more effectively but rather more outside the political arena, by submitting either to market forces inside Europe, or to the operations of some neutral, tripartite body. This was for most of them a preferred aim to the alternative of strengthening government against recalcitrant institutions which was only very reluctantly adopted in the later 1960s.

The senior ranks of the civil service can, therefore, be seen not merely as guardians of a balanced post-war settlement (as in each generation they defined balance) but as guardians of the state's interest in its continued existence – a role whose long time-scale inevitably caused them, collectively, to worry what other bargains politicians might propose, citing their electoral mandate. The state's interest might well conflict with the public interest if that were defined as 'what the public wanted'. The attempt to bring awareness of the state's interest to bear then necessarily involved the mandarinate in that higher level of competition where the national interest was now habitually determined. But, unlike all the rest of the field, mandarins did not address their claims to the public, only to ministers and their peers; and they tended, therefore, to argue that the public was at fault.

The political elite as a whole had invested its intellectual and moral capital in the idea of a post-war settlement. Coalition leaders and their senior officials, whether they were elected politicians, or civil servants with a departmental life of forty years, or wartime outsiders who returned to industry or banking, had drafted its various documents with reference to what the public interest as well as the national interest required. This they understood both from experience in the inter-war years and from actual surveys of home opinion in wartime.

Their conception of the state continued to be technocratic rather than party-political, Fabian rather than populist. Their models of inquiry derived from the tradition of parliamentary blue books and Royal Commissions. They would have endorsed L. T. Hobhouse's dictum: 'Ethical philosophy cannot construct the state without reference to established fact. We must start from the place in which we find ourselves. We must understand society, know how it works, before we can improve it.' Unlike reconstruction plans in the First

World War, theirs also took account of institutional opinion and hence, at one remove, the wishes of sections of the public these embodied. There is no reason to question recent historians' portrayals of the 1945 election as a sort of referendum, giving a charge to a more-trusted Labour party to implement what had already been planned.

But their perception of the public and indeed the national interest was not necessarily intended to satisfy demand, and certainly not demands as they accelerated in the age of working class economic emancipation. Although the element of tutelage was initially far stronger that it was to be by 1961, in laying down the canons of fairness and even egalitarianism, what may fairly be called a clerisy, assumed that they would still inquire and prescribe in this tradition in the future.

Over twenty years, their assumption met two long threats. First came public demand for higher consumption, accompanied by wage inflation and industrial indiscipline, and a rising, almost insatiable requirement for welfare and health benefits. Secondly, governments of the 1950s, only too aware that public expectation made it hard to practise economic management in a compartment separate from their electoral calculations, slowly abandoned the rigorous political morality established by Attlee and Cripps. In particular they slipped towards more or less permanent deficit financing, and began to build pre-election budgets into a cycle designed with much longer term considerations in mind.

Failure of the attempts in 1951 and 1957 to tie Conservative administrations down to stricter fiscal practice and curb what the clerisy saw as politicians' irresistible tendencies to evade responsibility, emphasised what was already becoming apparent for other reasons: that if the public did not behave with the restraint required, if trade unions could not, and if elected governments would not, the state as it was constituted had become inadequate. Search for an outside authoritative agency to do the job was, of course, an illusion; if guardians of the post-war settlement's principles such as the Bank of England were not listened to, how could a powerless body such as the Council on Pay Productivity and Incomes acquire the necessary authority?

To those who saw it as their function to manage, as neutrally as possible, a chaos of competing interests like driving pigs to market, the implications were worse even than the immediate handicaps. As criticisms developed on the left that elected governments had been too long in pawn to a mandarin elite (genesis of the Fulton inquiry, focused on the origins, selection and training of recruits to the civil service), it began to seem that they had helped create, not a balanced polity but one dominated by a Frankenstein monster of public ingratitude, wantonness and greed. Attlee had, of course, declared robustly that striking gasworkers ought to return to work and be grateful for what they had already gained, and there is no reason to suggest that the clerisy harked back to 1866 and Robert Lowe's gloomy prophesies about the tyranny implicit in a democratic franchise. Unfortunately for them, the language of obligation had worn out. By 1961, it was necessary to rethink quite fundamental propositions about the nature of authority in the British state and how its citizens should respond.

The authors of the post-war settlement had, at the very beginning, conducted a subtle manoeuvre which eliminated the need to ask such questions in wartime. By reasserting traditional Cabinet practice, ministerial authority, and Treasury financial control in the Machinery of Government Committee's report of 1941, they had not only determined the modes in which reform would be considered, but also had excluded any chance of establishing functional departments or an industrial parliament. In confirming the formal pattern of parliamentary democracy and of the state as it had grown up after the First World War, they permitted large informal extensions of the institutions' roles at the same time as they perpetuated their own.

Such was their success that, apart from a period of unease about the state's role in the mid and late 1940s among intellectuals as diverse as George Orwell and Friedrich von Hayek, fundamental discussion of the political economy confined itself to the argument about the proper limits of state controls – until these controls largely disappeared. The reversion to a more departmental structure after 1951 made no intrinsic difference to the way those in government operated a directive system under the cover of economic management. When it began to show symptoms of failure, would-be reformers were still able to conceive of reform from within, by extending their range of powers and instruments. They did not, initially, understand that their own functions, as well as the concept of an impartial omniscient state which they served, were at risk, although they did see, correctly, that the populism developing in party-political life implied a far-reaching change in the nature of parliamentary democracy.

The reformers imagined that by incorporating Britain in a larger economic environment and by tightening up the tried informal practices which bound government and governing institutions, the state could be strengthened sufficiently to do its current job without the political hazard of returning to more direct controls. Theirs was not a liberalising policy, nor one leading to greater public participation, but one that tended initially to reinforce existing patterns of action and institutions.

It may, in the long run, have been unfortunate that so much was achieved in an extraordinarily fluid period at the war's end which then set quickly in a particular mould before the 1950s began. Subsequently, the system could not easily be altered, even if it appeared no longer suitable to changing circumstances. Britain was saddled with a marvellous machine, able to eliminate most primary conflicts and many of the evils of the 1930s, but less suited to cope with dilemmas of the 1960s. This aspect of the post-war settlement outlived the political context and the physical presence of its authors, so that the generation in government after 1961 had not only to contend with the vast questions buried at its birth but had to do so with prescribed instruments they could no longer control.

The next volume will continue the narrative of events in the field of industrial politics through the period when governments attempted with increasing desperation to recapture the political and economic harmony and prosperity they saw rapidly slipping away, and into the crisis of the mid-1970s. It will ask whether that constituted a 'general crisis' in the political system, and whether subsequent trends down to the early 1980s amounted to a new departure or merely a variation in the old search for balance. The final volume will examine the mentalities of the various institutions and government departments studied here, over the forty years since 1940 – how these grew up and changed, and what were their influences on the nature of the modern British state.

Notes and References

INTRODUCTION

1. *Capitalism, Socialism and Democracy*, 2nd edn, Part II, Prologue, p. 61.
2. Most recently by Anthony Seldon in *Elite Oral History* (1985); see also the preface to his *Churchill's Indian Summer* (1981), and the introduction to R. K. Middlemas, *Power and the Party* (1980).

1 THE WARTIME STATE

1. PREM 1/431, 7.3.40.
2. TUC GC minutes, May 1943.
3. S. Pollard, *Development of the British Economy 1914–67* (p. 298). For general accounts of the war economy, see the official histories, H. M. D. Parker, *Manpower* (1954), W. K. Hancock and M. Gowing, *The British War Economy* (1949), R. S. Sayers, *Financial Policy 1939–45* (1950).
4. Martin Gilbert, *Winston Churchill* (1983), vol. 6, p. 331.
5. In addition he set up the Factory and Welfare Advisory Board, covering social conditions, and the short-lived Labour Supply Board.
6. 1940 material, in the Open University film *The Consequences of the Second World War*.
7. LAB 10/160, Tribe to Gilbert, 18.2.42.
8. Peter Mathias, 'History of the FBI' (unpublished MS), pp. 281–2. I am most grateful to Professor Leslie Hannah and the Business History Unit, London School of Economics, for access to these volumes.
9. FBI Defence Committee minutes, 1937–38 (quoted in Mathias, p. 287).
10. FBI Council to Arthur Greenwood, 16.7.40 (quoted in Mathias, p. 318).
11. PEP: *Government and Industry* (1952) p. 72. For a description of how the process worked in the Ministry of Food, see William Wallace, *Enterprise First* (1946).
12. In some complex industries such as building and civil engineering, National Consultative Councils served to co-ordinate the mass of organisations involved.
13. Later on in the war the TUC still feared to be a loser in this competition, and sought free access to other Ministries, beyond the narrow scope of sponsorship and MLNS (TUC FGPC 11/2, 24.7.44).
14. FBI to Kingsley Wood, 14.4.42; Executive Committee minutes 24.2.41 (quoted in Mathias, 'History of the FBI', p. 308).
15. Thus the FBI was able before Lend-Lease in 1941 to fend off state controls, acting as agent, via the Export Council, to encourage import substitution and export performance. In return for firms' co-operation, it could offer the bait of

favourable allocations – without which trade associations and firms might lose their overseas markets for ever (FBI Council minutes, March–October 1941).

16. FBI membership rose from 2800 to 4500 firms, 180 to 240 trade associations between 1939 and 1945.
17. See, for example, R. S. Sayers, *The Bank of England 1891–1944* (1976), vol. 2, p. 560.
18. They seem indeed to have been deeply worried, as late as January 1939, that Britain's financial resources would be inadequate for a European war (CAB 23/97, 2.1.39).
19. Sayers, *The Bank of England*, pp. 561–5.
20. Ibid., p. 568.
21. The resulting Exchange Requirements Committee gave the Treasury full control of foreign exchange and all gold transactions.
22. The most important may be listed: The Production Council, Economic Policy Committee, Food Policy Committee, Home Policy Committee, Lord President's Committee. The latter, chaired by Sir John Anderson, gradually assumed an overview role, under the War Cabinet, acting as co-ordinator of all major problems of planning and a court of appeal between competing Departments.
23. E. Durbin, *Problems of Economic Planning* (1949), p. 99.
24. MGO 6, CAB 87/72, 8.3.43.
25. 'The essence of the relationship is that the Department takes steps to ensure that government intervention in the affairs of an industry takes full account of its needs and of government policy towards it' (PEP, *Government and Industry* (1952) p. 72).
26. PREM 63/2, 19.10.42.
27. Close reading of the NJAC minutes makes clear that MLNS officials fostered this very specifically (see, for example, Emmerson to Hodges LAB 10/160, 26.11.41).
28. CAB 87/5, R (44); LP (43) 293. According to an MLNS report on the NJAC's workings: 'Government policy has been to deal with disputes on the basis of co-operation with organisation in the industry, to refer disputes to compulsory arbitration only after other means of settlement have been exhausted and to take legal action only in cases in which it can rely on the support of the constitutional elements [*sic*] among the workpeople, and in which the objects of those concerned are definitely mischievous' (LAB 10/160, 'Prices and Wages Policy', 8.6.42).
29. CAB 134/314, GOC (SC) 51/1, Appendix 4.
30. TUC AR 1941, p. 101; 1943, p. 131; FBI memorandum on relations with government, BT 64/2237, 1947; also BEC GPC minutes 26.7.50.
31. CAB 87/72, MGO 11, MGO 15, 18.5.43.
32. PREM 63/2 *passim*.
33. Max Nicholson used an unusually wide definition of the government centre; 'Treasury, Board of Trade, and Ministry of Supply, together with the CSO and Economic Section and the Lord President's Office, formed a steering committee responsible for economic policy as a whole' (PEP, A12/5, 1944–45). Beaverbrook put it more bluntly, accusing Churchill of running the government with 'three professors'. Cherwell, Keynes and Robbins. (Dalton diaries I, vol. 29, 14.2.44).
34. The 1940 Budget had already introduced purchase tax and dividend limitation. May 1940 brought 100 per cent Excess Profits Tax, followed by a supplementary Budget in July, and food subsidies a month later. Given Keynes' forecast of a

£400–£500 million deficit, compulsory savings and an excess earnings tax was discussed early in 1941: instead, post war credits were introduced. The April 1941 Budget instituted price stabilisation and made certain concessions to essential war workers. The first National Income White Paper and Keynes' plans for a 'social policy Budget' followed in November 1941, with PAYE in 1943–44.

35. CAB 87/72, MGO 21, 21.6.43, for example; also CAB 87/5, R (44), 25.2.44.
36. BT 64/3113, Memorandum on departmental functions, 19.1.43.
37. LAB 10/525 Alan Barlow to Ince (MLNS), 23.12.44 and again 9.1.45.
38. CAB 134/313, Kipping to Maud, GOC (RO), 51/8 (nd).
39. In Kathleen Burke (ed.), *War and Society* (1981), ch. 6.
40. PREM 4 63/2, 21.8.42.
41. cf. L. C. Carpenter, 'Corporatism in Britain', *Journal of Contemporary History*, vol. 11, no. 1, 1976; A. J. Marwick, 'Middle Opinion in the Thirties', *English Historical Review*, 1964.
42. T266/94, 30.11.50.
43. Norman retired in April 1944, and after a long discussion (in which Churchill rejected Niemeyer), Catto was chosen as Governor to face the new world, and Bretton Woods.
44. Cmd 5258, March 1941. By July 1943, 6 200 nuclei certificates had been issued by BOT and 3 500 factories closed; 257 000 workers had been transferred, mainly from cotton, hosiery, wool and carpet manufacture (FBI memorandum 20.10.43, quoted in Mathias, pp. 320 5).
45. Monckton papers, fol. 298
46. Dalton diaries I, vol. 29, 17.3.44. McGowan, Chairman of ICI, Monckton and Citrine who wanted a precise parallel to the TUC, all regretted that the merger did not take place (Monckton papers, fol. 316, 22.3.44).
47. Quoted in R. S. Sayers, *Financial Policy* (1956), pp. 46–7.
48. Dalton diaries I, f. 30, 1.9.44.
49. TUC, AR 1944, p. 370; Citrine memorandum, TUC, FGPC 11/2, 25.8.45; also TUC file 108.1, IV, Citrine's memorandum to the JCC, 14.1.46.
50. John Ramsden, *The Making of Conservative Party Policy: the CRD since 1929* (1980), pp. 95–8.
51. CRD, Hopkinson files, DCPS/11.
52. TUC FGPC, 28.9.43.
53. Eddersbury 1943; Skipton 1944; Chelmsford, April 1945; see generally, D. L. Prynn 'Common Wealth: a British Third Party of the 1940s', *Journal of Contemporary History*, vol. 7/1, June 1972.
54. LAB 10/525, Tribe to Ince, 27.12.44.
55. CAB 87/72, MGO 61 Committee report, 3.1.45.
56. CAB 134/312, GOC (RO) 50/88, 29.9.50, gives a Ministry of Supply view; MGO 21, CAB 87/22, 21.6.43, a BOT one. The latter specifically drew the wartime lesson about acting 'in such a way as to secure the confidence of opposing interests, e.g. producers and traders'.
57. CAB 87/72, MGO 30, 10.11.43; also MGO 59, and Dalton diaries I, vol. 31, 23.10.44.
58. Beveridge papers, IXa, 77.
59. A comprehensive catalogue is not possible here. Coal output fell off as early as November 1943, and the War Cabinet considered toughening up the Essential Work Orders (CAB 87/63, EC 43 27)). Strikes occurred in Coventry

engineering in clear contravention of the regulations, sometimes under the influence of Trotskyite groups (R. Croucher, *Engineers at War 1939–45* (1980)). Ministry of Supply controllers had sometimes to use what the SBAC disingenuously called 'Gestapo tactics'. At a personal level, Samuel Courtauld resisted the sequestration of his firm's dollar assets in 1940; ICI objected to breaking its cartel arrangements with IG Farben in Chile and Turkey (private information).

60. Attlee papers 45, fol. 172 (1945 nd).

2 ATTITUDES IN WAR

1. K. O. Morgan, *Labour in Power, 1945–51* (1984).
2. CAB 21/1581; CAB 65/17, WM (41) 20, 20.1.41. A paper prepared earlier, in 1940, by Gladwyn Jebb, on what the war was being fought for, was regarded as more than Churchill and Chamberlain could take and was not submitted to the War Cabinet at all.
3. Laski papers, Churchill to Laski, 25.3.42.
4. In early 1944, for example, Bevin argued against including in a published document any precise figure for 'full employment' such as 8.5 per cent unemployed (CAB 87/5, R (44) 8, 21.1.44). In May 1944, other Ministers, worried about the implications of deficit financing, managed to curtail the idea of debt management: 'we must guard against the dangers of undermining confidence in sterling in not only this country but abroad. It was necessary not only to be but to appear to be prudent in our financial policy' (Draft of the 1944 White Paper, CAB 87/5, R (44) 37°, p. 2, 9.5.44).
5. Labour Party RDR 265, April 1944: draft statement on full employment.
6. These holdings had grown at roughly £600 million a year, allowing Britain to run up an almost unmanageable trade deficit. UK reserves stood at only £250 million in May 1945, against overseas debts of £3 000 million.
7. BT 64/3113, memorandum on Industrial Efficiency, 11.3.43.
8. N. J. Vig, *Science and Technology in British Politics* (1968), p. 7.
9. cf. Lord Zuckerman, 'Scientific advice during and since World War Two', *Proceedings of the Royal Society*, A342/465.85, 1975; see Vig, p. 14, for Morrison's views in April 1944.
10. This explains the genesis of R. H. Tawney's well-known cautionary article 'The Abolition of Controls', *Economic History Review*, 1943.
11. IEP (41) 3, memorandum on Unemployment.
12. IEP (41) 4, memorandum by A. J. Baxter.
13. Post-War Issues, November 1941 (CAB 86/54, 1°, 11.11.41). Finance came first, industry second, labour third; then agriculture and food, rebuilding, house construction and transport.
14. IDAC men collectively saw their role in wartime as 'breaking down individualism and educating businessmen in many industries to work together' (Sir Hubert Henderson, *Tariff-making and Industrial Reconstruction* (1965), p. 75).
15. The most comprehensive statement of this thesis is to be found in the memorandum of BT 64/3113, 19.1.43.
16. BT 64/3113, memorandum of 19.1.43.

17. These arguments were, of course, put in an exaggerated form by F. von Hayek in *The Road to Serfdom* (1944).
18. 'It is preferable to leave money wages unchanged than link our currency to some fixed standard and force a reduction in the nominal rate of wages' (MLNS memorandum to PWIEC, November 1941). Also Tribe to Emmerson, 12.11.41; and LAB 10/160, Clay (BOT) to Tribe, 14.5.42.
19. Sayers, *Financial Policy*, p. 231; Susan Strange, *Sterling and British Policy*, p. 56. p. 56.
20. Strange, *Sterling and British Policy*, pp. 60–2.
21. This can be seen, for example, in the negotiations between trade associations and large firms, about the rate and timing of deconcentration and restoration of raw materials supplies, during 1945.
22. Mathias, 'History of the FBI', p. 328.
23. *The Organisation of Industry* (1944) p. 5.
24. BEC Council minutes B1/2/3, November 1942.
25. Samuel Courtauld, *Ideals and Industry* (1949) p. 2; for other opinions see W. Wallace, *Enterprise First* (1949); R. Glenday, *The Future of Economic Society* (1944).
26. R. K. Middlemas, *Politics in Industrial Society* (1979), pp. 295–6. The Nuffield Conference report was published under the title *Employment Policy and the Organisation of Industry after the War, A Statement* (1943).
27. Monckton papers, 55 (legal matters), pp. 167 76.
28. Joan Robinson wrote a pamphlet for Common Wealth in 1943, 'The Future of Industry', which attacked the drift towards monopoly, to the detriment of efficiency and the consumer.
29. Monckton papers, 55, p. 175.
30. Ibid., pp. 175–6.
31. This through Works Councils, apparently without threatening either trade union branches or lower management – precisely how, was not explained. Nor was the tension between raising low pay and maintaining differentials higher up, without creating wage inflation, recognised.
32. 'A National Policy for Industry', p. 13.
33. Turner and Newall Ltd. argued 'great care should be taken to see that industrialists are not stampeded under conditions of emergency into accepting principles which they would not accept in normal times' (Monckton papers, 55, p. 246).
34. Monckton papers, 55, p. 301.
35. Ibid., p. 315.
36. TUC EC 2, 14.1.42.
37. This had its own dangers, well demonstrated during the Greek civil war, when Churchill used Citrine to try and establish a liaison with Greek right-wing trade unions in 1944. From this cockpit the TUC was saved only by the counter-intervention of WFTU.
38. TUC Box 108, 12 JCC 175, para. 2.
39. The TUC's first substantive analysis of the effects of full employment did not occur until 1956 (see page 319).
40. 'The trade union movement will not be found unwilling, where it is shown to be necessary, to adapt its policies and its practices to the means of achieving full employment . . . There is no need to fear a [wages] spiral if the government can

convince the trade union movement that, in genuine pursuit of full employment, it is determined to take all other steps that are necessary to control prices, and convince it of the need to secure equivalent guarantees that wage movements will not be such as to upset the system of price control' (TUC EC 6/1, para. 13; also para. 15 and EC 6, 12.1.44).

41. TUC FGPC 12/1 *passim*, 26.7.43.

42. Beveridge asked the question in his negotiations with the TUC whether full employment would necessitate changes in union rules and practices, so as not to engender wage inflation; to which the TUC replied, obliquely: 'the greatest difficulty would be in getting trade unions to agree to the state having more authority over workpeople, on some expectation of full employment, and subsequently discovering that whilst the authority over workpeople remained, full employment was not in fact achieved' (EC 10/2, 10.3.44).

43. Had the TUC been aware that MLNS, recognising that the great gains made by the TUC would inevitably diminish private industry's profits after the war, hoped to link wage restraint to the promise of full employment, without price controls, they might have been more cautious.

44. Memorandum on post-war industrial relations and on wages policy, for PWIEC (LAB 10/160, January 1942). On the PWIEC, the Treasury accepted an unchallenged restoration of union rights, but argued that government must retain freedom of action on such questions as training which affected the labour market (CAB 87/63, EC (43) 3°, 21.10.43).

45. CAB 86/91 18°, 18.6.43.

46. Sir Norman Chester: 'Beveridge 40 Years Later', *The Times*, 1.10.82.

47. CAB 58/54, IEP (41) 4, p. 12, para. 27.

48. J. Ramsden, *The Conservative Making of Policy*, p. 96. The Post-War Problems Committee was appointed in July 1941, with Butler and Maxwell-Fyfe in charge, Topping as secretary.

49. Ramsden, *The Conservative Making of Policy*, p. 99.

50. PWPCC sub-committee report, January 1943, p. 2.

51. PWPCC minutes, 10.10.44.

52. Kenneth Harris, *Attlee* (1982) pp. 205–6.

53. After publication of the unhappily titled *Work: the Future of British Industry* (1944), Churchill's private advisors, Beaverbrook and Bracken, and the Emergency Business Committee dealt with the Manifesto. After the 1945 election disaster, Butler wrote privately to a few close contacts such as Aubrey Jones, 'who have not been condemned [later altered to "obliged"] to follow the narrow Party line and would help us with a wider outlook', asking for help: 'In my view it is quite essential that the Socialist Party should not develop into a totalitarian party due to weakness and hesitation of the side which we represent' (PWPCC minutes, correspondence file, 12.1.46).

54. T. D. Burridge: 'The Churchill–Laski Electoral Clash, June 1945', *Journal of Contemporary History*, vol. 12, no. 4, October 1977, p. 729.

55. RDR 265, April 1944, and 285, September 1944. The latter settled for a National Investment Board, which would control the whole capital market, maintain cheap money, and assist industrial stability.

56. RDR 250, December 1943.

57. RDR 206, April 1943.

58. In the genesis of this see RDR 203, April 1943; 237, October 1943 with Gaitskell's notes; and 251, December 1943.
59. RDR 251, December 1943.
60. RDR 285, September 1944; M. Kalecki, 'Employment in the UK during and after the transition period', *Bulletin of the Institute of Statistics*, December 1944. See also E. Schumacher, 'An Essay in the State's Control of Business', *Agenda* vol. III, no. 1, 1944. Generally K. O. Morgan, *Labour in Power 1945–51* (1984).
61. MLNS note to PWIEC, LAB 10/160 8.6.42. See also Bevin's own note (LAB 10/161, LP (4) 2/6, 22.12.41).
62. Lithgow to Forbes-Watson (BEC, correspondence files, 11.12.46).
63. cf. Attlee's speech to National Union of Manufacturers, 15.11.46, and Morrison's profuse notes for what was seen as an important, declaratory occasion (Attlee papers: 45, ff. 145–7).
64. BT 64/2275, document X (B); BT 64/3113 memorandum on industrial efficiency, 19.1.43; T161/1369 SI (O) 45 1° and 2°, 29.11.45 and 5.12.45.
65. MLNS, of course, wanted to keep Order 1305, as a safeguard against unions' monopoly powers so long as the expected shortages of skilled labour lasted. The TUC concurred: 'unless there was a curb on extravagant and unreasonable claims, sponsored by new elements with the least degree of protective machinery [a reference to shop stewards], sporadic and abortive strikes might result which would be beneficial to nobody' (TUC Box T559/89 C9/1A (Production Campaign); also January/February 1946 meetings of FGPC, and EC 7/1, 20.6.45).

3 BARGAINING FOR RECONSTRUCTION

1. CAB 87/71, WM 117 (42), 24.8.42. Officials may have been influenced by a notable article in *The Times* (27.3.42) analysing the lessons of the Haldane Report, and the 'need for concentration of authority'; also Laski's submissions to Churchill (PREM 4 63/2) and Cripps' to Anderson (CAB 87/31, memorandum, 24.8.42). Public debate was clearly unwelcome.
2. According to Bridges' advice to Churchill, a small Cabinet of Super-Ministers would be most undesirable. A full Cabinet of 15–20 was needed in order to handle a parliamentary majority, and prevent individual Ministers becoming easy targets. Churchill retained a fondness for the tight War Cabinet network, as his schemes for 'overlords' in 1951 indicates (PREM 63/2, Bridges to Churchill, 19.10.42).
3. CAB 87/41 44°, 7.3.44.
4. Dalton diaries, f. 21, 4.8.43.
5. CAB 87/5, Reconstruction Committee R (44) 1°, 3.1.44.
6. Whether the Commission should have powers, or remain a tripartite forum for discussion and dissemination of BOT wisdom was much discussed in the Post-War Employment Committee, some of whose proceedings foreshadow NEDC (CAB 87/63, EC (43) 7° and 8°, October 1943; CAB 87/72, MGO, 21°, 21.6.43; CAB 87/63, EC (43) 7°, 7.10.43).
7. CAB 87/72, MGO 1, p. 5, 25.1.43.
8. CAB 87/71 4°, 11.12.42; 87/72 MGO 6, 8.3.43.
9. For Bridges' view, see CAB 87/71 5°, 16.12.42; Sir Frederick Leith-Ross and Geoffrey Crowther argued for the Treasury location and cited the failure of the

US Economic Planning Board which had 'exposed the fallacy of a government introducing a key machine to pronounce upon economic policy' (ibid.).

10. CAB 87/71, Treasury memorandum MGO 24, p. 3, 27.8.43; also MGO 24 30°, 20.10.43.

11. CAB 87/63, EC (43) 16, 23.10.43.

12. After its agonising qualms of conscience, the Treasury had accepted that deficits were acceptable in bad years; but 'it would be impossible in the Treasury's view to justify any policy which rested on the basis of the *indefinite continuance* of unbalanced budgets. The altered conditions of the modern world would serve to increase rather than to diminish the importance of budgetary solvency.' This the Economic Section accepted, as it did the undesirability of devaluation or import controls (CAB 87/63, EC (43) 6, 16.10.43).

13. CAB 87/63, EC (43) 12, 20.10.43.

14. Labour Party, 1944 Association, 5°, 3.11.44.

15. Characteristically, Robbins fought a rearguard action: where nationalisation was used as a weapon against private monopoly, he argued, only certain firms should be taken over, not the whole industry, leaving others to compete with the state 'on the basis of free and fair competition' (CAB 87/63, EC (43) 8).

16. The TUC shunned the Labour Research Department's proposals on worker participation and rejected an over-arching definition of the public interest in public industry, preferring a straightforward list of limited objectives, based on mutual association between state, management and unions (TUC, EC 11/1, 6.4.44).

17. BT 64/3113, 1.1.43; CAB 87/63, EC (43) 4, BOT memorandum, 15.10.43.

18. CAB 87/71 16°, 10.6.43.

19. CAB 87/54, IEP (41) 3.

20. IEP (42) 2, p. 5.

21. 'Full Employment in a Free Society' took its final shape in committee between September and November 1943, and was published in February 1944; the Nuffield Conference took place in September 1943 and was renewed the following February; Civil Service attendance at both ceased in the autumn of 1943.

22. TUC assurances, with their insistence on price control as a prerequisite, were, in any case, largely unacceptable to industry.

23. TUC, EC 10/2, 10.3.44. The best account from Beveridge's side is in Jose Harris, *William Beveridge*, pp. 434–41.

24. CAB 87/63, EC (43) 1; LAB 10/160 *passim*.

25. CAB 87/5, R (44) 46°, 12.6.44.

26. CAB 87/63 EC (43) 6°, 26.10.43.

27. CAB 87/63, R (44) 6.

28. Ibid., para. 149.

29. LP, RDR 267, April 1944.

30. EC 13, 14.6.44.

31. TGWU *Record*, vol. XXIV, nos 273 and 274, June and July 1944. Beveridge himself continued to campaign for a better standard from 'outside'; although, as the 1945 election approached, he began to emphasise more strongly the need for reciprocal trade union responsibility (Beveridge papers IXA and VI, Politics, 12 and 13, 1944–45).

32. When Beveridge approached the TUC in November 1943 with three questions,

about the definition of full employment, the likelihood of wage inflation, and whether full employment could be achieved without great mobility in the labour market, the TUC replied: 'We are concerned to ensure that every worker shall be able, within limits determined only by the need to safeguard the reasonable freedom of others, to choose freely work which he prefers and for which he is trained, at rates of wages, and in conditions commensurate with his state and the nature of the work.' Beveridge gave the TUC to understand that he accepted this substantial extension of his original formulation, in which vacancies had simply been equated with job-seekers, regardless of their qualifications and expectations (EC 10/2, 10.3.44).

33. 'We are in fact concerned with the share of the product of labour which should accrue to workpeople in terms of goods and services, conditions of work and leisure as well as any possibility for individual and social development.' (EC 14/1, para. 4, 19.7.44). The programme fell short of interference with management (the TUC dismissed any idea of workers' control (EC 5/2, 9.5.45)), but it had a considerable influence on the drafting of *Let Us Face the Future*.

34. A. Booth: 'The Keynesian Revolution in economic policy-making', *Economic History Review* (second series) (1983) vol. 36, pp. 109–17.

35. The only British economist who became seriously worried about the inflationary implications of full employment at this early stage was D. H. Robertson (cf. his article 'The Problem of Exports', *Economic Journal* (1945) vol. 55).

36. CAB 87/5, R (44) 34°, p. 3, 24.3.44.

37. BEC MS B/32/CI, C487 Part I, 21.12.46.

38. To be fair, officials knew little of how restrictive practices worked, either among firms or unions. If they were naïve in hoping that both sides would reform, they were no more naïve than their Ministers (cf. CAB 87/63 EC (43) 22, EC (44) 6). 'An agreement to fix prices may be harmful,' the Cabinet were informed, 'but an agreement between a producer and a distributor fixing the price at which the latter may sell (RPM) is most probably harmless.' (CAB 630/6, GEN 80/42, CS (W) (45) 80, memorandum by Andrews, 4.10.45.)

39. CAB 87/5, R (44) 34°, 24.3.44.

40. Clay/Tribe correspondence, LAB 10/160, May 1942. In this they concurred with Keynes, who wrote in March 1944, 'I do not doubt that a serious problem will arise as to how wages are to be restrained when we have a combination of collective bargaining and full employment. But I am not sure how much light this kind of analytical method you apply can throw on this essentially political problem.' (Ibid.).

41. CAB 87/63, EC (43) 2, memorandum 15.10.43; 'What is important is to place the responsibility for any wage settlements fully and squarely on the shoulders of the parties most concerned.' (LAB 10/160, Clay to Tribe, 30.3.42).

42. Citrine gave a number of assurances to Beveridge including some about the TUC's power to eliminate unofficial strikes, by withholding strike pay, and by bringing 'fellow workers' disapproval' to bear, but there is no reason to think that Beveridge passed these on, or was even convinced by them. (Beveridge papers, IX A15, 10.11.43).

43. CAB 87/63, EC (43) 3, 15.10.43; CAB 87/5, R (43) 1°, 20.12.42.

44. During 1944, an official Committee, chaired by Sir Alan Barlow (Treasury) discussed how to increase the output of scientists from universities. From this developed the Advisory Council on Scientific Policy, under Tizard and Zuckerman.

45. CAB 134/376 gives the interesting debate on protection for the scientific instrument industry.

46. Dalton diaries I, f. 28, 4.2.44.

47. CAB 87/63, R (44) 6, para. 80.

48. CAB 87/63, EC (43) 9°, 29.10.43. The FBI's claim for rebates, tax concessions, and £400 million in state aid, went right back to 1941 (FBI Taxation Committee, 17.12.41).

49. BOT's defence of modernisation even at the expense of full employment is worth quoting: 'the need is to dissipate a national tendency to dislike scrapping and replacing. It is a question of psychology, and not of the state of profit and loss accounts' (CAB 87/63, EC (48) 4, 15.10.43).

50. CAB 87/5, R (44) 16, 21.2.44.

51. CAB 87/63, EC (43) 5; 87/5 R (44) 8°, 21.1.44.

52. CAB 87/63, EC (43) 18°, 9.11.43; CAB 87/63, R (44) 6 and Dalton diaries I, f. 32, 5.2.45.

53. See, for example, Barry Supple, 'Problems of the British Coal Industry' in *Arbeitskreis Deutsche England Forschung*, vol. 1 (1982) p. 22 *et seq.*; John Vaizey, *History of the British Steel Industry*, pp. 104–6.

54. MAP actually worked out a programme in 1944, in close consultation with SBAC (Avro, Rolls, Bristol and Handley Page) suitably tuned for either Labour or Conservative government, about which aircraft firms should be kept alive, and on what orders from BOAC and the new Air Ministry, in order to preserve capacity for Britain's strategic needs, and enable the industry to compete with US companies.

55. Even Beveridge and his retinue had to accept these realities and accommodate their report accordingly by assuming either that other Western countries would adopt similar policies, or, even more optimistically, the emergence of a new order of world management.

56. IEP (41) 4 and (41) 3, July 1941.

57. I am indebted to Stephen Gilliatt's unpublished thesis, 'Social Democracy and the Management of Reconstruction 1945–49', (University of Sussex D.Phil., 1983) for this analysis.

58. There had been no excuse for illusion, since the Atlantic Charter and the Mutual Aid Treaty 1942 (R. N. Gardner, *Sterling-Dollar Diplomacy* (1956), p. 186).

59. WP (44) 129, 3.2.44 and WD (44) 368, 3.7.44.

60. FBI, *Reconstruction*, p. 8.; Mathias, p. 339, quotes the FBI's correspondence with Dalton, January 1943, and its Trade Policy memorandum, 26.5.54, which gives an impression of desperation for anything which would protect sterling's value and stave off deflation.

61. PREM 4/17/10, 9.2.44.

62. WP (44) 145, 3.3.44.

63. CAB 87/72, MGO 44, p. 2, 3.3.44.

64. The figures he quoted can be found in GEN 80/19, COM/TOP 4, Cab 130/6, September 1945. 4½ million houses had been destroyed; internal disinvestment had been 2–3 times greater than in the United States; external disinvestment totalled $17.5 billion – six times that of the United States (and in terms of comparative national wealth, 35 times). Britain's export trade had fallen by two-thirds in volume, half in value, whereas that of the United States had more than doubled.

65. FBI papers. Reports on the Monetary Conference, November 1944–June 1945.
66. CAB 87/5, R (44) 37°, paras. 73–78, 9.5.44. See also Dalton diaries, I, f. 29, 17.2.44 on the evidence given by Catterns and Cobbold to the Cabinet Committee on External Economic Policy. Dalton thought then 'that the Bank was totally unconscious of post-war realities and in particular of our need to get very substantial assistance from the United States'. Two years later, in drafting the 1946 Act, Dalton would lose to Catto and the others on the Chancellor's powers over the Bank.
67. According to Hugh Dalton who, presumably, based his opinion on BOT surveys, Lord Melchett of ICI wanted IG Farben broken up so that it could not compete in research and development for five years. ICI's local agents in Ankara and elsewhere, even in 1944, were arranging to work together with Dupont (Dalton diaries I, f. 29, 21.1.44; I, f. 30, 10.7.44). Shipbuilders, according to Ted Leathers, were planning a similar form of collusion (ibid. I, 30, 10.7.44). As for the cotton factories, their managers 'want to live out their days in peace. They don't want to be bothered with new ideas or new machinery. The old stuff they are used to will last out their time. They are completely defeatist as regards the future and are only thinking of getting back to 1939' (ibid. I, f. 29, 31.1.44). Dalton, of course, was hardly an impartial observer.
68. It might have been expected from the record of individual academics serving the state that in higher education at least, rationality would govern post-war planning. Indeed, the 1944 Education Act, a bipartisan measure providing at last for a proper system of secondary education can be seen as a core achievement comparable to the 1944 White Paper. Yet once the Ministry of Education began to ask what was the role of the state in furthering technical education and the supply, for example, of trained engineers (in the Percy Report 1944), it became bogged down in ancient demarcation disputes between universities and colleges. A weak Ministry, outflanked by professional bodies and skilfully organised academic lobbies, had to struggle over more than a decade, until the White Paper on Technical Education 1956, promulgated by David Eccles. Rather like the parallel question of scientific manpower, these disputes were eventually resolved in favour of the universities, in favour of excellence and pure research, rather than technical training and applied research (cf. K. McCormick 'Elite Ideologies and Manipulation in Higher Education', *Sociological Review*, vol. 30, no. 1, 1982).
69. CAB 87/62, R (44) 6, p. 24.

4 MANAGING AUSTERITY 1945–47

1. cf. BT 64/2221, Wages Policy Working Party memorandum, 21.3.46; also LPC Industrial Sub-Committe, CAB 132/88, *passim.*
2. The FBI Organisation of Industry Committee Report, July 1944, shows members determined to resist the Boards, and any hint that trade associations might acquire compulsory powers. Each member trade association argued that it was responsible enough to warrant 'self regulation'.
3. cf. Arthur Deakin's speech demanding 'an effective place in the control and management of industry' (TGWU *Record*, vol. XXIV, no. 279, pp. 118–20, December 1944 and Biennial Delegate Conference 1945 minutes, pp. 16–29.)

4. Three substantial studies of the Labour government are now available: Roger Eatwell, *The 1945–51 Labour Governments* (1979); Henry Pelling, *The Labour Governments 1945–51* (1984); Kenneth O. Morgan, *Labour in Power 1945–51* (1984); also Kenneth Harris, *Attlee* (1982).

5. P. Addison, 'Attlee', *New Statesman*, 17.12.82.

6. MS Attlee, 71, ff. 232–3, on the 1948 dockers' strike.

7. Speech to the National Union of Manufacturers (MS Attlee 45, ff. 145–50, 14.11.46) with full notes from Morrison (Lord Privy Seal) and Cripps (Board of Trade).

8. IPA lecture, quoted in Bernard Donoughue and G. W. Jones, *Herbert Morrison* (1973), p. 343.

9. HC Deb, vol. 419, col. 2125, 28.2.46.

10. H. Dalton, *Memoirs 1945–60* (1962), p. 157.

11. Cab 134/503; MEP (46) 3, memorandum, 6.4.46 shows that civil servants warned Ministers against adopting too detailed targets which subsequent events might compel them to vary.

12. MS Attlee, 45, f. 59.

13. This dualism can be seen clearly in Harold Wilson's *A New Deal for Coal*, written in association with the party and the NUM while he was still a civil servant. He proposed that the NCB should own the mines and work them in the national interest without specifying how that interest would fit in with his aims of a board composed of men of 'administrative and technical ability'. See the Jay–Attlee correspondence, PREM 8/293, March 1946.

14. CAB 132/88, WM (46) 4 *passim*, November 1945 onwards; also T161/ 1369, SI (O) 46, 8°, 8.4.46 for the Treasury view.

15. CAB 124/929, July 1946.

16. LP 1944 Association, November 1944; this may be contrasted with the LP Research Department memorandum on privately-owned industry, September 1945.

17. Such as Morrison, who wrote, 'there is no question of regimentational propaganda or of political opportunism. The government need have no fear of truth told in a way the public will understand. The British public can be relied on in a national emergency, provided they know the state of affairs' (CAB 124/985, memorandum, September 1945. See also Max Nicholson to Bridges (CAB 134/503, MEP (46) 4, 17.4.46). For a full discussion of the uses of propaganda in this period, see A. Lawrence, 'Propaganda, Planning and the Economy' (unpublished M.Phil. thesis, Leeds 1982) and A. Wildy, 'Propaganda and Social Policy in Britain 1945–51' (unpublished D.Phil. thesis, Leeds 1985).

18. K. O. Morgan, *Labour in Power*, pp. 85–6.

19. CAB 129/4, CP (45) 260 and 314; HC Deb, 13.12.45.

20. CAB 129/1, CP (45) 112, 14.8.85.

21. It is interesting that the Treasury's own internal history of this episode, written in 1962, blamed not the Americans but only their timing in ending Lend–Lease after VJ Day. It shows, however, suspicion of the IMF, as embodying American influence, while Britain was trying to re-establish sterling and a new monetary order in Europe (T267/3 Treasury Historical memorandum no. 3 which is the main source of what follows). Susan Strange's picture of a benevolent USA facilitating the survival of the sterling area, in *Sterling and British Policy*, derives partly from the way the Attlee government depicted the USA in a favourable light in 1947 so as not to arouse fears of reneging on convertibility.

22. EMAs were intended to establish balance of payments equilibrium on a non-dollar

basis, and protect the home market with quotas. Being intensely restrictive, they were never popular with the countries Britain offered them to, France, Belgium, Sweden and Switzerland.

23. T. Brett, S. Gilliatt, A. Pople: 'Planned Trade, Labour Party Policy and US Intervention', *History Workshop Journal*, vol. 13, 1982.
24. Dalton diaries, f. 33, 7.12.45.
25. cf. Dalton diaries, f. 33: 'our retreat from the world would have been sooner, no election promises fulfilled, austerity worse than at the height of the war, high unemployment, with the near future as black as the pit'.
26. PREM 8/35 (Financial Policy), CP (45) 270, 6.11.45.
27. The FBI, however, had many reservations; memorandum by Sir Clive Baillieu, FBI/MSS200/F1/1/188, October 1945.
28. CAB 129/7, CP (46) 4, 8.2.46.
29. TUC Box T559, Production Campaign, *passim*; Tewson and Dukes to Isaacs, ibid. FGPC 5/1, 5.2.46.
30. The International Committee came under direct US political influence, exercised through the European Recovery Administration by AFL–CIO officials.
31. Oliver Franks, for example, was offered, successively, the NCB by Attlee, British Rail and BP by Churchill; for none of these did he have experience other than at the Ministry of Supply. Other notables had similar experiences, indicating just how administrative, rather than entrepreneurial, senior Ministers thought these jobs were.
32. CAB 130/7 *passim*, especially GEN 80/48, COM/Trade, 5°, 8.10.45.
33. Walter Lipgens, *A History of European Integration*, vol. 1 (1945–47); Alan Milward, in *The Reconstruction of Western Europe 1945–51*, gives a more significant role to nationalistic reconstruction of capital goods industries than to the European Recovery Programme.
34. Economic Planning Committee, CAB 134/503, MEP (46) 12.
35. CAB 134/503, 16–17 January; also Dalton diaries, f. 35, 17.1.47.
36. Sir Alec Cairncross, on Keynes, *Observer*, 5.6.83.
37. CAB 134/503, MEP (46) 3, 26.4.46.
38. The *Star*, 15.11.45. Another article in the *Observer*, 13.1.46, contained the phrase, 'unless the unions will support improvements of method, and not allow their members to obstruct them, it is of no use for the employers to be inventive'.
39. CAB 192/2, CM (45) 36, 30.10.45.
40. CP (46) 130, 3.4.46; CP (46) 148, 10.4.46.
41. CAB 132/88 *passim*.
42. CAB 134/503, MEP (46) 9, 22.10.46.
43. NJAC papers in this period appear deliberately to have been slanted to illustrate the link between wages and inflation; in a new departure, these were now handed to the FBI, even though they were not members of the Committee.
44. It referred specifically to the way intervention by the Truman administration, using the Taft–Hartley Act, had soured industrial relations and increased inflation in the United States.
45. Clive Baillieu to Sir John Woods, BT 64/2221, 11.11.46. The BEC was much impressed with the TUC's 'skill and leadership' during its 1946 Congress (MLNS/JCC 182 para. 12, 30.10.46).
46. TUC EC 6/4, 13.5.47; EC 7/4, 11.5.47.
47. CAB 21/2117, MEP (46) 17, 21.12.46.

48. BEC/EPB/C/500; FBI PA Advisory Committee, 6.5.47; TUC Box 567.1, May 1947.
49. EPB (47) 6, pp. 3–4.
50. T229 no. 63, CP17/04 No. 106, CP46/06; also PREM 8/642, Rowan (Treasury) to Attlee, 24.7.47.
51. K. O. Morgan, *Labour in Power*, p. 135.
52. 'You can persuade, encourage, inspire, but you cannot compel,' Cripps believed (C. A. Cooke, *Cripps*, p. 355).
53. This was confirmed by the reorganisation of NJAC and NPACI in July 1946. The composition of both was altered, to ensure a clear line of demarcation between them, and avoid embroiling BEC and FBI after their second failure to merge. NPACI still had executive functions, but NJAC now became a forum for discussion and mutual education: in Isaacs' phrase 'where government as a whole can communicate . . . the full facts about our economic situation and its implications' (Isaacs to Cripps, LAB 10/622, 11.10.46).
54. MS Attlee, Dep. 50, ff. 113–16.
55. TUC GC2 (Special), 5.11.46.
56. They may also have relied on the Bank's privileged relationships with other central banks which could override antipathies between their governments (as occurred with the Federal Reserve Bank and the Canadian Reserve Bank in 1945–46, 1947 and 1949).
57. Dalton diaries, vol. 34, 12.4.46.
58. Meeting with Ministers FBI MSS 200/F/1/1/215, 21.8.45.
59. Including the NFU, 245 trade associations belonged to it in 1946; and 4478 individual firms, three-quarters of British productive capacity (Mathias, p. 355).
60. 'Improving legislation' was the keynote in dealing with the first round of nationalisation. The FBI wanted to be sure that Ministers would not override Boards in the consumers' interests, nor alter the system of discounted freight rates when taking over road haulage. Co-ordination with Opposition MPs in the House of Commons brought concessions on gas and electricity tariffs for bulk users (Council minutes, MSS/200/F/1/1/188, p. 153).
61. BEC CF/47; BEC C487 II, 10.3.47.
62. MOI NIAC NIC 3–13, 6.8.47; also BEC/NJC 14 (CF487/II).
63. Mathias, p. 394.
64. A. A. Rogow and P. Shore, *The Labour Government and British Industry 1945–51* (1955) p. 44.
65. CAB 134/503, MEP (47) 1°, 7.1.47.
66. FBI memo, BT/4/2237, March 1947. This contained the phrase 'self-government is preferable to good government'.
67. TUC FGPC, 14.1.46.
68. TUC Box 557.1, NPACI (GC) 8, 5.11.46; also EC 3/1, 12.2.47.
69. Arthur Deakin (TGWU), Will Lowther (NUM), Charles Dukes (GMWU), Jack Tanner (AEU), Lincoln Evans (Steel) and John Benstead (NUR). All these unions were normally on the centre and right of the political spectrum. Tom Williams and Tom Yates later replaced Dukes and Benstead.
70. FGPC 5/1, 6.2.46; Tewson's speech, Production Campaign Conference of Executives; and Executive Report, 6.3.46.
71. K. O. Morgan, *Labour in Power*, p. 98.
72. In launching the Prosperity Campaign in March 1946, Ministers used charges of profiteering and poor management to coerce employers; yet they showed

themselves also sensitive to complaints that private industry could not comply unless government reduced personal taxation and convinced unions of the trade-off between union restraint and full employment (PREM 8/318, Production (misc.), March 1946).

73. TUC Box 527.9, 12.9.47.
74. MS Attlee Dep. 71. ff. 234–5; LP RDR 18, March 1946.
75. 'The Nation's Fight for Economic Survival', *TGWU Gazette*, vol. XXV, no. 239, November 1945.
76. CAB 134/503 MEP (46) 13 and 14, 14.11.46 and 27.11.46.
77. CAB 124/1006, 15 (48) 2, 12.3.48.
78. The idea originated in September 1945 as an exercise in presenting to Cabinet competing policies and the pattern of resource allocation that they required (CAB 129/6, CP (46) 32, memorandum by Morrison, 30.1.46). The first essay, in 1946, was kept secret, to protect Ministers from interest group and institutional lobbying.
79. Cmd 7046, p. 3. For an evaluation of the result, see Report by the COI, CAB 143/357, 6.1.48.
80. CAB 135/503, MEP (46) 15; memorandum by Sir Richard Clarke, 21.12.46.

5 CRISIS AND AUSTERITY 1947–49

1. Having been 500 000 at the end of January, unemployment reached nearly 4 million a month later. Production in some industries such as cars and cotton fell by over 50 per cent. The effect on the balance of payments and exports was catastrophic.
2. CAB 130/17, GEN 169/2, 31.1.47.
3. Ibid., GEN 169/3, para. 16, 3.2.47.
4. MS Attlee, Dep. 57, pp. 207–19. The signatories included all fifteen of the 'Keep Left Group'; Crossman, Foot, Callaghan, Whyte and Castle; Attlee reassured himself that it was only a whispering campaign.
5. MEP (46), 5°, 28.10.46.
6. CAB 128/10 CM (47) 65.
7. The deficit reached £450 million by July, against the *Economic Survey* forecast of £350 million for the whole year. The total deficit in hard currency was £600 million, against a £150 million surplus in Eastern Europe. Worse still, American wholesale prices had risen 40 per cent since 1945, and when the USA was running an $8 billion surplus.
8. T 267/3, No. 3, *Treasury History* (1962), p. 48, para. 53. This has to be read, of course, with the Robot affair in mind (see page 199).
9. BT 64/445 minutes of 7.8.47 and 28.8.47. Trade Associations were left to handle the cuts in investment aid, on the presumption that they knew best how to minimise damage (EPB (47) 11, 2.9.47).
10. CAB 129/19, CP (47) 146, 5.5.47.
11. T229/85, memoranda of 28.8.47 and 22.9.47.
12. TUC 110.449, p. 12. For Deakin's struggle see TGWU *Record*, XXVII, no. 319, June 1948; and TGWU Biennial Conference minutes 14, 1949.
13. CAB 129/36, CP (49) 193, 29.9.49.
14. NPACI minutes, 23.7.48.
15. CAB 130/35, February/March 1948. Report of the Working Party on the Economic Consequences of ERP.
16. K. O. Morgan, *Labour in Power 1945–51*, p. 272.

17. Cripps sent Plowden and Hall to meet Jean Monnet in June 1949, but the Foreign Office–Treasury–Attlee line already dominated Cabinet thinking. The Foreign Office had a valid enough reason for opposition, since it feared that, if ERP really did work, rapid recovery would allow the United States to withdraw from Europe, while the Soviet threat would remain. In any case, the Committee on European Economic Co-operation recommended the government not to participate in the European Customs Unions or the Schumann Plan.
18. Notes for EPB (47) 2, 16.7.47; and (47) 7, August nd.
19. TUC EC1 and 2, January/February 1948; EC8, 9.6.48.
20. FBI HEPC minutes, 12.12.47; also correspondence MSS 200/F/1/1/189, pp. 37, 48.
21. HEPC minutes, 4.2.48; also Walker file 79/3. The FBI gained further advantages from negotiations over the White Paper on incomes and prices in February 1948 (S. Blank, *The FBI*, pp. 96–100).
22. FBI members took their places on the JCP as individuals, not in a representative capacity, in order to avoid pointing to any one industry as 'uncompetitive'. ECA officials showed their bias by taking care to make sure that the TUC did accept the 'politics of productivity' (to use Charles S. Maiers' phrase) and brought over AFL–CIO leaders to exhort their British counterparts to the sort of efforts and anti-Communist activity which Irving Brown was fostering in French and Italian union confederations, and in the genesis of the DGB in Germany (cf. Henry Price, *The Marshall Plan and its Meaning* (Cornell University Press, 1955)).
23. One of Morrison's advisers wrote, 'Industrial unrest is a kind of social disease which people engaged in industry develop when they are exposed to certain types of grievances, without having sufficiently high morale to resist infection, or sufficiently good management and labour relations to deal with it on the spot, as soon as it takes shape' (JML (?) to Morrison, CAB 124/1196, 26.10.50).
24. FBI Draft Report on Inflationary Problems, 21.2.48; HEPC, 16.12.48; FBI Council minutes 1701; Annual Report 1947, pp. 10–11.
25. In the Labour Party, they had already been criticised as an extension of the corporate state which would allow unions and management together to gang up against government (LP, RDR 167, October 1948).
26. FBI circular, 10.5.49, answering *inter alia* an article in the *Recorder*, 5.5.49. Correspondence file, Walker to Austin 17.5.49, quoted in Mathias, pp. 447–8.
27. Trend to Kennet, chairman of CIC, T266/94, November 1950.
28. T266/94, Capital Issues Committee report, August 1950.
29. PREM 8/415, EPC (49) 72, Appendix, August 1949.
30. EPC (49), 35°, 14.10.49.
31. Even Bevan worried that the 1949 nationalisation list might frighten them (1944 Association meeting, where Bevan spoke of the need for partnership between the state and small businesses, 13.4.49).
32. CAB 21/2311, July 1948; MS Attlee Dep. vol. 72, ff. 205–8.
33. SI (M) (49) 47.
34. EPC (49) 164, 13.12.49.
35. PREM 8/1039 (especially GEN 300/1), 20.10.49; see also SI (M), (49) 38, p. 2.
36. LP RDR 201, 'Next Stages in Domestic Economic Policy', November 1948; also S. Taylor 'Democratic Socialism – a Restatement', RD 356, May 1950.
37. CAB 134/314, GOC (48) 31 (especially p. 3), 25.10.48. The first 'bonfire of controls' followed in November 1948, the second in March 1949.
38. GOC (49) 3°, 14.10.49.

39. GOC (RO) (51) 2° and 3°, 15.2.51 and 8.3.51. Morrison forecast the substance of their conclusions in July 1947 when he wrote wearily, 'Practical planning cannot be done in some remote Whitehall office and the result dropped on industry from above' (EPB (47) 5, 21.7.47).

40. CAB 134/314, GOC (SC) 51, 1, Appendix 4; also BT 171/191, for the BOT assessment, published by the Central Office of Information as *Government and Industry* (1948).

41. T236/1756, Bridges to Dalton, 11.11.47.

42. Sir Alec Cairncross and Barry Eichengreen, *Sterling in Decline* (1983), p. 142–9.

43. EPC (49) 72, Appendix, para. 11; also PREM 8/976, 3.8.49 (because these reports also went to Attlee).

44. PREM 8/976, 3.8.49.

45. Dalton diaries, vol. 37, 1.7.49; also MS Attlee Dep. 87, ff. 72–80.

46. Sir Roy Harrod, *The British Economy* (1963), p. 25; Sir Alec Cairncross, *Sterling in Decline* ch. 4 (1983).

47. PREM 8/973 8.9.49.

48. FBI HEPC 7.12.49.

49. T229/85 19.8.49.

50. EPC (49) 114, 15.10.49.

51. This was the line developed in 1956 by the Ministry of Labour who argued that wages had risen higher than output consistently through 1946–48 to the detriment of industrial costs and the export drive. The 1948–50 wages policy had then begun the process of matching wages to productivity increases, until the Korean War started. (MOL, NJAC/TUC box 108.22, III). In such ways, long after the event, reviews of history were pressed into justification for departments' contemporary conclusions.

52. Interview with Lord Plowden, D. Jay, *Change and Fortune*, January 1982 p. 203.

53. cf. The Labour Party's 'Inquest on the 1947 municipal elections', LP GS14/5–6, quoted in K. Morgan, p. 315.

54. Beveridge put the point rather more bluntly: 'If our present standard of living is to be justified, everyone should aim at producing 10 per cent more without asking for more wages.' The voice of Liberal England, appalled at the way full employment had already been taken for granted, thus joined the Treasury at last (*Daily Mirror*, 13.7.48).

55. EIU PRO 134/459, 1949 nd (I am indebted to Anthony Lawrence for this quotation).

56. See R. Jeffreys and P. Hennessy, *States of Emergency*, pp. 160–70. For another dispassionate comment see K. Morgan, pp. 375–8.

57. The draft Bill provided penalties of up to fourteen years' imprisonment for subversion or misleading propaganda.

58. TUC FGPC memorandum, 17.2.49; EC 3/4, January 1949: Comments on the 'London Committee for Workers' Control'. The TGWU conducted its own inquiry into Communist infiltration, in May 1950, and vindicated government action.

59. CAB 124/1196 memorandum by Morrison, 21.11.50.

60. Quoted in P. M. Williams, *Hugh Gaitskell* (1976), p. 172.

61. MS Attlee Dep., 86.1.

62. RG23/103 COI: Social Survey Report, November 1948.

63. General Election 1950: Electorate 34.2m. Labour 13.2m (46.1%) 315 seats; Conservatives 12.5m (43.5%) 298 seats; Liberal 2.6m (9.1%).

64. INF 12/245, memorandum, 23.7.49.

6 WHICH WAY IS JERUSALEM?

1. EPC (50) 4, report by Harold Wilson, 30.12.49.
2. According to his covering note, PREM 8/11183, it was prepared without official assistance. Yet it is reasonable to assume that in taking up so many of the questions BOT had had to lay aside in 1943–44, he had been considerably influenced by his department's ethos.
3. P. Williams (ed.), *The Diary of Hugh Gaitskell 1946–56* (1983), p. 330.
4. The proposal for worker-participation came, not from the TUC, but the party (RD 246, January 1949), with the aim of restoring faith in public industries among the workers themselves; it challenged, head on, Morrison's pre-war state corporative model and existing methods of appointment to their Boards; see also Wilson's December 1949 paper to the Fabian Society, 'Public and Private Enterprise', which harked back to his 'New Deal for Coal'.
5. CAB 21/2311, *passim* 1950/51.
6. TUC EC 7/4, 13.4.49; EC 3/1, 8.2.50.
7. PREM 8/1415, CM (49) 51°, minute 2, Appendix, p. 3, 25.7.49.
8. CM (49) 65°, 10.11.49.
9. Cripps, in CM (49) 65°; Morrison in SI (M) (50) 21, 5.5.50.
10. EPC (50) 76.
11. On the question of whether Gaitskell and Attlee manoeuvred in order to rout the left or whether Gaitskell's inexperience led to a disaster, historians of this government disagree. Kenneth Morgan takes the latter view, emphasising the 1951 budget as a watershed. This is, however, to see the rift between Gaitskell and the Bevanites as of recent origin, rather than as a symptom of more ancient and ideological rivalry.
12. PREM/1415, Part 4, Shawcross to Attlee, 7.7.51; J. C. R. Dow wrote caustically to Attlee that BOT's panaceas would scarcely affect the cost of living or wages, but were preferable to increasing food subsidies. Gaitskell approved this (EPC (51) 86, 18.7.51).
13. EPC (51) 17°, 19.7.51.
14. cf. CAB 130/70, GEN 380/4, 27.9.51.
15. LAB 10/662 and 664, 12.8.50: Emmerson wrote 'the department has the principal responsibility for wages policy, but the need to preserve its impartial status holds it back from any major role in pushing specific wage limitation policies'.
16. TUC file 110.44 II; EC (S) 3/1 May 1949; EC (S) 1/2, 5.10.49.
17. LAB 10/993, Rosetti to Sir Richard Gould, 11.9.50.
18. EOWG (50) 61, para. 34, 20.12.50 and LAB 10/933 *passim*.
19. CP (50) 71, Appendix, para. 5, 21.4.50. For the history of the gasworkers' claim, see PREM 8/1305, PC (50) 28 *et seq*, April 1950.
20. SI (M) (50) 7°, 16.9.50.
21. LP RD46, May 1951.
22. T124/1196, Gaitskell memorandum, 9.11.50. According to his figures, average earnings had risen from 101 to 134 between 1945–1950, against which the price index rose from 97.5 to 121 (1944=100).
23. TUC EC (S) 3/4, 6.2.51. Some publicity was given to this point of view at the TUC's Special Conference, February 1950.
24. TUC EC (5) 3/4, 6.2.51.

25. Speech at the United Nations, July 1951. In doing this, he warded off a challenge from Wilson, who had talked of laying a full employment Bill before Parliament.
26. P. Williams (ed.), *Diary of Hugh Gaitskell*, p. 489.
27. Supply officials argued that it should continue service in order 'to promote a vigorous and efficient structure likely to make an enduring contribution to full employment and a sound national currency', but Norman Brook declared that the Ministry of Defence was quite adequate and that Supply's claims to special skills of purchasing amounted to no more than gifted amateurism. It is hard to avoid the conclusion that he and his colleagues wanted a straightforward BOT/MOD demarcation, which would be easier to maintain once the Conservatives had denationalised the steel industry (CAB 21/2051, memorandum, February 1951).
28. GOC (SC) (50) 6, para. 2, 16.6.50.
29. GOC (SC) (50) 5, para. 10, 9.6.50.
30. GOC (SC) (50) 5, 9.6.50.
31. GOC (SC) (51), 26.2.51; the Board of Trade defended the Production Authority system on grounds of stimulating efficiency (similar to those put forward in 1943); the Ministry of Labour seems to have wanted the system eventually to complement its own labour market network (GOC (SC) (50) 2, Emmerson memorandum, 24.1.50).
32. The EOWG's second report may have had some influence, via hints about larger departments, on Churchill's planning of the Overlord system in 1951–52 (GOC (SC) (50) 5, 8.10.51).
33. Helsby to Attlee, MS Attlee Dep. 91, pp. 307–12, 27.10.49.
34. EPC (49) 137, 17.11.49.
35. Britain was, in effect, asking for aid under the pretence of helping Third World countries defend themselves against Communism by using their sterling balances for domestic use. The implied threat, to scrap the sterling system and leave them 'exposed', can barely have been credible in Washington in the summer of 1950, as Robert Hall admitted in a note explaining the manoeuvre as a way of avoiding direct aid 'which would be regarded by public opinion both in the USA and elsewhere, as yet another scheme of help for bankrupt Britain' (Dalton diaries I, f. 41, 26.6.51).
36. EPC (50) 40 and (50) 58, para. 27, 22.2.50.
37. T236/3070, 15.12.51; for the subsequent discussion, see T236/3240.
38. T236/3070, record of meeting, 2.1.52.
39. T236/3240, Clarke to Rowan, 12.2.52.
40. T236/3070, Cobbold to Butler, 7.1.52. Bolton had been advocating early convertibility and cessation of exchange control, both of which were far in advance of Cobbold's own thinking.
41. CAB (52) 10, 14.1.52; also 28.1.52, p. 46.
42. T236/3240, Cobbold to Butler, 13.2.52; for Thorneycroft's view, CC (52) 23°, 28.2.52; for Bridges', T236/3070, note, 8.1.52.
43. Anthony Seldon, *Churchill's Indian Summer* (1981), p. 171.
44. T236/3240, memo, paras. 40–1, 8.2.52.
45. Seldon, p. 172; Lord Birkenhead, *The Prof in Two Worlds* (1961), p. 288.
46. Cherwell wrote that it *could* work, in the long run. 'But in a hard-pressed community like ours, this form of rationing imports by the purse can scarcely ever be promulgated by Conservatives' (T236/3240).
47. T236/2340, p. 11, 22.2.52.

48. Seldon, p. 172.
49. There is no proper minute of this two-day meeting, but a summary appears in T236/3242. Apart from Butler, Lyttleton, Salisbury and Nicholson backed Robot; Cherwell, Woolton, Eden, Crookshank, MacDonald, Swinton, Maxwell Fyfe, Leathers, Thorneycroft, and Monckton opposed. What the remainder, who included Stuart, Macmillan, Dugdale, Gwillym Lloyd George, Peake and Florence Horsburgh thought is not recorded.
50. T236/3242, Cherwell memo, 18.3.52, Rowan 29.3.52.
51. The TUC's last successful action occurred in March 1949, when they persuaded the Dockers and Boilermakers to defer a demand for holidays with pay.
52. TUC EC7, 13.4.49; EC4, 8.3.50.
53. TUC file 110.44II, Woodcock to Tewson, 6.1.50.
54. The Board of Trade argued, cautiously, that it did not wish to break up cartels but merely to ensure 'fair trading'. Rather than attack this impeccable proposition, the FBI tried to circumvent it. Shawcross's Monopolies Commission would evidently be more stringent than Labour's mild Monopolies and Restrictive Practices Act 1948; the FBI therefore asked that its membership be restricted to government, industry and unions, with no representative of consumers or other, possibly ideologically-motivated, 'outsiders'. They also requested that the new body should not begin with an *a priori* definition of the national interest (and certainly not a hypothetical consumer interest) but allow this to emerge slowly as the result of a case by case examination, each on its individual merits.
55. On the question of location and land development charges, the FBI proposed detailed amendments to the Town and Country Planning Act, which were eventually incorporated into the Conservative amending Act of 1952 (Mathias, p. 512). The FBI also took on government over taxation policy, asking for higher investment and depreciation allowances, with support from the British Bankers' Association for investment priority over public industries (FBI, HEPC, 3.5.50; HEPC, 5.4.52).
56. In attempting to discipline three shop stewards in April 1950, the TGWU leadership provoked a much larger dispute, which left the administrators of Order 1305 with an almost insoluble problem of how to deal with an intra-union dispute.
57.

	1949	1950	1951	1952	1953	1954	1955	1956
Consumer Expenditure (£m)	8969	9461	10215	10766	11475	12160	13107	13821
Gross Domestic Capital Formation (£m)	1577	1700	1889	2106	2359	2552	2829	3103
Public Authority Capital Expenditure (£m)	1975	2062	2433	2883	3025	3108	8171	3438
Expenditure (£m)								
Furniture/Durables	467	530	526	476	560	653	664	615
Cars	91	94	90	124	215	271	354	282
Clothing/Footwear	1248	1293	1171	1153	1182	1267	1359	1413
Unemployment per cent	1.6	1.5	1.2	2.1	1.8	1.5	1.2	1.3
Cost of Living (1930 = 000s)	174.9	180.5	197.1	215.0	221.8	225.9	236.0	247.8

(SOURCE: A. H. Halsey, *Trends in British Society* Table 3.3 pp. 84–5; Seldon, *Churchill's Indian Summer*, pp. 501–2.)

58. | Gross Profits % | 1949 | 1950 | 1951 | 1952 | 1953 | 1954 | 1955 | 1956 |
    |---|---|---|---|---|---|---|---|---|
    | Private | 17.8 | 19.6 | 20.9 | 17.0 | 17.0 | 17.8 | 18.6 | 17.6 |
    | Public | 2.5 | 3.0 | 2.8 | 2.4 | 2.8 | 3.1 | 2.7 | 2.8 |

    (SOURCE: Seldon, *Churchill's Indian Summer*, pp. 501–2.)

59. At the election post-mortem held at Dorking in May 1950, party leaders settled in surprising harmony for what Kenneth Morgan calls 'a broad-based, classless appeal . . . a more dynamic version of consolidation, based on the mixed economy and planning through consensus, but with further advance well in mind also' (*Labour in Power*, p. 415).

60. PREM 8/1289, Anderson to Attlee, 2.5.50.

61. Jeffreys and Hennessey, pp. 181–90. As Chairman of the Electricity Board, Citrine was, of course, among those in the know, and he pressed for strongest measures, fearing actual sabotage in power stations in 1950–51. From outside, Deakin assisted by crying 'Reds' even though Special Branch and the Director of Public Prosecutions were more sceptical.

62. As the Labour Research Department noted, in 1950: 'the trade unions through the TUC, the trade associations through the FBI and NUM, the Chambers of Commerce through ABCC, and the banking and financial interests through the Bank of England are being linked more closely and openly to the central government, *as is required under a planned economy*' [my italics] (LPRD 246, March 1950).

63. About Labour's inheritance there is much argument; see T. Burridge, *British Labour and Hitler's War* (1976), pp. 164–72. For Labour's legacy, see J. France, *British Foreign Policy 1945–1973* (1981), pp. 185–6, which records Bevin's and then Morrison's communications with the Shadow Foreign Secretary, Eden, 1945–51.

64. The Conservatives immediately began a defence review which allowed Churchill in January 1952 to propose £250m of savings. Duncan Sandys, Minister of Supply, criticised the 1951 defence estimates as having been formulated 'on the unrealistic assumption that all necessary labour, materials and machine tools would be available when and where required' (CAB 129/48, CP (51) 27, The Progress of Rearmament Production, 26.11.51). As Morgan points out, actual expenditure, at £3 878m for 1951–4, fell far short of the £4 700m allocated (*Labour in Power*, p. 460).

7 PARTIES AND INSTITUTIONS, 1951–56

1. For a good description of the Research Department team, headed by Michael Fraser, see John Ramsden, *The Making of Conservative Party Policy* (1980), chs 5 and 6.

2. J. D. Hoffman, *The Conservative Party in Opposition*, pp. 137–42.

3. There were hints, however, of sterner measures than 'reliance on public opinion' in R. A. Butler's booklet, *Fundamental Issues* (1946).

4. R. A. Butler, *The Art of the Possible*, pp. 145–7.

5. This was evidently what Hopkinson had in mind, but it was anathema to those like Maxwell-Fyfe. The Research Department's view prevailed, partly because of the TUC's responsible conduct of its 1946 Congress (DCPS/11 Trade and Industry

(General)). This issue came up again before the 1951 election, but was dismissed (Box 3001, July 1950).

6. Ramsden, pp. 155–6; Butler p. 155. Evidence for the popularity of the housing pledge is to be found in a CRD Survey, 27.7.50.
7. 1950 Electorate 34.2m; Conservatives 12.5m, 43.5 per cent (293 seats); Labour 13.2m, 46.1 per cent (315 seats); Liberals 2.6m, 9.1 per cent (10 seats) majority 10. 1951 Electorate 34.6m; Conservatives 13.7m, 48.0 per cent (321 seats); Labour 13.9m, 48.6 per cent (295 seats); Liberals 0.7m, 2.5 per cent (6 seats); majority 17.
8. CRD Box 502, file E/FIG, 1950.
9. For this interchange see CRD Box 503, file E/F19, 2.5.51.
10. Ibid., July 1947 *et seq.*
11. CCO 4/4/287, 3.10.51; for Eden's views, see his speech at Liverpool, 4.10.46.
12. CRD Box 52, file E/F19, 2.5.51.
13. Ibid., note by CRD, July 1949.
14. Churchill once told John Colville that his policy was 'houses, red meat, and not getting scuppered' (A. Seldon, *Churchill's Indian Summer*, p. 30).
15. Quoted in Butler, *Art of the Possible*, p. 156.
16. CRD file IR172, policy document 1953; Ramsden, *Conservative Policy*, p. 176.
17. cf. M. Pinto-Duschinsky, 'Bread and Circuses' in V. Bogdanor and R. Skidelsky, *The Age of Affluence 1951–64* (1970), pp. 53–63.
18. For a detailed history of Churchill's illnesses, and the attempts to oust him, see Seldon, pp. 139–45; also James Stuart, *The Day Before Yesterday* (1968), pp. 145–7.
19. Bevan, Castle, Driberg and Mikardo were joined by Wilson and Crossman in the NEC election in 1952.
20. HPC R471, February 1953. A clearer standpoint can be found in *New Fabian Essays* (1952) edited by R. H. S. Crossman, especially in Austin Albu's essay 'The Organisation of Industry', which carried on what Wilson had tried to do at BOT, making the private sector accountable to national aims, with changes in company law to provide for worker participation and permanent dividend limitations without impairing the mixed economy. See also *The Anatomy of Private Industry*, Fabian Society Pamphlet, no. 145, 1953.
21. HPC R495, March 1955; see also R. H. Tawney, 'British Socialism Today' in *The Radical Tradition* (1964).
22. 1944 Association minutes, 15.12.56.
23. TUC AR 1952, p. 300; H. Pelling, *History of British Trade Unionism*, p. 234.
24. EC 2/2, 12.11.52.
25. TUC File 557.1, *passim.*
26. NPACI (GC), 1.8.50; also NPACI (GC), 30.3.50 and TUC AR, p. 548, 1949.
27. Production Committee 1/2, especially para. 20, 14.10.54.
28. Box 502, file 108.21, I/II/III; NJAC (GC) 5, 26.7.55; MOL JCC, 28.11.55.
29. Assailed because of his harsh 1952 Budget, Butler carefully assured the General Council that he would never use unemployment as lever to hold down wages. Given this sort of guarantee, and despite some doubts set off by the 1952 *Economic Survey*, the Economic Committee gave him in return assurances about productivity. When Butler later, in 1953, fastened on wage increases as 'unreasonable', he put the TUC in baulk: accepting that it was necessary to prevent inflation, they had nevertheless to defend their members' natural linkage between wages and the cost of living.
30. EC 7/1, notes on Labour Party Documents, 1953; also EC 5/2, 11.2.53.
31. EC 5/1, 10.2.54.

32. EC8, May 1954.

33. TGWU FGPC minutes, vol. XXX, p. 46, 1952.

34. When Deakin retired, Jack Tiffin was elected General Secretary, but died after a few months. The lay Executive had chosen Cousins as his deputy, and he then succeeded.

35. Plant bargaining really set in during the TGWU negotiations with Standard Motors between 1948 and 1951. Subsequently the rivalry of the car barons, Leonard Lord, Sir William Rootes, and the heirs of Lord Nuffield allowed it to develop rapidly in the early 1950s; by 1955, it had penetrated the aircraft and electrical industries. The annual round of *national* wage increases was, of course, now well-established.

36. After Vic Feather's disciplinary offensive during the Cold War period, anti-Communism declined in intensity. Woodcock never had much stomach for this sort of fight, in unions and in trades councils. No one attempted, in the years after 1951, to ask why the CPGB continued to win support among the rank and file in certain unions.

37. TUC FGPC (3) 11, memorandum on Industrial Disputes, 11.7.55.

38. TUC FGPC 10, 27.6.55.

39. TUC AR, p. 262, 1956.

40. BEC, AGM, 7.5.53.

41. BEC GPC item 1084, 28.9.55; general correspondence C1, C92, C1245.

42. BEC GPC, 23.9.53 *et seq*; see also the BEC President, Andrew Graham Stewart's speeches to 1954 and 1955 AGMs.

43. cf. the BEC inquiry into the 'functions and privileges' of shop stewards, which concluded that there was a clear correlation between the number of shop stewards and the frequency of unofficial disputes (GPC minutes, 22.3.55; 10.5.55). This argued that 'the ease with which instigators of strikes could, in conditions of over full employment, recover their jobs is a major factor in increasing their incidence'.

44. Eric Wigham, *The Power to Manage* (1973), p. 178.

45. By 1950, Britain had more or less recovered its 1938 export level. This level was maintained down to 1955, but represented a slowly declining percentage of total world trade, 23 per cent in 1953. By 1955 invisible earnings covered less of the import bill, yet defence and other overseas expenditure did not shrink, after the initial cuts of 1952, making the balance of payments problematic.

46. FBI, HEPC, 29.10.56; also 'Economic Problems and Policies of the U.K.' (FBI, October 1956).

47. FBI, GC. 8.6.55; correspondence with the Monopolies Commission, February 1955.

48. FBI Panel on Monopolies, 9.12.55; 30.1.56.

49. Mathias, 'The FBI', pp. 665–700.

50. FBI, GC minutes, 11.7.56; 10.10.56.

51. One of the first to take up this cause was George Schwarz: 'It is time that somebody reminded such bodies as the FBI and the TUC that they are not estates of the realm, charged with a share in the government of this country' (*The Sunday Times*, 23.12.51).

52. HEPC, 24.4.56, replying to Macmillan's letter of 20.3.56.

53. cf. Samuel Brittain, *The Treasury under the Tories* (1964) for an unflattering picture of both Cobbold and the Bank's activity.

54. The sterling area could no longer be an unmitigated advantage, and after 1952 probably absorbed more British capital in vast infrastructure developments like the

Volta Barrage in Ghana than the country could afford on a rational calculation. The Bank was consciously preparing sterling area countries in Africa for independence by training future Central Bank governors, and trying to implant the concepts of a common currency, common action in the international sphere, and a common interest in preventing emergent nations from excessive borrowing to fund rapid and unstable plans for industrialisation (as occurred of course in India in the 1950s and to a lesser extent in Ghana, Nigeria and Zambia). The intention of giving them sufficient financial strength not to have to depend on one or other of the super powers, or multinational corporations, can be seen as a subtle form of neo-imperialism, but its relative altruism and the choice of men who would ensure that their successors would not be white ex-patriates set it on a very different level from contemporary French, Belgian or Portuguese policies.

55. cf. H. G. Johnson, 'The Revival of Monetary Policy in Britain', *Three Banks' Review*, June 1956.

8 MEN AND ISSUES

1. For a very full analysis of these relationships, see Seldon, *Churchill's Indian Summer*.
2. Ibid., p. 109. The list included nine major problems of economic management, four of which were later the subject of inquiries by 'Padmore Committees'.
3. Ibid., pp. 102–6.
4. Sir Frank Lee, *The Board of Trade* (1958), p. 11.
5. Sir Edward Bridges, *The Treasury* (1964), pp. 177–9. The Royal Commission on the Civil Service, 1953–55, barely concerned itself with these issues, but only pay and conditions. D. N. Chester, however, conducted his own inquiry, in the 'New Whitehall' Series (RIPA, 1952).
6. Sir Thomas Dugdale followed closely the pattern established by Tom Williams of close, even corporatist contact with the NFU, a development enhanced in 1954 when the merger of Agriculture with Food effectively ended consumer representation. Until 1960–62, when the Macmillan government made Britain's first application to join the EEC, MAF concentrated on achieving maximum food production and safeguarded farming profitability with high guaranteed prices and assistance to small farmers.
7. After the war BEA and BOAC had been allocated virtual monopolies of all Britain's scheduled routes, though small loopholes were left for independent carriers. Far more than in the 1930s, the Ministry safeguarded the aerospace industry in the hope of staving off American competition, until the Comet disasters in 1954 destroyed Britain's primacy in design and manufacture. Subsequent delays in producing the next-stage aircraft, the Britannia, led BOAC to choose American models in the later 1950s. Similar attempts were made to protect British shipowners against American protectionism and the spread of flags of convenience. As far as domestic transport was concerned, the Ministry of Transport capitulated almost entirely to the views of industry (specifically the road transport lobby), and allowed the British Transport Commission to neglect railway innovation and investment for eight years, leaving a legacy of retardation which even Beeching's 1955 proposals could not remedy.
8. Sir Norman Kipping, *Summing Up* (1972), pp. 89–90.

9. For the whole debate, see CAB 134/794 (O), GEN 380 *passim* and CAB 134/787, Committee on Commercial Policy, 1952.

10. Seldon, *Churchill's Indian Summer*, p. 169.

11. Ibid., p. 183.

12. The diplomats of the time (according to Lord Sherfield (Sir Roger Makins) interview September 1982) believed that Monnet and Schumann only wanted Britain in the Coal and Steel Community if she would agree to monetary and political integration (Monnet hinted as much to Plowden in 1954). They also feared that the Eisenhower administration would use the ECSC as an excuse to withdraw its military presence from Europe, and clung, therefore, all the more strongly to Britain's 'special relationship', much as Baldwin had clung to American interest in resolving the problem of German reparations in 1923–24.

13. The ISB received protective advantages, through the Import Duties Advisory Commission. As in the 1930s, when the banks had put in Sir Andrew Duncan as chairman, the steel companies remained in the hands of the finance sector and proved (until the late 1960s) to be unwilling to take risks or go in for new investment and high technology. Thus, even after Korea, their capacity was often overstretched in the boom years, so that an illusion grew up that they need not rationalise production for a future when they would have to compete against European, American or Japanese producers.

14. Monckton papers, Box 49.

15. Lord Birkenhead, *Walter Monckton* (1969), pp. 279–80; Monckton papers, Box 2, correspondence, 1950–55.

16. Ibid., Box 49.

17. Sir Norman Kipping, *Summing Up* (1972), pp. 48–9.

18. Seldon, *Churchill's Indian Summer*, p. 200, n. 53.

19. Ibid., p. 203.

20. Private information.

21. This stance, which helped Monckton hold the NUR while fighting ASLEF, had some effect in diverting Eden's mind from thoughts of industrial relations legislation (Birkenhead, *Monckton*, pp. 300–3; David Carlton, *Eden* (1981), pp. 286–7).

22. NJC 193, TUC file 108–22, II, para. 37. For Monckton's overall policy, see Monckton papers, Box 4, general correspondence; including Watkinson's memorandum on industrial relations given to the Conservative Party Labour Committee, 28.1.54.

23. Monckton to Eden, 22.9.55 (Monckton papers, Box 5, general, 1955).

24. Macleod to Eden, 9.1.56; 13.2.56; 14.3.56 (Monckton papers, Box 5).

25. Stephen Blank, *The FBI* (1973), pp. 131–2; Macleod's notes for a speech by Eden in January 1956 Monckton papers, Box 6, 10–11, 9.1.56 read: 'There is no hope of any moderation in wage claims until we get more stable prices. When Cousins said, a day or two ago, that as long as prices rise, wages must rise too, he was no doubt talking economic nonsense, but it remains one of the awkward facts of life that we have to cope with.'

26. Beveridge Box IXA, item 59; item 90: 'The present danger of inflation and full employment'.

27. Private information, MOL official.

28. A. Seldon, *Churchill's Indian Summer*, pp. 160–1. Seldon's account of the transactions of civil servants and Ministers is of the utmost value to any study of the machinery of government in this period.

29. Quoted in Seldon, p. 167, n. 113, n. 114.
30. Hubert Henderson declared shortly before his death in 1951 that any level of unemployment less than 6 per cent was dangerous to equilibrium (Information from Lord Robert Hall). Butler subscribed in private to the view that unemployment ought to be more of a discipline (Butler to Monckton, Monckton papers, Box 2, 7.7.52).
31. Philip Williams, *Hugh Gaitskell* (1982), pp. 312–18.
32. Because the USA was assumed to be an ally so long as the Cold War lasted, overseas expenditure and conventional forces could be allowed to decline (and thus make balance of payments equilibrium easier to achieve). As Seldon points out (pp. 331–4) this represented a reversion to Neville Chamberlain's policy of asking what the nation could afford, rather than working from a concept of national foreign policy, as Attlee had done in Korea. As Britain opted out after the 1952 NATO Conference in Lisbon (Cmd 8475) so the USA moved towards 'massive retaliation' (Rosecrance, *Defence of the Realm* (1980), p. 196 *et seq*). This in turn allowed the government to rely on American strategic power and Britain's own nuclear bomb and V-bomber force (White Papers of 1954 (Cmd 9073) and 1955 (Cmd 9391)).
33. Butler had just raised Bank rate to 4.5 per cent and reintroduced hire purchase restrictions, to check inflation, as he told the Cabinet (Seldon, *Churchill's Indian Summer*, p. 175, n. 42). The younger officials of the Economic Section were, however, vociferous supporters of expansion (private information). The economic conservatives, led by Rowan until his retirement in 1958, relied on the Bank to back them up, and to press for convertibility as an antidote.
34. Eden, *Full Circle*, p. 278, admitted his responsibility. The Research Department looked on with grave concern, but had to acknowledge the importance of backbench forces, and the heavyweights of the Economic Policy Committee (Ramsden, *Conservative Policy*, pp. 177–8).
35. Seldon, *Churchill's Indian Summer*, p. 176; n. 47; Butler, *Art of the Possible*, pp. 177–9.
36. The Conservative share of the vote rose from 48 per cent to 49.7 per cent (though the total numbers fell) which gave them 344 seats, against Labour's 277, on a vote that fell by over 1½ million from 48.8 per cent to 46.4 per cent.
37. *The Economist*, 31.12.55.
38. Private information; see also E. Wigham, *The Power to Manage*, pp. 180–92.
39. David Kilmuir, *Political Adventure* p. 191.
40. The Iron and Steel Board continued pre-war practice and tended to reflect the wishes of Sir Ellis Hunter and the Iron and Steel Federation. In its fourteen years as a half-way house, it contributed to development, without enforcing rationalisation and without bringing in the newest technology. By the time of the second nationalisation, it was more backward in relation to UK competitors than it had been in 1951. (D. Burn, *The Steel Industry 1934–59* (1979), p. 153; J. Vaizey, *History of the British Steel Industry* (1974), pp. 150–79.)
41. In the row over steel prices in 1952, the Steel Board's chairman resigned at having to bow to a Cabinet ruling. (CC (52) 17°, conclusion). Sandys prevented the BTC from raising prices, in April 1952, when Maxwell Fyfe assured the Cabinet that there was a 'national interest in the cost of living' (CAB 128/24, CC (52) 44°, 22.4.51). In the same debate, Churchill refused to accept that a Board might raise its charges 'without the possibility of intervention by the government or parliament'.
42. Seldon, *Churchill's Indian Summer*, p. 195.

43. EPB (52) 7, p. 5, para. 14, 3.10.52. If spending were still to rise, then consumption must be cut back (CAB 134/794 *passim* (Employment Committee), 1951–52 and CAB 134/877, file, 1952).

44. CAB 130/71 (O), GEN 380/1 to 15, 1951–53.

45. T236/3242 *passim*, 1952–53.

46. Butler, *The Art of the Possible*, p. 166–7, quotes Eisenhower's attitude.

47. The Treasury agreed to support *transferable* sterling in the international market, thus making the pound in effect convertible for non-British holders, mainly in non-dollar areas such as the Middle East and Far East.

48. D. Carlton, *Eden*, p. 385.

49. CRD Economic Review, Box 502, 5.9.55.

50. In a paper on finance, trade and industry (Box 502, 3.2.54) in February 1954, the Research Department found itself uncertain whether or not to react positively to these ideas. It reviewed the state of economic management, full employment and the 1944 package, and asked how a Conservative government should deal with unemployment if it rose above the level which had become acceptable. CRD favoured tax reductions and fiscal stimuli, in other words, supply-side policies rather than budget deficits and the use of state industries' spending power. It was by no means clear, however, whether government could – or *should* – stop unemployment rising, as a deterrent to inflation (pp. 36–7). The only certainties appeared to be that it was 'politically impossible' to reduce wages, and disastrous again to devalue (p. 32). But nowhere did it address the question of whether full employment at current levels was compatible with growth.

51. No annual figure is given in the post-war *Annual Abstracts of Statistics* (HMSO) for what is now called the 'public sector borrowing requirement'. The table 'Exchequer Financing' does, however, give the overall budget deficit, less nationalised industries' capital requirements to 1959–60, then the total cash deficit or surplus.

	Overall budget deficit £ million	NIs capital requirements £ million
1951–52	−149	−131
1952–53	−436	−275
1953–54	−297	−310
1954–55	− 68	−175
1955–56	−141	−311
1956–57	−331	+ 15
1957–58	−212	+ 20
1958–59	−182	+ 19
1959–60	−314	+ 18

	Total cash deficit/surplus £ million
1960–61	−502
1961–62	− 32
1962–63	− 12
1963–64	−450

52. 'I knew that if we were to improve our position, I must in particular get my message across to the better-paid, skilled industrial workers who could be expected to benefit from the kind of society we wanted to create' (Eden, *Full Circle*, pp. 299).

53. Macleod–Eden correspondence, 9.1.56; Monckton papers, Box 6, general correspondence; Carlton, *Eden*, pp. 396–7.

54. Butler, *Art of the Possible*, p. 184.
55. CRD Economic Review, Box 502, 5.9.55.
56. P. Hartley, 'The Lost Vocation', *Journal of Contemporary History*, vol. 15, no. 1, January 1980.
57. Butler, *Art of the Possible*, p. 193; Selwyn Lloyd, *Suez*, p. 206; D. Carlton, *Eden*, pp. 425–6, 450–2.
58. NJAC October 1954, NJC 193 (in TUC File 108.22 II).

9 THREATS TO EQUILIBRIUM 1957–61

1. Because of the thirty year rule, prohibiting access to state archives after 1954, it becomes progressively harder to write about policy evolution and thinking inside the Treasury, BOT and MOL. Up to 1955–56, existing trends can be followed; but the next two years were sufficiently disruptive to prevent this for 1957–61. I have relied increasingly, therefore, on interview material, on the institutions' records of transactions with departments and after 1962 on departmental papers to and discussions inside NEDC.
2. Tax reliefs in the 1959 (pre-election) budget were planned with great care in relation to what was known of voting patterns (Ramsden, *Conservative Policy* p. 199, CRD File E/EF/1, Economic (General), Part II).
3. CRD/E/EF/1, J. Douglas to M. Fraser, 20.2.57.
4. Ibid. file ELA9, 'Trade Practices'.
5. Ramsden, *Conservative Policy*, pp. 193–5.
6. CRD file, Policy Study Group, 1957, quoted in Ramsden, *Conservative Policy* p. 213.
7. The debate in CRD started with the conundrum of employment with wages and price equilibrium, and took as its marker the position of mutual responsibility laid down in the 1956 White Paper (File E/EF/1, Part II). Later, however, CRD justified the earliest, voluntarist attempts at a wages policy and the work of the Cohen Council as an alternative to too strict monetary policy (Ibid., 4.7.58). After the 1959 election, its attitude hardened to the point of starting an inquiry into wage inflation, and the possibility of control by using monetary policy, which the Radcliffe Committee (1957) had evaded (Ibid., Part III).
8. CRD Files, Box 506; also CRD/ELA Trade Practices, November 1958.
9. CRD E/EF/1, 17.10.56.
10. Ibid., Douglas to Fraser, 16.11.59.
11. As one of his first acts as Chancellor, Thorneycroft set up an influential study group to prepare the party's evidence for the Radcliffe Committee. They reported in February 1958, after his resignation. Written by David Price, the Report mounted a skilful and damaging attack on the policies of the 1950s, castigating (by implication) both Butler and Macmillan. It put forward a more openly monetarist policy than Thorneycroft had essayed, and may have been intended to strengthen him, for it claimed that a 'true budgetary deficit' had existed ever since 1951–52 (meaning that only Labour governments had kept to the 1944 principles). It recommended heavy reductions in government spending, including 'so-called capital expenditure' on public industries, and it damned especially the housing programme of 1952–55 as a gross distortion of 'productive investment'. Slightly more to the Cabinet's taste, it advised support for employers in resisting wage demands, but it specifically blamed

Macmillan for letting down the EEF in 1957. It also criticised the practice of 'unsound finance' in certain Dominions – a crack at India for its threats during the Suez crisis – and proposed the establishment of a Committee of Commonwealth Central Bankers to curb it.

12. CRD File E/EF/1, 1958–60. A Committee chaired by Toby Low came out in favour of unit trusts and 'share-owning democracy'.

13. Quoted in Ramsden, *Conservative Policy*, p. 203.

14. A conclusion not substantiated by Butler and Rose in their study of the 1959 election, who pointed instead to the behaviour of the non-aligned centre which, they believed, thought it did not matter which party was in power, during the previous eighteen months (*The British General Election of 1959*, pp. 199–200).

15. As S. Brittan pointed out in *The Treasury under the Tories* (1964), p. 122, the Treasury developed the practice of publishing figures of the reserves at the lowest possible level, to induce caution in their political masters.

16. EPB (57) 11 & 12, 29.3.57.

17. British trade performance had been particularly poor the previous year. At the same time, the long transfer from sterling area to European markets accelerated, and exposed the fact that Britain's decline in exports was to be explained less by costs than non-price factors (EPB (57) 13, 29.7.57).

18. Macmillan cast around for alternative views outside government and consulted Monckton, now Chairman of the Midland Bank, hoping that he could give a conclusive answer to the Bank of England. Monckton had to disappoint him (Monckton papers vol. 11, pp. 46–7, August 1957).

19. Interview with Lord Thorneycroft, March 1981.

20. Interview with Lord Sherfield (Sir Roger Makins), September 1981.

21. House of Commons' debates, vol. 603, col. 41, 7.4.58.

22. Rowan made this point obliquely in his evidence to the Radcliffe Commission. In answer to a question by Cairncross about a common policy between Britain and the Six over reserves, Rowan said bluntly that Britain could not envisage either such a policy or economic integration.

23. Private information, Treasury official.

24. Cobbold did not want to lower Bank rate, but could not argue the real reason (which was to forestall an unwise Budget like that of 1955) and pleaded technical difficulties instead. Macmillan wrote that the Bank would bring ruin on itself and the nation: only if traditional, that is Keynesian, remedies were followed would the recession end. 'The Conservative Party will be re-elected, prosperity will be secured, the Bank of England will be preserved, and funding in 1960 will be easier than ever before'. Monckton reassured him that opinion among Midland Bank advisors supported a stimulus to consumption and confirmed the need for government deficit. (Macmillan to Monckton correspondence, Monckton papers vol. 11, pp. 46–7 February/March 1959).

25. Kennedy won, by a narrow margin, in November 1960. Some of his new advisers wanted Britain to devalue the pound; others forecast this and prepared to insulate the American economy against the consequences (interviews with Professor Sherman Maizel and Professor Milton Friedman, March 1984).

26. Lord Cobbold: evidence to the Canadian Royal Commission on Banking, Ottawa, question 4083, 1962.

27. According to Brittan, *Treasury under the Tories*, p. 232, the Treasury wanted an even tighter squeeze, but Lloyd resisted.

28. During 1960–61, the Treasury took care to try to educate both sides through EPB, but the way they objected to the appointment of Len Murray (EPB (60) 12, 2.9.60) suggests that they wished to exclude TUC radicals. Murray, in fact, did a great deal to galvanise the moribund EPB before it was subsumed into NEDC (cf. 'Notes on Growth', EPB (61) 4).

29. Sir Hugh Ellis-Rees's history of the 1947 crisis was completed soon afterwards, and its conclusions clearly reflect this 1961 standpoint. His codicil (p. 66) used the 1947 example to argue as a general principle against use of import controls which some bankers in 1961 apparently wanted (T 267/3, No. 3).

30. The Bank at first argued against the introduction of the special deposits scheme, detecting in its use by government a threat to its own power and status in the City; later, it made a virtue of it so long as it was allowed to run the scheme in its own way.

31. Cobbold had spoken out, for example, to bankers and at other annual dinners in 1957–59, and after retirement in his extensive and relatively outspoken evidence to the Canadian Royal Commission on Banking in 1962. But his slightly alarmist note only points up how little impact he made on a Prime Minister who was not, even in private, prepared to listen beyond the dictates of courtesy. This may explain why the Bank's quarterly *Bulletin* eventually became a preferred vehicle for guarded criticism.

32. The clearing banks, competing in the money market in the mid- and late 1960s, worried much less about government borrowing than about the share going to building societies rather than industry (see, for example, Monckton's view in note 24, above). Cobbold's own opinion was that bank rate was no deterrent until it reached 7 per cent (Canadian Royal Commission, minutes of evidence, question 4024, 1962). The Thompson Committee's recommendations on mobilising new sources of capital (1958) and Cobbold's own warnings about shrinking corporate profits after 1959 were largely ignored; it was only later that the Midland, Williams & Glyn's and Lloyds developed the interbank market.

33. Canadian Royal Commission, questions 4081–3.

34. cf. Cobbold's statement, that mass unemployment was 'the greatest failure on behalf of the fiscal and monetary authorities of any they could make in present circumstances' (question 4033). He added that the Bank had been left to carry too heavy a part of the battle against inflation, 'with insufficient support from the fiscal side' (question 4024).

35. In particular, it supported the ousting of Sir Bernard Docker, Chairman of the Birmingham Railway Carriage Company, and Sir Leslie Rowan, who had become Chairman of Vickers.

36. British Railways had been allowed, under the uninspired chairmanship of Sir Brian Robinson, to accumulate a backlog of debt, inadequate investment and poor industrial relations from which it looked almost impossible to escape. Added to a history of inter-union strife, caused by the long decline of the old craft union ASLEF and the NUR's growth, this record apparently condemned the railways to terminal decline. When Dr Beeching was appointed (having served already on the Prime Minister's special advisory group on transport) British Railways' modernisation programme had fallen five years behind, while its cost had risen almost out of control. Beeching's standing with the Prime Minister and Ernest Marples, the Minister of Transport, however, gave him unusual authority, though his assertion of the right of public industry chairman to manage eventually made him unpopular in Cabinet.

Aided by Sir Henry Benson (later a special advisor on industry to the Bank of England), Beeching chose to rationalise the network and its services, rather than cut each region by 10 per cent, as the Steddiford Committee had recommended. This in itself could only be a preliminary, and Beeching went far beyond his celebrated 'cuts' to try to pay equivalent salaries, regain management power and restore the autonomy which Morrison had originally intended. In spite of Marples' support, and that of the surviving Padmore Committees, however he could not escape the Chancellor's *démarche* in July 1961; hence his quarrel with Lloyd, for the investment cuts and pay pause came at the very moment when he had hoped to carry both NUR and ASLEF into a long-term, fair-wages agreement. Peace on that issue might have been a mirage, in any case, but the 3 per cent increase for 1962 which was all he could wring from Cabinet, looked to the unions like a betrayal and they called off the deal. ·

37. Business education, for example, was left to the BIM and the Ministry of Education who were jointly responsible for the institution of the first postgraduate business schools, in 1959–61. Scientific manpower policy and technical education likewise developed outside BOT, in ACPS, in the scientific lobby of men like Sir Solly Zuckerman and Sir Basil Blackett, and among Ministry of Supply officials such as Aubrey Jones, who became concerned about the technical backwardness of industry and its ability to supply defence requirements. Discussions about a Ministry of Technology achieved no more than the appointment of Lord Hailsham to the junior Ministry of Science, but Blackett and Zuckerman, both of whom had contacts with Harold Wilson and the Opposition, succeeded in planting the idea there.

38. This view appears clearly in Sir Frank Lee's evidence to the Radcliffe Committee. It drew on empirical evidence: when the Lancashire cotton industry was reorganised in 1958–59 (government providing grants to replace old machinery), neither Treasury nor BOT was able to ensure that spare capacity was reduced, any more than they had been able to enforce a similar bargain on the steel industry in the mid-1930s. State deficiencies, lack of expert knowledge of the industry and lack of business ability can be detected in government dealings with the aerospace industry. Macmillan had appointed Sir Percy Mills, who had helped him achieve the housing targets in 1952–54, in order to promote mergers among the aircraft producers. Rather than enforce nationalisation, as the Minister of Transport and Civil Aviation, Harold Watkinson, had intended to do, Mills distributed government development funds equally to Hawker–Siddeley and Handley–Page, thus facilitating an over-expansion which Duncan Sandys later had, with much forcible intervention, to curtail in the early 1960s. Civil atomic energy provides another instance: for Britain continued to suffer from the closed circuit of policy-making described in an earlier period by Margaret Gowing and Duncan Burn, so that it reached a condition of almost unique inefficiency by 1961 – a poor basis for the ambitious programme of advanced gas-cooled reactors (AGRs) in 1965 (cf. Roger Williams, *Nuclear Power Decisions 1953–78* (1980)).

39. Maudling, for example, seems to have known very little of the French system before 1961 (R. K. Middlemas, *Industry, Unions and Government* (1983), pp. 11–12).

40. Letter to the author, July 1981.

41. · Monckton papers 29, Macleod–Monckton correspondence, October 1957– November 1958; see also Nigel Fisher, *Iain Macleod* (1973), p. 111.

42. The main malpractices, according to MOL officials, were: endemic breaches of procedures and agreements, often with management connivance; inter-union poaching and demarcation disputes; low productivity (again, partly the fault of

management) and opposition to technical innovation and change. Specific evidence abounded: the TUC itself documented Communist Party and Trotskyite activities in the engineering industry, while the conditions of the car industry made Britain a by-word across Europe and North American. The almost anarchic conditions of the Ford plant at Dagenham which led Ford USA to contemplate closure of the plant were documented in MOL's own inquiries and a series of reports, above all that on the Briggs Motor Bodies Works in 1957. Even good private firms (like Birfields) in the engineering industry with a long history of good industrial relations could not isolate themselves from the prevailing climate at a time when the AEU was contesting the rise of the shop stewards movement, and the early combines, at Coventry and on Merseyside. In private, its General Secretary Carron could admit to abuses and provocation by political extremists, in firms like Hardy Spicer, but not in public. A pusillanimous EEF, weakened by the 1957 débâcle, avoided challenging either, even through the Procedure.

43. cf. S. J. Prais, *The Evolution of the Giant Firm in Britain* (1981). A notable case at this time was Courtauld's 'survival strategy' which involved taking over all rayon production. In turn, in 1961, ICI tried to take over Courtaulds. It failed but was left with a 20 per cent holding (Donald Coleman, *History of Courtaulds*, vol. 3 (1980)). Similar processes were at work in the car industry, most obviously in the BMC–Leyland merger in 1968 (K. Williams *et al.*, *Why Are the British Bad at Manufacturing?* (1984), pp. 217–39).

44. Evidence to the Royal Commission on Banking, Ottawa, question 4024, 1962.

45. In working out its policy towards European integration, the FBI consulted widely and consistently among its members after 1956, and kept in touch with comparable organisations in Europe. Sir William McFadzean (BICC) and Sir Hugh Beaver (Guinness) acted as the diplomatists. For a time, even after the Spaak Report, the FBI (under the influence of trade associations afraid suddenly of having to face up to a new competition) imagined that Britain might benefit from a reduction of European tariffs without losing the vestigial advantages of Commonwealth preferences (Council minutes, 13.6.56). Among industries, only farming and consumer goods were divided, while the majority, metal-working, engineering, chemicals, vehicles, construction and most textiles were in favour (Mathias, 'The FBI', p. 679 and Appendix I). Small business, mainly represented by the NUM, collectively opposed it, but the ABCC remained in doubt.

    When EFTA negotiations began in 1957, the FBI veered away from the EEC idea with its overtones of political and monetary integration. But the majority continued to hope that an EFTA–EEC grouping might emerge, as Thorneycroft had indicated was the government's aim (Thorneycroft to the General Council, 18.4.57). Britain grew more isolated, and in the remaining months before signature of the Treaty of Rome, the FBI's diplomatists scurried desperately around Europe trying to capitalise, against their own government, on the residue of goodwill among their German, Belgian or Dutch colleagues. By the end of 1958, they accepted defeat.

    The BEC stayed hostile to the EEC throughout, because they feared that France would insist on the forty-hour week, and harmonising of social policy, equal pay and paid holidays, with disastrous effects on the real cost of British labour. But once EFTA existed, they changed course. So did the NFU, as the FBI and BEC began to see EFTA as something which Britain could mould to her own advantage, and as a mass of manoeuvre *vis-à-vis* the EEC jointly to reduce tariffs. This had always been the FBI's intention, so their fury when, in May 1960, the government went ahead with the GATT–Kennedy round, cutting tariffs by 20 per cent and throwing away Britain's hypothetical advantage, is understandable (Council minutes, 13.7.60). Thereafter a general confluence can be observed, in which the industrial institutions, independently of government, prepared themselves for a British EEC application. (ICI's Planning Group, for example, set out in 1960 to plan the pattern of their future European factories on the assumption that EFTA was no more than a staging post.) At the top, in the Export Council for Europe (of which McFadzean became Chairman), FBI, ABCC, NUM and City institutions joined, together with the TUC, some months before Heath (then Lord Privy Seal) indicated in March 1961 that the government would, indeed, apply for membership.

46. Sir Archibald Forbes, a cautious President, prevented Council from outright opposition, but the FBI's characteristic strategy of indirect approach can be read in its protest that the measure was 'intrinsically bad for the financial and industrial structure of the country' (FBI General Council minutes, 12.11.57).

47. FBI evidence to CPPI, December 1957; BEC papers, general correspondence (CPPI), June 1958.

48. The EEF believed that Macmillan, then Chancellor, had promised them government support if they stood up to the AEU's wage claim. That was before Suez. After several months sparring, they felt uneasy when, in March 1957, Macmillan, then Prime Minister, announced in a speech at Leicester that 'in the long run, and for the common good, the umpire is better than the duel'. But it was not until the national engineering strike broke out, shortly before the Anglo-American negotiations at Nassau were due to start, and at a time when Macleod had become gravely worried about the pattern of wages on the railways, that they realised how little support would be forthcoming. Summoned to No. 10, the EEF leaders were virtually ordered by Macmillan and Macleod to settle on the best terms they could. The EEF Board was divided, as the Prime Minister probably knew. After this *démarche* it split, 42–18, and did, in fact, settle for what Carron and the AEU, by now extremely angry, would accept. For years, the conviction lingered that they had been betrayed by the great prestigiditator (E. Wigham: *The Power to Manage*, pp. 164–92; private information).

49. BEC, C500, Pollock to Kipping, general correspondence, 8.5.57.

50. 'We believe that inflation is inevitable so long as any government makes the avoidance of any significant unemployment a prime principle of policy, because this practice produces a chronic tendency to overfull employment. It is essential to restore labour mobility and workshop discipline, to stop hoarding of labour and to remove the temptation to employ unemployables. We cannot see how this can be done without some margin of unemployment' (AGM Report, p. 288, 1958).

51. Council minutes, item 1657, 28.10.59. In January 1961, they invited Woodcock to address a conference on collective bargaining.

52.

	1954	1959	1960
Unofficial stoppages	110	280	400
Days lost per 1 000 employees	49	173	291

53. BEC Council minutes, item 1728, 25.1.61 and items 1739–40, 26.4.61.

54. Ibid., item 1629, 28.1.59; item 1706, 26.10.60.

55. Ibid., item 1739, 26.4.61.

56. Ibid., item 1754, 26.7.61. If both BEC and TUC stood together, 'it might be possible to secure that departures from collective agreements would be the exception' (AGM, p. 310, 1962).

57. BEC statement, NC 18429, May 1961.

10 THE NEW OPPOSITION AND THE OLD

1. Economic Committee to BOT, 12.6.57 (EC 11/4). Having decided to support EFTA in October 1956, the TUC remained guarded until it could be certain that the British government would not succumb to supranational authority. The TUC found in national control over policy an antidote to what it saw as the conservatism of European institutions. Like the FBI, the TUC soon realised that EFTA could only be a stage, of immediate value to Britain's trade but inadequate compared with the EEC as a guarantee of stable trading patterns and high employment and prosperity (Research Department memorandum, 4.12.59, on EPB (59) 25 and 27).

2. EC3, 14.11.56; EC 13/2, 14.8.57. This inquiry continued into 1959. The AEU carefully explained the role and powers of shop stewards, and deprecated talk of a 'movement' like that of 1917–21. William Carron, the President, of course disliked Combine Committees and shop stewards' intrusion on the union's lay committees.

3. EC 3/6, 9.11.55. Research papers early in 1956 frequently stated that the TUC had to be more than a passive group acting on behalf of the most militant sections of the movement.

4. By 1957, unions headed the list of factors held responsible by respondents for the current economic situation (Gallup Report No. 20, August 1957). Anthony Crosland noted similar feelings in *Can Labour Win?* (1959).

5. TUC RD, Deakin's correspondence, March 1954, EC 8/2 para. 5, 21.2.56.

6. EC10, 11.4.56.

7. cf. Macmillan–Woodcock correspondence, March 1956; EC 10/1 paras. 34–37.

8. EC 13/1, 13.6.56, EC14, 11.7.56.

9. The questions were, briefly, about the relationship of prices, productivity and wages; the importance of the general level of demand; whether government could control demand; what were the most important factors in setting the trends of prices, wages and productivity; what was the effect of the collective bargaining system, and restrictive practices; and whether voluntary wage restraint was possible.

10. EC 1/6 and EC1, 9.10.57.

11. EC2 2/4 and 2/6, 13.11.57.

12. EC5, 10.2.60.

13. NJAC (GC) 2/1, 16.11.59, para. 14.

14. Production Committee 3/1, 15.4.59, para. 21.

15. TUC NI Committee 1/1, 1.7.60.

16. In the ETU, Communist activity continued for many years. Even after the party's hold on the leadership had been broken, Frank Chapple and those elected to the Executive in 1961 had to contend not so much with Foulkes' legacy as with the undoubted skill of CPGB members at local level in perceiving and exploiting grievances.

17. The TUC particularly disliked the party's 1957 scheme for the state to acquire an equity holding in six hundred leading companies (EC 8/2, 13.3.57), partly because public sentiment ran the other way, partly because it suspected that too wide state ownership would constrain the freedom of public sector unions to bargain with the government of the day.

18. LP RD 398, May 1958.

19. According to Harold Wilson 'this is not a substitute for traditional forms of nationalisation . . . [but] a new analysis of contemporary capitalism' (LPACR 1957,

p. 128). The settlement was made easier because Bevan now abandoned his fight for unilateral disarmament.

20. According to Michael Foot (*Aneurin Bevan*, p. 630), the Gaitskellites made a pre-emptive strike before the November Conference. Dalton diaries f. 51, and Douglas Jay (*Change and Fortunes* (1981), p. 272), argue that it was simply a move to confirm the Gaitskell–Crosland policy as the future 'radical' line. For Gaitskell's part see P. Williams, *Gaitskell*, pp. 556–80. Crossman (*Backbench Diaries*, ed. Janet Morgan (1981)) confirms the degree of personal venom. Dalton, never one for modest phrases, talked of the Party's 'massive bone-headedness' (Dalton diaries f. 51, entry for 13.7.60).

21. Williams, *Gaitskell*, p. 558, notes a TUC attempt to warn Gaitskell off the whole modernisation campaign. In 'Can Labour Win?', Crosland advocated a larger policy role for the PLP – inevitably to the TUC's detriment.

22. NEC Minutes, 16.3.60.

23. NEC Minutes, 13.7.60. Abrams had published his findings in *Socialist Commentary*, Summer 1960.

24. NEC Minutes, 23.11.60. For a general discussion, see Lewis Minkin, *The Labour Party Conference*, ch. 10.

25. cf. Gaitskell's speech to the 1944 Association (15.4.59). From the list of those who attended the 1944 Association meetings in the difficult years, 1959–61 (Jay, Wilson, Callaghan, Jenkins, Castle and Robens) it seems to have lost nothing of its significance as a conduit for influencing industrial opinion.

26. Among Labour's economists, Thomas Balogh favoured entry to the EEC as a means to overcome Britain's retardation and relative decline. He now deplored the GATT liberal trading system because it exposed Britain to the dilemma of deflation or devaluation, and he envisaged the EEC as a super-cartel, in which Britain would have greater autonomy to defend herself. This was at first a minority view, with which Nicholas Kaldor disagreed.

11 CONCLUSION

1. Gallup polls were beginning to reveal a pervasive fear of unemployment, inflation and decline in the standard of living. After the shock to expectations in July 1961, Gallup concluded that there was 'considerable support for the belief that Britain needs "more government planning and control of industry". Today, 45% [in contrast to 15% in October 1956] believe that there should be more planning. . .Only one in every four believes that the proper remedy for the present situation is to cut down on [government] expenditure' (Gallup Report No. 20, August 1961, p. 4; see also Tables 10, 13 and 44).

2. Plowden's committee investigating public expenditure control devised a new system (later called PESC) which was intended to force departments and their ministers to forecast expenditure and to budget resources against requirements for a much longer period than had been habitual; this new planning process would also enable the Chancellor to vet proposals in a more general context than the annual war of attrition between Treasury and spending departments (Cmnd 1432, July 1961). This will be discussed in Volume 2, Chapter 1.

3. 'Economic Reform' (1961) written for the Liberal Party Research Department (Beveridge Papers, IXA, Item 96).

4. PEP made two major studies in the late 1950s, one of European planning models (PWS 10, Box 52–3, Industry Study Group, 1957–59) which culminated in a report on Adaptation and Growth in Industry, a significant precursor to NEDC; and the other (PWS 13, Box 48, Trade Union Study Group, 1960) on the trade union movement, shop stewards and plant bargaining, which put wages policy foremost in any system of economic planning, but also gave indirect support for the sort of institutional reforms which Woodcock was trying to institute. It came down against legislation and can be seen as part of the trend of thought finally embodied in the Donovan Report, 1958.

Note on Sources

The public and private archives consulted for this volume are listed in the footnotes, using the acronyms given by the Public Record Office, or other archival classifications. These are as follow:

CABINET PAPERS (CAB): Cabinet Papers, and Cabinet and Cabinet Committee minutes, wartime and post-war Ministerial and official committees.
PRIME MINISTER (PREM)
DEPARTMENTS OF STATE:
  Ministry of Economic Planning (MEP)
  Ministry of Labour (LAB)
  Ministry of Labour and National Service (MLNS)
  Board of Trade (BT)
  Treasury (T)
OTHER:
  Economic Planning Board (EPB)
  Joint Consultative Committee (JCC)
  National Joint Advisory Committee (NJAC)
  National Production Advisory Committee for Industry (NPACI)
NON GOVERNMENT ARCHIVES:
  Conservative Party (CP), Conservative Research Department (CRD)
  Labour Party (LP), Research Department (LRD), Home Policy Committee (HPC)
  British Employers Confederation (BEC), General Purposes Committee (GPC)
  Federation of British Industries (FBI), Grand Council (GC), General Purposes Committee (GPC), Home Economic Policy Committee (HEPC)
  Trades Union Congress (TUC), General Council (GC), Economic Committee (EC), Finance and General Purposes Committee (FGPC), Production Committee (PC)
  Transport and General Workers Union (TGWU)

Gallup Reports and Social Surveys
The Industrial Society
Political and Economic Planning (PEP)
PRIVATE ARCHIVES:
C. R. Attlee, William Beveridge, Ernest Bevin, Hugh Dalton
(unpublished diary material), Walter Monckton.

Index

Addison, Christopher   46, 49
Agriculture, Ministry of (inc.
    Agriculture and Food)   6, 20, 28,
    33, 139, 249, 249 n6, 253
Aims of Industry   163, 279, 318
Aircraft industry   100 n54, 249 n7
Aircraft Production, Ministry of   23, 28,
    33–4, 53, 94, 96, 113
Air Ministry   6, 127, 139
Albu, Austen   223
American Federation of Labour (AFL)
    65–6
Amery, Leo   103, 212
Amory, D. Heathcoat   213, 251–2, 272,
    287, 289
  as Chancellor of Exchequer   294–6,
    305, 321
  and 1959 Budget   296–7
Anderson, Sir John   22, 28, 35, 58, 104,
    248
Andrew, Herbert   241, 253
Anglo-American Productivity Council
    (AAPC)   66, 113, 128, 150, 159,
    162, 228, 239, 251
Armstrong, William   270, 339
Army Bureau of Current Affairs
    (ABCA)   69
Assheton, Frederick   212
Attlee, C. R.   42, 45, 48–9, 53, 72–5,
    102, 104, 112
  as Prime Minister   114–19, 122–3,
    126–7, 129, 133–4, 138, 140, 151–
    8, 160–1, 165, 171–5, 177–9, 180,
    183, 186–7, 190, 209–11
  as Leader of the Opposition   217,
    222–5, 247, 329, 342–3

Baillieu, Sir Clive   143, 161
Bain, Sir Frederick   145
Balogh, Thomas   72, 223, 334 n26
Bank of England   9, 19, 141, 351, 353
  in Second World War   25–7, 37, 50,
    57–9, 99, 101, 104–6

under Labour governments, 1945–51
    141–2, 165, 181
under Conservative governments,
    1951–61   243–5, 270, 281, 293,
    296
  Governor of   37, 57, 293, 296
  Governor and Chancellor of
    Exchequer   141, 243–4
  relations with industry   58, 302
  relations with banking system   141–2
  and 1944 White Paper   106, 244–5
  and negotiations with United States
    123–4
  and sterling area   142
  and convertibility crisis 1947   153–5
  and devaluation 1949   171–4
  and Robot scheme   195–204, 243
  and US Federal Reserve Board   196–
    7, 243
  and government debt   244
  and convertibility   243–5, 270, 281,
    293, 296
  and inflation   267
  and credit control   297, 301, 301 n30
  and employment policy   302
  and 1961 defence of sterling   298, 300,
    301–2
Banking system
  in Second World War   24–7, 37, 58–
    9, 99, 103, 110
  under Labour governments   142,
    164–5, 196–8
  under Conservative governments
    244, 251, 296, 301–2, 302 n32,
    344–5
  and Bretton Woods   58
  and Bankers' Information Service   25
  and Commonwealth banks   26–7, 50,
    57, 101, 103
  and convertibility crisis 1947   155
  and exchange control   26–7, 57
  and full employment   87–8, 93–4
  and investment   106–9, 245, 302–3,
    310

and capital loan market 165
and export credit guarantees 253
Barlow Report 42, 99
Barnes, Denis 307
Beaver, Sir Hugh 312
Beaverbrook, Lord 20, 35, 41, 49, 103–4, 212
Beeching, Dr Richard 303 n36
Bevan, Aneurin 44, 73, 92, 126, 138, 171, 174, 180, 183, 186–7, 196, 204, 329
Beveridge, Sir William 13, 36, 44–5, 46, 49, 54, 60–2, 66–7, 69–71, 72, 74, 79, 81–2, 84, 87–9, 91–3, 95–6, 110, 112, 131–2, 188, 263, 340, 342
Bevin, Ernest 18–20, 30–1, 35, 38
  role in Second World War 21, 39–40, 42, 44–5, 48, 67, 94, 96, 102
  after 1945 112, 117, 120–1, 123, 126, 131, 133–4, 148, 153, 155–8, 160, 171, 173, 177
Birch, Alan 257
Birch, Nigel 268, 294
Blackett, Sir Basil 51
Bolton, Sir George 101, 199–203
Bracken, Brendan 212
Bretton Woods Agreement 124
Bridges, Sir Edward 29, 32, 36, 78, 82, 120, 132, 136–9, 141, 153–4, 168, 177, 195, 199, 202, 244, 247–9, 266, 270–1
British Broadcasting Corporation (BBC) 110, 176
British Employers Confederation (BEC) 21–2, 24, 31, 57, 112, 128–9, 135, 137, 143
  in Second World War 37–9, 59–64
  under Labour governments 139, 144–5, 180, 206–7
  under Conservative governments 232, 235–7, 259, 289, 299, 304–5, 312–15, 316
  organisation 38, 59, 312–13
  publications 237
  relations with FBI 39, 59, 142, 144, 235, 259, 312, 346
  relations with Conservative party 144
  relations with TUC 144, 236–7, 313–14
  and 1944 White Paper 93, 235, 314–15
  and 1956 White Paper 237
  and declining profits 312
  and CPPI 315

and European integration 310 n45
and labour legislation 236, 314
and restrictive practices 94
and shop stewards 236 n43
and wages and inflation 235–6, 262, 312–14
British Institute of Management 127
Brittan, Samuel 270, 296
Brittain, Sir Herbert 266
Brown, Ernest 17
Brown, George 329
Brook, Sir Norman 32, 121, 138, 190, 194–5, 206, 247, 249, 287, 296, 338
Boyd, John 331
Butler, R. A. 41, 48–9, 70–1, 188, 212–15, 247–8, 250–1, 261–2, 338
  as Chancellor of Exchequer 219, 221, 229, 236, 239, 243–5, 265–72, 276–7, 279, 281, 285–6, 288
  and Industrial Charter 213–15
  and Robot Scheme 198–204
  and 1955 Budget 269–70, 279

Cabinet organisation 78–81, 83
Cairncross, Alec 171–2, 338
Cameron Report 260, 262
Capital Issues Committee 26, 58–9, 99, 129, 141–2, 165, 206
Car industry 231–2, 255–6
Carron, Sir William 232, 309, 314, 324, 326
Catto, Sir Thomas 32, 57–8, 106, 141, 196
Central Economic Planning Staff (CEPS) 166, 169, 186, 248
Central Office of Information (COI) 137, 150, 176
Chamberlain, Neville 17
Chambers of Commerce 217, 241
Chandos, Lord *see* Lyttelton, Oliver
Chapple, Frank 324
Chemicals industry 100
Cherwell, Lord 41, 49, 51, 91, 104, 202–3, 212, 221, 248, 265
Chester, Norman 79
Chester, Sir George 157
Churchill, Winston 3, 17, 19
  and Conservative party 41–2
  as Prime Minister in Second World War 30–1, 35, 37, 41, 48–9, 57, 65, 68, 70, 72, 102, 112, 115
  as Leader of Opposition 212–19
  as Prime Minister 1951–5 192, 195, 192–204, 212–16, 219–22, 228,

244, 257–8, 260–1, 268–9, 273, 343
and overlords   45, 248–9
and reconstruction   48
and civil service   247–9
Civil Service (*see also under departments*, Labour, Trade, Treasury, *etc.*)
general   3, 6, 8, 11–14, 349–55
in Second World War   22, 29, 33–6, 44–5, 46–51, 53–7, 66, 74–6, 79–83, 87, 108; and machinery of government   79–83
under Labour governments 1945–51   112, 119–21, 136–7, 140, 168, 186, 192–3
under Conservative governments 1957–61   216–17, 247–9, 270, 277–9, 265–7, 288, 300
and Cabinet Office   121, 133, 136
and 1961 changes   337, 347
Citrine, Walter   18, 20, 35, 39–41, 43, 62, 64–5, 67, 72, 96, 113, 148, 317, 325
Clarke, Richard (Otto)   168, 171, 199–203, 267
Class structure and change   283–5, 328–9
Clay, Henry   101
Clayton, Will   123
Coal industry   100, 119 n13, 127
Cobbold, Cameron (Lord)   26, 101, 103, 142, 170, 200–3, 243–5, 277, 287, 294, 296 n24, 296–7, 298–300, 302, 302 n31,32,34, 310, 338
Cohen Council *see* CPPI
Cole, G. D. H.   89
Common Wealth   43, 69
Communist Party (CPGB)   5, 43, 65, 121, 151, 161, 163, 177, 204, 208 n61, 233, 233 n36, 325–6, 326 n16
Cold War, in Europe, effects of   158, 163, 172, 178
Committee of London Clearing Bankers (CLCB)   25, 58, 245, 296
Concentration of industry   310, 310 n43, 336
Conservative Party   3, 5, 17, 94, 112, 153, 193, 208, 210, 283, 337, 348
and electorate   72, 278–81, 283–5, 289, 296
and manifesto   72 n53, 212, 215
and organisation   41, 70–1, 212–15, 220, 278–81
and One-Nation group   216, 218, 286
and Tory Reform Association   49, 71
Research Department   41, 49, 71–2, 212, 215–16, 219, 270, 280–1, 284–6, 286 n7, 288–9, 348
relations with banking system   218
relations with civil service   247–9
relations with industry   214, 217–18, 240, 315
relations with trades unions   42, 217–18, 227–8, 230–1, 233–5, 278, 283–4, 286 n7, 286–7, 291, 308–9, 318, 324
in Second World War   41–3, 48, 69–72: and post-war problems   71; and state planning   41–2, 70–1, 140
in opposition 1945–51   212–19: and *Industrial Charter*   213–15
in government 1951–61: and Robot scheme   198–204; economic management   226, 278–81, 279 n50, 287 n11; industrial policy   217–18, 220–2; financial policy   218–19, 278; labour policy   257–8; policy-making   212–21, 285–6, 289–90, 297; and European integration   160, 251–2, 281–2, 334; and industrial relations   258–9, 261, 263
and full employment   226
and inflation   266–7, 278
and machinery of government   216–17, 225–6, 247–9
and nationalised industries   273–4
and wages   257, 259–62, 272, 278–9, 280–1, 286–7, 291
internal dissent   287–9, 299
and 1961 crisis   298–300
Consumerism   278–81, 334, 353
Cooper, John   232, 324
Corporate bias, theory of   1, 3, 5, 7–8, 11, 43–4, 81, 112–13, 134–5, 145–6, 209–10, 227, 242, 340–1, 344–7
Cotton industry   252
Council on Pay, Productivity and Incomes (CPPI)   287, 291–2, 298–301, 313, 315, 320 n9, 344
Courtauld, Samuel   60
Cousins, Frank   157, 183, 231, 233, 235, 262, 309, 320, 323–4, 326, 328–9, 331–3
Credit control   292, 295–7
Cripps, Sir Stafford   45, 53, 75, 84, 117–18, 120, 127, 131, 134, 137–8, 142, 145

as Chancellor of Exchequer 153–5, 157, 157–60, 165–7, 178–9, 180, 185–6, 196, 198, 346, 354: and devaluation 1949 171–4, 179; and productivity drive 176–7
Cromer, Lord 302, 338
Crookshank, Harry 202, 259
Crosland, Anthony 168, 184, 225, 328, 333
Crossman, R. H. S. 120, 329, 331

Dalton, Hugh 39, 49, 80–5, 91, 95, 100–1, 104, 112, 114, 165, 171–2, 330
as Chancellor of Exchequer 116–18, 120, 123–6, 129–31, 134, 137, 141–2, 153–6
Deakin, Arthur 121, 147, 150, 157, 177, 225, 231–2, 257
Defence, budget 185–7, 198–9, 203
Defence, policy 122, 160, 172, 174–6, 210–11, 211 n64, 269, 269 n32, 272
Defence, Ministry of 193, 275
Devaluation 1949 160, 165, 170–4, 189, 197–8, 292, 299
Dicey, A. V. 1, 82
Dollar Export Council 113, 251
Donovan Commission 258, 325, 346
Douglas-Home, Sir Alec 285
Dulles, John Foster 253, 277
Duncan, Sir Andrew 34, 39
Dunnett, Sir James 338
Durbin, Evan 28, 72, 120, 153–4, 184

Eady, Sir Wilfred 58, 91, 104, 141, 154, 198, 266
Economic Affairs, Department of 79
Economic Intelligence Unit (EIU) 150, 157, 166, 176
Economic League 163
Economic management, practice of 12, 53–5, 61, 82–4, 87–8, 90–1, 95, 97–9, 108–9, 132, 166, 169–70, 180, 188–9, 193–6, 248, 256, 265–72, 275, 279–83, 288–90, 316–17, 345
Economic planning apparatus 52, 75–6, 117–20, 132, 134, 136–8
Economic Planning Board (EPB) 113, 137–40, 166, 170, 180, 185, 190, 204 5, 235, 245, 292, 297, 300
Economic Survey: for 1946 113, 117; for 1947 132, 137, 145, 150–1, 170; for 1948 159; for 1949 176–7, 179; for 1950 185, 202; for 1952 188; for 1953 238; for 1954 270

Economy, changes in, and effects of in Second World War 26–7, 32–3, 50–1
in Korean War 175–6
general 122–6, 152, 159–60, 180–1, 188, 212, 230, 264–6, 283, 289, 336
external events and balance of payments 91–2, 97, 122–6, 187, 197–9, 256, 270–1, 287, 291–2, 297
competition from France, Germany and Japan 251, 261, 265, 271, 345
Eden, Sir Anthony 17, 65, 202, 214, 216, 221–2, 234–5, 241, 247–8, 252, 261–2, 269–71, 280–1, 283, 285–6, 294, 343
and trades unionists 262–3, 317
Education policy 110 n68, 221, 306 n37, 341
Eisenhower, Dwight D. 253, 277
Elections, general: 1945 112; 1950 179–80; 1951 208–9, 216; 1955 224–5, 270, 329; 1964 335
by-elections 280, 284
Electrical Trades Union (ETU) 177, 204, 232, 237, 318
Employment
full 11, 48 n4, 50, 52–5, 62, 64, 66–7, 71, 73, 75–6, 77–8, 87–91, 92 n32, 100–1, 104, 118, 126–7, 131–4, 151, 183, 192–4, 210, 235, 268 n30, 343–4, 349
and 1944 White Paper 46, 49, 54, 56, 58, 68–70, 77–8, 91–3, 95–8, 100–1, 105, 108–10, 127, 131, 134–6, 140, 145, 150–1, 165, 185, 193, 210, 213, 226, 247, 270, 274, 279, 283–6, 293, 316, 335, 341–2
and 1956 White Paper 226, 233, 237, 242, 261, 263, 271, 278, 280, 319
Engineering Employers Federation (EEF) 6, 22, 60, 232, 237, 255–6, 261, 272, 309, 311–12, 312 n48, 326
Engineering industry 97, 107
Engineering Trade Union (AEU) 177, 206, 232, 237, 256, 317, 324, 327
European Coal and Steel Community (ECSC) 241, 253
European Economic Community (EEC) 241–3, 253–4, 289, 310, 337
European Free Trade Association (EFTA) 241–3, 254–5, 281, 306

European integration and UK policy
160, 160 n17, 221–2, 235, 250–4,
295, 295 n22, 297–8, 304, 310 n45,
338–40
European Monetary Agreements
(EMAs) 123–5, 124 n22, 142, 154–
5, 158–9, 277
European Recovery Programme (ERP)
65, 157–9, 162, 162 n22, 171, 174–5
Evans, Lincoln 257, 325
Export drive 118, 125–6

Feather, Vic 147, 161, 177
Federation of British Industries (FBI) 4,
6, 19, 21–2, 24, 31, 90, 98, 100, 103,
105–6, 112, 126, 135, 137
Grand Council 59, 143, 237, 242:
HEPC 161
membership 38, 143, 311
publications 59, 61, 205–6, 238
organisation 38, 56–60, 143, 311:
Next Five Years conferences
143, 238, 309; Industrial Trends
Survey 311
sponsorship system 37–9, 59–64: in
Second World War: nuclei firms
38–9; reconstruction 59–61, 120;
industrialists 61–3, 89; and 1944
White Paper 92–3, 96–7, 108,
235, 311; under Labour
governments 1945–51 128–9,
139–40, 142–3, 145–6, 161–4, 172,
179, 180–2, 205–7; under
Conservative governments 1951–
61 205–6, 217, 235, 237–43, 255,
264, 289, 299, 304–5, 309–12,
316–17
and nationalised industries 163–4,
242–3, 273–4; and steel industry
142, 163, 205
and NEDC 309
and Board of Trade 250–1, 257, 305
and TUC 242–3
and capital market and investment
239, 242
and credit controls 311–12
and competitiveness, and industrial
policy 161–3, 239–41
and economic management 238, 242–
3, 264–5, 309–11
and European integration 241–3,
251–5, 309–11, 310 n45
and sterling area 238
and wages 311

Fergusson, Sir Donald 35, 81
Finance for Industry (FFI) 25, 99, 142,
144
Financial sector *see* Banking
Fisher, Sir Norman Warren 35
Food, Ministry of 59
Foot, Sir Dingle 45
Foot, Michael 183, 187, 332
Foreign Office 37, 123, 142, 222, 238,
241, 251, 253, 305
Foreign policy, UK 122, 155, 160
Franks, Sir Oliver 23, 35, 45, 245
Fraser, Michael 215, 285, 289
Friedman, Milton 93, 299
Fuel crisis, 1947 122, 131, 150, 152
Fulton Inquiry into Civil Service 353

Gaitskell, Hugh 72–3, 135, 138, 167,
171, 174, 178, 223–5
as Chancellor of Exchequer 180–1,
183, 188, 195, 197–8, 205–6, 209
and wages policy 189–92
and leadership crisis 328–33
General Agreement on Tariffs and
Trade (GATT) 101–2, 105, 125,
130, 144, 197, 240, 251–2
General and Municipal Workers Union
(GMWU) 323, 325, 327
George, David Lloyd 3, 5, 37
Gilbert, Sir Bernard 266, 270
Glenday, Richard 60, 105, 143
Gower, Sir Ernest 82
Governing institutions, theory of 7, 10,
37, 43, 78, 114, 344–7
Guillebaud Report 287, 303, 309, 314,
322, 326

Hacking, Sir Robert 70
Haldane, Lord 12, 44, 78
Halifax, Lord 17
Hall, Sir Robert 132, 138, 171, 190–1,
200–4, 248, 251, 266, 268, 270–1,
276, 285, 294, 296–7, 299, 338
Hankey, Lord 14, 35
Hare, John 300, 304, 338
Harrod, Sir Roy 172
Hayek, F. von 93, 348, 354
Heald, Sir Lionel 240
Heath, Edward 45, 240, 250, 285–7,
299, 305, 308, 338
Helsby, Sir Laurence 287, 300, 307,
338
Henderson, Arthur 114
Henderson, Sir Hubert 54, 81

Heron, Conrad 257
Hill, Dr Charles 285
Historiography, and politics 2, 43, 335
Hoffman, Paul G. 159
Hogg, Quintin (Lord Hailsham) 215, 285, 288
Home Office 20
Hopkins, Sir Richard 101
Hopkinson, Harry 212
Housing, Ministry of 98
  policy 186–7, 219–20, 250
Hudson, R. H. 103
Hull, Cordell 102
Hurcombe, Sir Cyril 79–80
Hyndley, Lord 285

ICFC 25, 99, 142, 144
Ince, Sir Godfrey 199, 247, 257, 263
Industrial politics, system of 2, 8, 349–55
  in Second World War 12–13, 22–4, 37–9, 43–5, 74–6, 178
  under Labour governments 206–7
  under Conservative governments 225–6, 283
  and competition theory 47–9, 74, 77–8, 108–9, 114, 220, 226, 245–6
  and 1961 rassemblement 344–7
  and the state 8–11, 93–4, 112, 114, 121, 140–1, 150, 168, 194–6, 210, 349–55
Industrial relations 60–3, 73, 308 n42, 325–6
  1947 White Paper on 134–5, 139, 151
Inflation 11, 17, 55, 57, 85, 87, 93, 95–6, 118, 125, 129–30, 156, 171–2, 187–9, 196, 206, 252, 264, 267, 288, 293–4, 298
Inland Revenue 298
Information, Ministry of 69
International Monetary Fund (IMF) 103, 105, 124, 302
Investment, industrial 50–1, 60, 62, 90–1, 96–9, 106–9, 127, 129–30, 161–3, 172–3, 264, 277–8, 292, 310
Iron and Steel Board 257
Iron and Steel Federation 241
Iron and steel industry 39, 100, 257 n13, 273, 273 n40
Iron and steel trades unions 232
Isaacs, George 199, 247, 257, 263

Jay, Douglas 72, 138, 153, 171, 174–5, 180, 183
Jenkins, Clive 324

Jones, Jack 183, 231–2, 323–4

Kaldor, Nicholas 72, 191
Kalecki, Michael 74, 349
Keith, Kenneth 302
Kennedy, John F. 298–9, 299 n25, 340
Keynes, John Maynard 13, 32, 35–6, 46, 50–1, 54, 58, 67, 74, 87, 91, 95, 97–8, 101–5, 108, 119, 122–5, 131
Kipping, Sir Norman 36, 113, 139, 143, 161, 251, 338
Korean War 122, 139, 160, 164, 169, 174–9, 197–8, 204, 206–7, 219, 239, 258

Labour, Ministry of
  Labour and National Service (MLNS) 18–20, 30–1, 33–4, 40, 42, 45, 51, 53–4, 56, 64, 68–9, 75–6, 80, 83, 85–6, 91, 100, 121, 144
  Labour (MOL) 249, 253, 286–7, 304, 317, 324: and labour market issues 88, 261–2; and full employment 89–90; and controls 121, 131; and codes of conduct 229, 235, 257; and labour legislation 307–9, 348; and trades unions 139, 229, 234–5, 307–9; and wages 95–6, 156–7, 174 n51, 189–92, 257, 263–4, 300, 307–9, 326
Labour Party 3, 5, 19, 70, 83–4, 105, 109, 111–12, 115, 337, 348
  Parliamentary Labour Party 42
  leadership 115–16, 330–4
  Economic Policy Committee 137–8, 145
  Home Policy Committee 72–3, 222–5, 329
  Research Department 42, 67, 72–3, 166, 191, 208
  organisation 42, 72
  relations: with banking system 73, 165; with civil service 120–1; with industry 73–4, 120, 128, 142–5, 208, 223 n20; with TUC and trades unions 42, 72, 116–17, 128, 133–5, 140, 208, 329–33
  and electorate 112, 176–7, 179, 182, 192, 208–9, 328–30, 333
  Manifestos 46, 74, 115, 166, 182, 192, 220, 233–5, 334
  1944 Association 85, 120, 144, 225

Labour Party *cont.*
 Keep Left Group   153
 Socialist Commentary   72
 XYZ Group   72
 in government 1945–51   141–211:
  Ministerial Economic Policy
   Committee   166–7, 174, 179, 185,
   197; and austerity   152–3, 156–8,
   172–3, 185, 197; and machinery of
   government   112–13, 165–6; and
   United States   122–4, 126; and
   Marshall Aid   157–9;
   achievements   209–11
 in opposition after 1951   222–5, 283–4
 internal divisions   92, 117, 135, 153,
   166, 174, 178, 180, 183–4, 186–7,
   187 n11, 191, 196, 208–10, 222–5,
   328–33
 issues: European integration   316,
   328, 334, 334 n26; industrial
   policy   117–18, 121, 130–1, 223–
   5, 329–31, 333–4; nationalised
   industries   85–6, 119, 129, 141,
   166–7, 183–5; planning   83–5, 92,
   117–18, 120, 169, 333–4; trade
   policy   102 3; wages   173 5, 191,
   329; worker participation   85, 184
   n4
Laski, Harold   48, 72–3, 83
Law, Richard   103
Lawther, Will   257
Leathers, Ted   202, 248
Lee, Sir Frank   199, 240, 247, 249–51,
   254, 256, 267, 291, 294, 297, 300,
   302, 305, 338–9
Leggatt, Sir Frederick   35
Lend–Lease   50, 58, 104, 122–3
Leslie, Clem   137, 179
Liberal Party   3, 216, 332
 and elections of 1950 and 1951   179,
   208
Lloyds of London   58
Lloyd, Selwyn   45, 281
 as Chancellor of Exchequer   288, 297–
   301, 307, 310, 314, 321–2, 326,
   334, 338
Location of industry policy   96, 99–100,
   205, 205 n55, 350
Lord, Leonard   256
Low, Toby   262, 287
Lyttleton, Oliver (Lord Chandos)   34,
   202, 213, 240, 244, 250, 252, 265

MacArthur, General Douglas   175, 186

MacDonald, Malcolm   203
Macleod, Iain   214, 229, 233, 262, 272,
   279, 285–7, 299, 307, 312, 316, 338
McGowan, Henry   62, 64
Macmillan Committee   25
Macmillan, Harold   45, 71, 213, 220,
   231, 237–8, 242, 250, 261–2, 269
 as Chancellor of Exchequer   268, 271–
   2, 280–2
 as Prime Minister   283, 285–90, 292
   n18, 292–6, 296 n24, 299–301,
   307–8, 312, 312 n48, 326, 337–8
Machine-tool industry   127, 254–6
Machinery of government   20, 27–35,
   32 n33, 77–83, 79 n2, 110–12, 138–9,
   247–9, 304
Makins, Sir Roger   268, 290–4, 313, 3??
   338
Management, industrial (*see also under*
   BEC, FBI)   4, 113, 128–9, 137,
   142–3, 157 n161, 232–5, 242, 255–6,
   292, 301, 303
Manpower policy   51–3, 75–6, 85, 99,
   121–2, 130–1, 133, 153, 175–6, 187
Marshall Aid   103, 130, 154, 156–60,
   162–3, 166, 171, 173, 175, 196
Maudling, Reginald   214, 286, 299,
   304–5, 338
Mayhew, Christopher   181–2
Maxwell Fyfe, Sir David (Lord
   Kilmuir)   71, 202–3, 208, 213–15,
   253, 263
Meade, James   52, 87, 119, 168
Messina Conference   253, 305
Meynell, Alexander   99, 101
Middleton, J. S.   72
Mikardo, Ian   74
Mills, Sir Percy   272
Monckton, Sir Walter   62–4, 218–20,
   228–30, 234–6, 247, 249, 254, 257–
   63, 267, 292 n18, 296 n24, 301,
   316
Mond, Sir Alfred (Lord Melchett)   64
Monnet, Jean   241
Monopolies and restrictive practices   54,
   62–4, 84–5, 87, 90, 92, 94–7, 118,
   127–8, 130, 183, 205
Monopolies Commission   83, 221, 238–
   40, 254, 274, 305–6, 310
Morgenthau, Henry   25–6, 50, 105, 210
Morrison, Herbert   36, 42, 45, 49, 73–4,
   86, 95, 116–18, 127, 129, 133–4,
   136–8, 150–1, 153–4, 156–7, 166–7,
   177, 180, 184, 186, 346

National Confederation of Employers
Organisations (NCEO) 4–6
National Economic Development
Council (NEDC) and Office
(NEDO) 45, 55, 139, 145, 254,
267, 289, 309, 312, 314–15, 322–3,
329, 334, 337, 339, 345
National Farmers Union (NFU) 6, 103,
139
National Joint Advisory Council
(NJAC) 18, 21, 45, 56, 60, 80, 113,
119, 133, 137, 139, 214, 218, 228,
235, 245, 257, 304–5, 307
and Joint Consultative Committee
(JCC) 21, 23, 38, 59
National Institute for Economic and
Social Research (NIESR) 35, 310
National Plan, 1965 329
National Production Advisory Council
for Industry (NPACI) 21, 23, 38,
60, 88, 113, 137, 139, 218, 228, 245,
254, 304–5
National Union of Mineworkers
(NUM) 17–18, 22, 65, 177, 217,
241, 273
Nationalised industries 61–2, 85–6, 91,
119–20, 129–30, 163, 166–7, 190–1,
194, 256, 259, 260–1, 272–4, 274
n41, 288, 292, 303, 326
and 1961 White Paper 272, 288, 303,
334, 337, 352
and British Transport
Commission 303 n36
Nelson, Sir George 39
Nicholas, Harry 232, 331
Nicholson, Max 32, 133, 192
Noel-Baker, Philip 190
Norman, Lord (Montagu) 25–7, 32, 35,
57–9, 141
North Atlantic Treaty Organisation
(NATO) 187, 199–200, 211
Nuffield College Conferences 60–1,
88–9

O'Brien, Tom 257
OEEC/OECD 197, 299, 310
Opinion, public 42–5, 70–1, 74, 110,
117, 148 n72, 152–3, 155–6, 179,
187, 212, 219, 260, 279–81, 283–4,
336
agencies 42, 69
appeals to 61, 68, 70–1, 74, 182, 191,
291, 333–4

management of 113, 120–1, 120 n17,
127–8, 136–7, 140–1, 144–5, 150–
1, 176–9, 208, 285–6, 346
research into 42–3, 46, 69, 173–4, 336 n1
on issues: Beveridge Reports 69–70;
Civil Service 351; industrial
relations 234–5, 237; strikes
318, 326; trades unions 278, 316,
320
Oral history 2, 8, 13–15
Orwell, George 93, 354

Padmore, Sir Thomas 249, 266, 273
Pannell, Charles 332
Parliament, sovereignty of 3, 44, 79, 82
Peake, Osbert 221
Phillips, Morgan 72, 178, 183, 331
Planning and economic overview 80–3,
112, 117–20, 136–8, 141, 297, 306–7
Playfair, Sir Edward 267
Plowden Committee report 290, 339
Plowden, Edwin 118, 137–8, 169, 171,
173, 175, 193–4, 200–4, 267
Political and Economic Planning (PEP)
36, 88–9, 310, 336 n1
Pollock, Sir George 259, 261, 309, 313,
338
Poole, Oliver 285
Post-war settlement 1–2, 7–8, 13, 47,
52–3, 55, 58, 63, 74–6, 78, 88–92,
109–13, 118–19, 204–8, 247, 249,
282, 315, 317–18, 341–2, 348–9
Powell, Enoch 214, 265, 285–7, 294,
338
Powell, Sir Richard 338
Press and television 132, 176, 228, 242,
337, 346, 351
Production, Ministry of 54
Production authority system 25, 80,
126, 138–41, 168–9, 194, 205, 217,
345
Production campaigns 127, 139, 150,
162

Radcliffe Committee 301, 311, 317, 321
Railway unions 233–4, 260, 263, 332
Reconstruction, post-war 7, 46–57, 74–
5, 77, 88–91, 101
Research, industrial 51, 128–9
Restrictive practices 95 n38, 107 n67
Restrictive Practices Court 240, 254,
305–6
Rickett, Sir Dennis 267
Robertson, Sir Brian 259

Robbins, Lionel 28, 32, 54–6, 66, 70, 79, 82, 84–5, 94–6, 98, 100–1, 109, 138
Robens, Alfred 273–4
Robinson, Joan 62, 224
Robot scheme 194–6, 197–204, 206, 219, 243, 248, 251, 265–6, 275, 293
Rooke, Sir William 30
Rootes, Sir William 232, 312
Roosevelt, F. D. 102
Rowan, Sir Leslie 170, 195, 200, 203, 266–7, 291, 293–4
Rowntree, Seebohm 87

Salisbury, Lord 251–3
Salter, Sir Arthur 202
Sandys, Duncan 273, 306 n38
Scanlon, Hugh 263, 323–4
Schumacher, E. F. 89
Schumann Plan 241
Science,
    role of 7, 51, 128–9, 306 n37
    research 51, 288; DSIR 99
    scientists, output of 97 n44, 110 n68
Second World War *see* World War Two
Shackleton, Sir Harry 39
Shawcross, Sir Hartley 205
Shinwell, Emmanuel 126, 131, 138, 153
Shipbuilding industry 107, 249 n7
Shone, Sir Robert 217, 273–4
Shonfield, Andrew 339
Simon, Sir John 25–6
Smith, Sir Allan 38
Sponsorship system 113, 139–40, 169, 217, 249, 254, 256
Stanley, Oliver 213
Sterling area 26–7, 56, 57–9, 97, 101–5, 123–4, 130, 142, 155–6, 158–9, 170, 197–9, 210, 219, 245 n54, 253–4, 295
Sterling, role of 53, 57–9, 67, 103–4, 123 n21, 185, 194, 197–9, 198 n35, 288, 290
    and convertibility crisis 1947 125–6, 152–6, 166
    and convertibility 272, 274–7, 291–2, 295, 302
    and Basle support plan 298–9, 302, 322, 340
Stock Exchange 26, 37, 58, 106, 245
Strachey, John 171, 330
Strauss, G. R. 171
Strikes
    in Second World War 21, 31, 45 n59, 76 n65

under Labour governments 120–2, 127, 150, 208: and emergency powers 161, 163, 177–8
under Conservative governments 190, 228–9, 233–4, 259–60, 313, 324, 326
Stuart, James 202
Suez operation, 1956 253, 262, 271–2, 278–9, 281, 291–2, 296, 319, 335
Supply, Ministry of 18, 22–3, 28, 31, 32–4, 37–8, 40, 53, 58, 113, 193, 193 n27
Swinton, Lord 202

Tanner, Jack 138
Tawney, R. H. 83, 119
Taylor, Stephen 168
Tewson, Vincent 135, 138, 147, 160–1, 204, 226, 228, 233–4, 257, 263, 317–18, 321, 338
Thorneycroft, Peter 198, 200, 218, 221, 238–40, 244, 247, 274, 280, 338
    as President of Board of Trade 249–56, 267, 269
    as Chancellor of Exchequer 264, 268, 272, 279, 281, 286–8, 287 n11, 291–4, 298, 313, 319, 321
Topping, Sir Robert 71
Trade associations 4, 23–4, 38–9, 60, 62, 80, 118, 182, 255–6
Trade, Board of
in Second World War 23–5, 40, 42, 51, 53–7, 59–63, 67, 75, 79–80, 83, 89–90, 101: and Regional Boards 55, 65
under Labour governments 1945–51 118, 133, 139, 154, 156, 169, 181–4, 189, 193; and devaluation, 1949 170
under Conservative governments 1957–61 218, 249, 275
Industrial Boards and Development Councils 80, 85–6, 94, 96–100, 113, 118, 128, 145, 163, 182, 194, 206, 217, 220, 250
industrial policy 55–6, 84–5, 97–9, 107–9, 128–9, 207, 250, 252–6, 297, 304–6, 306 n38, 309: investment policy 107–9; monopolies and restrictive practices 94–9, 130–1, 183, 205, 205 n54, 239–41, 254
and European integration 241–3, 251–4, 272, 305–6

and sterling area 295
and trade policy 101–5
and wages policy 95–6
Trade, patterns of UK 50, 52–4, 59,
61–2, 90, 95, 97–8, 100–5, 107–8,
185, 210, 239, 240–1, 250–5, 264,
277, 281, 295–6
and bilateralism 102–5, 124
and Commonwealth trade 251–2,
281, 306
Trades Union Congress (TUC)
membership 147–8, 317–19
headquarters staff 40, 146, 148–9,
328
publications 92, 149
Economic Committee 65–8, 92, 135,
146, 149, 204, 229–30, 232, 318–
19, 322, 327
General Council 18, 20–1, 39–40, 65,
96, 147, 227, 231, 257, 262–3,
316–17, 323, 325–6
Production Committee 146–7, 150,
162–3, 228–9, 322: prosperity
campaigns 127–8, 147, 149
and Labour Party 65–6, 68, 70, 73,
96, 114–15, 132, 134–5, 139, 223–
7, 230–1, 316, 321, 329–33
and Labour governments 1945–51
126, 134–5, 137, 139, 146–50, 154,
156, 161, 163, 172, 177–8, 184,
186, 188, 192, 204–6, 208
and Conservative governments 1951–
61 214, 226–8, 233–5, 258–9,
261–3, 278, 300, 303–5, 315–16,
319–21, 325, 327
in Second World War 17–19, 22–3,
29–30, 38–41, 44, 56, 61, 64–70,
88, 90, 100, 105: and CPPI 307,
320, 320 n9; and Board of Trade
149; and civil service 68–9, 146–
7; and Ministry of Labour 148–9,
230–1, 259; and shop stewards
148–9, 161, 207, 227, 231–2, 318,
322–3, 325–6; and Soviet Union
65, 113, 177; and economic
management practice 226–7, 264
and European integration 316 n1
and full employment 66–7, 89, 113–
14, 131–5, 148–9, 317, 319–21,
327: 1944 White Paper 92, 96,
110, 113–14, 149
and financial policy 149, 317
and industrial policy 149, 230
and labour legislation 316–17

and nationalised industries 120, 148–
9, 166–7, 184–5, 322–3
and planning 113–14, 119–20, 146–
50, 322
and wages policy 67, 96, 149, 156,
160–2, 173–5, 177, 186, 189, 192,
204, 206–7, 226–7, 229–30, 234–5,
261–2, 317–22
and worker participation 119–20, 149
Trades unions (*see also under individual
unions*) 17–19, 22–3, 29–30, 38–41,
65
composition of 228, 231–2, 323–6
Trades councils 41, 114, 178–9
Trades Disputes Act 1906 3, 18
Transport and General Workers Union
(TGWU) 147, 177, 230, 232, 323–
5, 327–8, 332
Transport, Ministry of 249, 249 n7
Treasury
in Second World War 18–20, 25–8,
32–3, 36–7, 40–1, 50, 53, 56–7, 68,
70, 75, 78, 84, 88–90, 94, 97, 99. 101
under Labour governments 1945–51
118, 121, 139, 141–2, 152–5, 170,
187
under Conservative governments
1951–61 217, 229, 239, 244–5,
288, 294, 329
relations with Bank of England 101,
106
and budgetary policy 92, 118, 130–1,
166–70
and devaluation 1949 172–4
and economic management 185,
188–90, 193–5, 206, 249, 264–72,
275–7, 287–8, 290–7, 304–5, 343
and European integration 251–3, 272
and external financial situation 122–6
and full employment 90, 131–2, 151,
268, 297
and investment 98–9
and machinery of government 78–84,
168–9, 192–4, 247, 249
and Marshall Aid 159
and nationalised industries 86
and PESC system 337, 350
and planning 136–8, 151
and Plowden Report 339
and Robot 195–204
and trade policy 102–5
and wages policy 86–9, 133–6, 156–7,
173–4, 185, 189–91, 257, 262–4,
271, 292–3, 306–9, 321, 343–4

Treasury *cont.*
  and 1961 crisis 298–301
  Overseas Finance Division 102, 104, 136, 155
  and tensions with Home Economic Division 170, 193–4, 197, 204, 244, 266–8, 271, 292, 339
Trend, Sir Burke 154, 338
Tripartism 64, 69, 75, 80, 113, 119, 127–8, 134–5, 138–41, 139 n53, 164, 168, 178, 206–10, 227, 235, 242, 245–6, 254, 257, 291, 304, 208–9, 314, 322, 334, 349
Truman, Harry S. 123, 158
Turner, James 139

Unemployment 295–6
United States 57, 66
  economic and trade policy 101–5, 187, 197–8, 210, 219, 240
  European recovery programme 157–8, 162, 171, 174–5
  Federal Reserve Bank 25, 57, 105, 290, 299
  loans to UK 103–5, 122–6, 276
USDAW (shop workers' union) 232
Uthwatt Report 42

Vinson, Fred 123, 210

Wages policy 156–7, 159, 173, 174 n51, 186, 188–94, 207, 229 n29, 232 n35, 258–9, 280, 293, 295, 298–300, 304, 316, 319–22, 324–6, 336, 349
  and 1947 White Paper 156–7, 161
Walker, D. H. 143, 163
Wallace, William 60
Warburg, Siegmund 302
Watkinson, Harold 258, 261, 306 n38
Watson, Forbes 144
Weir, Sir Cecil 34, 61, 142
Weir, Lord (William) 6, 39
Welles, Sumner 102
Williams, Tom 172
Williamson, Tom 257, 309, 314
Wilson, Harold 130, 138, 145, 155, 220, 223–4, 328–9, 332–3, 338
  as President of Board of Trade 163,

166, 171, 178, 180–4, 187–8, 195–6, 209
  and 'The State and Private Industry' 181–5
Wilson, Sir Horace 35
Wool textiles industry 39
World War Two
  Cabinet and War Cabinet 28–30, 34, 36, 38, 78, 110: Economic Secretariat 28, 53, 55–6, 63, 82, 84, 87–8, 90, 95, 100–1
  Committees: Machinery of Government 32, 34, 43, 47, 77–83, 101; Post-War Economy 29, 47, 52–3, 56, 77, 84, 95; Post-War Employment 78, 84, 89–90; Reconstruction 46, 95
  Coalition Government 32, 41–4, 46, 48–9, 68–9, 83–4, 109–10, 112–13
  economic overview 80–3
  emergency regulations 17, 20, 31, 41, 45, 52, 67–8, 86
  manpower organisation 18–22, 28, 31, 33, 51–2
  organisation 6–7, 19–20, 27–30, 43–5, 46–8, 75, 83–4
  outside personnel 30, 35–7, 47, 49
  reconstruction 30, 46–57, 74–5, 78–111
  sponsorship system 29–32, 38, 44, 83
  trade and industry 22–4, 31, 37–9
  wages and prices 32, 56–7, 67, 86, 89–91: effects of, as historic memory 114; comparisons with First World War 17, 23–4, 26, 29, 31, 37, 42, 46, 49, 52, 57, 108, 112, 340
World Federation of Trade Unions (WFTU) 65, 147
Woodcock, George 135, 204, 226, 229, 233, 287, 309, 313, 318–19, 323, 327–8 331
Wood, Sir Kingsley 27, 33, 57–8, 70, 131
Woolton, Lord 30, 35, 70, 202, 212–13, 215, 248, 260–1

Younger, Kenneth 120